More Praise for *Misquoting Muhammad*

"A comprehensive analysis of the most contentious issues that are now debated in the world. Professor Brown is one of the few scholars that is both at home in classical Islamic studies and the modern Islamic world. Displaying extensive research and a deep knowledge of the Islamic religious tradition, the author writes with verve and conviction."

Walid Saleh – Associate Professor, University of Toronto

"There are few books that combine passion with purpose more deftly than this. *Misquoting Muhammad* is brilliant, forensic and accessible, at once a delight to read, a beacon to herald, a vision to pursue."

Bruce Lawrence – Professor of Islamic Studies Emeritus, Duke University

"Erudite and provocative... compelling." *Literary Review*

"Superb... an essential read for anyone seeking to understand Islam and the Muslim world... fascinating." *Tribune*

"Brown ably navigates the cutting edge of Hadith studies while offering his able insight, encyclopedic knowledge [illegible]s, and awareness of the political con[illegible]dies... highly recommended." [illegible]'E Magazine*

"Exhilarating... Brown i[illegible] scholars in the field of Islamic Studi[illegible]who has the rare ability to sit at the fe[illegible] from Egypt to Malaysia for hours on end and translate that knowledge into something beneficial for his American audiences." *Los Angeles Review of Books*

"Brown possesses formidable knowledge of premodern Muslim scholars who sought to preserve accounts of Muhammad's teachings and practices... *Misquoting Muhammad* sheds light on the considerable dynamism and sophistication within the Sunni tradition." *Washington Post*

"An inside view into how key and controversial aspects of Islam took shape." *Asian Art Newspaper*

"Eminently qualified... Brown eloquently parses Islam's rich interpretive tradition." *Kirkus Reviews*

ABOUT THE AUTHOR

JONATHAN A.C. BROWN is Associate Professor of Islamic Studies and the Alwaleed bin Talal Chair of Islamic Civilization in the School of Foreign Service at Georgetown University. He is also Director of the Alwaleed bin Talal Center for Muslim–Christian Understanding. His other books include *Hadith: Muhammad's Legacy in the Medieval and Modern World* and *Slavery & Islam*, both of which are published by Oneworld.

Misquoting Muhammad

The Challenge and Choices of Interpreting the Prophet's Legacy

Jonathan A. C. Brown

ONEWORLD

A Oneworld Book

First published in North America, Great Britain and Australia by
Oneworld Publications 2014

This paperback edition published 2015
Reprinted, 2015, 2016, 2017, 2019, 2020, 2022, 2023

A CIP record for this title is available from the British Library

ISBN 978-1-78074-782-8
eBook ISBN 978-1-78074-421-6

Typeset by Tetragon, London
Printed and bound in Great Britain by Clays Ltd, Elcograf S.p.A.

Oneworld Publications
10 Bloomsbury Street
London WC1B 3SR
England

Contents

List of Illustrations

Islam in the Twenty-First Century
Series Editor: Omid Safi

ALSO IN THIS SERIES:

Inside the Gender Jihad, Amina Wadud
Sexual Ethics in Islam, Kecia Ali
Progressive Muslims, Ed. Omid Safi

For my beloved wife Laila,
who inspires me every day

'In every object there is inexhaustible meaning; the eye sees in it what the eye brings means of seeing.'

THOMAS CARLYLE
The French Revolution

Foreword

The Prophet Muhammad remains indispensable. The great debates of modern Islam – debates that, as this book shows, are great human debates – continue to be fought through the legacy of the Prophet, in his name, because of the Prophet, and in spite of him.

He is always present among Muslims. They continue to praise their Prophet and recall his virtues in sermons, devotional songs, and books galore. Today, as in centuries past, those who fear, are ignorant of, or hate Islam have zeroed in on the Prophet as the manifestation of their phobias, blasting him in books and YouTube clips. And so the Prophet's persona and legacy serve as vehicles for both the highest aspirations of Muslims and the most vicious vitriol toward them.

Salafis, Sufis, modernists, reformists, Wahhabis: whichever Muslim group, by whatever name one calls them, and in all their conceivable permutations, portray themselves as bearing the mantle of the Prophet. The Salafis claim to be the most authentic bearers of his authenticated words and deeds. The Sufis claim to be striving not just for the actions but also for the inner experience of the Prophet. Modernists talk about *Ijtihad,* or reinterpreting Islam according to what the Prophet would do and teach today. In short, they all claim to speak in Muhammad's name, quoting, misquoting, and contesting the legacy of the Prophet.

It is most appropriate that this book looks at the great questions of interpreting what Islam has meant and should mean through the lens of Muhammad. Perhaps until very recently, no Muslim had ever read the Qur'an with pure, naive eyes. Muslims had always read the Qur'an through the person and legacy of the Prophet, whether embodied in oral or written traditions, whether in inspired visions or through scholastic commentaries and commentaries on commentaries. It is the contested legacies of the Prophet that have been the prime commentaries on the Divine text.

In this book, Professor Jonathan Brown walks the reader through some of the more contentious modern debates in Islam today, such as whether women can lead communal prayers; what happens to Muslims who leave Islam; and the role of violence in the modern state. Readers will be surprised at what they find, sometimes pleasantly and sometimes not. It is not to be expected that all readers will agree with Brown's conclusions. Yet one has to admire the rigorous and methodical way in which he analyzes the textual evidence for the various positions held on these issues.

Misquoting Muhammad comes at an opportune time. The author has quickly established himself as the foremost scholar of the Hadith (prophetic traditions), combining the most rigorous aspects of the Western academic study of Islam with the best of classical Islamic scholarship. In this sense, his work recalls the best of biblical scholarship by exponents such as Bart Ehrman. Reading this book will be rewarding in many and different ways for Muslims and non-Muslims alike.

As a professor myself, and one reluctantly moving up in years, I cannot help but appreciate that Brown's book is also an important step in the career of an extraordinary scholar, one who is ready to bring the fruits of his formidable scholarship to a wider audience. Both the scholarly community and the general reading public are richer for his contribution.

Omid Safi

Preface

The title and the idea for this book was proposed by a crafty, teddy-bear-like friend of mine, who suggested writing a counterpart to Bart Ehrman's best-selling *Misquoting Jesus*. Though I still have not read the book, I have benefited greatly from Ehrman's other writings and could imagine what the book argued. I told my friend that I did not feel comfortable writing an 'unveiling Islamic origins' book, so he proposed framing the project more as 'contesting Muhammad.' This made much more sense, and thus the subtitle (for me, the real title) of the book emerged: the challenge and choices of interpreting the Prophet's legacy.

The contents of this book took shape starting in 2007, during my first year as a professor. At the time I was engrossed in the subject of forgery and looking at forgery in the Islamic tradition in a comparative light. Though this research ultimately made its way into chapter six of the book, the central themes of the volume originated not in my research but in my teaching and public lectures. It became clear to me that by far the most pressing questions befuddling both Muslim and non-Muslim audiences were how we should understand such-and-such a controversial Qur'anic verse, or such-and-such a provocative Hadith. During the question-and-answer time at talks I gave, I saw again and again the disillusioning clash between scripture and modernity acted out before me by individuals wondering how they should understand Islam today and what their relationship to the classical heritage of Islam should be. This book is not my attempt to give people *the* answers to these questions. Rather, it is my effort to lay out for the reader what some of the possible answers are and what their consequences might be.

I sit writing this in a bed and breakfast in Johannesburg, South Africa, Peter Tosh's 'Downpressor Man' playing on the music-video channel on a small TV. This city is a panoply of diversity. In the malls, people of all races and dress window-shop and wait for tables. Women in full face-veils and men with long beards and turbans stroll by without a passing glance from others. Back in the US, in the wake of the tragic Boston Marathon bombings, the media are still frenzied over distinguishing good, moderate Muslims from evil, extremist ones. No one of consequence ever acknowledges that 'good' and 'evil' in the American public square are too often not moral qualities or commitments to principle (a principled view might be, for example, 'The good person respects human life and protects the innocent at all costs; the evil kills and causes suffering ruthlessly'). Rather, they are tribal qualities. 'Good' corresponds to 'works to kill America's enemies' (American Muslims who joined the US military to fight in Iraq are thus good), and 'evil' means 'works to kill Americans or their allies or both' (Iraqi Muslims trying to defend their loved ones from random, dismembering explosions were evil). As for 'moderate' and 'extreme,' they map onto 'congruent with mainstream American culture' (Muslims who drink or don't cover their hair are thus moderate) versus 'clashes with mainstream American culture.'

I love coming to South Africa because it reveals so starkly how transient and fickle even our most fervent and supposedly absolute beliefs can be. Less than a quarter-century ago America's political establishment and its obsequious media considered Nelson Mandela to be a terrorist (he officially ceased to be for the US in 2008). Now perhaps no man in the world is more respected.* Many Americans and Western Europeans proudly trumpet the diversity of cosmopolises like London and New York without realizing that cosmopolitanism does not mean people of different skin colors all sitting around over wine at a bistro table complaining about organized religion. It means people who hold profoundly different, even mutually exclusive, beliefs and cultural norms functioning in a shared space based on toleration of disagreement.

As I ponder what this book I've written is about, I realize that it is as much as anything an expression of my desire to transcend the tribal and of my frustration at those who pass off cultural chauvinism and narrow-mindedness as liberalism, who use 'common sense' as a proxy for forcing one culture onto another on the pretext of imposing 'universal values;'

* In the time since this was written in May 2013, Mandela passed away.

who scoff at subservience to backward traditions when they see it in others but are blind to it in themselves; and who refuse to look at the cultural systems of others as – at least initially – equals that deserve to be judged by more than whether they drink beer, wear jeans, date or support some political agenda.

Johannesburg, South Africa

Acknowledgments

A number of friends and teachers assisted me in completing this book, but only I am to blame for its failings. Some read all or parts of it, and some lent expertise. Aunt Kate Patterson, Omar Anchassi, Rodrigo Adem, Matthew Anderson, Ovamir Anjum, Joe Bradford, Garrett Davidson, Robert Gleave, Matthew Ingalls, Tarek Al-Jawhary, Abdul Rahman Mustafa and Amine Tais suffered through readings and offered excellent suggestions and corrections. Jonathan Lyons in particular rendered me great service as a perceptive editor. Nuri Friedlander, Sher Ali Tareen and Maheen Zaman responded kindly to bizarre queries. Mohammed Fadel inspired me and upbraided me when necessary with his always animated discussion. Thomas Williams and my colleagues Jonathan Ray and Emma Gannage helped me with citations. Clark Lombardi has been a great friend and interlocutor, providing an elating elixir of legal expertise and outrageous humor. Abdul-Aleem Somers allowed me to use his massive library in Cape Town. My friends Asad Naqvi and Brendan Kerr, along with my sisters, have helped keep me sane. Sister Lucinda even hosted me in Kuala Lumpur. My brother-in-law Ben Ward came up with a surprisingly helpful list of suggested readings. I must extend my sincere gratitude to Umar Ryad for sharing his photo of Muhammad Tawfiq Sidqi with me, and Sherif Abdel Kouddous and his family for providing me with rare pictures of Shaykh Muhammad al-Ghazali, *rahimahu Allah*. I'm grateful to the Cosmos Club of Washington, DC for the use of the Writers Room and the library. Of course, I thank Omid Safi and Oneworld Publications for pushing me to write this book to begin with.

I remain a drop in the ocean of my great teachers, whom I will not name here because I do not want them tarnished by any opinions I express in the book. I owe great gratitude to my father, Jonathan C. Brown, and his wife Ayse for pushing me to write this book when it was lingering in the authorial limbo of the 'forthcoming.' They have never once turned me away when I needed help.

About my wife, Laila, I could say so much, but here I'll restrict myself to expressing my fully realized gratitude for her putting up with my long nights awake downstairs typing and thumbing through books, or clacking away on my laptop on the floor of our bedroom because I wanted to be near her. She has done so much to inspire me to crawl out of the classics into the cacophony of the modern world. She bore all my travels with remarkable patience (often right beside me). Our son Mazen I must thank for waiting an extra week to be born so that I could finish chapter five, and for being such a joy ever since. He has even volunteered an unsolicited finger or toe in typing. I am also indebted to my in-laws, Dr. Sami and Nahla, for the constant stream of information they provided about the unfolding events of the Arab Spring.

Over all my writings and thoughts hovers the memory of my late mother, Dr. Ellen Brown. This is the book she always wanted me to write. In the three years since she died, I have come to appreciate neglected facets of her personality: her everyday creativity, her patience, her integrity and her commitment to defending the autonomy of individuals regardless of who they were. She taught me to understand the perspectives of others, which is, in truth, no small accomplishment. Many cities of men she saw and knew their minds. With her passing, night fell and the roads of the world grew dark. But light and color return in the curiosity and smiles of children, in the gratitude for the treasures we have received and in the loving appreciation for what remains. I thank God for the blessings I have enjoyed in my life and hope that this 'dog on the doorstep' can be a useful servant of God.

Notes on dates, transliteration, abbreviations and citations

I have used a minimum of transliteration in order to make this book as accessible as possible. In the body of the text, I have used the following transliterations for Arabic words. The ’ character in the middle of a word represents a simple glottal stop, like the initial sounds of both syllables in ‘uh-oh.’ The ‘ symbol indicates the Arabic letter *‘ayn*, a sound absent in English but one that resembles the ‘aaaah’ noise a person makes when getting their throat checked by the doctor. In Arabic words, ‘q’ represents a voiceless velar sound produced at the back of the throat. It is non-existent in English, but one could most closely approximate this sound with the ‘c’ sound at the beginning of the crow noise ‘Caw! Caw!’ ‘Gh’ indicates a sound similar to the French ‘r,’ and ‘kh’ represents a velar fricative like the sound of clearing one’s throat. ‘Dh’ indicates the ‘th’ sound in words like ‘that’ or ‘bother.’ ‘Th’ represents the ‘th’ sound in words like ‘bath.’

I have omitted the Arabic definite article ‘al-’ unless it is an essential part of a construction, like the name ‘Abd al-Rahman, and have retained the Arabic connective nouns ‘ibn’ (son of) and ‘bint’ (daughter of) instead of abbreviating them.

In the Notes and Bibliography I have used the standard Library of Congress transliteration system, with the non-construct *tā’ marbūṭa* indicated by an ‘a.’ I use (ṣ) for the honorific Arabic phrase ‘May the peace and blessings of God be upon him (*ṣallā Allāh ‘alayhi wa sallam*),’ which is commonly said and written after Muhammad’s name.

Dates in this book will follow the Common Era format unless otherwise noted.

The only unusual citation conventions in this book are those for citing mainstay Sunni Hadith collections. I have followed the standard Wensinck system of citing to the chapter, subchapter of every book (e.g., *Ṣaḥīḥ al-Bukhārī*: *kitāb al-buyū'*, *bāb dhikr al-khayyāṭ*) except the *Musnad* of Ibn Ḥanbal, which is cited to the common Maymaniyya print. All translations are my own unless otherwise indicated in the endnotes.

1

The Problem(s) with Islam

A WORLD FULL OF GOD

Among the teeming and terrified crowd of protesters in Cairo's Tahrir Square in January 2011, a young man and an older man crouched huddled next to each other as bullets from the security services whizzed overhead. In the din, the two spoke of how the Prophet Muhammad had once declared that whoever dies speaking truth to a tyrant will die a martyr. They spoke of the great martyrs of the Prophet's day, who awaited those latter-day believers who would one day join them in Paradise. Seized by inspiration, the young man cried, 'I will greet them for you,' stood up and was shot in the head. 'I touched his blood with my hands,' the elder man, a famous Muslim preacher, it turns out, recounted later in a TV interview. 'It smelled like perfumed musk.'[1]

One of the first changes I noticed when I visited Egypt soon after Mubarak's fall was that Cairo's metro map had changed. The Mubarak station had been renamed and the dictator's name expunged from all maps and signs. Even the lists of station stops above the doors in the metro cars had been amended. They bore the station's new name, '*Shohadaa*' – The Martyrs. In the traffic-heavy Sadat station beneath Tahrir Square, posters of many of the martyrs adorned the walls in an impromptu memorial. Some were no more than enlarged photos. Others were photoshopped with roses and pious epitaphs such as 'Every soul will taste death,' a verse from the Qur'an. Looking at each poster in turn, I thought of how uncomplicated it is to honor and grieve for the fallen in the heady throes of an uprising and its triumphal denouement. I thought about how unifying and unified a people's religion can be in such times. For the vast majority of Egyptians, these dead young men and women were not martyrs for some secular cause in a disenchanted world. The very term '*shohadaa*' comes from the Qur'an and designates those who have fought and died in the path of God.

Whether in its charred streets or its bitter media battles, revolutionary Egypt was a world full of God. Everywhere one heard the words of His revelation, the Qur'an, adorning the banners of protesters or crackling with vintage piety from radios at sidewalk tea stands, recited by bygone masters. The Islam that Egyptians turned to in their common outpouring of grief and outrage seemed at times monolithic and as uncontested as the memorials to the martyrs on the metro walls. Reality was very different. Appearing on Egyptian state TV as the protests raged, one conservative Muslim cleric denied the haloes of martyrdom claimed for those protesters who had already died. Quoting a ruling by the Prophet Muhammad, he stated that, since they had been fighting fellow Muslims, in God's eyes no one who died in Tahrir was a martyr. He called on the protesters to go home and prevent the further spilling of Muslim blood.[2] This cleric's voice was only one among many. Since the first glimmer of protest in Egypt there had been deep contention over Islam's position on the obedience due a ruler and a people's right to rebel. As the protests against Mubarak grew, revolutionary barricades were turned into impromptu rostra, and along with Egypt's airwaves and mosque pulpits they carried the sparring voices of political activists and Muslim clerics of all leanings making competing claims about Islam. Some of the revolutionary youth and the Muslim Brotherhood protesters quoted a famous saying of the Prophet Muhammad: 'The best jihad is a word of truth before a tyrannical ruler.' Facebook posts countered this, especially from Muslims with more conservative, Salafi leanings. They warned of the inevitable chaos of revolution and quoted another saying of the Prophet: 'Civil strife sleeps, and God curses whomever awakens it.'

As Egypt's revolution turned from protests to parliamentary elections in the wake of Mubarak's ouster, Islam and Islamists dominated the media storm. The call for Egypt to be ruled by God's law, the Shariah, resounded. It resonated with millions, alarmed millions of others, and has not ceased. The press buzzed with decades of pent-up energy, and newspapers bubbled over daily with new controversy. Would the Muslim Brotherhood allow a Coptic Christian to be president of Egypt? Would the more conservative

Islamic party of the Salafis accept a woman as president, or holding any high position? Islam and calls for rule by God's law could no longer remain mere slogans or ideals that floated above the fray of politics and legislation. Public debates centered on the details of Qur'anic verses, such as God's command that Muslims 'not take unbelievers as friends and associates in the place of believers.' Editorials inquired about what would be made of the Prophet Muhammad's warning that 'No community will flourish if it entrusts its affairs to a woman.' All political camps proffered visions of what the details of Islamic law would mean for Egypt's future. Who spoke for Islam and how the scriptural sources of the religion would be interpreted were now pressing issues of policy.

In 2012, when a body of experts was convened to begin drafting Egypt's new constitution, the proper role of Islam was by far the most controversial issue at hand. A century earlier, the answer to this question would have come from only one source: the ulama of the Al-Azhar Mosque, Egypt's most famous center of religious learning and the heart of the state's religious establishment. The ulama (literally, the learned ones) are, as Muhammad once foretold, 'the heirs of the prophets.' For the past fourteen centuries these religious scholars have articulated the expansive and intricately detailed systems of Islamic law and dogma. While the ulama of Al-Azhar acquired a pastoral aura with their unmistakable charcoal robes and white and red turbaned fezzes, Islam has never had a formal clergy. Throughout the Islamic world the ulama did eventually take on the role of religious functionaries, but they have always been more rabbi than priest. Islam is a religion erected in a scholastic idiom of preserving the sacred knowledge of revelation and studying God's law. The ulama have thus always been scholars first and foremost. They penned the countless tomes that articulated the Shariah and served as the judges who applied it. They have been the shepherds who guide the Muslim masses and the chroniclers who record the history of the *Umma,* as the global community of Muhammad's followers is known.

In Egypt today, however, the ulama of Al-Azhar are not alone. In the meetings of the constitutional drafting committee they found themselves side by side with rivals who offered their own visions of Islam. There were ulama of the Salafi movement, scholars more acquainted with Egypt's prisons than with employment in the state's religious bureaucracy, and who often work day jobs as physicians and engineers. Most Salafis acquired their religious learning in the conservative Islamic centers of Saudi Arabia rather than in Cairo. There were others on the committee who claimed to speak for Islam as well but who had not passed through the traditional education of the ulama. Lawyers and academics who had graduated from Egypt's Western-style universities and earned recognition for their thinking on Islam, offered their own perspectives on the proper shape of Islamic law and the best ways to incorporate it into a democratic republic.

No one on the committee, not even secularists resolutely opposed to any state role for Islam, dared to make unsupported claims about what Islam is or what it demands of its followers. Whatever argument they hoped to advance, they had to reach back to the authority of the past, into the heritage built up by the ulama. They had to justify their claims, either by referring to Islam's foundational scriptures or by drawing on its millennium-long tradition of scholarly interpretation, which digested those scriptures to construct the edifice of Islamic law and theology. When the committee presented its draft constitution to the Egyptian people for approval, its second article confirmed that the primary source of legislation would be 'the principles of the Islamic Shariah.' These consisted of the religion's scriptural sources and the rational principles and methods of interpretation used to mine their meanings.*

Only a few months later, in the summer of 2013, Egypt spiraled into chaos and a military coup ousted the Muslim Brotherhood president Mohammed Morsi. Like Egypt as a whole, the ulama ranks fractured over contrasting visions of Islam and its proper relation to the state. Yet again the airwaves and social networks sizzled with invocations of the book of God and the words of His Prophet as devotees of the resurrected ancien régime battled Morsi supporters for the religious high ground. Tied intimately to the state apparatus and unmoved by attachment to Western ideals of democratic process, the senior Al-Azhar ulama welcomed what they saw as a return to stability. Ali Gomaa, a senior Al-Azhar cleric recently retired as Egypt's Grand Mufti, justified the coup with a parable expounded by the Prophet. The believers are passengers together on a boat; when one group starts drilling a hole in the hull they must be stopped by force or all will perish. Other ulama revealed the durability of that dimension of political consciousness that had made the Muslim Brotherhood so appealing to Muslims in the mid-twentieth century. The aged Hasan Shafi'i read

* Sadat added the present Article II to Egypt's constitution in 1980. The 2012 constitution added the definition for the 'principles of the Shariah' in Article 219, which was removed in August 2013. Article II remains intact. At the time of writing, the status of Egypt's constitution is in flux.

from the crinkled notebook paper of his prepared statement, lamenting Egypt's slide back into authoritarianism and warning desperately of the bloodshed he knew would ensue. Though he had risen to the upper levels of the Al-Azhar clerical hierarchy, he recalled his youth in the Brotherhood in the 1950s, when he had been arrested and tortured 'in ways that I had not even read about in history books.'

As Ramadan began and Egypt's summer neared the peak of its oppressive heat, supporters of ousted president Morsi gathered by the thousands for urban sit-ins. Addressing the crowds from makeshift stages, Brotherhood leaders inspired their supporters with stories of the Prophet and his Companions triumphing over their Meccan foes in battle during the Ramadan fast. When army bulldozers, shock troops and snipers cleared the encampments, leaving thousands dead in the streets, enlivened state propaganda flooded the airwaves. In an interview on a pro-coup channel, Gomaa opined that Muslim Brotherhood supporters were arch-extremists whom the state must fight and defeat at all costs. He cited the Prophet's teaching that those who attempt to fracture the unity of the Muslims must be fought, 'whoever they are.'[3] The Mubarak-era media, both television and print, invoked the Prophet Muhammad's sacred authority as they cheered the army's takeover of the government. Dramatic pro-army montages incessantly extolled Egypt's military as 'the best soldiers on earth,' an apocryphal saying attributed to Muhammad.[4] As the bloodbath continued, the military government issued a revised constitution that sought to remove much of its religious language. Yet Article II remained, perhaps too close to the bone to strip off. The principles of the Shariah remain the chief source of legislation in Egypt.

TAKING ISLAMIC SCRIPTURE AND ITS INTERPRETERS SERIOUSLY

In this book, I take the tradition of Sunni Islam* seriously and without apology. This is both merited and useful for a number of reasons. First and foremost, there is no doubt that the religious and civilizational edifice that the ulama constructed ranks among the greatest intellectual and cultural achievements in human history. It should be studied and appreciated in

* I am focusing on Sunni Islam because this book may be too long as it is, and many of the phenomena and developments discussed here are mirrored in Shiite Islam.

its own right regardless of whether one believes its claims to truth and regardless of any responsibility it might bear for contemporary crises.

Second, because the Islamic tradition formed the backbone of a world civilization, it necessarily dealt with challenges common to other religious and philosophical traditions. A study of how the Sunni ulama have tackled the challenges of interpreting scripture, applying law and guiding the laity quickly reveals that they were engaged in many of the same conversations as classical Greco-Roman philosophers, medieval Christians, Jews, Buddhists and the founders of the United States. One perennially pressing issue is the challenge of reconciling the claims of truth and justice made by scripture with what the human mind considers true and just outside it. Another is the challenge of deciding who speaks for God, balancing the need to circumscribe this authority with the danger that such controls can limit or distort God's message. A third challenge is determining the ultimate nature of truth and reality. Are those guardians who speak on behalf of scripture allowed to misrepresent surface facts for the greater good of their followers, or is such inaccuracy a betrayal of the truth they claim to hold paramount?

Finally, the solutions that the Islamic tradition produced for the global human challenges it faced offer valuable insights and reveal the limitations of Western discourse on reform in Islam. Some aspects of Islam that seem glaringly problematic today actually resulted from efforts to answer questions so fundamental that they have never been resolved definitively by anyone. Their answers are not so much right or wrong as they are choices between competing priorities, such as whether and when it is acceptable to tell a lie for a good cause.

Sometimes the solutions offered by the Islamic tradition to common challenges provide useful correctives. There is much exasperation among Western leaders over mobs of Muslim protesters failing to transcend religious chauvinisms and accept the dictates of 'reason.' Faced with this complaint, medieval ulama would observe that what one person insists is 'reasonable' is often no more than the conventions and sensibilities of their particular culture. It cannot be compelling to someone outside that culture without recourse to some transcending authority. Another common frustration with religion comes from atheists or skeptics who object that modern scientific discoveries contradict scripture and thus disprove its divine origin. This would perplex the medieval ulama. Many such discoveries are actually not that modern, they would point out, and they would add that they had reconciled their interpretation of Islam's scriptures to such empirical observations centuries ago. Responding to the frequent calls today for a 'Muslim Martin Luther,' medieval ulama would suggest that much of the violence and extremism found in the Muslim world results precisely from unlearned Muslims deciding to break with tradition and approach their religion Luther-like 'by scripture alone.'

Scripturae is the Latin word that Western Christianity adopted to translate the Hebrew and Greek for 'things written,' which Jews and early Christians had used to describe the sacred books of the Bible. We can sense something scripture-like in most religions, though composing one global definition for scripture seems impossible. Things we would call scripture are too diverse in content and form. Perhaps the best approximation comes from Harvard's William Graham, who describes scripture as a 'sacred and authoritative text.' More exact identifications, Graham suggests, must come from the lips of the beholder. What constitutes scripture for a particular group of people is whatever that community endows with religious salience. Scripture is something created by a community or tradition when it valorizes a text as 'sacred or holy, powerful and meaningful, possessed of an exalted authority... distinct from other speech and writing.'[5]

In the West we tend to think of scripture as a discrete, tangible holy book or a closed canon of such books. It would seem by definition to take written form. Most scripture does, although the Hindu Vedas and the Zoroastrian Avesta were transmitted orally by memory for centuries before finally being set down in writing. They are at heart 'oral scripture.' Scripture can also lack clear boundaries, with semi-canonical parts enjoying a status between the sacred and the profane. Even a body of scripture as well known as the Bible in Western Christianity is not monolithic or homogeneously scriptural. The King James Bible came to include thirty-nine books of the Old Testament and twenty-seven books of the New. The Catholic Latin Vulgate Bible, however, includes the additional fourteen (or fifteen) books of the Apocrypha, which Jews considered valuable but did not include in the Hebrew Bible. The exact demarcations of scripture can be contested even within one sect. Many English Protestants disliked the Apocrypha, while Martin Luther maintained its books were 'useful and good to read.' There can be total disagreement about what has the status of scripture to begin with. Stoic philosophers of the first century CE honored the *Iliad* and the *Odyssey* as scriptural vessels of philosophical wisdom, while at the same time the learned satirist Lucian mocked Homer for writing lies and passing them off as philosophy.[6]

Islam's scriptures were once oral but were set down in writing in time. The faith's scriptural foundation is made up of two parts. Its core is the Qur'an, which Muslims believe to be the unchanging record of God's revealed words, a small volume that can be gripped and memorized word for word. Around it are the teachings of the Prophet Muhammad, amorphous and contested. A saying of the Prophet or a description of his actions is known as a Hadith, and it is primarily over the Hadiths and their contents that Islam's sects and schools of thought have diverged. What one camp considers an authentic and compelling teaching of the Prophet, another considers a forgery. In light of this contest, the exact number of supposed Hadiths defies calculation. Though both Sunni and Shiite Islam have developed compilations of Hadiths that are relied on as authoritative references, these books enjoy no monopoly. The indistinct corpus of Hadiths in Sunni as well as Shiite Islam surrounds the solid nucleus of the Qur'an like a nimbus, its inner reaches made up of a narrow band of well-known Hadiths that circumscribe the established teachings and precedent of the Prophet. These are surrounded with layer after layer of more Hadiths, becoming less and less reliable and often more controversial as they stretch outward, until their muted light fades into profane blackness.

Islam's scriptures have always posed a great obstacle to Western attempts to understand the religion. The Qur'an's format and style would strike anyone accustomed to the Bible as unusual. It is non-linear, with no one narrative flow within individual chapters or across the book as a whole. This has confounded non-Muslim readers for centuries. Despite incalculable advances in scholarship on and awareness of other lands and cultures, Christian and European reactions to the Qur'an changed little between the eighth century and the 1800s. It has always been described as disjointed and incomprehensible. Writing in the mid-700s, John of Damascus mocked the Qur'an as a bizarre mishmash of heretical Christian teachings that Muhammad had cobbled together. Even Voltaire, who lauded Islam warmly when it suited his satirical ends (like belittling the Catholic Church or Jews), dismissed the Qur'an as full of contradictions, absurdities and patent scientific falsehoods.[7] Though he counted Muhammad as the most sincere of men (indeed one of the 'great men' who changed the course of history), Thomas Carlyle described the Qur'an as impenetrably befuddling, 'insupportable stupidity, in short.'[8]

The Hadith corpus fared better until the modern period, when these reports about Muhammad began attracting withering scholarly criticism from European orientalists. Western critics got off to a late start because, until the emergence of a historical-critical approach to the Bible in the late eighteenth century, European scholars thought of Hadiths as no different from any other type of historical report, like those compiled by antique historians about Julius Caesar. Christians who did grasp the essential scriptural character of the Hadiths, like a ninth-century Arab Christian engaged in anti-Islam polemics in Baghdad, dismissed their reliability, particularly when Hadiths attributed miraculous acts to the Prophet Muhammad. Such early attacks on Hadiths from non-Muslims in Baghdad were facilitated by the ulama's admission that they had themselves uncovered thousands and thousands of forged Hadiths.[9]

Whether due to the challenges of accessing Islam's scriptures or because of media bias, students have asked me more than once if Islam is a 'real' religion. This question is not absurd in the United States, where lawmakers and lawyers have argued in court that Islam is a cult undeserving of the legal protections afforded 'proper' faiths. Nor is the question unthinkable in the UK, where Tony Blair recently opined that 'there is a problem within Islam.'[10] In such an environment it is not easy to convince people to take Islam seriously as a religion. It is an even taller order to ask folk to treat it as it unquestionably deserves, namely as one of humanity's most accomplished and relevant intellectual traditions.

This is not to say that Western criticisms of Islam, as well as those coming from disapproving Muslims, are difficult to understand. Few things seem more repugnant than religious intolerance, luring young men to murderous deaths with carnal promises of virgins in Heaven, allowing polygamy and marrying teenage girls to old men. Though such practices might have been acceptable at some point in the past, few in the West would welcome them in this day and age. Speaking for a West proud of having cast off centuries of superstition and religious extremism, Tony Blair explained that such Muslim practices and values are 'not compatible with pluralistic, liberal, open-minded societies.' His words echo the common diagnosis, bandied about as self-evident truth by Western media pundits, that the Muslim world needs its own Reformation and Enlightenment.

It is often difficult, however, to distinguish those criticisms of Islam that are grounded in demonstrable moral realizations from those that merely mask cultural biases. Often Islam's most denounced barbarisms are nothing more than prosaic differences in dietary preference and dress. In the 2012 Oscar-winning film *Argo*, a mob of fanatical, screaming men with unkempt beards and women in headscarves storms the US embassy in 1979 Tehran. The American embassy staff are besieged along with the good, modern Iranians, beardless and with uncovered hair, who are waiting for visas for the US. The dangers facing the film's protagonist as he makes his way by air to the newly declared Islamic Republic are signaled by the flight attendants announcing forebodingly that the crew will collect any remaining alcoholic beverages. When he escapes Iran's airspace, his safety is marked by the attendant announcing that passengers are now free to imbibe.

Whether the subject is Iran, Egypt, Turkey or Tunisia, the narrative of Islam in the Western media and blogosphere is almost always the same. Tradition is gradually giving way to modernity. Black veils and prohibition mark the former. Flowing hair, Western dress and a good drink mark the latter. Open-minded, critical scholars are revealing cracks in the vaults of religious orthodoxy and allowing the light of modern reason to shine in. Islamists and the dragoons of conservatism might win battles, but in time the forces of liberal democracy will win the war. All they want, after all, is to live in a reasonable and tolerant country. News provides much of the fodder for this narrative, such as the taped testimonials of suicide bombers describing their desire to enter a Paradise with its seventy-two virgins promised to martyrs. Films like *Argo* and television serials reinforce and complement these images so routinely and unnecessarily that one hardly notices. A film with no logical link to Islam, *Taken* (2008), follows Liam Neeson as he hunts down the heartless Albanian (Muslim) syndicate that has kidnapped his teenage daughter until he finally finds the corpulent, yacht-owning Arab (Muslim) sheik who has purchased her, killing him only moments before this villain can deflower her.

The gratuitous anti-Muslim racism in *Taken* points to a larger realization. The West's problem with Islam is not at its core an objective matter of those who have achieved Enlightenment disapproving of those who have not, or of the modern, secular and liberal rebuffing the traditional, fanatical and conservative. It runs too deep into the past, with too much consistency and too much blindness to its own absurdity. Whether in its dispensation of Byzantium, Christendom (the Latin West) or in its modern form, the Christian Mediterranean/West has a problem with Islam per se. Even for the giants of Enlightenment thought, who built the intellectual foundations of modern secularism, religion was not the problem. Voltaire and Rousseau certainly called out the unparalleled dangers posed by intolerant and extreme forms of any religion, but Islam was inherently dangerous. Montesquieu wrote that 'a religion must temper the mores of men' in order to be 'true.' Islam did not meet this standard, in his opinion. Seemingly neglecting countless dynastic wars, the Crusades (with their array of heretical Christian, Muslim and Jewish targets) and the Reformation Wars of Religion, Montesquieu remarked that Christianity has nurtured peace, benevolent monarchies and liberal republics. Islam, by contrast, has fostered violence and despots.[11]

European lists of the affronts committed by Islam were well worn long before the budding of Enlightenment sensibilities. In fact, they go back to the earliest Eastern and later Latin Christian confrontations with Muslims. The themes of Muslim violence and excessive, dangerous sexuality loom large in the first Christian writings against Islam, such as those of John of Damascus in the mid-eighth century. Pope Urban II's call for the First Crusade in 1095 invoked the barbaric destruction supposedly wrought by the armies of Islam on the Holy Land. Martin Luther's invective against the Ottoman Turks draws on perennial tropes of Muslims' penchant for murder and their religion's disregard for 'proper' marriage.[12]

The Enlightenment's Republic of Letters elaborated a more supercilious air of moral disapproval. Its condemnation of Islam was a study in cognitive dissonance. The French Enlightenment critic of Christian backwardness, Pierre Bayle, did launch equally barbed comments against Islam. He decried the religion's unfair treatment of women, permission of spousal beating and divorce. Yet he seems not to have minded that France in his day denied married women the right to own property or divorce their husbands. His contemporary, Lady Montagu, who had actually frequented the harems of Istanbul and befriended Ottoman women, objected that ''tis very easy to see they have more liberty than we have,' since they enjoyed full rights to property and movement.[13] Only in 1938 did French women attain full capacity before the law, managing to acquire rights that the architects of the Shariah had granted women as early as the seventh century. In their efforts to bring the legal system of their Indian Muslim subjects closer in line with 'justice, equity and good conscience,' British colonial administrators remarked on what they considered the brutal and inhuman punishments meted out by Islamic law. Yet one awkward adjustment made by the British was to remedy how difficult they found it to sentence criminals to death in the Shariah courts they oversaw, since Shariah law acknowledged only five capital crimes. East India Company judges no doubt pined for justice back home, where in the 1820s British law listed over two hundred death-penalty offenses, including stealing firewood and poaching fish.[14]

Western antipathy for Islam has included contempt for the ulama. Even at the dawn of serious European study of the Islamic tradition in the late seventeenth century, it was already assumed that Muslim scholars had little to offer Europeans trying to dissect Islam and Islamic history. Voltaire proclaimed that Muslims had no knowledge of their own Prophet until the English scholar George Sale undertook a study of Muhammad.[15] As industrial wealth, scientific discovery and military might elevated European scholars to new heights of confidence, criticisms of Islam's scholarly tradition intensified accordingly. The benightedness of the East as a whole was not a matter of debate among European colonizers, but the medieval scholarly heritage of Islam attracted particular contempt. 'The entire native literature of India and Arabia' was not worth 'a single shelf of a good European library,' concluded the British historian Macaulay in the mid-nineteenth century.[16] In his immensely popular faux travel log, *The Persian Letters*, Montesquieu posed as a Persian visitor to France who, among many disillusioned reflections on his homeland, expresses his realization that Persia's ulama had never been able to answer any real questions of morality or religious profundity. They could do no more than quote scripture by rote.[17] Although he fawned over the romantic purity of early, Arabian Islam, the nineteenth-century French historian Ernest Renan concluded that the Persian and Turkish peoples who had borne Islam through the medieval period and into the modern world had adulterated it irretrievably. In particular, he considered the medieval scholarly traditions of Sunni theology to be irrational and intolerant, propagated by the ulama's dogmatic and barren educational system.[18]

Western scholarly and scientific development was, of course, eminently indebted to Islamic civilization in fields from medicine (Avicenna's *Qanun* was used as the standard medical textbook in Europe through the seventeenth century) to scholastic theology (Thomas Aquinas admitted relying heavily on Averroes to understand Aristotle). Yet Renaissance heralds of Europe's newfound scientific promise could not admit their vast indebtedness to the hated, infidel Saracens. Avicenna, Averroes and other undeniably prominent Muslims in the Western scholarly pantheon had to be uprooted completely from their 'Islamic' environment.[19] Avicenna the physician was not recognized as Ibn Sina the Islamic philosopher and mystic. Europeans embraced the Andalusian philosopher Averroes, who wrote such illuminating commentaries on Aristotle and Plato. They ignored that Ibn Rushd, as he was actually called, was the chief Shariah judge of Cordoba and a luminary of the ulama who spent two decades writing a comprehensive manual of Islamic law. To their own detriment, Europeans also neglected Ibn Rushd's groundbreaking reconciliation of religion and philosophy.[20] The credit that Muslim scholars would receive from pioneers of modernism like Henri de Saint-Simon and even numerous *National Geographic* issues would not go beyond their role in 'transmitting Greek learning' to the West.[21] When Western scholars have evinced an appreciation or admiration for Islamic scholarship, it is never for the religious sciences of law, language theory, exegesis, scriptural criticism or theology, which formed the voluminous core of the ulama's world.

This is a book about how a community has understood those scriptures that it considers its foundations. It is about a faith tradition that came to believe that God had revealed the truth to humankind in the form of revelation to His Prophet and that was then faced with the challenge of understanding what that truth meant in distant times and places, both as an ideal and as a practiced reality binding that community together. This is a book about a proud, at times overconfident tradition that had its cosmology of truth shattered by a confrontation not only with a more powerful civilization but also with a new stage in human history. It is about how that tradition has responded, sometimes turning inward to defend its integrity and sometimes adopting the novel and the strange. This is a book about how Sunni Islam was constructed and reconstructed, about the scriptures on which it was built and the ulama who built it.

In the end, this book is a sort of paean to an intellectual and religious tradition that nurtured a light of wisdom not only for its own adherents but for outsiders as well. As demonstrated by the many books and TV specials on Islamic science and the plethora of works on Sufism in Western bookstores, the scientific and spiritual treasures of this wisdom have been recognized. What I hope to bring forth in this book is Islam's contributions to an area at once profoundly theoretical but also eminently practical, namely the science of interpreting scripture, reconciling its claims of truth and justice with what is true and just outside its text. I hope to offer glimpses into the world of the ulama and their books, a world that I at first wanted to observe as an object of study but soon found to be an interlocutor that all too often showed me the limitations of the worldview I had grown up in and revealed my own intellectual arrogance. It was sitting at the feet of particularly capable ulama in Al-Azhar and elsewhere, watching them perform the delicate and controversial tasks of interpreting Islam's scriptures in a fraught time, that I really learned to think. Their story deserves to be told in its own right. Though I try to limit myself to narrating this journey, there are points at which I cannot keep silent and, as one says in Arabic, 'pour out my own bucket from the well.' I will begin this book as the ulama have always ended theirs, with the admission that I may well be wrong and that 'God knows best.'

2

A Map of the Islamic Interpretive Tradition

Lost in the urban chaos between the tangled lanes of Old Delhi and the leafy boulevards of the new city lies a Muslim graveyard, unexpectedly inhabited by both the quick and the dead. At its center is a school. When I came to visit the Rahimiyya Madrasa, I found its entrance down a narrow path lined with brightly dyed yarn hung to dry between tombstones, obstructed by an impromptu soccer match and guarded by a solitary goat wearing a recycled sports jacket. The school is the modern descendant of the seminary founded by the eighteenth-century family of scholars who now lie buried in the humble mausoleum around which the graveyard grew.

I had for some time hoped to stand there above one grave in particular and pay my respects. When historians try to map out the past, it is often to make sense of a present that, like the fluid chaos of Delhi's streets, offers glimpses of some elusive order that must be there but seems always just out of frame. As a historian, I had found a convincing order brought to the past in the writings of that one grave's occupant. The more I pondered the turmoil of Egypt's revolution, and indeed all the scenes of great intellectual struggle in the Muslim world, the more it seemed that the paths to the present day all passed sooner or later through this great scholar's mind.

In 1732, Shah Wali Allah, the scion of a learned clan of Delhi ulama, returned home from his studies in the distant Arabian cities of Mecca and Medina to take up his father's place teaching at the Rahimiyya Madrasa. The school lay just outside the city's colossal red sandstone walls, which extended impossibly far into the distance and stood in relief against the lush expanse of green stretching to the horizons of the Ganges plain. Women cloaked in scarlet and yellow, curtained palanquins carrying merchants and gentlemen, camels, carts and elephants strolled in and out of sight through the city gates. This was the grand capital that India's Muslim rulers had chosen five centuries earlier as their base from which to rule over a vast land, one quarter of whose population would one day enter the fold of Islam. The Muslim Mughal Empire that shaped Shah Wali Allah's world was held together by its Turkic warrior princes in fragile alliance with Hindu maharajas across northern India. The language of this blended ruling class, and Shah Wali Allah's mother tongue, was Persian. The artistic style of their palaces blended the thousand-pillar porticoes of Indian temples and the delicate ceramic tiles of Iran. It was indeed far from the craggy ravines and earthen-tone huts of Mecca, where Shah Wali Allah's religion had been born almost twelve hundred years earlier.

Yet Shah Wali Allah, perhaps more than any other mind of his day, seemed to epitomize the breadth and depth of Islam's intellectual tradition. Sitting in the sweltering humidity of the Delhi summer, the man who would become India's greatest Muslim scholar sat to write an intellectual history that explained how the single message delivered by the Prophet Muhammad in Arabia had resulted in the stunning plurality and dissonance of the Muslim intellectual landscape.

As fascicules grew heavy with the labor of his pen, Shah Wali Allah charted the ramose temperaments, priorities and concerns that shaped how the prophetic moment in Arabia spread and settled along the winding coil of history. He traced how the ulama, 'the heirs of the prophets,' had struggled to unlock the Qur'an and the teachings of Muhammad to give structure to a new and diverse world that they took it upon themselves to guide. He described the tension between their commitment to preserving the truth of revelation from the corruptions of human speculation on the one hand, and their acceptance that even the words of God depended on human minds in order to be understood on the other. His book enumerated different camps of scholars and how each had favored different vehicles for preserving and understanding Muhammad's teachings, from the living tradition of communal practice, to the interpretive principles underlying the Prophet's teachings, to the literal text of his words.

Shah Wali Allah wrote to bring order to his own intellectual world, which was racked by strife and dissent. Moving between his native Islamic heritage in India and his studies in Arabia, he had witnessed archetypal tensions between a confidence in human reason and a fideistic reliance on revealed texts; between the outward strictures of God's law and the mystical longing for God Himself; between following in the accumulated footsteps of those who had built the rich Islamic tradition over the centuries and returning to its origins in order to renew it.

Reading Shah Wali Allah's book today, the ideological sparring and dramas that continue to shape the Muslim world seem smoothed into order on the page as the author untangles them, tracing the roots of diversity and fragmentation in the Islamic community of his own day. Shah Wali Allah is a worthy guide to the rich terrain of Islamic tradition, leading his reader from the dawn of the faith to the cusp of the modern world, when the interpretive order that he exemplified was shattered. He wrote his book in the language of Islamic scholarship, Arabic, and entitled it *Al-Insaf fi Bayan Asbab al-Ikhtilaf*, 'An Evenhanded Elucidation of the Causes of Disagreement.'[1]

THE WORD OF GOD, THE TEACHINGS OF HIS PROPHET AND THE MIND OF MAN

'The slaves of God can do deeds that please the Lord of the Worlds, deeds that displease Him and deeds that cause neither anger nor approval,' explained Shah Wali Allah. This statement underlined the great questions at the heart of the Islamic tradition: how should God be understood, what actions please Him and how should human society be ordered to accord with His will? To find answers, Muslim scholars turned to three sources. First, there was the Qur'an, 'The Recitation' bestowed from on high upon Muhammad. Held to be the word of God in Arabic, it was revealed through the angel Gabriel to Muhammad intermittently over the course of his twenty-three-year prophetic career. It descended in verses and sometimes in whole chapters to answer questions, to inspire, to warn and to provide glimpses into the power of the divine and the nature of the unseen. It was the one intact moment of God's instruction to humankind. As the years passed, Muhammad ordered and reordered these separate transcripts into chapters forming a stream of divine consciousness, neither a strict chronology nor a linear narrative. The Qur'an lived privately in the recitations, prayers and scattered parchments of Muhammad's followers until the revelation was formalized in one official copy some twenty years after the Prophet's death.

Although the Qur'an was the epicenter of the Islamic movement, it was not a lengthy book. Shah Wali Allah memorized it by heart before he was seven years old (many Muslims still do the same today), and only a fraction of its verses provide details about Islamic law or dogma. The five daily prayers and the details of the Ramadan fast are found nowhere in the holy book. These were provided by Muhammad's teachings and his authoritative precedent, which explained and elaborated on the Qur'an. Known as the Sunna, or 'The Tradition,' Muhammad's collective words, deeds, rulings and comportment were understood to be the Qur'an's message implemented in one time and place by the living example of the infallible 'Messenger of God.' How the Sunna was communicated and implemented in subsequent generations would be a central cause of diversity in Islam.

The tendency of Western readers to assume that 'scripture' refers only to the book written by or revealed to a prophet and not to the prophet himself misunderstands the nature of scripture in Islam. The full systems of Islamic theology and law are not derived primarily from the Qur'an. Muhammad's Sunna was a second but far more detailed living scripture, and later Muslim scholars would thus often refer to the Prophet as 'The Possessor of Two Revelations.'

Alone, however, the revelation of the Qur'an and the Tradition or Sunna that accompanied it would be voices unheard. It was the minds of Muslims poring over this *'ilm*, or sacred knowledge, that interpreted it and mapped it onto earthly affairs. The meaning of the Qur'an's language and edicts had to be determined, and the myriad sayings of the Prophet placed within a hierarchy of rules and exceptions. Ultimately, human reason was thus a third source of guidance. It derived scales of equity and principles from the revealed teachings of the Qur'an and Sunna and then reapplied them to those two sources to ensure that they were understood properly. It scanned and digested the natural world that God had created, reading the Qur'an and Sunna coherently against its backdrop.

OBEY GOD AND OBEY HIS MESSENGER

A terrifying two-hour drive north of Delhi, along potholed roads plied by every kind of beast of burden and motor vehicle, takes you to the village of Kandhla, only a few kilometers from where Shah Wali Allah was born. The sight of enormous sows and porkers rutting in garbage at the issue of the old town's narrow lanes belies Kandhla's fame as a cradle of Islamic learning. Neglected and embattled, the town is still home to some of the old dynasties of madrasa scholars that intermarried with Shah Wali Allah's descendants and preserve his writings in vast private libraries. Sitting for the midday meal in one of these beleaguered but proud old houses, the Prophet's exemplars are ubiquitous. Beards are all long enough to be grabbed with a fist, as Muhammad's was. Food is raised to the mouth with the right hand only, plates wiped and fingers licked clean, as Muhammad would do. Water is drunk in three sips, each with words of prayer mumbled after it, and the satiated patriarch of the family recites the words of gratitude that his Prophet taught his followers in the distant world of Arabia over fourteen centuries ago. 'Praise be to God, who has fed us and given us drink and made us Muslims.'

When inhabitants of the Near East first began encountering the Muslims coming out of Arabia, they would remark how: 'Your prophet has taught you everything, even how to shit.'[2] This would seem strange to the multitudes of gentiles who had followed Paul's Christianity. For them, the notion of a prophet bringing an all-encompassing law, permeated with mention of pure or impure foods and times and places of ritual sanctity, would be difficult to grasp. For the Jews of Palestine and Babylonia, whose detailed law Christians believed Jesus had fulfilled, the Shariah of Islam would be much more familiar. Like the great second-century Rabbi Akiva, whose students observed his every gesture and once even stole into the toilet to watch how their master cleaned himself, Muhammad's body of actions was a living exemplar of God's law.[3]

During his lifetime, Muhammad's authority among his followers in the Muslim community of Medina was twofold. He was the political leader of the city, but more importantly he was the medium of God's word and the sole architect of a new religion. 'It is not for a believing man or woman that they should have any choice in a matter when God and His Messenger have decided it,' the Qur'an proclaimed (33:36). Disputes were to be brought before Muhammad, whom God instructed to 'judge between them according to what is just' (4:58) and 'by what God has revealed' (5:48). The Qur'an commanded the Muslims over and over to 'obey God and obey His Messenger.' 'If you dispute a matter, bring it before God and the Messenger if indeed you do believe in God and the Last Day,' the Qur'an ordered, 'that is more goodly for you and best in the end' (4:59). The Muslims around Muhammad tried to imitate him in every aspect of his life, seeing a lifestyle pleasing to God in the way he walked, ate and washed. This comprehensive mandate for religion would be a defining hallmark of the Shariah, or God's sacred law.

When Muhammad died in 632, his followers were devastated and confused. The Companions, as the generation of Muslims who lived with and learned from the Prophet became known, did not know who would lead them. Who now would explain what God expected from them? In a dispute that would resonate and deepen for centuries to come, the Companions arrived at a tenuous settlement on succession. Although a party of leading Companions believed that Muhammad's cousin, son-in-law and early follower Ali bin Abi Talib should lead the Muslims, the quarreling tribal factions among the Companions could only settle on the Prophet's oldest friend and senior lieutenant, Abu Bakr.

In this moment of transition, the broad foundations of Sunni Islam were unconsciously laid out. Political leadership would fall on whomever the community accepted – or whomever the community had no choice but to accept after this person had 'assumed authority over it,' as Shah Wali Allah phrased it euphemistically.[4] More importantly, it would be the Muslim community as a whole, advised and spoken for by the learned among them, who would carry and define the message of Islam for future generations. In matters of law, ethics and dogma in Sunni Islam, the consensus of the ulama, called *Ijma'*, would become 'the firm pillar on which the religion is founded.'

THE BEGINNINGS OF THE ISLAMIC INTERPRETIVE TRADITION

In Shah Wali Allah's day, Jerusalem was a small provincial town in the Ottoman Empire. It remained close to Muslim hearts, but its medieval heyday had long since passed. Travelers making their way from Damascus to Baghdad or Egypt – even those voyaging from as far away as India – rarely made it a station on their journey. An Ottoman judge in Jerusalem's Shariah court thanked God when a Sufi dervish foretold that he would be transferred to a proper city.

For Christians, however, Jerusalem had never ceased to be the *axis mundi*, the center of the world. When the Frankish monk Arculf visited Jerusalem over a thousand years earlier in the 670s, he described an awesome city of grand and elegant stone. But the rude structure of awkward pillars and wooden planks that the 'Saracens' had erected atop the Temple Mount where Solomon's majestic Temple had once stood was built in 'a crude manner,' he recalled. Only twenty years later the same space would host the iconic Dome of the Rock and the massive Al-Aqsa Mosque, raised by the Arab rulers of Jerusalem to commemorate the place from which the Prophet Muhammad ascended to tour the heavens. When Arculf visited, the Muslims were still desert strangers encamped in a holy land.[5]

Within decades of Muhammad's death, his Companions, men and women who had been shepherds and merchants in the harsh earth of Arabia, sat in the palaces of Damascus and Cyrenaica. By 650, Muslim armies had advanced across North Africa and into Central Asia. In 711 they crossed into Iberia in the west and into the Indus valley of Shah Wali Allah's native India. Yet the Bedouin troops who flocked to the victorious banners of Islam and settled in the new garrison cities of Egypt, Syria and Iraq knew little about the religion in whose name they fought. The farmers of Mesopotamia and the merchants of Bukhara who converted to the triumphant faith would never know the prophet who was the epicenter of this movement, and who now lay interred in the mosque of Medina. In this nascent civilization, it was the Companions of the Prophet, settled in the new cities of the Muslim empire, who were the representatives of Islam. They had to instruct their followers and meet the new ethical, theological and legal challenges that confronted them in strange lands.

They faced unprecedented crises. In 656 the original succession crisis sparked by Muhammad's death plunged the Muslim community into a civil war that would not finally abate until 692, when the Umayyad family of the Prophet's tribe finally established uncontested authority over the new Islamic empire from their capital in Damascus. Yet the impious ways and unjust rule of the Umayyads bred bitter resentment among many Muslims. The radically different opinions about who had truly inherited the Prophet's authority to define God's law on earth only grew more pronounced. One camp, the emergent Shiah, held that Ali and the descendants of the Prophet through him should be the spiritual and political leaders. What became the Sunni majority held that the Muslim community, the *Umma*, as a whole would come to consensus on those worthy of political or religious authority. As Umayyad power weakened, these contentions broke forth once more into strife in the 740s. A new dynasty, descended from the Prophet's uncle Abbas, drawing support from the lands of Persia and claiming to rule in the name of the Qur'an and Sunna, crushed the decadent Umayyads and built a new capital city at Baghdad. Under the looming shadow of the Abbasid Caliphate, the sects of Sunni and Shiah Islam gelled into their recognizable forms.

Throughout these decades of conflict, the powerful forces of cultural chauvinism, sectarian certainties and political ambitions began encroaching onto the religious message of the early Muslims. The text of the Qur'an had already been fixed, but the uncontested authority of the Prophet's voice remained dangerously inchoate. Eager to insinuate their ideas and customs into the new religion, parties from every religious and political direction began placing their messages in the Prophet's mouth. Hadiths – reports of the Prophet's words or deeds – were forged by the thousands. Supporters of the Umayyad dynasty forged a Hadith in which the Prophet foretold that Mu'awiya, the first Umayyad caliph, would enjoy the intimate company of God, seated below His throne in the heavens, as recompense for the abuse his opponents dealt him in this world.[6] Mu'awiya himself encouraged his followers to forge Hadiths detracting from the standing of his opponents, the Shiah supporters of Ali and his descendants.[7] A concocted Hadith in which the Prophet supposedly foretold the founding of Baghdad was dueled over and spun by forgers for and against the Abbasid caliphs, some manipulating the forged Hadith to say that the dynasty's capital was 'as firmly planted as an iron stake in the earth' and others that 'it will sink faster than an iron stake in sandy ground.'[8]

The great challenge facing Muslim scholars amid this chaos was to resist the forces tugging at and impacting Islam and to preserve the religion in its true form. As the Qur'an cautioned, earlier communities such as the Christians and Jews had gone astray when they had allowed their own inclinations and speculations to lead them away from God's revealed truth. 'Hold fast to the rope of God together, and do not break apart' (3:103), the Qur'an had warned.

It was the bond of devotion to the sacred knowledge, *'ilm*, revealed to Muhammad that held the Muslim community together during these afflictions. Throughout years of brutal civil war, every year during the Hajj season trickles of Muslims from across the fractured empire would converge on Mecca in a great sea of white-clad pilgrims. A crucial assumption shared by the Muslims was that the revelation given to Muhammad was not relevant only to his lifetime and the founding Muslim community in Medina. The Prophet had been sent as 'a mercy to all the worlds' (21:107).[9]

The Qur'an, compiled into official form and promulgated by the third Muslim ruler, Uthman, around 650, was understood to be an inexhaustible mine of guidance and truth – 'an elucidation of all things,' as it called itself (16:89). The relatively short holy book was seen as a spark of divine potential, the seed from which a holistic way of life and belief would bloom thanks to the efforts of scholars to unlock its meanings through the lens of Muhammad's Sunna and their own reason.

Islam was thus a totalistic vision. The founding generations of Muslims, spread across a wide expanse, would not understand their religion as merely one part of their life, separate from daily etiquette, the rules of commerce or the courts. In time, Muslim scholars would develop a five-tiered model for marking the status of any conceivable act in God's eyes. 'Required' (*wajib*) acts would be rewarded by God in the Afterlife, and failing to carry them out would result in punishment by God and perhaps in this life by state authorities as well. 'Recommended' (*mandūb*) acts were rewarded by God but not required for Muslims. If a person avoided 'Disliked' (*makruh*) actions, God would reward him or her, but committing them was nonetheless allowed. The 'Prohibited' (*haram*) acts carried the threat of punishment by God in the hereafter and possibly in this life by the state. 'Permitted' (*mubah*) was a narrow category of acts that had no value, positive or negative, in God's eyes. All conceivable words and deeds had some ruling under God's law, and, as an early Muslim scholar explained, it was not permitted for a Muslim to undertake anything without determining what that ruling was. To do this they had to ask the ulama.[10]

Yet who were the ulama of these first generations of Islam, and how were they to guide their fellow faithful in belief and practice? 'In every city a leading scholar arose,' wrote Shah Wali Allah, and often more than one.[11] The leading scholar of Iraq's bustling port city of Basra was the revered Hasan Basri (d. 728). Widely sought out for his piety and knowledge, Hasan was turned to for explanations about how Muslims should understand their religion and how they should interact with a startlingly diverse environment of Nestorian Christians, Jews and Persian Zoroastrians. Hasan had been raised until adolescence in the household of one of the Prophet's widows, whom his mother served as a maid. Living in Medina, Hasan had learned from senior Companions like the Prophet's son-in-law Ali bin Abi Talib and his servant Anas bin Malik. He had gathered together the sayings and descriptions of the Prophet from those Companions he had met, learning from them also how to implement the values and mindset of a Muslim when new questions arose.

When asked about how a Muslim should pray, whether or not a novel type of food or drink was permitted or how to settle a commercial dispute, Hasan looked for answers in the Qur'an, his knowledge of the Prophet's rulings and the opinions and principles he had learned from the Companions he had known. On one occasion, a man came to Hasan unsure of what to do because, when one of his slaves had run away, he had sworn to cut off the slave's hand in punishment when he found him. Must he fulfill this gruesome oath? Hasan recalled that the Companion Samura, who had settled in Basra, had told him that the Prophet used to encourage charity and forbid mutilating prisoners, and that the Prophet had once said, 'Whoever kills a slave, we will kill him; whoever mutilates a slave, we will mutilate him.'[12]

Unlike Christianity, in which a priest was invested with his office in a ritual presided over by senior clergy, Islam has no formal priesthood or process of ordination. Nor did the medieval Islamic community erect any stable institutions of learning producing graduates marked for religious distinction. Instead, the emergence of the Muslim scholarly class took place through the society's valorization of *'ilm* and the community's recognition of those deemed to possess it. In the early Islamic period, a gradual consensus formed around who these major pious figures were who, like Hasan Basri, carried this knowledge. The networks of the teachers and students that radiated outward from these early figures defined the ranks of the ulama. Like the Christian tradition of apostolic succession, a Muslim scholar derived his or her authority from the chain of teachers that linked them back to the font of *'ilm*, the Prophet. Like Rabbinic Judaism, it was the transmission of sacred knowledge that created the authority to interpret God's scriptures and endowed individuals with it.

ABU HANIFA AND THE PARTISANS OF REASON

Tracing Islam's movement out of Arabia, Shah Wali Allah described how, as different Companions settled in different cities, varied approaches to understanding Islam's teachings emerged. Not only did each group of Companions bring with them their own recollection of the Prophet's Sunna as well as their own understanding of the Qur'an, they also faced starkly divergent local environments. These early Muslims were a small minority compared to the huge native populations, and the specific customs, foods and climates of each region began impacting their lifestyles.

In Kufa, a new Muslim garrison city in southern Iraq founded next to the ancient Persian metropolis of Hira, the Companion 'Abdallah bin Mas'ud became a pillar of instruction and guidance, passing on much of his learning to his disciple 'Alqama bin Qays. As those few who had actually known Muhammad died off, the next generation, known as the Successors, picked up the mantle of leadership. Kufa soon looked to Ibrahim Nakha'i as one of the most learned. He gathered together the traditions passed on by 'Alqama as well as those of the Prophet's favorite wife, Aisha, renowned for her perceptive understanding of Islam. Nakha'i's most famous student was Hammad bin Abi Sulayman, who in time passed his learning on to his talented disciple of eighteen years, a Kufan silk merchant of Persian descent known as Abu Hanifa (d. 767). He would become the epicenter of a great scholarly movement in the city, which would eventually be one of the four Sunni schools of law.

Abu Hanifa developed a unique perspective on how to answer the question of what God expected from Muslims in the interpretive chaos that reigned after the end of prophecy. Surrounded by the jostling cultural and political flux of cosmopolitan Kufa, he turned to the Qur'an, those Hadiths he knew for sure to be reliable, the teachings of the Companions who had settled in Kufa and then his own reason. For him, the Qur'an was the anchor of any true understanding of God's will. Unlike the flurry of spurious Hadiths, the holy book remained an unchanged record of God's instruction. Its verses and commandments were certainties that could not be dropped or altered by anything less than certain. Only the most reliable Hadiths, which did not contradict the evident truths of Islamic practice as Abu Hanifa understood them, could be allowed to alter how a Qur'anic ruling was interpreted.

When asked, for example, if a person performing their ritual ablutions before prayer had first to formulate the intention to do so, Abu Hanifa said no. The Qur'an merely commanded those preparing for prayer to 'wash your face and arms to the elbows, and wipe your heads and feet to the ankles' (5:6). It never mentioned forming an intention. A person who happened to submerge themselves in the nearby Euphrates would thus be, quite accidentally, ready to pray. Confronted with a Hadith in which the Prophet supposedly stated, 'Deeds are determined by intentions,' Abu

Hanifa chose not to admit it as evidence. Far from being a well-known teaching of the Prophet, this Hadith had reached Abu Hanifa from only one person, who had heard it from only one person, who in turn had heard it from only one person, from only one other person, who had supposedly heard it from the Prophet.[13] How could a decision affecting the validity of an act performed at least five times a day by every Muslim depend on a report known to so few?

Shah Wali Allah's discussion of the stereotypical punishment of cutting off a thief's hand for stealing reveals the complexity of how Abu Hanifa dealt with problems of law. One might imagine that, if presented with a question such as 'How should a thief who has stolen loaves of bread from a baker be punished?' Abu Hanifa and the young scholars who congregated around him would look first to the Qur'an. It states clearly, 'The thief, male or female, cut off their hand as a punishment for what they have earned...' (5:38). But Abu Hanifa would also remember that his teacher Hammad had heard the great Nakha'i tell that the Prophet only ordered this punishment if the item stolen was worth more than ten silver coins. Moreover, earlier Kufan masters had ruled, on the basis of a well-known Hadith from the Prophet, that 'There is no amputation for stealing the fruits [of a palm tree] or its heart.'[14] But Abu Hanifa and his colleagues would still not have found a clear answer to the question of the loaves of bread in the Qur'an, the Hadiths or the Companion rulings at their disposal. How could they use these sources to cover new territory and resolve the question?

Abu Hanifa developed a systematic form of analogical reasoning, called *Qiyas*, to extend the ruling of one situation to another based on a shared legal cause (*'illa*) – that feature for which God or the Prophet had judged the situation in a certain way. By understanding what lay behind the rulings of the Qur'an and Hadiths, these rulings could be extended to unknown situations that shared the same legal causes. Abu Hanifa understood that the Prophet had ruled out the severe punishment of amputating a hand for stealing the yield of a palm tree because the fruit would soon rot anyway. It was too ephemeral to merit such a harsh response. He thus concluded that the theft of any foodstuff, such as a loaf of bread, that would quickly rot would not entail losing a hand.[15]

Of course, *Qiyas* was a precarious process. The Qur'an and Hadiths rarely explained clearly the legal cause of a ruling, and it was left to scholars like Abu Hanifa to derive it from context. Some disagreed with his *Qiyas* in the case of date palms, arguing that the reason the Prophet had prohibited amputating a hand for stealing dates from trees was that in Medina such exposed fruit was considered semi-public property.

More importantly, there may be no *reason* at all for a ruling. This was especially the case in the rules revealed by God and His Messenger on matters of ritual. God had forbidden pork in the Qur'an, calling it 'filth' (*rijs*) (6:145). The Prophet had also instructed Muslims to wash out seven times any dish that a dog had drunk from. Did that mean dogs were ritually filthy too? Abu Hanifa and the majority of Muslim scholars used analogy to conclude that dogs were unclean. If one slobbered on your clothing, you could not pray in it. One scholar, Malik, disagreed. The Prophet allowed Muslims to use dogs in herding and to fetch game in hunting, Malik observed, so how could they be filthy? Malik concluded that the command to wash dishes drunk from by dogs was merely 'done out of worship' (*ta'abbudi*), an arational act of obedience performed for the sake of God alone and unrelated to dogs' ritual cleanliness or lack thereof.[16]

Important to Abu Hanifa's method for deriving law from scripture was the concept of *Istihsan*, or 'seeking the best.' Sometimes the systematic application of *Qiyas* led to a result that Abu Hanifa and his circle considered unjust or harmful. So an alternative analogical maneuver was sought out. When it came to the question of women selling their breast milk, at first Abu Hanifa and his circle of disciples found themselves forced to prohibit it. This was inevitable, due to two *Qiyas* analogies they had already developed. First, milk was a bodily fluid, like semen, and Abu Hanifa held that these fluids were impure when they left the body. Much like wine and other impure substances, these fluids could not be bought and sold. Also, Abu Hanifa had concluded, humans cannot sell parts of their bodies – the Prophet had forbidden 'weaves' made from human hair, for example – so selling a woman's milk could not be allowed either. This was a problematic ruling for parents who could not find sufficient breast milk for their children, however. Abu Hanifa and his circle thus engaged in *Istihsan* and drew a third analogy based on a separate scriptural command, namely the Qur'an's statement that Muslims could consume the forbidden substances of pork and carrion in cases of necessity (2:173). Since infants had to consume the milk of their own species to survive, breast milk was an absolute necessity. Prohibition of its sale could be lifted, just as pork was permitted for a starving adult.[17]

In effect, *Istihsan* presupposed a scholar referencing some notion of equity or justice outside the boundaries of the literal texts of the Qur'an and Hadiths. But the whole point of analogy was extending the wisdom of these scriptures to new situations while remaining true to the revealed truth of the Prophet's message. What place did an outside standard of fairness have in restricting this process? This would be a great cause of later controversy.

Abu Hanifa's method of elaborating the Shariah, further developed by his leading students like Abu Yusuf and Muhammad Shaybani, became extremely influential in Iraq. Both these students found places in the Abbasid court in Baghdad, with Abu Yusuf appointed as the first chief judge of the empire. Shah Wali Allah described how Abu Hanifa came to exemplify the approach to the Shariah taken by a broad trend known as the *Ahl al-Ra'y*, the Partisans of Reason.

MALIK AND THE AUTHORITY OF CUSTOM

Shah Wali Allah had been a late addition to his family. His father, Shah 'Abd al-Rahim, had long been one of the most respected ulama in the Mughal realm, and his talents and austere piety had won him and then cost him royal favor decades before his most famous son was born. When Shah Wali Allah was five, his father placed him in the school he supervised, and by seven the boy had memorized the Qur'an. He mastered Arabic and Persian letters soon thereafter and was married at fourteen. A childhood spent studying at his father's feet meant that by sixteen he had completed the standard curriculum of Hanafi law, theology and logic along with arithmetic and geometry. A year later, Shah Wali Allah would recall poignantly, his father and greatest teacher 'voyaged onward to the abode of God's mercy.'

The young student's ambition to seek *'ilm* remained strong, and by nineteen he had exhausted the knowledge of Delhi's scholars. So Shah Wali Allah voyaged across the Indian Ocean to perform his Hajj pilgrimage and pursue his studies in the holy cities of Mecca and Medina. In the Prophet's mosque in Medina, at the feet of scholars from across the Muslim world, he studied a book to which he became exceedingly attached and which he viewed as the foundation for understanding the Prophet's Sunna. It was the *Muwatta'*, the 'Well Trodden Path,' of the eighth-century scholar of Medina, Malik bin Anas.[18]

Medina in Malik's time was far from the booming trade and imperial politics of Kufa, Basra and Baghdad. Its quiet date groves hummed with the calm of a home whose occupants had moved on to a wider world. There, in 'The City of the Messenger of God,' another approach to formulating Islamic law and belief was developing contemporaneous to that of Abu Hanifa. Malik had grown up in Medina and learned from its most esteemed scholars like Nafi', a learned servant of a famous Companion of the Prophet, and the early Hadith collector Zuhri, who had actually met some of the more longevous Companions. Malik collected the Hadiths transmitted from the Prophet in the city as well as the legal and doctrinal opinions of Companions like Umar bin Khattab, the second caliph. Leaning against a column of the Prophet's own mosque, only yards from where the Prophet himself was buried, Malik sorted through this material, organized it by topic and recorded it in his *Muwatta'*, the earliest surviving book of Hadiths and Islamic law. Consisting of approximately 1,800 reports, 527 are Hadiths of the Prophet, 613 are rulings made by Companions, 285 are the rulings of Successors and the remainder are Malik's own opinions. The book covers wide areas of Muslim life, from performing one's ablutions for prayer to irrigation law, from Hadiths affirming God's complete control over man's destiny to Hadiths describing Hellfire.

Unlike the cosmopolitan soup of Kufa, Malik saw Medina as the bastion of the pure Islam the Prophet had originally taught. He believed that the customs and practices of Medina's scholars were the true vehicle of the Sunna and a peerless guide to how to live as a Muslim. The strange Hadiths circulating in Damascus or Egypt seemed suspicious to Malik, and in some cases even Hadiths he heard from his own teacher, Nafi', who had heard them from the caliph Umar's son, who had heard them from the Prophet, were not definitive for him. One such Hadith quoted the Prophet telling Muslims that a buyer and seller can rescind or cancel a transaction up until they part company. But this was not the practice of the people and scholars of Medina, for whom a sale became final once the two parties verbally agreed on it. Because the Hadith was 'not acted upon' in Medina, Malik and his students did not accept it as defining the Prophet's teachings.[19]

In a use of reason similar to Abu Hanifa's *Istihsan*, Malik pioneered a mode of thinking about laws that became known as 'blocking the means' (*sadd al-dhara'i'*). This prohibited something otherwise legal because it was a slippery slope to a known evil or prohibited result.

The Qur'an forbade Muslims from engaging in *Riba*, which Muslim scholars understood as any kind of interest-bearing transaction such as loans in business. The Qur'an explicitly condemns excessive usury as exploitative to the poor, but Shah Wali Allah explained that Islamic law considered even mild interest harmful. It prevents people from focusing on agriculture and manufacture, 'the roots of profit,' he claimed.[20]

Even in the early Islamic period, however, Muslims lending money felt that charging interest was as essential a part of business activity as it is today (at the very least, it represents the opportunity cost of the lender's money – what he could accomplish with it were it available and not with the borrower). Muslim scholars thus developed what became known as 'the double sale,' in which the borrower approaches a lender with an offer to buy some item from him, for example, a bolt of cloth, for some cost, such as 100 gold pieces. Since the buyer (i.e., the borrower) does not have that sum available at the time, he agrees with the seller (i.e., the lender) to pay him 125 gold pieces in a year's time – buying the cloth on credit and paying a premium for receiving it right away (credit purchases were allowed by the Prophet and were essential in activities like farming in which revenues come only at harvest time). In theory, the borrower can keep the cloth or sell it to whomever he wants for whatever sum he wishes. But the lender 'offers' to simplify matters by taking the bolt of cloth off the borrower's hands right away for its actual value of 100 gold pieces. The borrower/buyer agrees and thus departs with 100 gold pieces in his hands and a duty to pay the lender/seller back 125 gold pieces in one year's time. An interest-bearing loan has been accomplished.

Since buying on credit with a premium was permitted by the Prophet, and since it was permitted for parties who had completed one transaction to engage in a second one whenever they wanted, there was no technical reason to ban this 'double sale.' Neither the first nor the second sale on its own was prohibited, nor was combining them. Just as a merchant is not forbidden from selling a knife to a customer simply because the customer *might* intend to murder someone with it, the majority of Muslim jurists looked at the legality of each *act* and not the possible future intentions of the actor. The 'double sale' soon became widely allowed and practiced. In fact, it ultimately became the basis of modern Islamic finance, which accomplishes the same process through almost instantaneous platinum transactions arranged by the bank lender.[21] But when Malik looked at the 'double sale,' he saw only a clear plan to violate the spirit of God's law. The 'double sale' was a means to precisely the interest-bearing loan that God and the Prophet had forbidden, and Malik prohibited it.[22]

THE POWER OF REASON: THE GREEK LEGACY AND ISLAMIC THEOLOGY

Seven hundred years before Shah Wali Allah's time, a renowned Muslim scientist named Biruni was dragooned into the service of Mahmud of Ghazna, the first of the Turkic warlords who came to plunder North India's riches. Mahmud's army, Biruni recounted with sadness, 'destroyed the verdant land and scattered the Hindus to the wind and memory.' Biruni took advantage of his conscription to learn Sanskrit and translated books of Indian theology and astronomy into Arabic. He recorded the strange and incredible peoples, places and mores he encountered during his stay among the Hindus. Many of his observations, he knew, would defy his readers' belief. As a devotee of Aristotle and the Greek sciences, Biruni knew that 'hearing reports of something is not like seeing it directly.' Unlike sense perception, the fragments of data and impressions one hears from other people rarely if ever convey certainty. But as a follower of Muhammad, Biruni also knew that nothing of his religion, born in time and carried down through the years in text and tradition, could ever survive without relying on the testimony of earlier generations and 'the immortal tracings of the pen.' Shah Wali Allah could only echo his predecessor. Anything you know that came from someone else, he wrote, must have come via some medium out of the past.[23]

Shah Wali Allah understood that inheriting the teachings of the Messenger of God meant handling sacred knowledge that originated in the realm of the unseen. He offered his audience some striking examples. 'On the Day of Judgment the Earthly World will be brought forth in the form of an old woman, black-and-white of hair, blue-eyed and teeth bared, hideous in form,' read one Hadith. 'God will bring you into the Gardens of Heaven, and you need do no more than wish it, and you'll be carried on a ruby steed, who will fly with you wherever you desire,' read another. No doubt profound meaning lay veiled in metaphor behind these words of the Prophet as he described the Afterlife, and Shah Wali Allah knew the great controversies that had swirled around such uncanny Hadiths. But he also knew the fundamental position of Sunni Islam: one must affirm the truth spoken by the Messenger of God.[24]

Early Christian opponents of Islam had pounced on such beliefs. 'We put no faith in such silly tales,' the Byzantine Emperor Leo III had written in a letter, mocking the Muslims' belief in a Heaven full of carnal delights such as perpetual virgins and rivers of milk and honey. How could Muslims trust any tenets of their faith, he asked, when they so often relied on mere tenuous attributions to Muhammad?[25] This letter, part of an exchange with the Umayyad Caliph Umar bin 'Abd al-'Aziz around the year 720, illustrates the centrality of the question of epistemology, or how and from where we attain knowledge. The great challenge of the Muslim ulama was to answer the questions: 'How do we know God?' and 'What is right and wrong in God's eyes?' Now, as the ruling class of an expansive Islamic empire, they had to justify the sources of their sacred knowledge to outsiders and substantiate their answers to a broader and more contested audience.

The Qur'an had encouraged Muhammad and his followers to use their reason, to scan the heavens and appreciate the ordered infinity of God's creation. But the Qur'an also cautioned against trusting too much in reason when pondering matters of the unseen, for the Devil is forever urging man to 'say about God that which you do not know' (2:169). Reason and rationalization offered a deceptive and alluring window for indulging one's own fancies and desires. This had been the bane of earlier peoples gifted with prophecy by God. Overconfident in their own speculations about the nature of God and His law, they ignored the revealed books sent down to them. The Qur'an warned Muslims, 'If you heed most of those in the world, they will lead you astray from God's path. They do but follow supposition, they do but conjecture' (6:116). Belief, prayer and practice must be built on firm instructions revealed by God. All else is too subject to abiding human whims and interests.

This presented a quandary. The Qur'an had been preserved unaltered since the death of the Prophet, the foundation of Muslim faith and practice.* But this foundation did not provide all the answers to theological questions or the necessary details for basic rituals and laws. These could be found in plenty in the teachings attributed to Muhammad, but the Hadiths inundating the garrison cities of the Near East were very often totally made up, frequently deserving of suspicion and at best transmitted from the Prophet by a fraction of that great plurality of Muslims who memorized the Qur'an by heart. If the Qur'an warned Muslims against following mere supposition, and if 'supposition can never take the place

* The majority of Western scholars also affirm the Qur'an's date of origin and overall textual integrity. See Behnam Sadeghi and Mohsen Goudarzi, 'Ṣan'ā' 1 and the Origins of the Qur'ān.'

of truth' (53:28), how could Muslims 'know' anything about God or their duties to Him from a source as questionable as the Hadiths?

Furthermore, at the very moment at which Muslims were reminded to cling tightly to God's authentic revelation and avoid outside influences, they were confronted with the stunning diversity of the Near Eastern philosophical heritage. The Muslim ruling class found itself face to face with the logic of Aristotle, the cosmology of Plotinus and the theologies of Christianity and Zoroastrianism. The challenges raised by polemics like Leo III's letter were but early salvos in an embattling barrage.

In Baghdad and Basra particularly, a group of Muslim scholars arose to confront these other systems and came to be known by the general moniker of the Mutazila. By wading into interfaith debates, however, these Muslim intellectuals implicitly accepted the terms of their opponents. As a result, they were permanently affected by their opponents' methods and philosophical assumptions.

To defend Islam in this environment, the Mutazila school of thought based its understanding of Islam on sources that it felt could stand up to the skepticism of internal and external critics: the Qur'an, reports about the Prophet that were universally agreed upon, other items of complete consensus among Muslims and, finally, the proofs of reason.[26] This species of reason, though, was not the common sense of a Bedouin pondering the night sky. It was the regimented and logical reasoning of the Aristotelian heritage, thought to be able to reveal profound truths and unmask falsehood without recourse to religion at all.

The Mutazila first had to develop a suitable vision of theology. The Qur'an magnified God as 'glorified above all ascribed to Him' (37:180) and as totally beyond our mental conception. Indeed, the most central theme in the revelation to Muhammad is God's *Tawhid*, His absolute and transcendental unity. But the holy book also described God in terms humans could understand. He is seated on a throne 'above the heavens and the earth.' He speaks to prophets, is 'closer to man than his own jugular vein' and will come before us on the Day of Judgment among ranks of angels.

This presented a serious problem for the Muslim rationalists. As the Latin Christian philosopher and devotee of Aristotle, Boethius (d. 525), and later Maimonides (d. 1204), Aristotle's greatest Jewish champion, both observed, 'there cannot be any belief in the unity of God except by admitting that He is one simple substance without any composition or plurality of elements.'[27] In the Greek philosophical tradition, to be in any location, like on a throne, above anything or closer to something than something else, a thing must be bounded within a certain space. In other words, it must be a body. A body must exist in a space greater than it – it thus cannot be the creator of *all* space. Furthermore, an entity that consists of any composite elements, like an entity possessing a 'hand' or even 'speech,' needs a greater power to assemble it and thus cannot be the greatest or only eternal entity. Finally, motion entails change for Aristotle, and in his view nothing that changes can be eternal.

Plato's conception of the ultimate source of all creation was 'The Good,' one and unknowable. Aristotle understood the notion of God as changeless, pure reason, which generated the cosmos but is removed from its flawed particulars. Immersed in the Hellenistic heritage, the Mutazila conceived of God as simple, unified, distant and eminently just. His justice made Him subject to reason. He could only ask of humans what was fair, and man could grasp the objective realities of right and wrong with his mind. Man had to have free will, the Mutazila argued, because if man were not able to choose between right and wrong God would be punishing or rewarding him for something outside his control.[28]

The Mutazila's epistemology and theology shaped the way they understood the Islamic scriptures. The God of Abraham was far too personal and tempestuous for Hellenistic philosophers. Not surprisingly, the Mutazila thus read the seemingly anthropomorphic verses of the Qur'an figuratively. God's coming in ranks of angels was thus not to be taken literally. It was only a figurative allusion to the signs of His power.[29]

While their fundamental commitment to the truth of the Qur'an obliged the Mutazila scholars to negotiate such problematic verses, they had no such duty with Hadiths. For them, any Hadith that they saw as contradicting the Qur'an or reason had to be rejected outright as a forgery. One such Hadith quotes the Prophet as revealing how 'God descends to the lowest heavens in the last third of the night.' From there He grants the wishes of those who remain awake in prayer. The Mutazila rejected this as absurd because it entailed God moving and thus being a body subject to change. In another Hadith, the Prophet recounts how Moses confronted Adam in Heaven, rebuking him for robbing all his future descendants of life in the Garden of Eden. Adam replied that Moses, as a prophet of God, should know that it is not fair to blame him for something that God had ordained. 'So Adam bested Moses in the argument.'[30] This was preposterous and could never have been taught by Muhammad, the Mutazila asserted, because man has free will and cannot escape blame by claiming that some act 'was written.'

SHAFI'I AND THE BEGINNINGS OF SUNNI ISLAM

'O Commander of the Believers, do not do it!' Malik had once pleaded with the Abbasid caliph. The ruler had proposed making Malik's *Muwatta'* the basis for an empire-wide code of Shariah law. But the scholar of Medina explained that each region of that realm had forged its own path for God's law, and this diversity could not realistically be undone.

Shah Wali Allah appreciated this story, and he used it in his writings to demonstrate how the world of Islam in the eighth century was a very localized one. Abu Hanifa only left Kufa to make his pilgrimage to Mecca, and Malik only left Medina to visit nearby Mecca as well. Despite the expansive diversity of the Muslim empire, its scholars clung to the parochial spaces of their own cities. When a certain view on law became established in an area, scholars there 'clung onto it by their teeth,' Shah Wali Allah remarked.[31]

Malik's most famous student, however, was a very different creature and a symbol of an interconnected new day. Muhammad bin Idris Shafi'i was born in Gaza, studied for many years with Malik in Medina, served as the Abbasid governor in the Yemeni city of Najran, traveled to Baghdad to study with Abu Hanifa's acolyte Shaybani and others and ended his days settled in Egypt. His travels showed Shafi'i how isolated and idiosyncratic the local schools of Islam really were.

Oddly, despite this undeniable multivocality, in debates over law and dogma consensus (*Ijma'*) was the most powerful proof that Muslim scholars could invoke. Quoting an early Muslim scholar, Shah Wali Allah explained how, when the 'leading and best of the people' came to a consensus on an issue of law or dogma not specified in scripture, that opinion carried the day.[32] But often both sides in a scholarly dispute claimed consensus, as occurred in contentious correspondences between Abu Hanifa's student Abu Yusuf and Awza'i, the leading scholar of Beirut.[33] Aware of these absurdities, Shafi'i rejected most claims of consensus as fanciful, though he affirmed the soundness of the concept. Only the most basic, core elements of Muslim faith and practice were in fact agreed upon by all, such as the five daily prayers or the prohibition on wine – 'the roots of sacred knowledge, not its branches,' he explained.[34]

In light of this disagreement, what could provide a thread of unity for the scholars' interpretive efforts and serve as a common standard of proof? Shah Wali Allah explained that Shafi'i 'took law from the source.' The answer was to return to the Hadiths of the Prophet.[35] All the regions and varied scholars believed firmly that they were adhering to the Prophet's Sunna in the sense of his overall precedent. But they had different notions of how that Sunna was understood and proven. For Abu Hanifa it was through the strong, established Hadiths available in Kufa, then through the teachings of the Companions who had settled there. Although he carefully collected Hadiths, for Malik there was no better record of the Sunna than the practice of the people in Muhammad's own town.

But, as Shafi'i had pointed out, all these supposedly accurate understandings of the Sunna disagreed with each other. He believed that only by obeying strictly the actual words of the Prophet as transmitted in Hadiths could a true and unified vision of the Sunna triumph. This was the mantra of a dynamic but highly conservative new group with which Shafi'i identified. Calling themselves the *Ahl al-Sunna wa'l-Jama'a*, 'The People of the Sunna and the Collective,' their vision of the faith would become known by the abbreviated name of Sunni Islam.

Shafi'i threw himself into arguments not only with other students of Malik and the disciples of Abu Hanifa but also with the Mutazila. His aim was to raise the Hadiths to the role of the primary lens for understanding the Qur'anic message. Shafi'i criticized the Kufans for following analogical reasoning when they should heed the words of the Prophet first and foremost. The notion of *Istihsan*, he decried, was tantamount to an assumption that God had not provided clear guidance on an issue. He further attacked their principle that no Hadiths other than those considered eminently reliable by Abu Hanifa's circle could be used to govern the interpretation of Qur'anic verses.

The Mutazila bore the brunt of Shafi'i's campaign. For Shafi'i, their skepticism about Hadiths was heretical. In debates, the Mutazila asked him how he could put mere reports transmitted 'from so-and-so, from so-and-so' on the same level as the Qur'an. Some even rejected the idea that anything other than the Qur'an and reason be used as a basis for law at all. They based this on the Qur'anic verse in which the book described itself as 'an elucidation of all things.' Shafi'i responded that the Qur'an, in fact, ordered Muslims to obey the Prophet. After his passing from the world, the only way now to know his teachings was through reports of his words and deeds. If Shafi'i's opponents claimed that they could derive the full range of Islamic law and doctrine from the Qur'an alone, he asked, then how did they know how to pray or fast? Neither is described in any detail in the Qur'an. There must be some source for God's instructions to man outside the pages of the Qur'an by which these details were known, and Shafi'i argued that this source was the Hadiths.[36]

The Mutazila opponents of this argument were pious and learned Muslims, however, and they countered that core Islamic practices like prayer were indeed drawn from outside the Qur'an – from the living tradition of the Muslim community, which handed down these sacred customs generation after generation by consensus. This did not mean that Muslims should heed individual Hadiths on every particularity of the Shariah.

Shafi'i admitted that making Hadiths the primary source for the minutiae of a law covering everything from sales to marriage and divorce would mean relying on a source less certain than the Qur'an or living tradition. But the Prophet had sent individual Companions to distant settlements to teach Islam to their inhabitants, and these communities had relied on these solitary sources. If one could achieve confidence in the authenticity of a report from the Prophet, then was it not better to follow the Prophet than one's own fallible reason?

The new epistemology and interpretive method proposed by Shafi'i and the early Sunnis inverted that of the Kufans and Mutazila. The Qur'an was *not* the most powerful source for understanding the Islamic message. Certainly, it was the word of God and thus peerless in its ontological standing. But, as Shah Wali Allah explained, early Sunnis held that 'The Sunna rules over the Book of God, the Book of God does not rule over the Sunna.'[37] The Qur'an and the Sunna functioned in tandem. Like a locked door without a key, the Qur'an could not be accessed without the Sunna. The Qur'an contained the totality of God's message, but the Sunna explained, adjusted and added to it in order to convey God's complete guidance.

Hadiths of the Prophet could specify and restrict the Qur'an, as in the case of punishing a thief. They could also explain vague Qur'anic commands, for example, by detailing the specific motions and words that make up the Muslim prayer. Hadiths could also add new rules onto those already mentioned in the holy book. The Qur'an forbids men from marrying their mothers, sisters, daughters, nieces, aunts or mothers-in-law (with corresponding prohibitions for women), adding 'And other than that has been permitted for you' (4:23–24). Hadiths add that a man cannot take both a woman and her aunt as co-wives.[38] For the early Sunnis, there could be no contradiction between a Hadith authentically transmitted from the Prophet and the Qur'an. They were two halves of the same revelation. The Hadiths were just explicating the true meaning of the holy book.

Shah Wali Allah explained how Shafi'i's vision of law erased regional boundaries and built on a common body of Hadiths, Companion rulings and regimented reasoning. Finding the answer to a new question about how to act or adjudicate would begin with consulting the verses of the Qur'an and reliable Hadiths together. The local practice of Medina or the teachings of Kufa had no weight. If nothing in the Qur'an, Hadiths or universally agreed-upon positions among the early Muslims could be found to address the question, then the scholar could search for a ruling by a leading Companion or use strict analogical reasoning based on a Qur'anic verse or Hadith.

Shafi'i's use of reason in deriving law was more restricted than Abu Hanifa's broad *Istihsan*. In particular, he favored a form of analogy known as 'manifest analogy' (*qiyas jali*: in the Western intellectual tradition, a fortiori or 'by the stronger' reasoning). Here, the presence of some factor in mild or moderate form in one case entails that another case where it exists in extreme form would share the same ruling. Shafi'i's followers used this approach in the question of whether women could lead men in congregational prayers. No Hadith of any reliability dealt with this subject, nor had the Companions formalized an explicit rule. Hadiths did explain, however, that in congregations of men and women, the women lined up behind the men to pray. Since women could not be in the *same* rows as men, a fortiori they could not be *in front* of them leading the prayer.[39]

Shafi'i and his followers also innovated a new interpretive method for deriving rules from scripture. Known as 'Negatively Implied Meaning' (*mafhum al-mukhalafa*), it held that if the Qur'an or Hadiths made a positive statement about a thing, then the negative held true for all else. For example, the Qur'an encourages those agreeing on a loan to set down their agreement in writing and to 'take two witnesses from among your men or, if there are not two men, then one man and two women.' If one of the two women became confused, the Qur'an explains, the other could remind her (4:282). Because the Qur'an specifies women as possible witnesses in the case of financial matters, Shafi'i concluded these were the *only* cases in which women could serve as witnesses in court. According to Negatively Implied Meaning, ordering Muslims to take women in one situation meant forbidding them in all others (with the exception of cases of necessity, such as exclusively female domains, for example, witnessing childbirth). Abu Hanifa, on the other hand, did not accept Negatively Implied Meaning. He allowed female witnesses in all areas of law except some cases of capital or severe corporal punishment, which he disallowed based on a Kufan consensus against this.[40]

Although a main pillar of Shafi'i's legal methodology was the rejection of custom or local practice as a constitutive source of law, this did not mean that he or his followers denied any elasticity in the Shariah. Along with Abu Hanifa, Malik and all luminaries of law, Shafi'i acknowledged that local custom (*'urf*) tailored the edges and contact surfaces of Islamic law in any particular locale. Shafi'i, for example, followed the above-noted prophetic Hadith that a buyer and seller had the right to annul a sale 'until they had parted company.' But what does 'parting company' mean? When the seller leaves the buyer's stall? When they both leave the market at the end of the day? The definition of parting company was left up to local custom to decide.

THE COLLECTION AND CRITICISM OF HADITHS

The coalescing of the 'People of the Sunna and the Collective' in the time of Shafi'i saved Islam from oblivion. So Sunnis like Shah Wali Allah believed. Christians, Jews and misguided Muslims like the Mutazila had all believed in God's revelations, but they had strayed from the pure teachings and clear precedent of His prophets. In reminding his readers of this point, Shah Wali Allah drew on the well-stocked Sunni arsenal of anti-Mutazila evidence. A Hadith portrayed the Prophet predicting the Mutazila fault with tailored exactness, damning their dismissal of Hadiths with more than a hint of scorn for their elitism: 'It's as if there's a man, his stomach full, lounging on his couch and saying, "Stick with the Qur'an. What you find licit in it, consider it permitted. And what you find prohibited in it, consider it prohibited."' 'But what God's Messenger has forbidden,' the Prophet adds as a rejoinder in the Hadith, 'it is as if God has forbidden it.'[41]

Shafi'i had brought up this Hadith no fewer than three times in just one of his debates with the Mutazila.[42] Yet for all his disdain for his opponents, it was not intellectual elitism that made the Mutazila suspicious of Hadiths. It was the problem of rampant Hadith forgery, and their objection was valid. If Muslims were really to set aside reason and local custom and instead derive the details of a comprehensive legal and ritual system from a myriad of Hadiths, how could they tell if a Hadith was really the words of the Prophet?

The answer given by Sunnis like Shafiʿi would define Sunni Islam and become its hallmark. The *Isnad*, or chain of transmission, would be used to verify Hadiths and guarantee the authenticity of sacred knowledge. Muslims need not accept Hadiths blindly. In fact, they should not accept any instruction or claim uncritically. Rather, they only had to obey a Hadith if they found an *Isnad* demonstrating that it had been transmitted reliably from the Prophet. 'The *Isnad* is part of the religion,' proclaimed a Sunni contemporary of Shafiʿi. 'If not for the *Isnad*, whoever wanted could say whatever they wanted.' Another early Sunni wrote that preserving unbroken chains of transmission for their scriptures and sacred knowledge was what set Muslims apart from followers of other religions. Shah Wali Allah devoted a whole book to celebrating this. 'If the *Isnad* had not been a basic principle,' he wrote of Islam, 'then the Shariah would not have survived.'[43]

In order to determine if an *Isnad* was reliable, Shafiʿi proposed a critical method that had been developed by a network of ulama in Mecca, Medina, Iraq and northeastern Iran, all of whom specialized in Hadiths. Among them was Shafiʿi's own teacher, Malik. Although not himself an important contributor to this science of transmission criticism, Shafiʿi gives a useful summary of its methods. 'If a trustworthy person transmits [a Hadith] from another trustworthy person until the chain ends with the Messenger of God, then it is established as being from the Messenger of God.'[44] To be trustworthy, Shafiʿi explains, a Muslim had to be well known as honest, transmit a Hadith they had heard exactly as they heard it and be clear about the source from whom they heard it.

More importantly, the Hadiths that this person recounted to others had to be corroborated by what other respected Hadith scholars also transmitted. If this person narrated Hadiths that broke with what others narrated, he or she could not be trusted. A chain of these reliable transmitters, each reporting the Hadith from their teacher, et cetera, had to extend unbroken to the Prophet himself. During Shafiʿi's time, these chains usually stretched from three to five or six people back to Muhammad. A break in the chain, like a person not remembering who told them the Hadith or quoting a person they had never met, made the Hadith unreliable.[45]

A Hadith that met these requirements was considered 'sound' (*sahih*). If it was widely transmitted through many circles of Hadith scholars, then it was also deemed 'well known' (*mashhur*). A Hadith with some flaw in its chain of transmission was termed 'weak' (*da'if*). It was the strength of the *Isnad* chain that determined if a Hadith should be heeded, since it meant that the Hadith had been authenticated as the words of the Prophet. The Hadith 'Deeds are determined by intentions' may have been only transmitted by limited *Isnad*s, but those *Isnad*s were reliable, concluded Shafi'i. Unlike the followers of Abu Hanifa, then, Shafi'i felt compelled to accept this Hadith as binding. One of his close colleagues in Baghdad, in fact, once said that this Hadith should be included in every chapter of law books.[46]

In his discussion of the collection and criticism of Hadiths, Shah Wali Allah explains the crucial fact that, like law and theology, Hadith transmission and study had remained localized until Shafi'i's time in the late 700s. Abu Hanifa and his followers in Kufa had thus allowed Muslims to consume non-intoxicating amounts of alcoholic beverages other than the grape wine, *Khamr*, forbidden in the Qur'an (drunkenness itself they forbade by *Qiyas* and due to a sound Hadith stating that *intoxication* from any drink is prohibited).[47] They had never heard the Hadiths, widely circulated elsewhere, that 'Every intoxicant is forbidden,' and 'Whatever intoxicates in great quantities, small quantities of it are forbidden.'

During Shafi'i's generation, scholars had begun traveling more widely. In what became known as 'Travel in the quest for sacred knowledge,' Muslims devoted to collecting the Prophet's word plied the dusty roads of Iran and Arabia in search of Hadiths. One of Shafi'i's students in Baghdad traveled to Damascus, Basra and Kufa to study with ulama and hear Hadiths. He even ventured as far as the terraced green mountains of Yemen to study with the great Hadith masters of the trade entrepôt of Sanaa. Named Ahmad Ibn Hanbal, this scholar compiled his Hadiths into a great collection known as the *Musnad* and became one of the most archetypal and revered figures in Sunni Islam.

PUTTING REASON IN ITS PLACE IN SUNNI THEOLOGY AND LAW

Shah Wali Allah arrived in Mecca in the fall of 1730, several months before the start of the annual Hajj. It was normal for scholars to spend months or even years living there in studious retreat as 'neighbors' of the House of God. When the sacred days of Hajj arrived, the Indian wrapped himself in the two plain white cloths that signified the sanctified status of a pilgrim and made his way with thousands of others toward the massive stone cube, draped in black cloth, towering at the center of the Haram Mosque. Each pilgrim repeated over and over Abraham's call, 'I heed your call, O God I heed your call! I heed your call, O You without partner, I heed your call! All praise and blessings are yours, and all dominion. You have no partner!' The Kaaba was the sole destination of the pilgrims, the anchor of the rocky ravines of Mecca and the axis of the Muslim cosmos. Following the Abrahamic ritual that Muhammad had taught his followers, the wheeling throng circumambulated the Kaaba seven times. The persistent among them tried to press through the crowd toward the Kaaba and kiss the smooth Black Stone embedded in one of its corners. This was not required of the pilgrims, but as Shah Wali Allah wrote in his own instructions on Hajj, it was done 'out of imitation of the Prophet.'[48] Indeed, one of the Hadiths that Ibn Hanbal had included in his *Musnad* quoted the Caliph Umar's words as he had approached the Black Stone: 'I know you are but a stone that cannot hurt or help, and if I had not seen the Messenger of God kiss you I would not kiss you.'[49]

The preference for relying on Hadiths over rational devices such as *Istihsan* was a hallmark of the emergent Sunni school as a whole. More than any other sect, it took to heart the Qur'anic warning against an over-reliance on man's frail reason in understanding God and morality. As one of Ibn Hanbal's contemporary admirers in Baghdad wrote in defense of the Sunni creed:

> We do not resort except to that to which the Messenger of God, may God's peace and blessings be upon him, resorted. And we do not reject what has been transmitted authentically from him merely because it does not accord with our conjectures or seem correct to reason... we hope that in this lies the path to salvation and escape from the baseless whims of heresy.[50]

It is not surprising that the method the Sunni scholars used for sorting sound from forged Hadiths made no mention of examining the *meaning* of the Hadith in question. Both the followers of Abu Hanifa and the theological school of the Mutazila (many followers of Abu Hanifa's school, in fact, subscribed to Mutazila theology) had used the Qur'an, the consensus of the Muslims and reason as criteria for determining if a Hadith was authentic or a forgery attributed to the Prophet. Its contents had to be tested against these criteria. If a Hadith contradicted any of them, it could not be true. It had to be a forgery regardless of who was claiming the Prophet had said it.

For the nascent Sunnis, this was outright heresy. First of all, this proposition opposed their vision of how the two scriptures of Islam functioned: Hadiths, as the units that composed the Sunna, explained and added to the Qur'an. What seemed to be contradicting the Qur'an might really be explaining its true meaning, as was the case with the Hadith informing men that they could not marry a woman and her aunt at the same time. Second, human reason, with its limited understanding of reality and its inability to grasp God's power and truth, was not fit to act as a litmus test for the wisdom of a prophet. As Shah Wali Allah remarked, when it comes to knowing what is best the Messenger of God is 'more trustworthy than our own reason.'[51]

The Sunni solution to the problem of authenticating Hadiths was to try and remove reason from the process, focusing on tracing and evaluating their chains of transmission instead of examining their contents. Sunni Hadith scholars researched and compiled volume after volume, with titles like *The Book of Reliable Transmitters* and *The Great Book of Weak Transmitters*, which listed entries on Hadith transmitters. Each identified the transmitter's teachers, students and the evidence for his or her reliability or lack thereof.

Reason could never be totally excluded, however. Biases and sensitivities cannot be shut off. Sunni Hadith critics could not help pausing at reports that seemed *to them* to be impossible, outrageous or contrary to what they considered the established teachings of the Prophet. But unlike rationalists, the Sunni Hadith critics did not consider examining the meaning of Hadiths to be an independent avenue of criticism. It was only a subsidiary of critiquing *Isnad*s. A glaring problem in the meaning of a Hadith was only a symptom of a diseased, flawed chain of transmission. Perhaps a less than stellar transmitter in the *Isnad*, or a lapse of memory from a reliable person, had allowed the mistake to slip through. The critic only had to find the crack.

On rare occasions, we find glimpses of the wheels of reason turning behind the pages of Sunni Hadith-transmitter criticism. The most famous of all Sunni Hadith scholars, Bukhari, listed as evidence of one transmitter's unreliability a Hadith he had narrated in which the Prophet purportedly warned, 'The signs of the Day of Judgment will appear after two hundred years.' This could not be true, Bukhari observed, since those two hundred years had passed without incident.[52]

It makes sense that such remarks were rare. Admitting that the door to man's frail reason could not be closed completely would mean that the Sunnis' claim to preserving the Prophet's true teachings might still be colored by subjectivity. Bukhari might well have concluded that 'after two hundred years' could mean after two hundred and fifty years or five hundred years. These meanings would pose no problem for the Hadith's authenticity. Even in later centuries, when Sunni scholars tried to set up rules regimenting criticism of the meanings of Hadiths, they could never overcome the simple fact that what one person considers unreasonable another finds sensible.[53]

In their extensive travels in the quest for Hadiths, scholars like Ibn Hanbal collected thousands and thousands of reports attributed to the Prophet. Sometimes they might collect a dozen or even several dozen transmissions of the same statement, its chains of transmission intertwining and converging through a web of pious ancestors back to Muhammad (the *Musnad* contains seven transmissions alone of the Hadith of Umar kissing the Black Stone). These would all be analyzed and compared with one another to determine their individual and collective soundness. Ibn Hanbal's *Musnad* contained some 27,700 transmissions, roughly a quarter of which were repeated versions of Hadiths.[54] He sifted these from around 750,000 transmissions he had come across in his travels.

Although Ibn Hanbal acknowledged that there were many Hadiths in his *Musnad* that suffered from some flaw or weakness in their *Isnads*, he felt they were all admissible in elaborating some area of the Shariah. He explained that, as long as a Hadith was supported by an *Isnad* reliable enough to show it was not a patent forgery, 'then one was required to accept it and act according to the Prophet's words.' 'A flawed Hadith is preferable to me than a scholar's opinion or *Qiyas*,' he added.[55] Muslims were, Ibn Hanbal reminded his students, commanded to take their religion from on high and not rely on the flawed faculty of reason.

Ibn Hanbal's legal opinions thus built on the vast corpus of Hadiths he had amassed, seeking to flesh out every detail of law with a prophetic precedent. His acceptance of dubious Hadiths led to unique legal rulings. All other ulama held that Muslims must convene their communal Friday prayer during the time period allowed for the daily noon prayer (beginning when the sun passes its zenith and ending when shadows are the same length as the objects casting them). Ibn Hanbal, however, allowed Friday prayer to be held as early as mid-morning due to an unreliable Hadith to that effect (today, Ibn Hanbal's opinion is used to allow Muslims in the West more flexibility in scheduling Friday prayers).[56]

Ibn Hanbal's strict adherence to Hadiths did not mean that he disregarded the use of reason altogether in law. He used *Qiyas* if there were absolutely no other grounds for arriving at a ruling. When Muslims die, for example, their bodies are brought enshrouded to the mosque, where they are placed in front of the congregation and a short funeral prayer is performed. But what if more than one body is brought, such as the body of a woman and a man? There were not even any weak Hadiths or Companion rulings in this situation, so Ibn Hanbal concluded by analogy that the bodies were placed in the same order as people follow when lining up to pray.[57]

The early Sunni view of the proper relation between reason and revelation had its greatest impact on the understanding of theology. If reason was not fit to play a constitutive role in determining right and wrong in law, it certainly had no place in informing our understanding of God's nature and the ultimate reality of the heavens and the earth. Rational presuppositions about what was and was not acceptable for the proper conception of God had led the Mutazila to introduce figurative readings of anthropomorphic Qur'an verses and to reject wholesale Hadiths describing God in physical or familiar terms. The early Sunnis opposed this wholeheartedly. To convey this point, Shah Wali Allah quotes the writings of a famous Sunni Hadith collector named after his native city of Tirmidh, which today sits perched overlooking the winding Oxus River between Uzbekistan and Afghanistan. Abu 'Isa Tirmidhi explained that true scholars knew that Hadiths 'dealing with God's attributes and the Lord most high's descending every night to the lowest heavens, these narrations have been established and are to be believed.' Sunni ulama must teach 'that one should not fall into error concerning such Hadiths or say "How could this be?"' The correct approach to such Hadiths, wrote Tirmidhi, is to 'take them as is without asking how.'[58]

For the Sunni school of thought, God 'established Himself on the throne,' and one could point upward to where He ruled 'above the heavens and the earth,' as the Qur'an described. Hadiths foretold how, on the Day of Judgment, believers would be granted a beatific vision of their Lord, seeing Him 'like you see the moon on the night of its fullness.' These things were and would be, and man could not understand how. God's hands, eyes and speech were real, although man could never grasp their true nature or description, for 'there is nothing like unto Him' (42:11). God was all-powerful, all-knowing and beyond our conception. Muslims should simply affirm what the Qur'an and the Prophet told them about God's nature and not plumb the depths of these questions.

This did not mean that one could not accept explanations for Qur'anic verses or Hadiths. As long as they could be traced back to the Prophet or one of his early followers, explanations could be heeded because they reflected revealed teachings, not human speculation. Ironically, these often resembled the figurative explanations that the Mutazila arrived at through their philosophical lucubrations. Asked about the Qur'anic verse 'And He is with you wherever you are' (57:4), the Companion Ibn 'Abbas did not take it literally. He explained that this meant God is aware and cognizant of you wherever you are. Similarly, a Hadith describing how God 'draws near to the believer by an arm's length' is explained by Companions as referring to the nearness of His mercy as opposed to physical movement.[59]

Just as they added to the Qur'an in law, the founders of Sunni Islam believed that Hadiths could add new tenets of theology. Though they are not mentioned in the Qur'an in any obvious way, the Hadiths compiled by scholars like Ibn Hanbal predicted phenomena such as 'The Punishment of the Grave.' These Hadiths described how man's Afterlife begins in the grave even before the resurrection on the Day of Judgment. Believers would find the grave peaceful and blessed, while unbelievers or sinners would be tortured in fearsome ways. Other Hadiths foretold the return of Jesus at the end of time. Along with a messianic figure descended from the Prophet and known as the *Mahdi*, he will battle the Antichrist and usher in a period of peace and justice before the end of the world. Literal belief in these Hadith-born tenets of faith became a hallmark of early Sunni theology, while the Mutazila dismissed them as fable or considered them allegorical.[60]

THE GREAT CONVERGENCE OF SUNNI ISLAM

Delhi during Shah Wali Allah's time was far too unstable and war-torn for the Mughal court to justify throwing lavish, lantern-illuminated public festivals. But royal festivals there were nonetheless. Funds might better have been used bolstering the city's defenses against Afghan invaders, who several times during Shah Wali Allah's life sacked the city and massacred thousands of its inhabitants. At least this chaos spared the great scholar invitations to participate in palace religious debates. They might have cost him more than time. The Mughal emperor who had made observing such matches his passion had invited Hindus, Jains and even Jesuit priests to participate. He had little sympathy, unfortunately, for ulama he chose as representatives of Islam.

The Abbasid caliphs had set the model for public debates on religion. At one held at the caliphal court in the 830s, a Mutazila scholar took on an intimidated representative of the embattled Sunnis on the issue of whether man brings about his own actions (the Mutazila stance) or whether God does (the Sunni one). When the Sunni let his arm dangle at the elbow and asked, 'Who is moving this?' – he expected the answer to be God – the Mutazila responded, 'Someone whose mother is a whore.' The caliph approved.[61]

For several decades in the early ninth century, the Mutazila enjoyed tremendous favor at the Abbasid court in Baghdad, but their power was not always so humorously exercised. Ibn Hanbal was tortured and imprisoned, and other Sunni scholars were killed for refusing to embrace Mutazila beliefs. In 848, this changed. The new Abbasid caliph, Mutawakkil, embraced Sunni beliefs. He brought the leading Sunni scholars out of prison and sent them to the great cathedral mosques of Baghdad. There they narrated Hadiths to the crowds, reciting their full *Isnad*s back in time through chains of great scholars to the Messenger of God. Their Hadiths stressed the immediacy and closeness of God, including such prophetic sayings as the promise that believing Muslims would behold their Lord directly on the Day of Judgment.[62] The ascendancy of the 'People of the Sunna' brought with it the steep decline of Mutazila fortunes. By the eleventh century they were few in number and limited to scholarly circles along the Silk Road in Baghdad, Iran, the mountains of Yemen and the oases of Central Asia.

The triumph of what would become the majority school of thought and sect in Islam was the most remarkable development in the ninth through the eleventh centuries. The phrase that this network of scholars used to refer to itself, 'The People of the Sunna and the Collective,' referred to their belief that they alone followed the true Sunna of the Prophet and the united path of the Companions. Although they began as a small, conservative and ideologically xenophobic network of scholars obsessed with collecting and evaluating Hadiths, the Sunni mantra of the primacy of revealed text over reason would attain a paramount place among the populations of cities like Baghdad and would eventually draw other schools under its banner.

Seated in the sprawling mosques of Baghdad, Isfahan and Samarqand, narrating the words of the Prophet to their enraptured audiences, the Sunni scholars had terrifying popularity among the masses. The movement's doctrine of political quietism, based in the belief articulated by Ibn Hanbal and others that Muslims should never rebel against their Muslim ruler regardless of his heresies or iniquity, made Sunni Islam eminently acceptable to the rulers of the Muslim empire as well. The combination of popular and state support proved unbeatable.

During this time of tremendous ferment and productivity in Islamic thought, ninth- and tenth-century scholars traveled, taught and disputed along the Silk Road that linked the Mediterranean, the Middle East and Central Asia. There were many more luminaries of law than just Abu Hanifa, Malik, Shafi'i and Ibn Hanbal. Awza'i of Beirut, Tabari of Baghdad and Thawri of Kufa developed their own approaches to the Shariah and attracted followers. The legacies of Abu Hanifa, Malik, Shafi'i and Ibn Hanbal, however, flourished above all others. Through a combination of chance, the efforts of talented scholars who preserved and further developed their bodies of law and occasional sponsorship from Muslim rulers, by the twelfth century the schools of thought around these four names emerged as the four accepted *madhhab*s, or schools of law, in Sunni Islam.

If the triumph of the 'People of the Sunna' meant that the vast corpus of Hadiths now superseded the Maliki reliance on Medinan custom and the Kufan laws derived from analogical reasoning and *Istihsan*, then how could the Hanafi and Maliki schools continue to adhere to their bodies of law under the Sunni umbrella? Shah Wali Allah pondered this question in particular as he looked back on the first three centuries of Islam. He saw an eerie, symmetrical unity in what had been for those involved an age of bitter disagreement and venomous dispute. He explained how Kufan scholars like Abu Hanifa had developed a comprehensive body of legal rulings using rational methods to extend the limited texts of the Qur'an and acceptable Hadiths to a limitless number of real or hypothetical situations. The early Sunnis had prioritized clinging tightly to the words of God and the Prophet, fearing an indulgence in speculation and reason.

This limited their ability to find answers to new legal questions. As the Sunni scholars of the 800s unified the regional pockets of Hadiths into a vast reservoir, this new wealth of scripture enabled them to expand their law as well to cover almost all areas of life.

This meant that the Hanafi and Maliki schools were then able to back their law up with the newly amalgamated wealth of Hadiths too. They did so by mining the voluminous collections of Hadiths gathered by scholars like Ibn Hanbal for Hadiths that would support their rulings. In Egypt, a scholar named Tahawi defected from the Shafi'i school to the Hanafi and proceeded to compile two vast Hadith works that explained how his adopted school's body of law obeyed Hadiths to the letter. Abu Hanifa and his followers had, for example, maintained that a Muslim who murdered an unbeliever (*kafir*) could be executed as punishment on the basis of the Qur'anic edict of 'A life for a life' (5:45). Tahawi explained that a Hadith in which the Prophet commanded that 'A believer is not executed for an infidel' should be understood as applying only to unbelievers with whom the Muslims are at war, not ones living under a peace agreement. Tahawi supported his argument with narrations of this Hadith that made reference to the context of being at war.[63] An eleventh-century Maliki judge in Lisbon, then a provincial center of learning in Andalusia, named Ibn 'Abd al-Barr did the same service for Maliki law.

Each *madhhab* was an ocean of diversity and constant scholarly activity. The Hanafi school was based on the often contrasting opinions of Abu Hanifa, his two main disciples Shaybani and Abu Yusuf, as well as a more independent student named Zufar. The Maliki school built on the opinions of Malik and his senior disciples, who often disagreed with him and each other. Shafi'i's long years of travel and intellectual maturation led to two whole eras in his legal opinions, 'the Old' and 'the New,' both of which were incorporated into his *madhhab*. Ibn Hanbal's close attention to Hadiths led him to change his opinion on legal issues as new Hadiths were uncovered, and the Hanbali *madhhab* thus enjoyed a wide range of opinions even at its founding level.

The foundational legal manuals of each *madhhab* were expanded on, abridged and commented on in depth over the centuries. Like an accordion, the books of the *madhhab*s were sometimes summarized into terse epitomes (even rendered in poetry to aid memorization), then these laconic booklets would be explicated by a new generation of scholars in a new, larger book before being abridged once again.

The leading scholars of each generation felt qualified to extend the interpretive methods of their school to novel issues, such as the tobacco newly discovered in the Americas (most schools have permitted smoking or considered it 'disliked,' though consistent minorities have argued for prohibiting it) or the use of new military technologies like gunpowder.

Far from a myopic or rigid body of law, the Sunni Shariah tradition thus became a swirl of stunning diversity. Not only were there four distinct schools of law, but each school also had a range of opinions on any one question. Furthermore, the recorded legacies of the extinct *madhhab*s of scholars like Tabari and the ancient opinions of scattered Companions and Successors added to the body of legal knowledge. The statement 'the Shariah says...' is thus automatically misleading, as there is almost always more than one answer to any legal question.

Each *madhhab* conquered its own territory over time. The Hanafi school proliferated among the Turks of Central Asia, becoming dominant in India and later in the Ottoman Empire when Turkic Muslim dynasties established themselves in those climes. The Shafi'i school, based in Egypt and Yemen, spread through Indian Ocean trade to Southeast Asia, where it is the monopoly *madhhab* until today. The Maliki school spread with Malik's students from North Africa to the west, becoming the exclusive *madhhab* from Andalusia to West Africa and even east to the Sudan. The Hanbali school was predominant in Baghdad through the fourteenth century, but otherwise it simmered only among scholarly circles in Jerusalem and, when the Crusaders drove many of its ulama to flight, in certain districts of Damascus. Always a minority movement, it became increasingly influential in the eighteenth century, when the isolated Hanbalis of Central Arabia formed the powerful Wahhabi movement.

The undeniable diversity of the schools of law presented a potential challenge to the ulama, who all believed that the Shariah was the unified law of God. They explained this inconsistency by upholding the unity of the Shariah as the idea of God's law, while acknowledging that humans will necessarily come to different understandings of *fiqh*, or the actual law as derived and applied in this world. Although scholars from different *madhhab*s would argue and write spirited polemics against one another, they recognized each other's legitimacy. Their approach to the unity and diversity of the Shariah was best expressed by the twelfth-century Hanafi scholar of Central Asia, Abu Hafs Nasafi: 'Our school is correct with the possibility of error, and another school is in error with the possibility of being correct.'[64]

In fact, within the greater Shariah system this diversity became a strength. The Shariah courts of the medieval and early modern Islamic world reflected and took advantage of it. In a region with multiple coexisting *madhhab*s, such as Egypt (where the Shafi'i, Maliki and Hanafi schools proliferated), a couple who wanted to marry without the permission of the woman's father could go to the Hanafi court, whose judge would allow this, unlike the other schools of law. A Muslim woman in Bosnia in the eighteenth century whose husband had disappeared overseas without a trace abandoned the local Hanafi school and declared herself a follower of the Shafi'i *madhhab* before the judge. While the Hanafi school required her to wait the average lifetime of a man before her marriage was dissolved, the Shafi'i opinion that had gained ascendancy in that period (there were two opinions in the school) allowed her to remarry after only four years on the basis of the caliph Umar bin Khattab's ruling.[65]

Rulers could take advantage of this diversity as well. The Mamluk sultans of medieval Cairo appointed chief judges from each *madhhab* to keep an array of authorities on hand to legitimize their policies. The Maliki judges in particular proved useful when the sultan wanted to execute heterodox troublemakers, since their *madhhab* did not allow a chance to repent for someone convicted of the capital crime of apostasy.[66]

A functioning legal system needs to be predictable, however, so there were also efforts to rein in and order this interpretive plurality. Scholars like the tenth-century Ibn Mundhir of Nishapur compiled books of *Ijma'*, listing the points of law on which all schools agreed. After the eleventh century it became effectively impossible to start a new *madhhab*, with one Baghdad scholar composing a poem on how the four schools' founders 'Are our proofs, and whoever is guided by anyone other will go astray.' In thirteenth-century Cairo, the accusation that a senior scholar was trying to found a new school of law prompted a rebuke from the sultan himself.[67]

Within each school of law, the multiplicity of opinions was regimented by developing a hierarchy of authoritative scholars and texts to use as references when answering legal questions. Generations of scholars sifted through the array of opinions in their *madhhab*, highlighting the well-founded ones and marginalizing the anomalous. Through this process, in the thirteenth and fourteenth centuries schools identified what was the 'official opinion' (*mufta bihi*) or the 'relied upon' one.

Whether a scholar could go outside the four *madhhabs* and adopt the anomalous position of a Companion or extinct *madhhab* was a vexing question that would boil over in controversy time and again from the thirteenth century onward, particularly in Shah Wali Allah's day. A scholar writing in fourteenth-century Damascus emphasized the importance of the cumulative process of review and correction that the four *madhhabs* each offered. If one tried to bypass them and go back to the Qur'an, Hadiths or the sometimes erratic rulings of the early Muslim generations, one might end up adopting the mad ruling of Hajjaj bin Arta, an eighth-century scholar who ruled that a thief's severed hand should be hung around his neck.

Though Muslim rulers might benefit from Shariah flexibility, in the thirteenth century large Islamic states saw restraining it and systematizing Shariah justice as part of strengthening their centralized authority. Of the Sunni law schools, only the Hanafi one allowed judges to accept appointments under the condition that they only rule by one school. It was fortunate that the dominant Sunni states of the late medieval and early modern periods identified as Hanafi. As the Ottoman Empire reached the full bloom of its power in the 1500s, Shariah court judges were restricted to ruling only by the principal decisions of the Hanafi school unless the sultans issued edicts otherwise (though the state's efforts to ban dodges like the Bosnian wife's recourse to Shafi'i law failed in practice). Regulation need not come from the state, however.[68] Throughout Maliki-dominated North Africa and Spain, the judges in Shariah courts limited themselves to ruling only by the official position of the Maliki school of law.

LEGAL THEORY AND ITS DISCONTENTS

The books that a young Shah Wali Allah carried to and from his daily studies in Delhi did not differ dramatically from the curricula followed in madrasas in Ottoman Istanbul or even in the Shiite seminaries of Isfahan. Like his cohorts in all these centers of learning, he plodded through dense works of Arabic grammar, law and theology. The text at the center of the page would be explicated by multiple commentaries running between its lines and around its margins, often composed by some legendary master scholar from Tamerlane's court in Samarqand. All this would be unlocked and clarified, the students hoped, by the teachers at whose feet they sat.

The scholarly ether that permeated all these subjects was the language of logic. The convoluted procedures of Aristotelian definition and syllogism became second nature to students like Shah Wali Allah, and they employed logical jargon like 'specific accident' and 'a thing in its essence' with almost instinctive ease. Logic had become the lingua franca of Islamic scholarship and the glue of ulama culture. One of the senior scholars at the Ottoman court grilled newcomers seeking employment in Istanbul's learned hierarchy with a set of questions such as proving how the logical definition of 'proposition' did not collapse under the contradiction of the Liar's Paradox. The most epic scholarly dual in the collective memory of North India's ulama was the near-mythic disputation on language, logic and theology held between the two most vaunted scholars of Samarqand, which had resulted in the loser's death from despair.[69]

Shah Wali Allah cursed the extinct heresy of the Mutazilites as much as any self-respecting Sunni. But, as the ubiquity of Greek logic in its curriculum betrayed, Sunni Islam had long ago adopted much of the heresy it had once fought so fiercely. Ironically, the great and unbridgeable dispute between the rationalist Mutazila and the traditionalist Sunnis resulted in a synthesis of the two schools. It began with an early tenth-century Mutazila scholar from Basra named Abu Hasan Ash'ari, who had a dream in which the Prophet bid him embrace the teachings of Ibn Hanbal. He became their most avid defender and soon began using the Mutazila's own rationalist methods to support the tenets of Sunni theology.

Although he began by adopting the Sunni approach of affirming belief in anthropomorphic verses of the Quran and Hadiths without asking questions, Ash'ari soon adopted the Mutazila's method of figurative interpretation. Consulting the metaphors used in Arab poetry at the time of the Prophet, he established that when scripture mentioned God's 'hand,' it was a reference to His power. His 'face' should be understood as a metaphor for His essence. God's 'sight' alluded to His unerring watchfulness over creation. His 'descent in the last third of the night' was His mercy upon the pious.

For Ash'ari and the early Sunnis, the great heresy of the Mutazila was their confidence in human reason. In matters of theology, this had led them to defend God's justice at the expense of His power. By insisting that God was rational and that right and wrong were objective realities, they had made God subject to reason and His actions hostage to concepts outside of Him. Ash'ari and his followers countered by erasing limits on God's power and making His actions the very definition of right and wrong. For Ash'ari, God knew the most insignificant act and ultimate destiny of every creature. In fact, Shah Wali Allah notes, Hadiths like the debate between Adam and Moses made it clear that God had predestined each soul for Heaven or Hell before the world even began. If this seemed to entail an injustice for those humans who would be punished in Hellfire for sins they were predestined to commit, this was immaterial. Our feeble minds cannot grasp God's knowledge or ultimate justice. How can we hope to explain how God can both know what we will do before we do it and still hold us accountable for that choice afterwards, when words like 'before,' 'after' and time itself are His creations?

In their conception of law and ethics, the Mutazila believed that universal notions of right and wrong could be ascertained by reason. For Ash'ari, this was simply untenable. There were no universal rights or wrongs. Concepts of just or unjust, laudable or despicable were nothing more than personal predilections or the customs of a particular culture. One might think that basic maxims like 'justice is good' or 'senseless killing is wrong' are truths accessible universally by human reason. But, as a later theologian proposed, imagine a person suddenly coming to earth without any culture, upbringing or background. They might not come to those conclusions at all. Such notions may be extremely widely held, but they are the products of culture, convention and education, not first principles of reason. The essential rightness or wrongness of an action was determined solely by God's revelation to humankind and the legal scholars' derivation of the Shariah from it.

In such beliefs Ash'ari and his school of theology might seem mindlessly regressive, but the ulama were constructing the Shariah project as a language and system designed to unify a cosmopolitan world that seemed too diverse to explain. Among the Hindu nobility of Shah Wali Allah's India, many Rajput noblewomen considered throwing themselves onto the funeral pyres of their dead husbands to be an honor and a duty. Yet for Muslims, suicide was strictly prohibited. In Ash'ari's own lifetime, a Muslim ambassador from the Abbasid caliph in Baghdad traveled through what is now southern Russia and witnessed the burial of a wealthy Viking chief. Placed on the chief's longboat in the river along with his body was one of his slave women, who was ritually raped by six warriors before being stabbed and strangled to death as the ship was set ablaze. When the polite but aghast Muslim observer asked how the Norsemen could conduct such burials, they responded with equal confusion: how could Muslims let their dead loved ones be eaten by worms beneath the ground?[70] Where were universal notions of propriety, rights or morality to be found in such a world?

Imperial diversity was not new, of course. Roman jurists in the geographical heyday of their empire had found themselves adjudicating similarly polyglot peoples. They concluded that even disparate cultures generally shared core values, sometimes even due to the natural makeup of the human species. Sunni theologians and jurists also accepted readily that people tended to behave according to *'Ada*, or the common course of nature and society, such as love for family and a desire for self-preservation. Such reliable generalities were strong probabilities admissible in shaping the details of law or for governing procedure in courts. Based on the standards of *'Ada*, the claim of an impoverished man who insisted that he was actually wealthy but had loaned all his money to a rich man who had then refused to return it, would not even be entertained by a Shariah judge. But such generalities were not eternal moral truths, uniformly knowable to man's reason and able to trump the revealed laws of God.[71]

Ironically, in their attempt to construct a more universal epistemology for law and theology, the Ash'ari school was deeply influenced by the Mutazila. In the tenth and eleventh centuries, the Sunni legal scholars who followed the Ash'ari school of theology began examining the epistemological roots of knowledge and the derivation of law through the rationalist lens of the Mutazila in order to articulate a science of moral epistemology and legal theory (*Usul al-Fiqh*).

Since the sources of Islamic doctrine were revealed texts, much of this science involved investigating the nature of language. What is the basic feature of an imperative command? What determines the meaning of words in general and in the Qur'an or Hadiths in particular? What emerged as the 'Majority' (Ash'ari) school of legal theory, for example, held that the meaning of words was determined by their use in Islam's scriptures, while the legal theory developed by the Hanafis held that the meaning of terms came from their original meaning in pre-Islamic Arabic.

Legal theorists of the tenth and eleventh centuries developed tiers of certainty based on the Late Antique philosophical heritage. Their vision paralleled Aristotle and other philosophical schools such as the Stoics. 'Certitude' (*yaqin*) was the rare level of knowledge that came from unimpeachable sources, needed for areas such as theological beliefs. 'Probable supposition' (*zann*) was the more realistic level of certainty that people needed for daily life or for determining right and wrong acts. Like Aristotle, they concluded that certitude comes through sense perception or the First Principles of reason (such as 'the whole is greater than one of its parts' or 'X cannot be X and Not-X in the same way at the same time').[72]

Aristotle, however, was never a follower of revelation. The past was a grab bag of interesting particulars, not a source of truth. He had no place for scripture. How could the concept of a revealed source of authority, like the Qur'an and Hadiths, be fit into this worldview? Christian Church Fathers such as Augustine and Jewish scholars like the great rabbi of tenth-century Baghdad, Saadia Gaon, faced the same challenge of reconciling the Bible and the Greco-Roman heritage. Muslim legal theorists followed in their footsteps by adding another source of certainty to reason and sense perception: infallibly accurate transmissions from a divine source.[73]

This allowed the all-important place for the Qur'an and those Hadiths that were attested widely enough to be considered 'widely and diffusely transmitted' (*mutawatir*), or so well known that they could not possibly be forgeries. Such reports were so well verified that their truth came across like sense perception. In this new scale of certainty, the standard, less well-known Hadiths used to establish most Shariah laws were still considered acceptable, since the Late Antique philosophical tradition only required a strong probability as opposed to certainty in judging actions.[74] Law thus stood in stark contrast with theological doctrine, which required epistemological certainty.

The most challenging task was finding rational justification for the infallibility of *Ijma'*, the consensus of the Muslim community. The Hadiths in which the Prophet spoke of this, like his saying that 'My community will never agree in error,' were themselves only known through limited numbers of transmissions and thus offered no certitude. Sunni legal theorists tried to solve this problem by arguing that *'Ada*, the normal functioning of human society, made it impossible for a whole community to agree in error that an event had occurred or a statement been made. Sunni scholars argued that, since the ulama had come to consensus that the Prophet had affirmed the *Umma*'s infallibility, the authenticity of this Hadith was certain and the basis for *Ijma'* established.

Counterintuitively, the formal, rationally derived schools of theology and legal theory emerged after the *madhhab*s and the tenets of Sunni theology. These new sciences were used to justify rather than to correct or replace Sunni bodies of law and dogma. In the case of Sunni theology, this presented a serious challenge. The epistemological framework that these Sunni legal theorists had adopted required that tenets of faith such as the nature of God, the events of the Day of Judgment and the fate of the soul after death be derived from epistemologically certain sources of revelation, such as the Qur'an. But the Hadiths that conveyed these beliefs could not meet the standard for massive transmission. Some legal theorists solved this conundrum by arguing that the Muslim community as a whole had come to consensus on these beliefs. They were therefore known with certainty. Moreover, although a particular Hadith about the Punishment of the Grave might not be established with total certainty, all the varied Hadiths mentioning this article of faith collectively raised this tenet above the possibility of forgery, the ulama claimed.

Beginning in the tenth century, these legal theorists derived *Qawa'id*, or doctrinal principles and procedural maxims for navigating the array of legal opinions on any one issue and to guide them in addressing novel questions. Sometimes these maxims came from the Prophet himself, but more often they were logical rules or principles distilled from the decision-making processes of the early generations of jurists. One maxim stated that 'Certainty is never removed by doubt.' Analyzing their *madhhab*'s law, Hanafi scholars concluded that this was the basis for their refusal to annul the marriage of a woman whose husband had vanished or been absent for years. Her marriage to him was known with certainty, and it could not be overturned by the mere probability that he was dead until this was ascertained for sure or the average human lifespan had passed.[75] Another maxim stated that 'Difficulty calls for easing.' On this basis, the Hanafi judge in Bosnia allowed the woman with a missing husband to take her case to the Shafi'i court to be decided according to that school's more lenient ruling.[76]

SUFISM AND INSPIRATION FROM GOD

At fourteen, even before he acquired his prodigious learning, Shah Wali Allah became a disciple of the Sufi path. The young scholar's given name was actually Ahmad. At his birth, however, intimations felt on a visit to the shrine of a powerful Sufi saint had left his father convinced that the child enjoyed a rare intimacy with the Creator. He gave him the title by which he would become so well known: *Wali Allah*, 'the friend of God.' In time, the honorific used for those with prestigious spiritual lineages was added to his name as well: *Shah*, or 'king.'[77]

The ideal of *Ihsan*, or 'perfecting' one's faith and conduct such that one was constantly conscious of God, had been the highest level of religion that Muhammad had taught his followers. But, like Islam's legal and theological traditions, this singular teaching had branched out into tremendous diversity over the centuries, a phenomenon that Shah Wali Allah sought to trace and explain in his writings.

While in Mecca, Shah Wali Allah ventured into the barren desert to pay homage to the grave of one of the Prophet's Companions named Abu Dharr Ghifari.[78] Even during the Prophet's lifetime, some of his followers had been more inclined than others to intensive devotion, pious abstemiousness and pondering the divine mysteries. Abu Dharr was among those who cultivated a heightened spiritual state, and his constant awareness of God led him to an ascetic lifestyle far more austere than what Islam required. Some of the Prophet's Companions chose this path because they had absorbed the profound aura of blessings around their master and perhaps even heard him explain deep truths not shared with all.

The tradition of spiritual and ethical devotion that reaches above and beyond the required duties prescribed by the Shariah is known as *Tasawwuf*, or Sufism. In addition to being a leading jurist and Hadith transmitter in his day, Hasan Basri was also seen as a founding figure in this 'science of purifying the heart.' When later Sufi masters traced their teachings and practices back to the Prophet, in just the same way that a Hadith's chain of transmission ensured its authority, their *Isnad*s of Sufi teachings most often passed through Hasan to the Prophet's son-in-law Ali, proclaimed by Muhammad to be the gate to the city of his prophetic knowledge.

In the ninth century, this spiritual inheritance was claimed by great Sufi icons who sought the constant presence of God. For some, like the martyred mystic of Baghdad, Hallaj, ecstatic union with the divine led to moments of spiritual intoxication and utterances that struck more sober ulama as heretical. What became orthodox Sufism was exemplified by Hallaj's fellow Baghdadi of the early tenth century, Junayd, who famously declared that 'Our Science is bounded by the Qur'an and Sunna.'[79]

For those who cultivated a constant God-consciousness, the pious elect whom the Qur'an referred to as *Awliya' Allah* (the Friends of God), the constraints of the earthly world meant nothing. As Shah Wali Allah described them (and himself), they could know the future, exist in a constant state of ritual purity and some would set out on travels without any provisions, trusting completely in God. As one Hadith foretold, for those whom God chose as His saints He becomes 'the ears with which they hear, the eyes with which they see, the fist with which they grasp...'[80] For them, the rules of nature could be broken, and they could work miracles such as curing the sick, folding space and traveling to Mecca and back for a daily prayer.

After their death, these saints only grew in power and station. The same Hadiths that established the Punishment of the Grave established that the souls of the dead are still conscious and active, and in other Hadiths the Prophet tells how: 'The prophets are alive, praying in their graves.'[81] Saints were thought to be no different, as able in death to answer invocations for assistance as they had been in this earthly life. Especially after the 1100s, their graves became centers of pilgrimage for the masses of Muslims seeking their *Baraka*, or blessing. The Mughal sultans who ruled Delhi may have held the reins of temporal power, but they believed that it was the Sufi saints of India, living and dead, who truly upheld their sovereignty. Delhi had a special gate built for the road to the distant city of Ajmer, where the patron Sufi saint of the Mughals, Muin al-Din Chishti, was buried. Every year the greatest of the Mughal sultans would make the four-hundred-kilometer pilgrimage to Ajmer – on foot – to pay homage at the Chishti shrine.[82]

For the elite Sufis, their path was not merely the pursuit of superior conduct and consciousness of God. It was the unveiling of reality itself. The Qur'an called God 'the light of the heavens and the earth,' and proclaimed that 'everything will perish except His countenance.' The material world was simply dark nothingness illuminated by the creative light of God. It was a shadowy and corrupted reflection of God, the only true Reality. Human souls were stranded particles of God's divine breath, tormented by their distance from the wellspring of existence. As the thirteenth-century Sufi poet Rumi wrote, humankind's cry of isolation was like the reed flute's song. Ever since it was cut from the reed bed, it has yearned to return.

This Sufi cosmology was formalized by a unique Sufi master, the thirteenth-century Andalusian Ibn Arabi. In his profound writings, he described how God had brought about creation because He was 'a hidden jewel and wanted to be known.' Creation reflected His simultaneous unity and limitless creative power, but only humankind, by choosing to worship Him fully, could most fully know and reflect God. For Ibn Arabi, Muhammad was not simply a prophet and guide. As the best of humankind, he was the best of creation, the ultimate reflection of God's perfection. Muhammad was more than just a man. He was a cosmic reality, the ideal 'perfect human' who existed throughout time to fulfill the purpose of creation and mirror God.

What these theosophical Sufis understood but could not proclaim publicly was that these truths transcended Islam's Abrahamic horizons and the legal and theological traditions of the ulama. The metaphysical reality that creation was an emanation, an overflow, of God's perfection, growing darker and less real the further it extended from Him; that human souls were caught too far out in this tide and yearned for the divine shore, traced its roots to Plato and a later mystical interpreter of his philosophy in Rome, the influential third-century philosopher Plotinus. Such awareness led some Muslim mystics to acknowledge that truth lay embedded in other religions, even if they had gone egregiously astray. The leading Sufi of Delhi in Shah Wali Allah's day was Mazhar Jan-e Janan, who affirmed that Krishna (in Hinduism, an avatar of the god Vishnu) had been a prophet and that the Hindu Rig Veda was divinely inspired scripture even if Hindus in his own time had descended into polytheism.[83]

In the twelfth and thirteenth centuries, as the schools of law were solidifying into their guild-like form, a number of Sufi masters emerged whose teachings attracted wide attention. Among them were a Hanbali scholar in Baghdad, renowned for his piety, named 'Abd al-Qadir Jilani; a Moroccan saint who settled in Egypt, Abu Hasan Shadhili; and the Bukharan Baha' al-Din Naqshband, who gathered together the wisdom of Persia's Sufi masters.

The mystical insights and methods of spiritual and ethical discipline taught by these masters were organized by their senior disciples into regimented Sufi orders, or 'paths' (*tariqa*). Sufi orders centered on the devotional exercises and liturgical poems (*wird*) penned by the masters to focus aspiring Sufis on God, the Prophet and greater piety. Many orders gathered together for group recitations of these poems or merely for chanting the names of God. Some, like the Mevlevi *tariqa* of Anatolia (the famous 'whirling dervishes,' the order founded on the teachings of Rumi) developed dances that focused them on God's majestic oneness and the order of the cosmos. Other, more extreme and controversial orders sought to demonstrate their spiritual ecstasy by walking on hot coals or eating snakes live, as the stunned Moroccan traveler Ibn Battuta observed the frenetic Rifa'i Sufis do in southern Iraq around 1330.[84]

The person of the Sufi master, who had learned from a succession of predecessors back to the order's founder, and from him back eventually to the Prophet, was all-important. The master, or shaykh, could diagnose the seeker's spiritual illnesses and prescribe the proper steps to moving along the Sufi path. In the Shadhili order, for example, this might first entail repeating any of the five daily prayers that the novice had performed without truly remembering God, or going a whole month without backbiting. Like the schools of law, these Sufi paths proliferated in certain regions. The Naqshbandi order predominated in Central Asia and had a huge impact in India, while the Shadhili gained many followers in North Africa and Egypt.

Mainstream Sufism stressed its adherence to the Shariah in common mantras like 'Without Shariah, the Truth lying at the end of the Sufi path is heresy.'[85] Although antinomian orders like the Rifa'is used claims of religious ecstasy to justify outrageous practices, treading the Sufi path in one of the mainstream orders began – at least in theory – with committing oneself to observing the Shariah fastidiously.

Yet the Sufis' objective of proximity to God and the notion that this closeness could grant access to mystical truths, received directly from the Divine, in addition to claims that Sufi masters inherited esoteric knowledge from early figures like Ali, created a source of *'ilm* that competed with the books of Shariah jurists. As one early Sufi, Bayazid Bistami, once told a Hadith scholar: 'You take your knowledge dead from the dead, but I take mine from the Living One who does not die.'[86] Shah Wali Allah himself encountered the Prophet many times in person in the spiritual dimension explored by Sufis. The Sufi tradition thus added experiential knowledge, or taste (*dhawq*), to the existing sources of knowing truth – revelation and reason. This experiential knowledge, however, generally concerned insights about God's nature or spiritual realities. It rarely intruded into law. When a man in the thirteenth century saw a vision of the Prophet in which he told the man where to find buried treasure and issued him an exemption from paying the required *Zakat* charity tax on the loot, the leading scholar called to judge the case was unimpressed. This man's vision of the Prophet could not contend with sound Hadiths requiring the charity tax be paid.[87]

THE ICONOCLASTS AND ISLAMIC REVIVAL

Shah Wali Allah's two-year sojourn in Mecca and Medina was life-changing. Not only was the twenty-nine-year-old Indian exposed to scholars and students from distant lands, Kurdish Sufi masters and Basran Hadith experts, he was also drawn into the vortex of a revivalist current that would transform far-flung corners of the Muslim world. Seated in the study circles clustered around the pillars of the Prophet's mosque in Medina, he was introduced to the impassioned writings of a scholar from Damascus of four centuries earlier, a man who had waged a one-man campaign against the heresies and corruptions he saw around him. Controversy led to this scholar's imprisonment in Cairo and then eventually in the citadel of Damascus, where he died in 1328.

Ibn Taymiyya has certainly been one of the most controversial figures in Islamic history. Many have lionized him as Islam's greatest reviver, yet just as many others have condemned him as an unleasher of interpretive chaos. Loved or reviled, Ibn Taymiyya rose up in a jeremiad against almost every institution and tradition of Sunni Islam as it had accrued in his day. Although an accomplished Hanbali jurist, he broke not only with his own *madhhab* but also with all four Sunni *madhhab*s on sensitive issues when he believed that these schools had not followed the clear evidence of the Qur'an and Hadiths. Ibn Taymiyya worked to unmask the charlatanry of fire-walking Sufis like the Rifa'is and personally destroyed sites of local superstitious pilgrimage around his native Damascus. He passionately rejected Ash'ari theology as a Greek solution to Greek problems that should never have concerned the Abrahamic revealed tradition. In his resistance to rigid loyalty to the *madhhab*s, his critique of the excesses of Sufism and his rejection of Ash'ari speculative theology, Ibn Taymiyya brought together important strains of iconoclastic opposition to the powerful medieval institutions of Islamic thought. Shah Wali Allah devoted a treatise to defending him and praised him as one of the great scholars of Sunni Islam.[88]

The intellectual threads that intertwined in Ibn Taymiyya's voluminous writings were not new. Ever since Abu Hasan Ash'ari's pioneering development of the Sunni science of speculative theology, there had been a prominent strain of conservative Sunni scholars who had rejected his school of thought. Particularly numerous among Hanbali ulama, they represented a continuity of the original traditionalism of early Sunnis like

Ibn Hanbal. They rejected any rational speculation in theological matters, seeing no need to euphemize the anthropomorphisms in the Qur'an and Hadiths. These traditionalists rejected the Ash'ari philosophical conceptions of God that made such scripture problematic to begin with. As a leading Hanbali scholar of Damascus, Ibn Qudama, wrote, God never required Muslims to understand the exact meaning of anthropomorphic images invoked in scripture. Lay Muslims understood instinctively what God meant when the Qur'an said, 'God established Himself on the throne,' and all that the ulama had to remind them was that, whatever image occurred in their mind when they heard God's words, it can never even approximate God's untrammeled power and glory. Where the Ash'ari theologians used reason and an analysis of Arabic metaphor to hammer out specific explanations for God's 'hand' and 'face,' the traditionalists such as Ibn Qudama and Ibn Taymiyya trusted in the instinctive understanding of the average believer.[89]

Many Muslim scholars had also been alarmed by the excessive practices found in some Sufi orders. A famous twelfth-century Hanbali scholar of Baghdad, himself a committed Sufi, wrote a detailed criticism of all the ways in which the Devil had led Muslims astray. Much of his criticism was directed at the superstitions, unsanctioned forms of worship and moral laxities of the rabble who claimed to be Sufi devotees. Several decades later, an outraged Shafi'i scholar in Damascus wrote a book describing all the forms of *Bid'a* (heretical innovation in ritual and practice) that had proliferated in his region, specifying the local shrines that the populace frequented for petitioning bygone saints. By Ibn Taymiyya's time, some ulama of Cairo and Damascus had become increasingly disturbed by the theosophy of Ibn Arabi as well, seeing it as disguised pantheism, or the belief that creation is infused with the divine.[90]

Finally, the four Sunni schools of law had become so institutionalized and guild-like that several prominent scholars in Ibn Taymiyya's small circle in Damascus rebelled against their rigid and decadent scholarly culture. By the twelfth and thirteenth centuries, the ulama had taken to wearing distinctive robes with pronouncedly wide sleeves as well as cloths draped over their turbans in order to distinguish themselves as a clerical class. Iconoclastic critics like Ibn Taymiyya saw in this the creation of a priestly caste following specific codes of law with blind devotion, ignoring the living impulse of the Qur'an and the Sunna as well as the primordial equality of believers.

From the time of Ibn Taymiyya in the fourteenth century onward, Sunni thought would be characterized by a great tension between the institutional traditions of the *madhhab*s, Sufi orders and Ash'ari theology on the one hand, and an austere iconoclasm on the other. This second strain would coalesce in the time of Shah Wali Allah into a powerful impetus to renew and revive Islam, to return to the pure faith of the Salaf, or the righteous early Muslims.

This impulse stemmed from an acute sense that Muslims had abandoned or adulterated the message of Islam. The cosmopolitan world of seventeenth-century Istanbul had been jolted by a conservative fundamentalist movement known as the Qadizadeli that preached against coffee drinking and tobacco smoking, and in northern India in the same period Shaykh Ahmad Sirhindi claimed to be the 'renewer' of the Islamic *Umma* in the new morning of its second millennium. He decried Sufi groups that had incorporated elements of Hindu ritual and imagery, and he called for an orthodox denunciation of India's infidel majority (as opposed to Jan-e Janan's more sympathetic view). A Moroccan scholar sojourning in the Songhai Empire of Mali in West Africa told its ruler, newly committed to an orthodox implementation of Islam, that his supposedly Muslim people had to renounce their local pagan customs or be compelled to do so.[91] Such forces culminated in a set of powerful revival movements that sprang up in previously marginal parts of the Muslim world: India, Central Arabia, West Africa and Yemen.

It was actually Sufism that helped spark these eighteenth-century calls for revival. Shah Wali Allah's father was a Naqshbandi Sufi master and his first shaykh, and his immersion in Sufism led him to pore over seminal mystical works that stressed how the Sufi's supererogatory commitment to pious excellence transcended the *madhhab*s and brought a more direct connection with God. The true Sufi recovered the station of the exemplary original Muslims, who had predated the stagnation of the *madhhab*s and the dissipation of the faith.[92] What Shah Wali Allah encountered during his stay in Mecca and Medina was a rejuvenated and intensive study of Hadiths, which allowed him to immerse himself in the records of the Prophet's words and furnished direct scriptural means to return to the original Sunna.

When he settled back in Delhi to teach in his late father's madrasa, Shah Wali Allah devoted himself to reviving what he understood to be the true Islam. He denounced the popular practices and superstitions that he believed the Muslims of India were borrowing from Hinduism and other religions. Like Ibn Taymiyya, he rejected the speculative theology of Ash'ari and advocated the straightforward acceptance of God's description of Himself. Moreover, he felt that the ulama should not encourage or allow the masses to venerate unduly the saints, both living and dead, or to forget that God alone has the power to answer prayers.[93]

Shah Wali Allah also wrote hundreds of pages explicating how India's ulama should break free of their chauvinistic loyalty to the Hanafi school of law and recognize how its legal rulings sometimes ignored authentic Hadiths. This issue was crystallized in the seemingly mundane question of how and when a Muslim should raise their hands toward their ears during daily prayers. Shah Wali Allah and other revivalists believed that Hadiths made clear that this must be done multiple times in a prayer, while India's loyal Hanafi scholars insisted that it should only be done once. They argued that Abu Hanifa and the many generations of scholars who developed his school after him had taken into account all the evidence from the Qur'an and Hadiths in formulating their laws on issues such as the mechanics of prayer. They could not have missed applicable evidence. But Shah Wali Allah responded that sometimes they might have done just that, and to him and other revivalists, refusing to even consider that possibility meant preferring the Hanafi school of law over Hadiths and treating the Hanafi scholars of yesteryear like infallible priests, an error condemned by the Qur'an.

The debate over raising hands in prayer was not merely academic. One of Shah Wali Allah's disciples was almost beaten to death in Delhi's great mosque for raising his hands and, so the uniform Hanafi congregation there thought, adulterating the known prayer taught by the Messenger of God. Although he hoped to reform Islam in India, Shah Wali Allah understood the importance of tact and strategy. His criticisms of popular Sufi practices, like musical gatherings, were balanced and subtle. Perhaps in response to what he saw befall his student in the mosque, he wrote that in a public situation one should follow the local custom and not bring strife upon oneself by raising one's hands in prayer – despite the strong evidence that this was the correct Sunna. The uneducated masses should not involve themselves in such issues and should simply follow the local *madhhab*. Shah Wali Allah was not a militant, and his reform efforts were attempts to educate society and correct the life of the mind.[94]

Mecca and Medina in the early 1700s were crucibles of revivalist thought. Others who studied and taught in the twin shrine cities alongside Shah Wali Allah similarly devoted themselves to a renewed reverence for Hadiths and to rejecting obedience to a *madhhab* (known as *taqlid*, or 'imitation') if it meant stubbornly refusing to even consider that the *madhhab* might include rulings that contradicted clear evidence from the Qur'an or Hadiths. Others in the same study circles reached similar conclusions about the need for a return to the Qur'an, Sunna and the righteous Salaf, including the Arabian Hanbali scholar Ibn 'Abd al-Wahhab.

Unlike Shah Wali Allah, some revivalists envisioned purifying Islam as a mission that must be carried out by force. Particularly in West Africa and Central Arabia, they saw themselves as being in the exact same position as the Prophet's founding community over a millennium earlier: the lone messengers of monotheism carrying God's word to their pagan surroundings by force of arms. In the barren desert of Najd in Central Arabia, Ibn 'Abd al-Wahhab perceived the superstitions, grave visitations and sinful lifestyles around him as no different than the pre-Islamic, polytheist Arabs that Muhammad had battled. The alliance he formed with the ruling Saud family in the town of Dir'iyya, known as the '*Muwahhid*' movement, or those calling for restoring *Tawhid* (called 'Wahhabis' by their detractors), engaged in a violent conquest of Central Arabia that forced their revivalist message on the tribes they defeated.

In what is today northern Nigeria, in the late eighteenth century a Muslim scholar named Usman Dan Fodio too looked at the supposedly Muslim communities around him and saw only neglect for the Shariah, such as public nudity for men and women and surviving animist religious customs such as venerating sacred trees. Like Ibn 'Abd al-Wahhab, he gathered followers and, after local rulers tried to terminate his preaching, eventually declared a jihad against them. As his movement grew, it used force of arms to bring the peoples of the region back into the fold of true Islam, an Islam that, in truth, they had never known. Dan Fodio was eventually declared Caliph of the new Islamic state of Sokoto (which survives today as one of Nigeria's states).

At the root of these militant revival movements was the question of *Takfir*, or declaring someone who claimed to be a Muslim an unbeliever. Unlike followers of other established religions, whose faiths Shariah law uniformly allowed them to practice in peace alongside Muslims, those Muslims who either announced their apostasy from Islam or were declared unbelievers faced an unpleasant fate. Based on Hadiths in which the Prophet stated that 'Whoever changes his religion [from Islam], kill him,' and that 'one who leaves his religion, forsaking the community' should be punished by death, leaving Islam was a death-penalty offence. This was agreed upon by all the Sunni schools of law (though the Hanafis only punished women apostates with prison).

Sunni ulama had historically been excruciatingly cautious about declaring Muslims to be apostates, following the general principle that 'Those who pray toward Mecca are not to be declared unbelievers.' Only someone who explicitly declared his renunciation of Islam, actively participated in the rituals of another religion or denied some aspect of Islam that was 'known essentially as part of the religion,' like rejecting the requirement to pray five times a day or the finality of Muhammad's prophethood, was declared an unbeliever. Even a Muslim who drank alcohol, ate pork or fornicated was still Muslim. He was just a sinner. What would push him outside the pale of Islam would be *believing that it was permissible* in Islam to drink wine, eat pork or fornicate.

The soldiers of the Wahhabi movement and the Sokoto caliphate, however, shifted this lens in a slight but hugely consequential way. Many of the traditional customs of West African Muslims or Central Arabian Bedouins were certainly prohibited and deemed heretical by the Shariah. Wahhabi and Sokoto leaders would duly write to such communities, advising them to desist. When they refused – sometimes because they had no real idea about Islam to begin with and sometimes because, they rightly argued, many ulama approved of their practices – the revivalists interpreted this as the fatal belief that something clearly forbidden in Islam was permissible. While a more patient and realistic scholar like Shah Wali Allah would see this as an occasion to educate, the militants saw these wayward folk as non-Muslims who could legitimately be brought under Muslim control or, worse, as apostates worthy of death.

TWILIGHT OF AN ERA

In 1762, Shah Wali Allah died at the age of fifty-nine. During his lifetime, India's Mughal Muslim dynasty had gone from controlling almost all the subcontinent into a precipitous decline. The scholar's life coincided with a period that would later be referred to as the Twilight of the Mughals, when the increasingly hapless emperors in Delhi lost themselves in poetry and wine as their realm spun out of their control. In 1757, five years before Shah Wali Allah's death, a small and previously negligible band of foreigners who had been operating trading stations on India's coasts orchestrated the defeat of a Mughal vassal in Bengal. Within ten years, the Mughal emperor had acknowledged the British East India Company as its local 'representative' in most of northeast India, and the Company administered Shariah courts and collected taxes in the emperor's name. By 1818, the political machinations and seemingly unstoppable British armies, led by legendary generals such as the Duke of Wellington, had gained control of most of India and left the Mughal emperor a ruler in name alone.

In 1798, the turbaned ulama of another historic metropolis of Islam, Cairo, also found themselves under the rule of strange foreigners in bizarre, tight-fitting uniforms. That year, Wellington's implacable foe Napoleon had landed an expeditionary force in Egypt in an attempt to challenge Britain's control of trade routes to India. A Muslim scholar who witnessed the dramatic defeat of the Mamluk armies by the French at the Battle of the Pyramids remarked with grudging respect the foreigners' discipline, efficiency and bravery.[95]

The colonial expansion of European powers heralded a new age for the custodians of the Qur'an and Sunna. No longer would the words of God and Muhammad or the interpretive sciences that the ulama had developed be paramount in the arena of law or society. An East India Company administrator who became a leading European scholar of Islamic scripture considered the Hadith corpus to be 'confused, if not contradictory.' He identified what he saw as Muslims' uncritical approach to scripture, along with the Shariah (especially its treatment of women and family), and the fatalism of Sunni theology, to be primarily responsible for the 'barbarous' state of Islamic societies.[96] Napoleon's secretary in Egypt described how the future French emperor had feigned an interest in Islam to curry the support of Cairo's ulama. In truth, however, Muslim dress and customs were silly to the French. Napoleon, the secretary noted, really looked upon all religions as 'the work of men.'[97] The pole of the intellectual and spiritual world of Muslims was shifting.

3

The Fragile Truth of Scripture

The young Egyptian doctor could not believe the Prophet had said it. The Hadith contradicted everything he had learned about disease and standards of hygiene in Cairo's modern Qasr Al-Ayni Medical School. 'If a fly lands in your drink, push it all the way under, then throw the fly out and drink. On one of the fly's wings is disease, on the other is its cure.' Such were the words of the Prophet as Tawfiq Sidqi found them.[1]

Sidqi was a committed Muslim. He had memorized the Qur'an as a boy and wrote regular contributions to Cairo's burgeoning journal scene, defending Islam against Christian missionary efforts in Egypt during the 1890s and the early 1900s. But even after sharing his doubts with his mentor, the great Muslim reformist scholar Rashid Rida, the young doctor could not escape an alarming conclusion: the Hadiths of the Sunni tradition were little more than fable. The Sunna as a whole, he would write in a controversial 1906 article, was only ever meant for the Arabs of the Prophet's time. From that point on, Muslims were meant to rely on the Qur'an and reason alone to find their way.

Another protégé of Rida in Cairo, Mahmud Abu Rayya, was similarly disturbed by the supposedly *sahih* Hadiths he read. The Hadith of the Fly was found in the *Sahih al-Bukhari,* which Sunnis claimed was 'the most authentic book after the Qur'an.' The book and its compiler, Bukhari, who had been a leading student of Ibn Hanbal, enjoyed almost sacred status. Yet another troubling Hadith from this collection told how, when the Devil hears the call to prayer, 'he flees, farting.' Abu Rayya could not accept that the Prophet would say something so vulgar and ridiculous. Still another Hadith quoted the Prophet telling his followers that, after the sun set, it went before the throne of God and prostrated itself. This Hadith came from the *Sahih Muslim*, a Hadith collection considered second only to *Sahih al-Bukhari* in reliability. Like the Hadith of the Fly, this report was clearly scientifically impossible. Sidqi died of typhus in 1920, at the age of only thirty-nine. Writing about his late classmate, Abu Rayya recalled how he had been called a *kafir*, an infidel, for doubting a Hadith from *Sahih al-Bukhari*.[2]

A CRISIS OF CONFIDENCE

Medieval Muslim scholars had looked at these same Hadiths with perplexity. Ninth-century Mutazila scholars had dismissed the Hadith of the Fly as absurd because it seemed rationally impossible for both a disease and its cure to coexist on the same object. A twelfth-century Sunni judge from Cordoba wondered what the Devil 'farting' could mean, and medieval ulama found the Hadith of the Sun Prostrating puzzling. How does the sun, an orb, prostrate itself? It has no knees or joints. Like Aristotle and Augustine, Muslim scholars knew the earth was a sphere.[3] In the course of one of their basic duties – calculating prayer times in various locales – they had noticed that the sun is always visible somewhere, rising and setting at different times depending on latitude and longitude. When would it be free to engage in this prostration before the throne of God?

Though Sidqi, Abu Rayya and these medieval scholars pondered the same perplexing segments of scripture, their reactions could hardly have been more different. Whereas Hadiths like that of the Fly collapsed Sidqi's and Abu Rayya's faith in the reliability of the Hadith corpus as a whole, they had posed little threat to medieval Sunnis. These classical scholars had dismissed the Mutazila's objection to the Hadith of the Fly as the byproduct of their heretical empowerment of human reason over a submission to revealed text and divine knowledge. Medieval Sunnis further affirmed that Hadith's authenticity and the truth of its contents by noting that antidotes to snake venom often used flesh from the snake itself. The Cordoban judge pondering Satan's flatulence noted that it might well be a rhetorical device intended to express the Devil's intense hatred for the call to the remembrance of God. Others speculated that perhaps this was a desert allusion to his rapid flight, just as horses inevitably break wind if they bolt into a sudden run (a fact omitted in films, no doubt due to its undramatic effect).[4] While Sidqi and Abu Rayya agonized over what they could only conclude was a crude medieval forgery foisted on the masses before the discoveries of modern astronomy, the prominent thirteenth-century Damascene scholar Nawawi concluded that the Hadith of the Sun Prostrating must be referring to a metaphorical prostration – the sun's submission to God's will through the order of His creation. As the Qur'an reads in a highly poetic passage: 'The stars and the trees bow down' (55:6).

Sometimes medieval exegetes simply admitted that they had no answers to explain perplexing Hadiths. But this was their failing, they felt, and no more than an unsmoothed wrinkle in the pages of scripture. In the fifteenth century, Ibn Hajar convened his finest students in Cairo to assist him in completing his monumental, fifteen-volume commentary on *Sahih al-Bukhari*. When they came to a Hadith recounting how 'God created Adam, and he was sixty arms tall,' and that, after Adam fell, 'mankind has continued to shrink since that time,' Ibn Hajar noticed a problem. The houses he had seen carved out of cliffs by ancient, bygone peoples were the same size as those in his own time. Their inhabitants had not been any taller than his fellow Cairenes. Ibn Hajar admitted frankly that 'to this day, I have not found how to resolve this problem' and promptly moved on to the next Hadith.[5]

For the pre-modern ulama, problematic or confusing Hadiths were interpretive challenges to be overcome with the confidence of mandarins who had inherited God's revelation and labored to understand it fully. For Sidqi and Abu Rayya, they precipitated a clash between, on the one hand, the certainty espoused by the new behemoth of 'modern science' and the hegemony of globalizing Western sensibilities, and on the other, a suspicious, archaic religious tradition, a tradition that must have been the work of men.

Like all faith communities, Muslims' approach to their scriptures has been influenced by their epistemological worldview. This is that lens that a person or group of like-minded people habitually apply to the world around them, to the history they read and the beliefs they hold. It dictates what are the primary truths against which other claims and data are tested. In the epistemological worldview of modern Western historians, events must be explained through material or social causes. Claims of some miraculous occurrence *must* be fabrications or delusions. Yet, inconceivable for academics in today's disenchanted world, in the seventeenth century even the most skeptical Jesuit historians had no compunction reporting that they had seen the blood of a long-dead saint liquefy again before their very eyes. They had expected no less. To them, the world was still a theatre of God's power where miracles could occur.[6]

For an individual or a community, a commitment to the primacy of scripture opens up endless possibilities for its interpretation and facilitates reconciling it with elements of outside truth. Medieval Muslim scholars interpreted the Qur'an and Hadiths so that they would remain true both in relation to one another and to the rational and empirical realities that the ulama perceived outside these texts. Any Qur'anic verse or Hadith whose literal meaning seemed problematic could be negotiated. When a community's commitment to scripture is shaken or lost, however, crises of contradiction quickly emerge and threaten the canonical worldview built around those scriptures. Its weakness can be revealed in quotidian moments of common life, as in the case of a British schoolboy who, in the 1880s, heard that 'Darwin had disproved the Bible.'[7]

CANONS AND READING SCRIPTURE WITH CHARITY

The Gospels, Shakespeare's plays and the Constitution of the United States are not just revered tomes, mere works of literature or meditations on law and justice. Each is part of a canon, a set of texts deemed authoritative by its community of readers. For Western European civilization from the fourth century until the early modern period, the Bible was the recognized vehicle of God's truth. It remains so for many to this day. Shakespeare's works are the measure of literary achievement in the English language, graciously bearing aphorisms on love and mortality. His grammar cannot be 'wrong' or his neologisms cheap. For Americans, the Constitution is the prized and venerated source of order and good governance. It is framed in the modern museum-temple, the conscript fathers who drafted it lionized anew with every heavy biography devoted to one of their number.

Canonical texts may not always be above criticism, but critiquing them has its limits and its costs. Although criticizing Shakespeare's oeuvre is permitted in the academy, one cannot say it is bad English. Some might argue for revisions to the American Constitution on matters such as the right to bear arms, but no American in public life could say that the Constitution is not suited for running a garden club, let alone a nation. Such opinions would be dismissed as absurd if not offensive within the canonical communities whose very identities are formed in part around these texts.

The possibility of trenchant biblical criticism today only highlights the Bible's previously fortressed canonical status. Before serious criticism of the scripture began in Germany in the late eighteenth century, one could not say that the Bible was historical invention or utter nonsense (at least, not without dire consequences). The appearance of the historical-critical study of the Bible and the fall of the Bible from scriptural canon to mere literature among scholars has been one of the great events of modern Western history.

Canonical works are assumed to be complete wholes endlessly pregnant with useful meaning. Virgil was *the* poet of imperial Rome, that idea of an eternal city that has long outlasted the city's greatness itself, the vision of sovereign glory to which Jove gave 'empire without end.' Virgil guided Dante through the Underworld and Purgatory in a world ruled by Rome's Christian, Germanic heirs, and he still protects protagonists in Hollywood adventures (*The Core*, 2003). When the emperor Constantine converted to Christianity, he expounded publicly on how Virgil had predicted the coming of Christ (Gibbon muses sarcastically that Virgil was 'one of the most successful missionaries of the gospel'), and later in the Middle Ages men of letters would flip to random lines in the *Aeneid* in superstitious divination.[8] All this despite the fact that Virgil had left his famous poem unfinished.

The flawless relevance of the *Aeneid* inheres because, when communities endow certain texts or bodies of material with authority, they commit themselves to interpreting those texts with charity, to extending them the benefit of the doubt. The notion of a canonical work or 'a classic' is intimately linked to a commitment to making sense of that text and affirming its worth to the community.

When a work becomes canonical its internal order and logic are guaranteed by the collective will of the canonical community. Its consonance with the known truths and reality outside the text is similarly committed to. What Frank Kermode referred to as the Principle of Complementarity is the willed assumption of the community that has invested value and meaning in a text that the text *must* make sense within itself and against its extratextual surroundings.[9] It cannot suffer from senseless internal contradictions. It cannot clash with what is known to be true outside the text. What the biblical scholar Moshe Halbertal termed the Principle of

Charity is the willingness of a canonical community to read its texts in the best possible light and in a way that defuses or elides contradictions with truth or order.[10]

The charity extended to a text reflects its canonicity and can increase as its status solidifies. By the third century BCE, the orally transmitted epics of the *Iliad* and the *Odyssey* were already centerpieces of the Greek cultural landscape. The literary scholar Zenodotus, the first chief librarian of the Library of Alexandria, worked to compile the first critical edition of Homer's epics. This was a fluid point in the two texts' development, and when Zenodotus came across verses that he felt described the gods inappropriately he simply rejected the verses as inauthentic or offered a 'correct' amendment.[11] In the centuries that followed, many Greco-Roman philosophers came to look to the *Iliad* and *Odyssey* as more than literary works; they saw them as primordial storehouses of philosophical wisdom. Now endowed treasuries of meaning, they required even more charitable readings. The many and bizarre behaviors still ascribed to the gods in these two epics had to be reconciled with extratextual ethical teachings. Stoic philosophers such as Heraclitus (writing around 100 CE) thus read scandalous behavior by the gods allegorically. Mars' and Venus' adultery in the *Iliad* represented the peaceful melding of Strife and Love.[12]

To those outside the canonical culture, all this can seem like obliviousness or naiveté. Outsiders see gross imperfections or jarring inconsistencies in the text. But within the canonical community a canonical text cannot include desultory details or oversights, regardless of how clearly these protrude to outsiders. In the Gospel of Mark, Jesus' capture at Gethsemane is punctuated by the odd mention of a 'young man' wearing a linen shirt who is also grabbed by the Roman guards but who flees naked, leaving the gown behind (Mark 14:51–52). Random and pointless to some, this detail cannot be so within the worldview of the biblical canon. It must carry meaning and must accord with the greater narrative of Jesus' life, teachings and the drama of his death and resurrection. Biblical scholars and exegetes have devoted great efforts to unlocking the meaning behind this youth's appearance, with some associating him with the robed youth who tells the women who discover Christ's empty tomb that he has risen. A medieval manuscript, supposedly written by Clement of Rome, offers the explanation that this episode is a vestige of a second, fuller Gospel that Mark had written after leaving Rome for Alexandria. The manuscript includes a segment telling how Jesus had earlier resurrected the youth and told him to meet him that night to be baptized, still wearing his burial gown.[13]

As Augustine, Saadia Gaon and the Muslim legal theorists appreciated, the sources of knowledge for 'Peoples of the Book' are scripture, the light of reason and the perceived realities of the outside world. But God's word intrudes into man's world as no equal partner. Revealed scripture makes unmatched claims to truth and authority over society. Alongside scripture, members of society also identify truths and realities outside its pages, either in first principles of reason, experienced observation or embedded cultural norms. Which source is supreme, requiring the others to be tailored to its claims? The answer to this question determines the canonicity of scripture within a community's epistemological worldview.

A canon of texts is stable as long as it holds its weight against the other sources. The great danger looming over a canon is the turning of a new epistemological era, when the community no longer grants its text sufficient charity. The early fourth-century Church Father Eusebius believed with all his heart that the Old Testament was revelation prefiguring the coming of Christ. He was still the child of the Greco-Roman milieu, however, and Abraham's face-to-face encounter with Yahweh in the Book of Genesis (18:1–2) presented a problem. Eusebius felt that 'Reason would never allow that the uncreated and immutable substance of Almighty God should be changed into the form of a man.' But neither can he allow that 'Scripture should falsely invent such a tale.' Eusebius therefore concludes that Abraham must not have encountered God Himself, but rather the Logos – the constructive and rational emanation of God in creation.[14]

Thirteen hundred years later, the iconoclastic Jewish philosopher Spinoza (d. 1677) refused to extend such charity to the Old Testament's anthropomorphisms. For him, the text was not the preserved word of God. It did not deserve to be made sense of at any expense. It was dishonest chauvinism, he argued, to insist on reconciling the Bible with regnant extratextual philosophies. The Old Testament was suited to a specific place and time, for an ancient people who did not find anthropomorphism or the admissions of a 'jealous God' objectionable. That world found nothing odd about forbidding cooking a lamb in its mother's milk, though Augustine thought the verse too absurd to be anything but allegory and

Maimonides could only explain it as an ethical reminder not to cook an animal in a substance that should have nourished it.[15] Spinoza dismissed figurative interpretations for biblical passages like this as the affected gymnastics of readers whose notions of truth had moved on beyond the ancient Hebrews but whose sentimental attachment to the canon left them unwilling to read its texts honestly.

Spinoza represented the beginning of a new epistemological era in how the Bible and religion would be viewed in the West. For him, true religion is attainable by reason and is no more than the eternal moral truths of loving God and one's neighbor. The Bible was a book born in history like any other.[16] Eusebius' teacher, the great third-century Alexandrian exegete Origen, had acknowledged that the Old Testament contained many passages that, if read literally, would be heretical or absurd. He thus read almost the whole Old Testament as moral, spiritual or Christological allegory. The impossible and ridiculous episodes of the Old Testament existed precisely so that believers would *know* that the book should not be read literally.[17] By contrast, in some of the first openly patronizing (and posthumously published) writings about the Bible, the eighteenth-century German scholar Hermann Reimarus mocked as childish and ridiculous this biblical world of seas boiling, asses talking and men flying through the air. Like Spinoza, Reimarus demanded that the Bible be taken for what it said, not what Christians extracted from its passages as the 'true,' intended meaning. Both Spinoza and Reimarus acknowledged that the Bible might reflect greater moral or spiritual truths present outside its pages, but its laughable text certainly did not *contain* them.[18]

Of course, canonical cultures are not monolithic. There are always heretics and contrarians, and private doubts abound even among the publicly faithful. Cicero could not understand how two Roman augurs, charged with state soothsaying duties, could refrain from laughing when they met one another. Yet canons and their infrastructures reveal themselves plainly. When we look at the frame of reference within which a history is told or unfolds, we can sense clearly the basic legitimizing principles of a system, and we can make out an epistemological era's foundations. For all the superciliousness of the Roman elite, the political, legal and cultural world of Rome was still played out under the auspices of Jupiter Capitolinus, and Cicero required skeptical priests to keep their debates over the gods private. As Gibbon mused, they 'concealed the sentiments of an atheist under sacerdotal robes,' but they concealed them all the same.[19] Similarly,

Voltaire did not want to share his skepticism about the Bible with the masses of the poor, for whom Christianity provided both a rare comfort and 'that necessary fear that prevents secret crimes.'[20]

Medieval Islamic civilization boasted its share of renowned heretics and freethinkers. The eleventh-century poet Ma'arri gained acclaim for his cynical agnosticism, jibing that 'The people of the earth are of two types: those with reason and no religion, and religious folk with no reason at all.' But such skeptics still abided by or concealed themselves within the confines of Islam's canonical culture. Ibn Sina (Avicenna) upheld for the masses the Shariah ban on wine while holding that he, as a philosopher, could enjoy it. The grand vizier of the Ottoman sultan Sulayman the Magnificent was not convinced of Islam's exclusive claim to salvation, and he shared this in private. But he still carried out his duties to prosecute a jihad against the enemies of his religion and endowed the gorgeous Rüstem Pasha Mosque to be constructed in his name.[21] The very fact that we still speak comprehensibly about 'Islam' as a geopolitical unit or the 'Muslim world' reminds us that, until well into the modern period, this epistemological system saw no new viable framework for society and politics. It remains the world of the Qur'an and the Prophet.[22]

Neither do epistemological eras transition overnight. Western civilization did not progress from purely religious to purely secular. It has never been purely either. But the dominant canonical culture built around the Bible and the public cult of Christianity was the overarching framework of the medieval West, and it faltered irreversibly in the mid-nineteenth century. In France in particular 'the hour was come' even sooner, concluded Carlyle. And it came with startling speed. Philosophism and the French Revolution tamed a Church that just decades earlier had been able to deprive Jansenists of a Christian burial. In Britain, the very universities that once required conformity to religious orthodoxy and that elaborated its details began producing minds who argued for the Bible's and Christianity's marginalization in public and even private life. In the 1840s Queen Victoria publicly attended the theatre in Lent – unheard of – and in 1862 no less than a bishop of the Church of England published a book claiming that the Pentateuch was 'fictitious from beginning to end.'[23] Islamic thought in the twentieth and twenty-first centuries has shown how fierce resistance to the fall of a canonical culture can be, but this fierceness belies the great changes that may well be at hand.

THE TURNING OVER OF AN ERA

Sidqi, the young Egyptian doctor, and his intellectual comrade Abu Rayya seemed to teeter on the edge of an epistemological era. What separated them from their counterparts among the medieval ulama was not necessarily a lack of faith or a desire to believe. In fact, swimming against the tide of modernity, Sidqi may have been more tenaciously committed to Islam than a scholar like Nawawi (d. 1277), who lived celibately (unusual for a Muslim scholar) and cerebrally, writing and teaching his whole life in a Damascus madrasa. What differed was what formed the patent background of reality in their respective worlds and where they identified their storehouses of truth. What separated them was the extent to which they were committed to the maintenance of a canon of scripture. Surrounded by reverence for the Shariah, respected universally as a leading member of the ulama in a city studded with madrasas, confident in a secure Abode of Islam that had recently recaptured Jerusalem from the Crusaders and whose Mongol interlopers would soon convert to Islam themselves, Nawawi never had cause to doubt the eternal veracity of the Qur'an and its interpretive tradition.

Sidqi, on the other hand, stares back at us in anxious discomfort. He poses nervously before an image-capturing device invented by an alien, infidel civilization, which occupied his country but whose sciences he had learned eagerly and whose vest and bowtie had become irresistible markers of status among Egyptians. The Europeans touring Cairo in his day offered dismissive insights like 'Islam and good order are incompatible,' and modernized Egyptians left the ulama aghast with casual calls for laws and mores to be based on modern customs, not on the Sunna of the Prophet. Other young effendis less pious than Sidqi freely mocked the Sunna as 'stupid' and 'evil,' a blasphemy unthinkable only years earlier.[24] In Sidqi's photograph, only his fez and moustache remain to mark his 'Muslim-ness' in an ensemble, typical of young Egyptian professionals, that symbolized an attempt to achieve a hybrid, modern Islam. Sidqi longed to cling to his religion and to the civilization it had created, but for him, and for many, its canonical culture had been shattered. Islam had to be rescued from its sunken and ill-fitted medieval shell. It had now to conform to precepts as undeniable as the bowtie: those of the modern West.

In Shah Wali Allah's day, two great camps of Sunni thought contended with one another: those we might term the Sunni traditionalists, who believed that the institutions of the triad heritage of the *madhhab*s, speculative theology and Sufi orders represented the true embodiment of Islam; and the iconoclastic 'Salafi' revivalists, who called for bypassing what they considered rigid and often misguided traditions to return to the Qur'an and Hadiths, the pure Islam of the Prophet's community.

Figures like Sidqi and Abu Rayya introduced a new school of thought, that of Islamic modernism. It was built on the conclusion that true Islam could only be saved by radically overhauling the entirety of pre-modern Islamic tradition. Those who took Islamic modernist directions believed that the modern world had brought an unprecedented clarity to the true, original and eternal nature of their religion. Islam had always been modern, they contended, and it had to be returned to its proper form. As Abu Rayya once boasted, 'I am more knowledgeable than Abu Hanifa or Shafi'i.' He announced that it was his mission to rescue true Islam from its medieval darkness.[25] It was no coincidence that this 'true Islam' accorded with the main sensibilities of the omnipresent modern West.

READING SCRIPTURE SO IT'S TRUE

Medieval Muslim scholars understood well that communication through the medium of language was inseparably influenced by the assumptions that surrounded the speaker and their audience. In the case of God's revelation to Muhammad, connection to this formative moment of communication was increasingly strained as the audience receded further and further away from the speaker's voice in space and time. The conservative ethos of the ulama's culture, with its chains of transmission and decrial of 'heretical innovation in religion,' served to anchor them in the original moment of God's address to humankind and in its founding constellation of assumptions. Their task was to preserve the immediacy of the revelation in later times, to draw on their ties back to the origins of their tradition and grasp the intentions of the Lawgiver.

The conviction that the Qur'an and its application in the Sunna together embodied truth, and thus had to be read in that light, was core to the pre-modern Islamic interpretive tradition. The Qur'an describes itself as a book that 'falsehood does not approach either from before or from behind, revelation from the Most Wise, the Most Praised' (41:42); the Prophet's Sunna, as contained in the totality of the Hadith corpus, is in his own words 'a path gleaming white, its night like its day.' The assumption of the infallibility of the combined Qur'an and Sunna and their congruence with truth is so ubiquitous in the Islamic tradition that it rarely appears explicitly. One does find it, however, articulated in Sunni legal theory through the notion of *lahn al-khitab*, or the 'perceptive understanding of a textual address.' Shared by both the Majority (Ash'ari) and Hanafi schools of Sunni legal theory, this was 'the interpretation of a text in the manner on which its truth depends.' To paraphrase the eleventh-century Ash'ari legal theorist Juwayni, *lahn al-khitab* is the interpretation of a text that makes it congruent with other truths.[26]

Shah Wali Allah's intellectual history showed how the Sunni interpretive tradition was both unified and polyglot. It coalesced from many voices into a system of agreed-upon certainties from which increasingly attenuated probabilities extended in diverse but ordered branches. Its sturdy core, formed from the great roots of scripture and early practice, in turn brought order to their more erratic strands. As Nawawi explains, when the ulama have arrived at certainty about a stance derived from the Qur'an and Sunna as a whole, all individual Qur'anic verses and Hadiths must be interpreted to accord with it. Origen and Augustine would have understood him perfectly. He was restating the central pillar of scriptural hermeneutics, the reciprocal movement in which, as Leo Lefebure describes, 'We interpret the part in light of the whole, and then we reinterpret the whole in light of our new understanding of the part.'[27]

To maintain concord within their interpretive system, the medieval ulama read an address by God or the Prophet with the understanding that 'it was permitted to derive from within the text some implication that specifies its meaning.' For example, the Qur'an orders Muslims to perform ablutions before their prayers if they have broken their state of ritual purity by using the bathroom, or 'If you have touched women' (addressing Muslims as a whole but using men as examples, 5:6). The ulama, though, exempted touching close family members, such as one's mother or father. They did so because the Qur'anic text here implies that the issue at hand is sexual arousal. This implication is derived from the overarching system of values and rules communicated by the Qur'an and Sunna, of which every specific 'text' (Qur'anic verse or Hadith) forms a part.[28]

There are plentiful counterparts in the Hadiths. One of the groups condemned most vehemently in the Qur'an is the *Munafiqun*, 'The Hypocrites' of Medina who entered Islam formally but who worked openly to undermine Muhammad's message and leadership. In God's eyes, they were the worst of the unbelievers, and the Prophet was even forbidden to pray for them at their funerals. Labeling someone a *Munafiq* or hypocrite is thus no small matter in Islam. In one famous Hadith, the Prophet warns his followers that 'The signs of the hypocrite are three: if he speaks, he lies; if he makes a promise, he breaks it; if he is entrusted with something, he betrays.'

This boded very badly for Muslims. Few humans can really hope to be free of such faults throughout the course of a lifetime. Does God, then, condemn anyone who lies, breaks promises or violates a trust as severely as He dooms hypocrites in the Qur'an? A ninth-century Hadith scholar who studied with Bukhari and whose own collection of Hadiths serves as a document of early Sunni Islam, offers a clarification. Abu 'Isa Tirmidhi reminds us of Hasan Basri's explanation of this Hadith. He had noted the difference between 'Hypocrisy of Action' and 'Hypocrisy of Disbelief.' The latter only existed during the time of the Prophet. It was insidious dissimulation in the very face of God's Messenger, and it was this hypocrisy that the Qur'an condemned so stridently. For the rest of humanity, hypocrisy was simply one's actions not living up to one's commitments or stated values.[29] There was no clear statement in the Qur'an or Hadiths that directed Hasan or Tirmidhi to this interpretation. There seems only to have been a profound belief, drawn from the aggregate ethos of early Islamic teachings, that the hypocrisy described in the Qur'an and the hypocrisy confronting everyday Muslims were two distinctly different species. It was not fair to tar both with the same brush.

As these examples suggest, the charity that Muslim scholars granted passages from the Qur'an and Hadiths in order to read them as part of a greater, encompassing system of truth meant that their literal meaning was often set aside altogether. The Qur'an states that 'The polytheists are naught but impure (*najas*), so let them not approach the Inviolable Mosque [of Mecca] after this, their year...' (9:28). Some early scholars like Hasan Basri had leaned toward a literal interpretation of this verse, advising Muslims to perform ablutions after shaking hands with a polytheist. By the eleventh century, however, the ulama had come to consensus on the doctrinal maxim of 'Adamic purity' (*taharat al-adami*), based in part on the Prophet's interactions with unbelievers and his allowing them into his mosque. Non-Muslims, like Muslims, are thus inherently pure, and their sweat, tears and saliva are ritually innocuous. As Nawawi explained, the

Qur'anic verse was referring to the impurity of polytheistic *beliefs*.[30] This verse was thus shifted out of its literal sense to accord with the overarching system of legal principles established by its interpreters. That one had to move from the evident meaning of a text to a secondary meaning because compelling evidence required it was known as *Ta'wil*, or interpretation.

Even the earliest Muslims understood that literal meanings could, in fact, be dangerous. In a series of verses chastising the Jews and Christians of Medina for not following the sacred laws revealed to them or submitting to the Prophet's judgment, the Qur'an declares: 'And whoever does not rule by what God has revealed, truly they are the unbelievers' (5:44). This verse has echoed violently among militant revivalist groups in the modern period. It literally condemns as *kafir*s – unbelievers – those who do not rule by the law revealed by God, the Shariah. The Companion Ibn Abbas, who was so prized for his exegesis of the Qur'an's language that he was dubbed 'The Rabbi of this Nation,' offered a crucial specification. 'It is not the unbelief that they think it is, namely the unbelief that places someone outside the Muslim community. Rather it is an unbelief other than that unbelief.' Distancing this Qur'anic verse from accusations of apostasy was crucial in the first decades of Islam, which saw the emergence of the extremist Kharijite sect. This group believed that anyone who committed a serious sin was an apostate deserving of death (if someone really believed in God, how could they disobey Him?). Kharijites assassinated the fourth caliph, Ali bin Abi Talib, after accusing him of not ruling by God's decree. Ibn Abbas confronted the Kharijites with his explanations, and some four thousand eventually recanted their extremism.[31]

Empirical reality could also require figurative readings of scripture. As the elaborate references to the zodiac in Homer's epics remind us, our modern esteem for the scientific method should not obscure the manifest reality of nature in pre-modern life. The Qur'an referred to both its own verses and the details of God's ordered creation in nature as complementary 'signs' (*ayat*) revealed together for man to ponder (45:2–6). Augustine had preached the same to his congregation. 'Let your book be the divine page, that you may hear it. Let your book be the world, that you may behold it.' Like Augustine, the medieval ulama were careful to read the two sets of signs in accordance with one another.[32]

In the case of one Hadith found in Tirmidhi's canonical Hadith collection, the facts of nature required abandoning the literal meaning for a figurative one. The Prophet is quoted as saying, 'Two months of festival do not fall short, Ramadan and Dhu'l-Hijja' (the month in which Hajj occurs). The Islamic calendar, prescribed in the Qur'an, is a lunar one in which the new moon appears either every twenty-nine or every thirty days depending on when the moon is sighted. A month 'falling short' thus generally refers to it containing only twenty-nine days. Like other months, Ramadan and Dhu'l-Hijja frequently 'fall short.' The Hadith is thus literally and undeniably contrary to fact. Ibn Hanbal had therefore opined that it meant no year could pass when *both* of these months fell short (hardly true, other scholars objected). Tirmidhi leaned toward the simpler metaphor that, even when these two months 'fall short,' they are nevertheless 'complete' in their spiritual value.[33]

Human nature can be as empirically daunting as planetary motion. In one famous Hadith, the Prophet proclaims that 'None of you believes until I am dearer to him than his parent and his child.' This is a tall order indeed. Many Sufis to this day seek to achieve this level of devotion to the Prophet's person and precedent. Yet even an unusually pious individual would find it difficult to love the Prophet more than their own parent or child. Khattabi (d. 998), a pioneering Shafi'i legal theorist and theologian from Bost (modern-day Lashkar Gah in Afghanistan), explains that the 'love' referred to in this Hadith is not our naturally occurring affection (*hubb al-tab'*). Rather, the Prophet intended it as 'love by choice' (*hubb al-ikhtiyar*). Khattabi concludes this because a person's love of himself and his kin is part of his nature, and 'there is no way to overcome that.' Love by choice, however, is the conscious decision made by one's higher functions for reasons that may seem superficially unnatural but that are truly best, much like the sick person who chooses to take bitter medicine in order to be cured. Thus, it is as if the Prophet is saying that one's faith is not perfect until 'he prefers what I choose for him over the folly desired by his parents or children.'[34]

THE ISLAMIC SCIENCE OF EPISTEMOLOGY AND INTERPRETATION (*USUL AL-FIQH*)

One could object that these readings of the Qur'an and Hadiths contradict what the texts explicitly 'say.' But texts themselves do not *say* anything. What they *say* and what they *mean* is determined by the reader in the unavoidable and sometimes unconscious act of interpretation. Although often associated with postmodern literary theory, this empowerment of the reader's interpretation over the author's intent is no novel assertion. Responding to the rhetorical query 'What is the Torah?' Talmudic rabbis replied simply, 'It is the interpretation of the Torah.' Even if God himself voices disagreement from the heavens, the Torah means what the majority of the rabbis say it means.[35] Erasmus remarked on the counterintuitive fact that it is the interpreter of God's words who truly wields the 'force of divine law.' The caliph Ali echoed this. Confronting the Kharijite rebels, who based their violent claims on what the Qur'an 'said,' Ali alerted them that 'This Qur'an is but lines written between two covers, it does not speak, rather it is but men who speak for it.'[36]

With speaker and listener separated by an interpretive gulf, there is no escaping the inherent ambiguity in language. An intended meaning may be conjured by the speaker in light of how he or she assumes the audience will understand it, but actual meaning is ultimately defined by the hegemonic power of the audience's worldview. There is no way to deny these influences or meld them seamlessly. Once you speak or write, it is the audience who decide your meaning. It is the station to which they have assigned the text they read that determines its worth.

No use of language, regardless of how much care is taken in crafting a phrase, is unambiguous or immune to (mis)interpretation. Although he wrote much of the United States Constitution, James Madison still argued that the meaning of laws in the new republic could not be fixed with certainty until they were contested and discussed. All laws, he wrote, regardless of how finely worded, 'are considered more or less obscure and equivocal' until they are interpreted. Language is an imperfect medium for communicating the ideas of one mind to the mind of another. Madison offered that, 'When the Almighty himself condescends to address mankind in their own language, his meaning, luminous as it must be, is rendered dim and doubtful by the cloudy medium through which it is communicated.'[37]

This does not mean that there are no boundaries to interpretation or that no interpretation is wrong. But those boundaries are set by the community reading the text, not by something intrinsic in the text or by the fact of the text itself. The allowable distance between what appears to be the literal meaning of the text and its outer limit of interpretation is determined by the charity extended to it. For the Qur'an and Hadiths, interpretations were valid as long as they accorded with the overall message of God and His prophet as understood by the ulama. To the Muslim community, the Qur'an was 'not touched by falsehood, neither from before nor from behind,' so interpretation was allowed as long as it rendered a meaning understood as true by that community. Muslim scholars expressed this through a general principle, dubbed *Qanun al-Ta'wil* (the Rule of Interpretation), which required adhering to the evident meaning of a text until some significant evidence required otherwise. Sometimes violations of this rule are called out, and ulama have at times dismissed each other's interpretive arguments as 'affected' (*fihi takalluf*) or 'arbitrary' (*fihi ta'assuf*) when they deviate too far from the evident meaning or do so without cause.

The texts of the Qur'an and Hadiths provide immensely rich interpretive ground. The two scriptures are heterogeneous, one the word of God and the other of an inspired man. They run from rock solid in authenticity to little more than rumor. They span two decades of the Prophet's career, and are thus elastic in their points of reference. In their interactions within themselves, with each other and in the florid mold of classical Arabic, the Qur'an and Hadiths are inexhaustibly polyvalent. Moreover, Hadiths were not merely reports of the Prophet's speech. They also included descriptions of his conduct, practice and even his silence. If an action was done in his presence or some opinion was voiced and he remained silent, this was understood as conveying his approval.

The type of interpretive activity we have seen so far was carried out almost instinctively by the first generations of Muslim scholars, such as Hasan Basri. By the early 800s, Shafi'i had offered his singular contributions to the science of weighing evidence, and by the late 900s the Sunni science of legal theory was reaching maturation. Its study of moral epistemology and the rational derivation of law from scripture took as its main subjects the great questions of ascertaining the historical reliability of scriptural texts and then mining their meaning.

Medieval Muslim ulama approached interpreting the Qur'an and Hadiths via two axes, that of attestation (*thubut*) and that of indication (*dilala*), each spanning the range of epistemological reliability (between doubt, probability and certitude). 'Attestation' was the historical reliability and authenticity of a proof text; a verse from the Qur'an was automatically considered 'certain in its attestation' because of the holy book's historical intactness, while the vast majority even of *sahih* Hadiths were only 'probable in their attestation.' They were simply not widely transmitted enough to create total philosophical certainty regarding their authenticity. Those

Hadiths that were declared *da'if* (weak) or, more egregiously, *mawdu'* (clear forgeries) fell short even of that level.

'Indication' concerned the ambiguity or precision of a text's meaning. Qur'anic commands like 'Give in charity from what We have granted you' are only 'probable in indication' even if they are historically authenticated. We know that God issued this command, but what does it mean? Do we give all our money, or only some? Do we give it every day or only once, and to whom? The Hadith 'A father is not punished by death for killing his child' is also 'probable in indication,' since it is unclear if it addresses all instances of infanticide. How would it relate to the Qur'anic command of 'A life for a life' (see chapter five)? The Hadith is also 'weak,' so it does not even reach the level of being 'probable in its attestation.'

Knowing the indication (i.e., meaning) of the Qur'an and Hadiths ultimately rested on the ulama's understanding of the phenomenon of language, and this occupied a large portion of the science of legal theory. Books in this genre drew on the first science developed by Muslims, the study of Arabic grammar, to catalog types of speech and evaluate the ways in which grammar affected meaning. A particularly important issue was the division between the literal (*haqiqa*) and figurative (*majaz*) registers of language. The sentence 'The lion is the king of the jungle' uses 'lion' in its literal sense; 'The knight is the lion of the battlefield' uses it figuratively. Both the literal meanings and accepted figurative uses of words were set by their uses in the Islamic scriptures, pre-Islamic Arabic poetry and in the uncorrupted Arabic of the first century and a half of Islam.

Much discussion was devoted to the various types of figurative speech: figurative 'reduction' (*nuqsan*), such as the Qur'anic command to 'Ask the village' (in other words, the people of the village, not the physical structures); metonymy (an example both in English and the Qur'an is 'going to the bathroom' as metonymy for certain activities that take place therein); or by personification or metaphor of entity (*ista'ara*), like 'the wall wants to fall.'[38]

Of great importance was the question of how one should understand an imperative phrase in language. Although the dozens of leading ulama who dove into this debate often differed, a general conclusion emerged in the eleventh century that, all things being equal, an imperative command was 1. general, 2. meant as an obligation (as opposed to a recommendation), 3. meant only one time (as opposed to performing the act more than once), 4. did *not* require immediate action and 5. implied an accompanying command for anything necessary to carry out the original command.[39] Prohibitions carried similar negative features.

Context could alter any of these aspects, and the science of legal theory devoted volumes to evaluating and weighing the relationships between different units of communication. The ulama ruminated on the nature of 'general' (*'amm*) statements and what marked them, for example, the Arabic definite article 'the' (*al-*), a universal qualifier like 'all,' or a general pronoun such as 'him who' or 'whoever.' Looking at Hadiths, which often described the Prophet's actions and not his words, they concluded that his actions cannot convey general commands because their meaning is unclear.[40]

General speech was altered and opposed by 'specific' (*khass*) language, like the Qur'anic command to perform ablutions after touching members of the opposite sex, which was understood as not including close family members. Another type of specified language was 'delimited' (*muqayyad*), namely a phrase that denoted a particular, specified meaning but did not exclude all else. While close family members were totally excluded from the intended meaning of the above Qur'anic verse on touching, the Qur'an's 'delimited' order to 'free a believing slave' in order to expiate certain sins did not mean that non-Muslim slaves are somehow excluded from the Qur'an's advocacy of manumission.

Muslim scholars elaborating legal theory graded scriptural texts along a spectrum according to the clarity of their indication (*dilala*). An 'equivocal' (*mujmal*) text was so unclear that it could not be acted on without clarification (such as the command 'Pray!'). 'Evident' (*zahir*) texts had more than one possible interpretation, but one was what we would call the evident, immediate, common-sense meaning. If we hear a person calling out 'Help me!' from a lake, that person might mean that they need investment advice. But it is most probable that they need rescue. Similarly, the 'impurity' of pagans in the Qur'an is figurative and not literal. Finally an 'unequivocal text' (*nass*) is one whose interpretation was ineluctable and could mean only what it seemed, like a proper name or a number like '3' or '5.'[41]

Shifting away from the evident meaning of a passage or from the literal to the figurative registers in scripture lay at the root of many inter-Sunni disagreements. When adherents of the Sunni Maliki school of law ruled that a sale contract became final with verbal agreement of the parties and not, as the widely known Hadith stated, 'when the two parties part company,' they invoked the shift from literal to figurative registers, from the evident to the derivative meaning. The 'parting company' mentioned in the Hadith, the Malikis held, meant 'parting through their verbal agreement,' not literally leaving one another's presence. Opponents responded by citing the Rule of *Ta'wil* and accusing the Malikis of a far-fetched interpretation: one cannot abandon the evident meaning of a text for no compelling reason. In the Arabic language of the Prophet's time, 'parting company' meant physically leaving someone's presence unless some evidence suggests otherwise.

The Majority school of legal theory, developed out of Ash'ari's combination of Sunni traditionalism and Mutazila rationalism, envisioned an interpreting hierarchy of concentric spheres. Similar to the postmodern emphasis on the power of the interpreter/reader, the outer spheres controlled those within, and the outermost interpretive layer was the most powerful. Just as the translator exercises power over the speaker by determining the meaning of a speech as he translates it, the Sunna controls the Qur'an because it is the lens through which the holy book is understood. The consensus of the ulama then controls the interpretation of the Sunna because it decides which understandings of the law ultimately enjoy total authority, and nothing supersedes it. Specified units of scripture supersede the general in their authority because they act to clarify it, and the delimited supersedes the unqualified. In both cases, the former tells you the real, intended meaning.

Interestingly, the Hanafi school of legal theory often took the opposite tack. It was rooted more closely in Abu Hanifa's original embrace of the Qur'an as the rock of authentic revelation in a sea of opinion and unsure Hadiths. Only the most reliable Hadiths could specify the Qur'an, and statements that could be acted on without specification held greater power than other items of scripture that sought to specify them.

Differences in managing the relationship between general and specified passages from the Qur'an and Hadiths as well as their relationship with derived Shariah principles could lead to bitter divisions. The Salafi surge led by Ibn Taymiyya and militarized by some of the eighteenth-century revival movements objected forcefully to forms of worship engaged in by Sufi orders over and above Muslims' prescribed five daily prayers. These included group recitation of poems praising the Prophet, sessions chanting the names of God and sometimes swaying or dancing while doing so.

The defenders of these practices justified them by pointing to Qur'anic verses such as 'Remember God often' and 'O you who believe, call God's peace and blessings down upon the Messenger most generously.' They further noted an authenticated Hadith in which, after being told that he was the relative of Muhammad who physically resembled him the most, the Prophet's cousin Ja'far began dancing on one leg in glee. The Prophet did not object. All this evidence, supporters of Sufi practices claimed, was general and unrestricted. God's commands to remember Him and praise the Prophet were unlimited, and the Prophet's condoning of Ja'far's dance showed that dancing for religious purposes was permissible. What, then, could be prohibited about pious Muslims gathering to repeat the names of God, praise the Prophet and sway as the heady airs of proximity to their Lord took control of them?

On the contrary, ulama like Ibn Taymiyya who opposed such practices argued that worship was an inherently limited field of activity in Islam. 'The assumption in matters of ritual worship is that something is forbidden,' one of Ibn Taymiyya's influential students argued, 'until some textual evidence is provided justifying it.' The Qur'anic commands above were general, but in matters of ritual worship even something fitting under a general order was not legitimate unless the Prophet or a Companion had performed that act. Critics of Sufi rituals cited opinions like that of the Companion Hudhayfa, who taught, 'Do not engage in worship by any means not engaged in by the Companions of God's Messenger.' Evidence permitting one type of ritual action could not be used to allow similar forms by analogy. Ja'far had danced, but the Prophet's approval could only be interpreted as permitting those particular movements done by Ja'far, not dancing in general.[42]

THE LANGUAGE OF GOD AND THE RHETORIC OF HIS PROPHET

When James Madison remarked on the ambiguity inherent in the use of language and the inevitability of interpretive exercise, he was discussing the precise, legal language of courts and legislatures in the former British colonies of America. This was a narrow linguistic field designed to articulate law in all its obscurities and detail. The Qur'an, on the other hand, has never been a legal manual. Its language ranges from apocalyptic warnings about doomsday to mystical ruminations about man's longing for God; from broad ethical commands to, occasionally, more specific instructions on the division of inheritance and manslaughter. The Hadiths are often more exact in their formulations of duties and obligations, but they are still expressed in the idiomatic, highly rhetorical flourishes of seventh-century Arabic. One of the chief interpretive challenges facing the medieval ulama was thus deriving concrete laws and tenets of belief from scriptures more kerygma than legalese.

The prophetic language of the Hadiths is consistently hyperbolic. We often find the phrase that someone who commits a certain sin or holds some incorrect belief 'Is not from among us,' for example. 'Whoever carries arms against us is not from among us,' the Prophet warns in one such Hadith. Does this mean that a person committing this act ceases to be a Muslim, leaving the faith for doing so? Recognizing the hyperbolic flair in the Prophet's rhetoric, the medieval ulama understood this phrase as a type of preventative rebuke (*zajr*) and not a formal excommunication (*takfir*). Tirmidhi explains that this is not an accusation of unbelief but rather indicates that the person was simply 'not following the path of the Muslims' in committing such acts.[43] Condemning certain actions to perdition is also common in Hadiths. 'Whatever [robes] extend lower than the ankles go into Hellfire,' the Prophet admonishes. This does not mean that the wearer is condemned to perdition. Khattabi explains that the Hadith should be interpreted as meaning that this action or habit is considered to be among the behaviors of people condemned to Hellfire. Furthermore, other Hadiths make clear the reason behind this declaration. Wearing one's robes so low that they drag on the ground was boasting about one's wealth, since it assumed that one had spare clothes and enough servants to wash the soiled ones. In one narration of this Hadith, the Prophet condemns 'dragging one's clothes arrogantly in the dust' but excuses those whose robes droop low without that intention.[44]

The difficulty of mining legal content from rhetorical language contributed to divergent interpretations and sometimes lay at the root of bitter disputes among the medieval ulama. Horrified by what he saw as the saint worship prevalent among the Sufis who frequented the shrines and mosques of the 'Friends of God' in Damascus and its environs, Ibn Taymiyya interpreted the *sahih* Hadith 'Do not tighten your saddles (i.e., travel) except to three mosques: the Haram Mosque, the Al-Aqsa Mosque and my mosque' as a clear prohibition on traveling to any locations other than Mecca, Jerusalem and Medina with the intent of worshiping there. Khattabi, however, and most other ulama, had not taken this Hadith literally. Instead, they understood the Hadith as a tribute to the status of these great places of prayer. Khattabi felt that its legal import was that, if one had sworn an oath to pray in a specific mosque, praying in any mosque would fulfill it – except these three prophetic mosques. One had to fulfill one's oath to pray there. Others had interpreted the Hadith as meaning that one could not hold extended prayer vigils (*i'tikaf*) in any mosque other than these three. The Hadith seemed so hyperbolic that even Ibn Taymiyya had to squint through its rhetorical flair and shift it from its evident meaning. He still allowed traveling to other places for purposes of trade, study or just for visiting, provided the intention was not solely worshiping in a mosque or saint's tomb there.[45]

THE QUR'AN: VALID FOR ALL TIMES AND PLACES

The Medinan scholar and descendant of the Prophet, Ja'far Sadiq, was one of the pillars of sacred knowledge in the eighth century, revered by Sunnis and Shiites alike. When he was asked how the Qur'an, 'despite the passage of generations, only increases in its freshness,' he replied, 'Because God did not make it for one specific time or one specific people, so it is new in every age, fresh for every people, until the Day of Judgment.'[46] To borrow a phrase from Frank Kermode, the holy book was stamped 'Licensed for exegesis.' The Muslim community came to an early consensus on treating the book as a revelation that spoke to those beyond its original audience. They deemed it, in the phrasing of modern ulama, 'good for all places and all times.'

Interpreting the Qur'an's message simultaneously within history and outside of history presented a daunting challenge to the ulama. For them, it was both a book revealed over twenty-three years in a particular region and a source of eternal law. They could never deny that the Qur'an's verses were obviously revealed in time and often in specific contexts. Many verses pronounce on concrete, time-bound matters. 'The power of Abu Lahab will perish, and so will he perish,' the Qur'an declares, predicting the grizzly end of one of the Prophet's inveterate Meccan foes. Such a specific verse, referring to one mortal in one place, cannot be applied to any other person or case. Yet the holy book also contains innumerable verses that ring out like decreta for all time: 'A life for a life,' 'And do not kill the life that God has declared inviolable except by just right' (5:45, 6:151).

More often, the valence of verses was not clear or agreed upon. Qur'anic verses rarely mention the historical circumstances that occasioned their revelation, and many verses could be read as either universal laws or particular instructions. They could appear to be one type to one school of ulama, but another school might conclude otherwise. The nature of Qur'anic commands and rulings has been endlessly debated and is one of the primary causes for the tremendous variety within Islamic law and dogma.

Sunni legal theorists since the eleventh century have phrased the tension between the specificity or generality of Qur'anic verses as the tension between the 'Generality of the Language' (*'umum al-lafz*) and the 'Specificity of the Reason for Revelation' (*khusus al-sabab*). The capacity of the Qur'an to address audiences and circumstances beyond its Arabian context depended on the maxim, developed by these medieval legal theorists, that 'Consideration is granted to the Generality of the Language, not to the Specificity of the Reason for Revelation.'[47] 'No compulsion in religion' (2:256) was a Qur'anic command revealed in Medina when a child from one of the Muslim families who had been educated in the town's Jewish schools decided to depart with the Jewish tribe being expelled from Medina. His distraught parents were told by God and the Prophet in this verse that they could not compel their son to stay. The verse, however, has been understood over the centuries as a general command that people cannot be forced to convert to Islam.

Even an elementary understanding of the meaning of Qur'anic verses often depended on grasping the specific circumstances of their revelation. The shortest chapter in the Qur'an reads, 'Indeed we have given you the *Kawthar*. So pray to your Lord and sacrifice. Indeed, the one who derides you, he is the one cut off.' Even the approximate meaning of such a passage does not become clear until read in the light of reports of *Tafsir*, or reports from the early Muslim community about the meaning of Qur'anic words and verses as well as the contexts in which they were revealed. Similar to Hadiths, *Tafsir* reports provide a variety and sometimes a cacophony of explanations, as the Companions or Successors tasked their memories or speculated about the original setting of God's revelations. More rarely, Hadiths from the Prophet himself offered explanation. Struggling to understand what this '*Kawthar*' was that God had granted Muhammad, medieval ulama identified no fewer than sixteen opinions, with well-known, authenticated Hadiths providing the strongest account that it is a river in Heaven. They further disagreed on the command to 'sacrifice,' with some early ulama interpreting it figuratively as a command addressed to all Muslims telling them to hold their hands folded at the lower neck, where a ritual offering's throat is cut, during their daily prayers. And who was this 'derider'? *Tafsir* reports seem to concur that it was an enemy member of the Prophet's tribe in Mecca who had mocked him for having no male children who survived infancy. Hence his line was 'cut off.'[48] The genre of *Tafsir* reports that explained when and why a Qur'anic verse descended came to be known as *Asbab al-Nuzul*, or 'Reasons of Revelation.'

Often Qur'anic verses appeared to be so general that scholars could refer to them without knowing or mentioning their original context at all. This was sometimes because the wording of the verses made their general import obvious. The verse about punishing thieves was revealed on the occasion of the Companion Safwan having his valuable cloak stolen, but the phrasing of the verse, with its extension to male or female thieves, clearly indicated a more general rule.[49] Similarly, the verses at the beginning of the 'Chapter of the Believers' seem to float outside of circumstance:

> Felicitous are the believers. Those who humble themselves in prayer, who turn away from vain talk, who render their charitable tithes, and who guard their chastity, except from their spouses and those their right hands possess (concubines), for indeed they are blameless. But those who seek beyond that, they are the transgressors. (23:1–6)

The generality of these verses left medieval ulama free to reach their own conclusions about the sexual constraints referred to in the last two. Shafi'i understood these verses as a general prohibition on stimulating the penis outside of licit sex (marriage and concubinage). This led him to forbid masturbation, and other schools concurred. But in light of the dearth of Hadiths on masturbation, Ibn Hanbal and his school did not see this verse as relevant and thus considered masturbation to be merely disliked or even totally permissible for those who lacked the circumstances to marry.[50]

More often, there were substantial clashes over what a Qur'anic revelation originally meant. Hence there was disagreement over whether and how applicable it was to new situations. For example, some classical ulama understood the following verse as a prohibition on Muslims who had committed fornication from marrying anyone other than fellow fornicators: 'The fornicator marries only a fornicatress or a polytheist woman, and a fornicatress marries only a fornicator or a polytheist man. And God has forbidden that for the believers' (24:3). Khattabi disagreed. Most scholars, he explained, read the verse along with *Tafsir* reports from prominent Companions, which explain that this verse had been revealed when a particular Muslim man asked the Prophet's permission to frequent some well-known pagan Arab prostitutes. The Qur'an provided the response: a sincere Muslim must not do such a thing, for this only befits a fornicator or a pagan. What might seem like a general rule condemning Muslims guilty of fornication to a caste of sinners – surely an unjust punishment for youthful indiscretion – is thus shown actually to be a response to a specific man's licentious request. Other ulama expanded it to a repudiation of prostitution in general.

The question of whom a fornicator could marry arose in the first place because of an ambiguity, absent in the English translation, over the crucial distinction between 'marrying' and 'having sex with' in Arabic. How the ulama understood this Qur'anic verse goes back to the different approaches to language adopted by the Majority and Hanafi schools of legal theory. The Majority school considered the Arabic word '*yankihu*' in the verse to mean 'marries,' based on its definition in the Islamic legal lexicon. The Hanafis, however, used the original Arabic definition of 'has sex with.' For them, the above verse would read: 'The fornicator only *has sex with* a fornicatress or a polytheist woman...' The verse becomes a condemnation of Muslim men having sex with polytheist women, using the elliptical logic of Arabic rhetoric to say that having sex with a polytheist woman makes a Muslim into a fornicator.[51]

HADITHS AND INTERPRETING THE LIFE OF THE PROPHET

Grounded in the prosaic moments of everyday life, and many thousands of times more numerous than Qur'anic verses, Hadith reports were even more entwined in historical context. Muslim scholars labored endlessly to determine if specific Hadiths addressed specific situations and persons, or if they constituted general commandments.

One consequential example of the thorny process of Hadith interpretation concerns mourning for the dead. In its treatment of death and burial, the Islamic tradition shares many features with Protestantism: a sense of the potential danger inherent in the undue veneration of the dead, and unease over the thin line between grief and railing against God's decree. Numerous Hadiths caution against excessive mourning, warning, 'He is not from among us who beats his cheeks or rends his garments, calling out the invocations of the Pre-Islamic Age of Ignorance.'[52] A set of sound Hadith narrations via the Companion Ibn Umar reports a direr admonition from the Prophet. When Ibn Umar's father, the second caliph, was mortally wounded by an assassin, he reminded his family that the Prophet had admonished: 'The dead are punished for the weeping done over them.'

But Aisha, the Prophet's widow and a pillar of religious authority in Medina, disavowed this report. Ibn Umar, she concluded, had erred or misunderstood the Prophet's words, for he had actually only said this concerning a Jewish man or woman (narrations from Aisha differ) whose funeral he had passed in Medina. The Prophet had said to the mourners, or about them (again, narrations differ), 'You/they mourn and s/he is being punished in the grave.' In other words, the dead unbeliever's tragic fate had been sealed, and the grief of mourners availed nothing. The punishment that God was inflicting was not caused by their mourning. In another narration, through the Companion Ibn Abbas, Aisha explains that God *increases* the torment of the dead unbeliever *through* his family's lamenting. In the version reported by another Companion, Aisha explains that the dead person was being punished for his own sins and faults.

Although some early ulama interpreted this Hadith literally, submitting that God could treat the souls of the dead however He wished, most heeded Aisha's qualifications. The importance of recognizing the limited application of this warning from the Prophet rested on its clash with a central Qur'anic principle, which Aisha invokes in most narrations of this Hadith: 'No bearer of burdens will bear the burdens of another' (6:164). God would not punish a soul for the actions of others.[53] At most, then, Nawawi notes, this Hadith warns Muslims against *instructing* their family to mourn for them publicly, which was a custom among Arabs of the Prophet's time, since God might well hold the dead person accountable for that egotistical stipulation. This was the interpretation of the majority of the Sunni ulama. Furthermore, Nawawi and others remind us that the 'weeping' forbidden here must be understood as loud, histrionic wailing, not normal tears of sadness.[54] Such natural expressions of grief must be allowed, notes Nawawi, because authentic Hadiths tell of the Prophet shedding tears at the death of his own infant son, Ibrahim, and also describe his close friend and successor Abu Bakr breaking into tears upon seeing Muhammad's body. Indeed, tears for the dead were 'a mercy,' the Prophet had explained.[55]

CHANGING TIMES AND THE REASONS BEHIND SCRIPTURAL LAW

When God or the Prophet decreed a ruling for a specific reason, what happened if that reason ceased to apply? Would the ruling still continue to be compelling for Muslims? In matters of ritual and worship, Islam's strict conservatism counted obsolescence as a badge of authenticity, a mark of guarantee that God's last revelation remained unaltered. When he arranged with his Meccan enemies to allow the Muslims to journey from Medina to perform the Hajj one year, Muhammad instructed his followers to move vigorously through the various stations of the pilgrimage, walking briskly in their seven transits between the small hills of Safa and Marwa near the Kaaba. He hoped to show the Meccans that years of war, travel and hardship had not sapped the Muslims' strength. The ulama preserved this 'brisk walking' (*raml*) as a well-established, recommended act. Years after the Prophet's death the caliph Umar remarked on Hajj, 'What is this for, this brisk walking... now that God has empowered Islam and negated unbelief and the unbelievers?' He answered himself with pride. 'Regardless of this, we will not abandon something we used to do in the time of the Messenger of God.'[56]

Outside of ritual matters, though, the disappearance of the original cause for some scriptural ruling proved more complicated. The Qur'an, for example, specifies eight groups who are eligible to receive the charitable tithe (*Zakat*) collected annually from Muslims as part of their religious obligation: the indigent, the poor, those in bondage or debt, travelers, those laboring in God's path, workers compensated for collecting and dispensing the *Zakat* and 'those whose hearts are to be reconciled' (*al-mu'allafa qulubuhum*) (9:60). This verse was revealed as the Muslims achieved their final victory over the Meccans and moved to establish their control over Arabia as a whole. The cryptic last group of *Zakat* recipients refers to the Meccan elite and the nobility of nearby tribes that had opposed the Prophet to the bitter end, embracing Islam only when its triumph became a foregone conclusion. In a decision that proved controversial even among his loyal followers, Muhammad decided to direct much of the spoils of war and charity collected to this group to help them retain their wealth, standing and thus their loyalty to their new community. It was a decision justified by the strategic fragility of the Muslims' situation.

But was this Qur'anic command valid beyond the strategic circumstances that occasioned it? Medieval ulama differed. The Hanafis and some Maliki scholars felt that the need to garner the support of such folk had disappeared. They deemed the *Zakat* category of 'those whose hearts are to be reconciled' to be defunct. The Hanbalis and Shafi'is both maintained that the category was still valid even centuries after the imperial expansion of Islam, though the Shafi'is rejected giving any *Zakat* funds to non-Muslims from this class. Although it might not seem necessary in a civilization reigned over comfortably by Muslims, surprising needs could arise. The sixteenth-century jurist and Sufi of Egypt, 'Abd al-Wahhab Sha'rani, recalls a Jewish man who had converted to Islam and received no aid or attention from his supposed newfound brethren. Ostracized by Cairo's Jewish community, he was on the verge of apostatizing once again when Sha'rani arranged for him to receive some financial assistance from the *Zakat* collection.[57]

THE INTERACTION OF THE QUR'AN AND HADITHS IN TIME

Although the medieval Sunni tradition developed an astoundingly deep and regimented hermeneutic system, it cultivated no unified study of the relationships between the individual proof texts of the Qur'an and Hadiths. One rarely comes across books, such as the one composed by the Hanbali scholar of Baghdad, Ibn Jawzi, identifying all the ambiguous Qur'anic verses that are explained by other verses in the holy book.[58] Instead, each school of law and theology proposed its own set of relations between the sea of Qur'anic verses and Hadiths. These varied visions of how Qur'anic verses related to each other, how Hadiths related to each other and how the two bodies of scripture interacted was often what created the divergent interpretations of the schools.

Shah Wali Allah's history provided a glimpse of how Qur'anic verses, Hadiths, Companion rulings and the use of analogy built on, superseded or elucidated each other in a process of interpretation that varied with each scholar's mind or temperament. Eventually this interpretive flood settled into the more standardized channels of the four Sunni schools of law. In this process, one absolutely defining question in the interpretation of the Qur'an and Hadiths is how they fit together, both internally and with each other.

The minutiae and subtle variations of Hadith narrations could weigh heavily in these calculations. For example, the majority of Sunni scholars understood the Hadith that 'A believer is not killed in punishment for the death of an unbeliever' as prohibiting the death penalty for a Muslim who had murdered a non-Muslim. But Hanafi scholars did not accept this Hadith limiting the general Qur'anic edict of 'A life for a life.' They located versions of the Hadith that place it within the restricted context of warfare and treaties, giving it the circumscribed meaning that a Muslim would not be executed if he had killed a non-Muslim from another polity with whom the Muslim state had no treaty arrangement. The uniform principle of 'A life for a life' was preserved.

The Qur'an and Hadiths appeared over the lengthy time span of the Prophet's career, which increased the potential facets of interpretation. It was self-evident to even the earliest generations of Muslim scholars that the beliefs and law taught by Muhammad had evolved over the course of his preaching, growing gradually from simple to more ornate. Muslim ritual practices and proper conduct oscillated at the margins, their details marked by small changes, sometimes with no consequence, sometimes placing heavier loads on the believers and sometimes lightening them.

From an outside perspective, one could observe that it was impossible to maintain the unity of the Prophet's teachings without seeing them as evolving within a temporal frame. An authenticated Hadith quoted the Prophet teaching that 'Whoever says "There is no deity but God" will enter Paradise,' which seems to obviate not only the totality of Islam's ritual and legal requirements but also the religion's exclusive claim to salvation as a whole. It is thus no surprise that the early scholar and teacher of Malik, Zuhri, explained that the Prophet had said this in the early days of his mission before the pillars of prayer, fasting, charity and other laws had been revealed.[59]

The notion that aspects of the Qur'an's message and the Prophet's teachings developed over time was expressed through the concept of *Naskh*, commonly translated as 'abrogation.' Looking back at their mature bodies of law, the Sunni legal theorists of the tenth and eleventh centuries described *Naskh* either as God 'replacing a ruling established by the lawgiver's address with another ruling' or as 'a temporal indication of a ruling's duration.'

Some cases of abrogation in the Qur'an and Hadiths were unmistakable in the texts themselves: the Qur'an's command to Muhammad and the Muslims to turn their faces away from 'the direction of prayer that you faced before' (Jerusalem) to a new one, one that 'pleases your heart,' the Sacred Mosque in Mecca (2:143–50); Muhammad's command to his followers that, 'I had prohibited you from visiting graves, but visit them, for indeed in visiting them there is a reminder [of death].'[60]

Many of the other instances of *Naskh* that the ulama identified were less obvious, relying on *Tafsir* reports to offer explanations for when a verse was revealed or Hadith transmitters recalling when the Prophet made a statement. Often, such historical details were barely intimated, and it was just the agreement of scholars that determined if abrogation had occurred. Numerous reliable Hadiths described the Prophet instructing his followers to perform ablutions after eating food cooked by fire. But other authenticated Hadiths note that, during his time in Medina, the Prophet had eaten a cooked lamb and then prayed without renewing his ablutions. Tirmidhi remarks that this is widely agreed upon as the 'latter command of the Messenger' and that it abrogates the earlier Hadiths. Indeed, no schools of law required ablutions due to eating cooked food.[61]

Such consensus on abrogation was rare. The intangible and ambiguous indications of abrogation meant that there was often little beyond inclination to justify a scholar's decision to classify a Qur'anic verse or Hadith as 'abrogated' or 'abrogating.' Zuhri had explained the Hadith about all monotheists entering Heaven as an instance of *Naskh*. Other early ulama explained it as a reference to the well-known Sunni tenet that, in fact, all monotheists would eventually attain salvation. Non-Muslim monotheists and sinful Muslims alike would simply have to endure punishment in Hellfire for some period of time before God relieved them.

One example shows the tremendous consequences of differing perspectives on when verses were revealed, how abrogation could occur and how context determined the meaning of a Qur'anic verse. The Qur'an's command that 'retaliatory punishment has been prescribed for you concerning those killed, a freeman for a freeman, a slave for a slave, a woman for a woman...' (4:178) seemed to clash with the sacred book's principle of 'a life for a life.' The Hanafi school of law argued that the two verses had to be understood in light of context and *Naskh*. The first verse was revealed to correct the erroneous demand of a powerful Arab tribe that had earlier warred with a smaller tribe in Medina. When they sought to reconcile, the stronger party was insistent that, for every one of their slaves killed, a freeman from the opposing tribe be put to death; and for every woman killed, an enemy man be put to death. The Qur'anic verse then came down, overturning this line of thinking and establishing parity between parties in a blood dispute: 'a freeman for a freeman, a slave for a slave...' The Hanafis held that this verse, in turn, was clarified by the verse testifying 'a life for a life.' The other Sunni schools of law, however, deemed the 'freeman for a freeman, a slave for a slave' verse to be the definitive command that actually *replaced* the egalitarian order of 'a life for a life.' As a result, unlike the Hanafis, the other schools did not permit a freeman to be executed as punishment for killing a slave, though other harsh punishments might be appropriate.[62]

Abrogation brought into sharp contrast the dissonance between the science of legal theory articulated by the medieval ulama and the bodies of law that their *madhhab*s had developed. From the earliest days of scholars like Hasan Basri, it was clear that the Qur'an had abrogated the Qur'an, some verses superseding others, and that the Sunna had abrogated the Sunna, with some Hadiths overruling others. The Hanafi school of law and the rationalized legal theory of Abu Hasan Ash'ari both upheld the principle that something that is only epistemologically probable cannot overrule something epistemologically certain. Mere authenticated Hadiths thus could not abrogate Qur'anic verses. But the bodies of substantive law in all the Sunni schools demonstrated countless instances of this occurring. All schools of thought were able to overcome this theoretical block by turning to the axis of indication rather than that of attestation. Qur'anic verses might be entirely certain in their *attestation*, but they were not necessarily so in their *indication*. Hadiths could thus effectively overrule the Qur'an not through abrogation but through specification (*takhsis*, or *bayan* among Hanafis), explaining the intended meaning rather than replacing it.

Regarded from the outside, the flexible function of abrogation worked as a stunning multiplier of interpretive possibilities in the Islamic scriptures. The possibility of one Hadith simply replacing another one reduced drastically the challenge of maintaining consonance within the body of scripture overall. Instead of laboring to reconcile two scriptural passages, if any evidence suggested that one appeared later than the other, one could simply declare that abrogation had occurred. The following verse, for example, was generally thought to have been revealed after the Muslim conquest of Mecca in 630:

> When you meet the unbelievers in battle, smite their necks until you overcome them, then bind them as prisoners, either then setting them free out of munificence or for a ransom, until the war ends... (47:4)

Other verses, however, command the Prophet that 'It is not for a prophet to take prisoners until he has triumphed in the land' and to 'Fight the polytheists altogether as they fight you altogether' (8:67, 9:36). Some early ulama read these second two verses as abrogating the first one above, entailing an end to taking prisoners and commanding a total, merciless war with the enemies of Islam. Others interpreted the first verse above as abrogating the second two, providing a new ruling in the last years of the Prophet's career that encouraged sparing the enemy soldiers, keeping them as prisoners and even freeing them out of beneficence.[63]

It is in the Islamic rules of war, in fact, that the doctrine of abrogation has been most consequential. The Qur'an's commandments on conflict and warfare range from passive forbearance to declarations of open war. This befits a document that unfolded over more than two decades of preaching, persecution, incipient conflict and finally declared war and truces. The reasons of revelations tell of a slow escalation. Non-violent instructions to 'dispute with [the Meccans] in the best way' and declare 'Unto you your religion, unto me mine' (16:125, 109:6) give way to permitting Muhammad and his followers to fight the Meccans after being driven from the city into exile in Medina: 'Permission is given to those who fight because they were wronged, verily God is most able to give them succor, those who were driven from their homes unjustly, for but saying, "Our Lord is God"' (22:39). Yet even war with the Meccans and their allies was restricted by principles of proportionality:

> Fight those who fight you, but aggress not, verily God loves not the aggressors. And slay them wherever you find them, and drive them from whence they drove you, for strife is worse than killing... So fight them until there is no strife and religion is God's alone. And

> if they desist, then let there be no attacks except upon the oppressors. (2:190–93)

In a rare instance of agreement, the classical ulama declared all these verses, along with their clear principles of proportionality and non-aggression, to be abrogated by the 'Sword Verses,' the moniker for a few decontextualized segments of Qur'anic verses suggesting unrestricted offensive war, such as 'Fighting has been ordained for you' (2:216) and 'Slay the polytheists wherever you find them' (9:5). In all, a total of 124 Qur'anic verses were considered abrogated by the 'Sword Verses.'[64] Jihad for the expansion of the Abode of Islam thus became a collective duty for the Muslim polity according to all Sunni schools of law. Leading medieval jurists ruled that the caliphs must undertake jihad at least once a year against the most proximate foe (based on analogy to the annual collection of the *jizya* poll tax from non-Muslim subjects), though the Prophet's treaties with the Meccans meant that extended truces were allowed.[65]

Jihad was understood as the unceasing quest to 'make God's word supreme,' as Hadiths described, through the ongoing expansion of the rule of God's law on earth. This was not envisioned in any way as a quest for forced conversion, which never featured in the Islamic conquests. The Qur'anic edict of 'No compulsion in religion' governed the interpretation of Hadiths like the authenticated report of the Prophet declaring, 'I have been commanded to fight the people until they testify that there is no god but God and that Muhammad is the Messenger of God, establish prayer and pay the charity tithe.' Read in light of the Qur'anic prohibition on coerced belief, this mission to extract confessions of belief was not interpreted literally. Rather, it was understood as referring either only to Arabia's pagans (not followers of monotheistic religions) or as a metaphor for the conquered non-Muslims agreeing to submit to Muslim rule.[66]

Some pre-modern Muslim scholars recognized how a recourse to abrogation could excuse laziness in engaging the leitmotifs of Islam's scriptures. Only after Sufism had permeated Sunni thinking on law, creating a loftier sphere from which the law could be regarded, did perspectives emerge putting the theory of abrogation in its place. The Sufi jurist Sha'rani considered all four Sunni *madhhab*s to be one great school of law, offering each believer a range of positions on any issue and thus the choice between relaxed or more stringent rules on any one issue. For him, claims of abrogation were the recourse of those mediocre and narrow-minded jurists whose hearts

God had not illuminated with His light. They could not perceive all the interpretive possibilities in the words of God and the Prophet or appreciate that a diversity of opinion was a mercy. By taking the shortcut of stamping Qur'anic verses or Hadiths 'abrogated,' such ulama had restricted the interpretive plurality that God had intended in the Shariah. For Sha'rani, only when a Hadith included the Prophet's own clear abrogation, like his report about visiting graves, could it be considered *Naskh*. Shah Wali Allah was similarly skeptical of the ulama's excessive indulgence in abrogation to explain the relationship between Qur'anic verses or Hadiths. In all but five cases, he found explanations for how to understand the relationship between scriptural passages without recourse to abrogation.

Conscientious thinkers like Sha'rani and Shah Wali Allah were aware of how even the learned could be led astray. Sha'rani was fond of the story of David's complaint to God. While building the Temple, everything David constructed would crumble. God spoke to him, 'My house will not be erected by the hands of one who has shed blood.' David pleaded that he had only fought wars in God's name. 'Indeed,' God replied, 'but were those who died not also my servants?'[67]

INTO THE WEEDS: THE CASE OF RAISING ONE'S HANDS IN PRAYER

It is not logic that is the life of the law but experience, observed Oliver Wendell Holmes.[68] Certainly, one cannot appreciate the complexity of the Islamic interpretive tradition until one experiences its application at least in part on an issue. Appreciating the thousands of volumes written by medieval Muslim scholars is impossible without mustering the patience to trace a few of their paths. The controversy over raising one's hands in prayer might seem a triviality, but nothing was more important to Muslim scholars than the means by which God was worshiped. It almost cost Shah Wali Allah's friend his life. Moreover, this debate crystallized the tension between loyalty to *madhhab* (especially the Hanafi one) and the evocative call to submit to the original evidence of the Qur'an and Sunna. Hanafis claimed that their school's interpretive tradition had taken all the relevant Hadiths, Qur'anic verses and Companion opinions into consideration in formulating its law. Revivalist Salafis considered this a sacralization of institutions outside the Qur'an and Sunna.

This controversy in the time of Shah Wali Allah has its roots in the primordial disagreement between the Kufan tradition of Abu Hanifa and the early Sunni school, which later blossomed into the Shafiʿi and Hanbali *madhhab*s and eventually brought the Hanafis under its sway by forcing them to justify their law with Hadiths too. The Shafiʿi and Hanbali schools, which emerged from the original Sunni clique and identified most closely with its Hadith-centered ethos, both saw raising one's hands at multiple points in the prayer as an indication of a true commitment to following the Prophet's teachings. The Hanafis viewed these schools as obsessive literalists who did not recognize how Abu Hanifa had accurately assessed the true shape of the Sunna through his legal methods.

In reality, however, the debate over raising one's hands in prayer was just as much about two teams stubbornly defending their colors as it was about the proper approach to the Prophet's legacy. It caused such strident dissension because each side in the dispute seemed to enjoy strong support from the Hadith corpus. At Hajj one year, Abu Hanifa met the leading scholar of Beirut, Awzaʿi, and the two debated whether one should raise one hands toward one's shoulders only when beginning the five daily prayers, or also before bending over to bow and then also when standing erect again. Awzaʿi presented his evidence: he had heard Zuhri narrate from Salim, from his father Ibn Umar that 'The Prophet, may God's peace and blessings be upon him, would raise his hands toward his shoulders when the prayer opened, upon bowing and upon rising up from it.' But Abu Hanifa countered with his own formidable Hadith evidence: his teacher Hammad had learned from the Kufan jurist Nakhaʿi that he had heard from ʿAlqama, who had heard from Ibn Masʿud that 'The Prophet only lifted his hands at the opening of the prayer.'[69]

Both of these Hadiths appear to rest on solid, authenticated chains of transmission and seem clear in their meaning. And they also completely contradict one another. The issue of raising one's hands in prayer thus provides an ideal example of the very frequent clash between contrasting Hadiths. A defining claim of Sunni Islam was that no two authentic Hadiths could actually contradict each other (just as they could not contradict the Qur'an). Apparent contradiction thus meant that the ulama either had to prove that some of the Hadiths were unreliable, or they had to find how the Hadiths fit properly together. If this could be achieved through the interpretive means we have seen so far, such as specification, this was ideal, since Sunni ulama generally favored incorporating as much of the great mass of scriptural evidence into the interpretive process as possible. Khattabi explains that, 'If they can *both* be acted upon, it is not permitted to interpret two Hadiths as contradictory.'[70] Next, if no interpretive reconciliation can be reached for two reliable Hadiths, one should look for signs of abrogation. If none is evident, then one should examine the two *Isnad*s to identify which one is more reliable in terms of its transmitters and the corroboration it enjoys. If no substantial difference can be found, then one takes the Hadith that seems closest to the overall message of the Qur'an and Sunna.[71]

The debate on raising hands in prayer offers a glimpse of how the stunning number of Hadiths, each ramifying into narrations differing in minute details, Companion opinions and scholarly analyses, could grow up around an issue like an intertwined trellis of argument. The works of two scholars, the Shafi'i Hadith prodigy Abu Bakr Bayhaqi and his earlier counterpart, the Hanafi Abu Ja'far Tahawi, provide a model intellectual duel. Seeing how they navigated and utilized this mass of information demonstrates the interpretive richness inherent in the Sunni tradition.

Bayhaqi stands out as the perfect champion of the Shafi'i school. He had compiled his massive *Sunan* (published today in ten volumes) to collect, organize and analyze all the scriptural evidence backing up the Shafi'i school's body of substantive law. This was needed to fend off the increasingly skilled Hanafi polemicists such as Tahawi, who had mastered the science of Hadith collection and criticism, originally exclusive to the armory of the Sunni network that developed it. The tremendous service that Bayhaqi rendered the Shafi'i school in doing so led one leading scholar to observe that 'Every follower of the Shafi'i school owes Shafi'i himself a favor. Except Bayhaqi. Shafi'i owes him a favor.'

On the issue of raising one's hands in prayer (and, in fact, the shape of prayer in general), the Qur'an is silent. But Bayhaqi lists dozens of versions of almost a dozen different Hadiths, narrated from the Prophet by Companions like Ibn Umar, the Prophet's servant Anas bin Malik as well as others via the caliphs Abu Bakr and Ali. He follows these with the rulings of Companions and Successors such as Hasan Basri. Ibn Umar's narration of a Hadith from the Prophet was deemed decisive by a number of leading ulama, such as Malik, Awza'i and the Meccan Sufyan bin 'Uyayna. Their transmission of the Hadith via the *Isnad* of Muhammad → Ibn Umar → Salim → Zuhri sums up the contents of all these reports succinctly: 'The Messenger of God, when the prayer opened, used to raise his hands toward his shoulders, and also when he moved to bow at the waist and when he rose up from that bow. And he would not raise his hands between the two prostrations [the often televised act of Muslims kneeling and touching their forehead to the earth twice].'[72]

But what of the Hadith evidence against raising one's hands multiple times in prayer? Bayhaqi provides a lengthy chapter devoted to neutralizing it. Hanafi evidence consisted principally of two Hadiths, each with its own web of narrations emanating from the Companion and Successors who transmitted it. The Companion Bara' bin 'Azib is quoted observing, 'I saw the Messenger of God, when he began the prayer, raise his hands, and he did not repeat this.' To dispute this Hadith, Bayhaqi deploys the Sunni science of Hadith criticism. The Successor, Yazid bin Abi Ziyad, who supposedly transmitted this report from the Companion in question, was declared unreliable by Ibn Hanbal and his close associate and fellow master Hadith critic of Baghdad, Ibn Ma'in. Bayhaqi finds earlier criticism from the famous Meccan scholar, Sufyan bin 'Uyayna, who actually heard this Hadith from Yazid. He observed that Yazid was unreliable, particularly on this Hadith, because he allowed his students to influence his transmissions. They would prompt him until he assented that the Hadith specified that the Prophet only raised his hands once. Another criticism by Sufyan bin 'Uyayna notes that Yazid only transmitted this Hadith after he had been afflicted with senility.[73]

The second and better-known Hadith was the one Abu Hanifa had cited to Awza'i at Hajj. The base and trunk of the *Isnad* tree came from the Companion Ibn Mas'ud, who described the Prophet's manner of prayer and then proceeded via his student 'Alqama bin Qays (hence, Muhammad → Ibn Mas'ud → 'Alqama bin Qays). From him the transmissions radiated outward among the ulama of Kufa, including to Nakha'i, who then transmitted it to Hammad bin Abi Sulayman, Abu Hanifa's teacher.

Bayhaqi musters the collective expertise of the Sunni Hadith critics against this evidence. The senior Hadith critic of Baghdad, who took his cognomen from the city's cotton district, Daraqutni, analyzed the range of narrations via Abu Hanifa's *Isnad* and concluded that some error or forgetfulness had affected Hammad's narration of the Hadith from Nakha'i. Every other scholar narrating it from Nakha'i cited the originating authority as Ibn Mas'ud, not the Prophet, and transmitted the report with an incomplete *Isnad* (namely, Nakha'i quoting Ibn Mas'ud, whom he never met, without naming his intermediary). This version of the Hadith, Daraqutni explains, therefore suffers from both an unreliable, broken *Isnad* and also only represents a Companion's opinion, not prophetic precedent.[74]

In truth, there were too many narrations of Ibn Mas'ud's Hadith from the Prophet to deal with in such a particularized, technical manner; Daraqutni's critique only neutralized one cluster of narrations (those from Muhammad → Ibn Mas'ud → 'Alqama → Nakha'i), and many other Successor scholars had narrated the same Hadith from 'Alqama. Bayhaqi thus introduces early scholarly opinions that dismiss altogether the Kufan version of the limited, one-off hand raising. Ibn Mubarak, a contemporary of Malik from Khurasan in northeastern Iran, is quoted saying that he simply could not accept the Hadith from Ibn Mas'ud as authentic, since he had heard so many narrations of the Hadith describing the Prophet's numerous hand raises via Muhammad → Ibn Umar → Salim → Zuhri. He had come across so much evidence of this Hadith, in fact, that he remarked, 'It's as if I'm seeing the Messenger of God himself raising his hands in prayer before me, due to the sheer number of Hadiths and the quality of their *Isnads*.'

Bayhaqi concludes that, assuming the *Isnads* back to Ibn Mas'ud are reliable, this Hadith can only be explained by Ibn Mas'ud having forgotten or mistaken what he saw the Prophet do. Raising one's hands at the opening of prayer, before bowing and after standing straight again is so well established via Hadiths of the Prophet, reports about how the first four 'Rightly Guided' caliphs prayed and from the opinions of other leading Companions, that Ibn Mas'ud's report simply cannot be true. Bayhaqi himself introduces the possible explanation that, if Hadiths like Ibn Mas'ud's were historically reliable, they must be cases of abrogation. They must represent some earlier form of the prayer before the Prophet gave it its final shape. He notes that in the early days of the Prophet's mission other aspects of the prayer had differed as well, like placing one's hands between one's thighs while bowing instead of leaning on one's knees.[75]

Bayhaqi's opponent in this debate was the Egyptian Abu Ja'far Tahawi, who had begun his studies at the feet of his uncle, a leading student of no less than Shafi'i himself. The nephew, however, chose not to follow in his family's footsteps, and he embraced the rival Hanafi school of law instead. As the school favored by the imperial authority in Baghdad, the Hanafis controlled the Shariah courts in the Abbasid province of Egypt. Working as a court clerk, Tahawi was sought out by Hanafi colleagues and his opponents alike for his mastery of Hadiths. Tahawi's experience with the early Sunni methodology of Hadith criticism and the vast accumulation of Hadiths he heard from all the ulama who visited Egypt made him a formidable Hadith critic, able to engage his Shafi'i and Hanbali opponents in their own science.

The main challenge facing Tahawi was how to explain why the Hanafis had not acted on the many Hadiths, mostly through the Companion Ibn Umar, that clearly described the Prophet raising his hands at multiple points in the prayer. Here, Tahawi's tactic was to catch the early Sunnis (and their Shafi'i and Hanbali descendants) up in their own game, arguing that they were just as guilty of selectively acting on Hadiths as they accused the Hanafis of being. The majority version of Ibn Umar's Hadith includes the final phrase 'and he [the Prophet] did *not* raise his hands between the two prostrations,' which was an important point for Shafi'is and Hanbalis, who indeed did not raise hands at this point in the prayer and would have excoriated anyone who did. But Tahawi contends that it is not clear who actually said this last clause. Evidence suggested that it might merely be the opinion of some later transmitter passing on the Hadith. In fact, Tahawi introduces another version of Ibn Umar's Hadith that describes the Prophet raising hands while seated between the two prostrations. The Shafi'is and Hanbalis accused the Hanafis of ignoring Hadiths that did not accord with their *madhhab*, but, Tahawi points out, the accusers were themselves guilty of this. Why did the Shafi'is and Hanbalis not follow this command to raise their hands between the prostrations as well, Tahawi asks, turning the accusation of selectivity in following Hadiths back on them.[76]

The Hanafi school, argues Tahawi, did not lumber clumsily through all these contradictory details in the varied narrations of Hadiths. 'We know that hands are raised only at the opening of prayer,' he asserts. Tahawi acknowledges that there are many Hadiths through other Companions describing the Prophet raising his hands at multiple points in the prayer. But these are moot, Tahawi claims, since he cites narrations describing senior Companions like Ali and Umar only raising their hands at the opening of prayer. This, he argues, demonstrates the understanding of the Prophet's Sunna after his death, which necessarily reflected its final, abrogating form. Raising one's hands at the opening of the prayer alone represents the Prophet's true Sunna.[77]

Examined from a distance, Tahawi's and Bayhaqi's arguments are often mirror images of one another, relying on the same techniques and arguments. Both had argued that all evidence for the opposing position was abrogated. Like Bayhaqi, Tahawi also attempts to draw distinctions between brief and thus inaccurate observations of Muhammad's practice on the one hand and extended experience with him on the other. Responding to a Hadith transmitted from one of the more junior Companions that reports the Prophet raising his hands at numerous points in the prayer, Tahawi quotes Nakha'i that, if that minor Companion had seen the Prophet do his prayers only once, Ibn Mas'ud had seen him fifty times.[78]

Hadith criticism was a science designed by the early Sunnis, and Hanafis like Tahawi had to convince their opponents by playing by their rules in order to be accepted. But Tahawi also fights back against what he feels are the inaccurate rules in Hadith criticism, such as requiring contiguous, complete *Isnad*s even during the generation of the Companions and Successors, when such obsessively exact transmission practices were rare. On the count of Nakha'i narrating Hadiths from Ibn Mas'ud without specifying his intermediary source, Tahawi argues that this was the common Kufan method (in fact, he and other Hanafis argued that it was universally accepted before the early Sunnis challenged it). Nakha'i would tell his students from among the nascent Sunnis, who often demanded complete *Isnad*s, that if he said 'Ibn Mas'ud said...' that meant that Nakha'i had heard this report from Ibn Mas'ud via multiple intermediaries whose large number made specifying them unnecessary and tedious.[79]

Both Bayhaqi and Tahawi used the evidence of scripture and the accepted tools for manipulating and analyzing it masterfully to pursue their own positions. Judging from a distance, it is very difficult to distinguish the victor. The volumes written on the issue of raising one's hands in prayer over the centuries could occupy whole library shelves. An entire wing would have to be devoted to the hundreds of other such debates over issues, from performing ablutions to the technicalities of divorce and the propriety of visiting saints' graves. Shafi'i was right, it seems, in declaring that consensus exists only on the basics of Islamic dogma and law, not on its details.

THE SUMMER OF THE LIBERAL AGE

Notarizing away in the Shariah court of Fustat ('Cairo' proper would not be built for another forty years), Tahawi could not have imagined the epistemological crisis into which the Hadiths of the Fly and the Devil Farting would pitch his countrymen a millennium later. He had debated over too many Hadiths, dodged too many scholarly ripostes and seen too many litigants swear too many oaths before judges to maintain any illusion about achieving certainty in the law. But he and his contemporaries were also too confident in the Shariah and its scriptural bases for reservations about the cilia and murky minutiae of that system to cast doubt on its overall form. Whether in law or theology, Muslim scholars accepted that the religion they taught the believers was at best an imposing thicket of probabilities built around a core of certainties. The elements 'known necessarily as part of the religion' were the bedrock of Islamic dogma and practice, those items that rested on epistemologically unshakable foundations and enjoyed true consensus support. Like all matters, the ulama often disagreed on how far this list stretched, but the agreed-upon core did not vary: God's unity and transcendence, His main attributes, resurrection and the Day of Judgment, the finality of Muhammad's prophethood, the requirement of ablution for prayer, the five daily prayers, *Zakat*, the fast of Ramadan, the pilgrimage to Mecca, the basic structure of Islamic marriage and divorce, the impermissibility of intoxication and fornication, and so on. To reject those articles 'known necessarily as part of the religion' was to cease being a Muslim.[80]

Tahawi certainly hoped to convince all Muslims to pray as the Hanafi school prescribed, but as long as Muslims performed the five daily prayers according to any acknowledged *madhhab* their faith was valid. The ulama harangued their flocks from Friday mosque pulpits with Hadiths that brought the Prophet's warnings of Hellfire and good tidings of Paradise to the very ears of his followers. But if a member of the congregation refused to believe even a *sahih* Hadith this would amount to no more than a sin or deviance. Only denying the authenticity of a Qur'anic verse or a massively transmitted (*mutawatir*) Hadith would make one an unbeliever.[81] Mosque preachers or popular storytellers at Sufi shrines could enrapture audiences with the many esteemed Hadiths from the *Sahih* books of Bukhari and Muslim describing Muhammad's ascent through the seven heavens on his miraculous night journey, when God 'took His servant by night from the Sacred Mosque of Mecca to the Farthest Mosque' in Jerusalem (Qur'an 17:1). One version describes him leading all the great prophets in prayer in the heavens; another had him touring the Gardens of Paradise destined for the felicitous. Some imply that he actually saw God, others that he merely beheld the 'Furthest Lote Tree' in Heaven. If a Muslim chose not to believe some of these narrations, or denied the contrasting, sometimes contradictory details of Muhammad's ascent, a scholar like Bayhaqi could do no more than reprimand him as sinful or misled. Only the general outline of the Prophet's miraculous night journey, referred to in the inerrant Qur'an, was a required tenet of faith.[82]

In stark contrast to Tahawi's time, Egypt of the early twentieth century was at a historical nadir of confidence in Islam's scriptures. It was an era of intense colonial influence and intellectual liberalization. The writings that Sidqi and Abu Rayya produced and the milieu that received them would have been unthinkable only decades earlier. Never has Egypt or the wider Muslim intellectual world seen a more willing acceptance of Western approaches to the study of Islam and the definition of its doctrine.

The one man to whom the Islamic modernist cause owed the most was the visionary scholar who inspired both Sidqi and Abu Rayya. Muhammad 'Abduh (d. 1905) was a classically trained Maliki jurist, but one who had spent time in Europe and possessed a peerless and creative reformist bent. Under the watchful eye of the British 'Veiled Protectorate' of Egypt, in 1899 the Egyptian king appointed 'Abduh as Grand Mufti, in charge of issuing Shariah rulings for the government. In part this was to mollify the British High Commissioner, who supported 'Abduh's modernizing zeal. As Grand Mufti, 'Abduh undertook dramatic efforts to reinterpret Islamic law according to modern precepts. While pre-modern ulama had derived legal rulings from an extensive body of scripture, including unreliable Hadiths as well as Companion opinions, 'Abduh felt that only clear Qur'anic verses and the most solidly reliable Hadiths were compelling. In their absence, he ruled according to *Maslaha*, or public interest, which in his mind tended to dovetail with state modernization agendas.

'Abduh's approach in many ways revived the rationalism and Hadith skepticism of the medieval Mutazila, and he left as his legacy for generations of like-minded reformists a reordered interpretive system in which a direct engagement with the Qur'an overshadowed the Hadiths, consensus or the four vast pools of substantive law. During his tenure as Grand Mufti, 'Abduh permitted individual Muslims and the Egyptian state to receive interest from bank deposits (since he argued that the *Riba* prohibited by the Qur'an was only excessive usury, not simple interest itself) and issued controversial fatwas allowing eating non-Halal meat and the collection and display of artwork and statues depicting human beings (the fear that Muslims would lapse into idolatry no longer applied, he argued).

Western intellectual influence in early twentieth-century Egypt was so profound that it extended into the study of Islam itself and enjoyed strong currency. A book by Europe's leading scholar of Islam, which dismissed the Sunni Hadith corpus as wholly historically unreliable, was used in the curriculum of Cairo's vaunted Al-Azhar seminary. The Arabic Language Academy, formed by the Egyptian king in 1933 and which would eventually symbolize not only the sanctity of Islam's sacred language but also the very stuff of Arab nationalism, originally reserved no less than one quarter of its board of scholars for European orientalists.[83]

The Sunni approach to interpreting scripture and its mind-numbingly detailed application on issues like raising hands in prayer carried little weight in this atmosphere. For Sidqi and Abu Rayya, the richness, voluminous complexity and frequently incapacitating depth of the medieval Sunni interpretive tradition were merely more nails in its coffin. The more one explored this heritage, they concluded, the more it revealed the benighted assumptions of the medieval world. They looked at it as Renaissance humanists such as Erasmus had looked at the Christian scholasticism of Aquinas and Duns Scotus: it was an obsolete system stuck in a self-involved and overly intricate discourse of 'subtle trifles' that did not address the real problems at hand or reflect God's simple, original message to humankind.[84]

Sidqi and Abu Rayya had run up against the historical fact that, in truth, the Shariah had always been just as much a civilizational project as it was an impulse of religious conscience. The shop owners and farmers who had notarized land sales in Tahawi's court had acknowledged the Shariah as much because it was the law of the land as because it was God's law. Wherever it came from, it provided the legal lubricant and protection for society's moving parts. It had been constructed to bring a unified order to a polyglot expanse, to furnish the infrastructure of a civilization that had joined regions never bundled together before. But now the world had a new order. It was mapped, nationalized and administered by the white-skinned and pith-helmeted colonizers, as foreign and as unaccommodating as they were undeniably alluring.

At many crucial junctures in their Shariah construction project, medieval Muslim ulama had relied on the argument that principles such as the ultimate reliability of Hadiths or the infallibility of the Prophet had to be accepted or else the whole of the Shariah would be lost. It was an argument from consequence, a parade of only one horrible, that no one in their world could accept, namely the loss of the civilizational project itself. In Egypt of the early twentieth century, however, for many people that no longer seemed so bad. Conservative ulama who responded to ʻAbduh, Sidqi or Abu Rayya by parroting their medieval forefathers were arguing for a vision of religion that the world seemed to have outgrown. As he sought to understand his faith through reason, the twelfth-century Christian scholastic Anselm of Bec had professed that one had to believe in order to understand.[85] In Cairo of Sidqi's day, and in many other metropolises of the Muslim – now colonized and/or modernizing – world, many did not believe enough anymore.

4

Clinging to the Canon in a Ruptured World

UPSTARTS AT THE END OF TIME

Cosmopolitan Istanbul attracts visitors with the iconic hilltop mosques and romantic bazaars of a past it has tried hard to escape. Republican Turkey's fraught relationship with its Ottoman, Islamic ancestry has long been on display in the neighborhood clustered around the weathered domes of the Fatih Mosque. Off the main tourist route, located as it is in an area that guidebooks label 'conservative,' the Fatih Mosque was built by Mehmet the Conqueror when he took the city in 1453. It quickly became the beating heart of the Ottoman Empire's religious establishment. Generations of ulama flocked to its famous 'Eight Madrasas' from as far as Cairo and Samarqand to teach and study, departing only to staff madrasas in provincial metropolises like Belgrade or Shariah courts in Baghdad or Cairo.

Today, the environs of the Fatih Mosque are cheery and peaceful. When I first visited, the sun had not yet vanquished the predawn chill of the Istanbul spring, and the old men who remained in the mosque after the dawn prayer sat huddled in the mosque's sole heated room. I had come to attend the lessons of one of them, a man in his eighties who was the last surviving student of an Ottoman scholar who had refused to accept the modern world.

When Mehemmet Zahit Kevseri taught there in the years before the First World War, the Fatih madrasas still basked in imperial pride, despite the Ottomans' extensive modernization of the state's educational system.

Before he fled the Republican militias of Mustafa Kemal Ataturk, Kevseri had been the most senior instructor in the Ottoman clerical elite. He may well have helped formulate the last declaration of jihad by the caliph of an Islamic empire in November of 1914. Ironically, it was the graduates of that empire's Europeanized military academies (too successful for the sultan's own good, it turned out) who ultimately freed Istanbul from foreign occupation in 1922. They considered the conservative ulama to be a clerical barbarism and a prime impediment to progress. The antipathy was mutual. The secular, westernized republic that Ataturk and his cadre inaugurated wiped away all traces of the Islamic caliphate that Kevseri knew and embodied everything he despised.

In the winter of 1922 Kevseri arrived in Cairo, a penniless exile, and eventually found work cataloging the Turkish and Persian manuscripts in Cairo's royal library. He lived dispossessed and frugally until his death in 1952, not two weeks after a military coup by young, nationalist, secularizing officers had toppled Egypt's monarch, the last potentate of the Ottoman world. For thirty years Kevseri had lived in Cairo, writing at home and teaching students in an impenetrably high literary Arabic lightened by the labial delicacy of his Turkish accent.

And he had raged. He had raged against Ataturk's abolition of the caliphate, God's shadow on earth and Muhammad's rightful successor. He had raged against Egypt's stupid, bewitched reformists, whose aim of matching the Western powers was matched only by their need to please them. He had raged most of all against the modernist ulama, who 'tore up our religion to adorn our earthly world,' not realizing that 'our world does not endure, and now neither does what we have torn up.'

For Kevseri, there was no modern world. There was only a glorious past that endured into the present until it was ripped away. There was only God's law, the truth of Islam and the countless tomes penned by the great ulama of its halcyon days. In his modest apartment in Cairo, Kevseri answered fatwa requests from around the world and taught his students. For them he was a living relic of that past. Few of its minds had ever been his equal. He was an ocean of knowledge, his students recalled. It seemed as though the whole heritage of the Islamic past floated at his command as he scribbled countless journal articles, raging against all that was distorted around him, quoting from memory vanished pages from the imperial libraries of Istanbul.[1]

THE TREASON OF INTERPRETATION

Scripture is fragile only if the community of its readers lacks the will to affirm its truth. When a canonical community fragments, those segments that continue to cling tightly to their scripture and the belief system surrounding it can fight fiercely against those who seek to break away. At these moments of epistemological rupture, approaches to scripture that had never previously been controversial in and of themselves can overstep the new lines demarcating treason to the rump canonical community. For centuries Sunni scholars had critiqued freely, sometimes viciously, Hadiths from the esteemed *Sahih Bukhari* and *Sahih Muslim* collections. It was only when the foundations of the classical Sunni tradition were challenged in the modern period by the Salafi movements and even more so by the appearance of Islamic modernists, that a skeptic like Sidqi was called an 'unbeliever' for rejecting the Hadith of the Fly. Similarly, for well over a millennium the Catholic Church had sensed no great need to declare the Latin Vulgate Bible unified and immune from textual criticism. Only after some Protestants had made the scripture the center of their occasionally critical study was questioning the Bible's unity or content declared anathema at the Church's Council of Trent in 1546.

In such periods of crisis, even methods of reading scripture or interpretive devices with impressive pedigrees can become dangerous if utilized as vehicles for new epistemological worldviews. Spinoza argued that the books of the Old Testament had not been written by their supposed authors. To justify his conclusion, he invoked the writings of the twelfth-century rabbinic exegete Ibn Ezra as precedent. Despite such medieval testimonium, Spinoza was excommunicated from Amsterdam's Jewish community. Some fifty years later, the Cambridge divine Thomas Woolston wrote what he insisted vehemently and to his last day was a defense of the Bible in his modern age. He argued, like his paragon Origen, that the Old Testament must be interpreted allegorically in order to be acceptable. Just as Origen had read biblical verses considered absurd in his own day figuratively (how could the Devil actually have taken Jesus up a mountain so high that he could see *all* the kingdoms of the world, Origen asked), Woolston argued that the miracles in the New Testament, which were obviously scientifically impossible, must be interpreted allegorically as well. They were, he wrote, no more than the curing of 'the Blindness and the Lameness of our Understandings.' Copies of Woolston's book sold so well that Voltaire complained about not being able to find one. Yet the Cambridge scholar was dismissed from his teaching post and fined so heavily that he died in a debtor's prison.[2]

The fate of Spinoza and Woolston is hardly surprising. Yes, Ibn Ezra (and Martin Luther, for that matter) had opined comfortably and without incident that Moses did not write the last part of Deuteronomy. It was probably penned by his successor, Joshua. Nor was skepticism toward biblical miracles new. A seventh-century Christian commentary on the Bible, *De Mirabilis Sacrae Scripturae,* offered natural explanations for them.[3] But Spinoza was arguing that *nothing* in the Old Testament was written by Moses. Woolston was teaching that *none* of the miraculous works of the historical Jesus ever occurred, that they were unimportant and that even considering their occurrence literally was to misunderstand Christianity altogether. All that mattered was the ethical and religious teachings encoded metaphorically in Jesus' life.

The cases of Spinoza and Woolston offer a clear distinction between the *cognitive content* of an idea or a component of a scholarly tradition and the *ideological purposes* to which it is put to use.[4] The main route for introducing change to a conservative interpretive tradition is to employ veteran tools from its repository to advance unprecedented ideas. But one must do so without seeming to break the coherence of that system or pandering too obviously to external agendas. Overloaded or pushed too far, even the most indigenous interpretive scheme will run aground.

With Spinoza and Woolston, what opponents and timid supporters alike knew mattered was the worldview preached in their writings, not the formal legitimacy of their interpretive methods or even the particular conclusions they reached. The *De Mirabilis* offered a natural explanation for miracles that denied any direct divine interference with nature's laws. But the book only did so to affirm the natural law of the Christian God in an ordered Christian universe. Woolston, by contrast, mercilessly mocked the comic image that a literal reading of the New Testament miracles created. He scoffed at the priesthood who taught it and the laity who believed it. Ibn Ezra and Luther believed that, whoever wrote the last part of Deuteronomy, it was indubitably the inspired and compelling word of God; Spinoza dismissed this as naively untenable.[5] The religious leadership of Amsterdam's Jewish community and the Anglican state establishment saw Spinoza and Woolston for exactly what they were: proponents of a new epistemological worldview that threatened religious orthodoxy and the social sensibilities, and hierarchies, that it represented.

HERESY ACCEPTABLE: RUPTURES IN CANONICAL COMMUNITIES

Scriptural communities are not homogeneous. The turning over of new epistemological eras is rarely quick or decisive. Even the most undeniable historical transformations, such as secularization in the West, only slowly engulf the phenomena they replace. The fourteenth-century proto-Protestant Lollards of England announced a suspicion of Church sacraments and considered marriage to be out of the hands of priests. But five hundred years of gradual social and legal evolution passed before civil marriage received full legal recognition in Britain in 1833.[6]

Worldviews split at ruptures in commonly acknowledged truths, diverging and coexisting in tension. Cosmopolitanism can exist side by side with an atavistic longing for an insulated, 'authentic' tradition. The Hellenistic Mediterranean world produced Jewish communities of both types, Platonic philosophers like Philo of Alexandria and the hermetic community of the Dead Sea Scrolls.[7] Microcontexts coexist in stark contrast. The pious but disquieting peripatetic teacher Giulio Vanini was executed for heresy and atheism in the zealous French city of Toulouse in 1619. Meanwhile, a professor in the University of Paris flourished while mocking the Bible as absurd and dismissing Heaven and Hell as fables drummed up to scare simpletons.[8]

The attitudes of Egypt's political and cultural elite in the liberal heyday of the early twentieth century may have created unprecedented space for the establishment of a modern banking system, women's rights movements or for young effendis to dismiss the Sunna as stupid. But the turn of the epistemological era would not be as dramatic as Islamic modernists like 'Abduh or Sidqi would have hoped. Leading defenders of Al-Azhar traditionalism in the 1930s rebutted criticisms of the Hadiths of the Fly and the Sun Prostrating. They offered the latest scientific studies attesting that flies carried powerful antibodies and invoked the rich figurative possibilities of classical Arabic. They accused modernists like Sidqi of being so enamored of Western scientism that they were summarily and ignorantly dismissing the Islamic interpretive heritage. The famous Muslim revivalist scholar

Rashid Rida ('Abduh's chief acolyte, though much less enamored of Europe) riled provocatively against the appointment of European orientalists to the Arabic Language Academy and their 'twisted' presentation of Islam.[9] The use of orientalist books in the Al-Azhar curriculum triggered influential defenses of the Hadiths and Sunna. 'Abduh was attacked mercilessly in the popular press as a westernized hypocrite who 'went to Europe but never to Hajj' and died a broken man.[10]

In modern Egypt, what had unfolded as internal dynamics between the secular/scientific and the scriptural/clerical in Spinoza's Amsterdam and Woolston's England was being rehashed as part of the agonistic dynamic between the colonizer and colonized, 'co-opted' elites and 'authentic' tradition. In the 1930s the Muslim Brotherhood arose to challenge the notion that 'Islam and organization can never coincide' and to drive imperialism first from the hearts of Egyptians and then from Egypt itself. Arabic nationalism rolled back calls like that of Egyptian reformists in the late 1930s to follow Turkey's example and write Arabic in a Latin script. Most importantly, the powerful, popular Islamic revival of the 1970s and 1980s reintroduced at least a formal respect for Islam and its scriptures in public life.

In part as a civilizational riposte to Western encroachment and in part due to state support as a bulwark against communism, Islamic-inflected discourse came to dominate the Egyptian public square by the 1990s. Since then, modernist rethinking of scripture like Sidqi's advocacy of 'Islam is the Qur'an Alone' or Abu Rayya's wholesale indictment of the classical methods of Hadith criticism have come only from a few diehard Islamic modernists and have found purchase only among elite and liberal circles in Egyptian society.

Yet the tremendous influence of westernization, the modern and the secular has not waned. As a result, since the mid-twentieth century discourse on Islam in Egypt and other centers of the Arab world has reflected the intense contest over the proper sources of norms and beliefs. A publicly recognized commitment to the Shariah and Islam's scriptures competes with the hegemonic expectations and gravitational pull of the modern West. Ring-fenced and embattled, the symbols of Islamic identity – the Qur'an, the Shariah and the person of the Prophet – occupy a station made all the more sacrosanct by its precariousness. Media, the state, secular Arab intellectuals and international actors alternately encourage or oblige segments of the ulama to reconcile the Qur'an and Hadiths with the firmest tenets of neoliberal economics and democracy. State-appointed muftis and state-employed clergy usually comply. Meanwhile, more conservative ulama, particularly those in opposition to the state, champion interpretations of the scripture and the Shariah that preserve the pre-modern heritage. Sometimes they reimagine an atavistic tradition more conservative than any that actually existed.

In an Egypt straddling an epistemological fault, the balance that has emerged between the canonicity of scripture and liberalized interpretation has proven precarious. The late Nasr Hamid Abu Zayd, once a professor of Arabic literature at the University of Cairo, discovered this when he produced a postmodern restatement of Sidqi's modernist call to base Islam on the Qur'an and human reason alone. Abu Zayd applied the philosophy and literary criticism he had learned from European postmodernism to the Qur'an, acknowledging that the book was divine but insisting that the meaning of its text shifted with language and social context. Its specific rules and references are thus not fixed in their meaning according to the classical understanding of Muslim scholars. In 1993 a colleague accused Abu Zayd of apostasy on the basis of his writings, and within two years an Egyptian court concurred. Threats on his life led the scholar into exile in the Netherlands. Oddly, Abu Zayd's approach shared much with pre-modern Islamic interpretive methods. But in his reading of the Qur'an his lodestar was the postmodern literary theory of Europe and not the native Islamic ethos of venerating God's word. This colored him irreparably as an agent of Western influence.

In 2007 controversy also highlighted sensitivities around the Hadiths and the persona of the Prophet. An Egyptian pundit mentioned tangentially in an article that the Prophet Muhammad had not been born circumcised, a statement that ran contrary to widely believed miraculous reports that he had been. Acrimony from conservative Muslim groups gathered steam, and public outrage resulted in the writer's dismissal. Yet this religious outrage was more an inflamed reaction to perceived attacks on Islamic tradition than an expression of Islamic tradition itself. Whether or not the Prophet had been born circumcised had never before been a question of any great consequence among Muslim scholars. Although many pre-modern ulama had affirmed the reliability of Hadiths describing the Prophet as having been born preternaturally circumcised – one of the miraculous signs of his mission – many leading ulama had considered those Hadiths baseless. Among these skeptics were Ibn Kathir and Ibn Qayyim, both students of

Ibn Taymiyya and among the definitive references for conservative Muslims in the Arab world. The outrage at the journalist was a novel byproduct of modern insecurities about the Islamic canon.[11]

In modern Egypt, and perhaps anywhere in the Muslim world, no two issues have proven as controversial as the great knots of women's status and religious violence. No topics more succinctly embody the incredible tension between submission to scriptural tradition and the call to replace it with secular mores, between the perceived influence of Western imperialism and a rally to resistance through championing claims of authentic, indigenous identity. Women's persons have tragically often been the field on which these and other questions have been contested, and violence is the ultimate form that such contesting can take.

SLAY THE UNBELIEVERS WHEREVER YOU FIND THEM: JIHAD AND (RE)INTERPRETING SCRIPTURE

Around the year 1300, Osman Ghazi and his band of Turkic warriors lodged with a Sufi dervish in the wilds of Anatolia. The founder of what became the Ottoman dynasty dreamed that the moon exited the holy man's mouth and passed into his own chest. A great tree sprang forth from the warrior's breast, its branches arching over the whole world.

The pre-modern Shariah tradition was sprawling in its diversity. One of its common threads was the quiescent but universal assumption that Islam's eventual destiny was manifest. Regardless of the infrequency, infeasibility or even undesirability of holy war against non-Muslim foes, all schools of law agreed that it was the collective duty of the Muslim polity to expand the borders of the Abode of Islam.

This pre-modern jihad narrative was terminated abruptly with the arrival of the European powers. The might of industry and totally restructured organs of state and society allowed the armies and navies of Britain, France, Russia and the Netherlands to occupy great swaths of Muslim land. This ended any pretense of the ancient dynamic in which the Abode of Islam existed in a state of constant, impending expansion into non-Muslim territory, with peace and truces mere exceptions to this rule. From North Africa to India, the ulama and Muslim rulers of the nineteenth century faced an upturned balance of power in which colonial rulers claimed legitimate sovereignty over their holdings according to a system of treaties and legal understandings that they had constructed and which only they had the military force to challenge with any hope of success.

Faced with the irresistible might of the colonial regimes, some Muslim scholars reconsidered the obligation of jihad. This would have been a tall order for the interpretive methodology of the pre-modern ulama, as the duty of jihad was a Shariah stance that enjoyed uncontested consensus in a legal system that considered such consensus binding. Reformists like 'Abduh and Rida, however, developed a perspective on the Shariah that allowed them to break loose of the constraints of this consensus culture. They built on the medieval revivalist Hanbali school of Ibn Taymiyya and its notion that consensus really only existed among Muslims at the time of the Companions. After that it was simply impossible to verify. Rida retooled this idea to argue that later agreements could overrule all earlier claims of consensus as long as they promoted clear public interest (*maslaha*) and that, in the modern world, consensus could only be declared by those Islamic thinkers who truly understood the political and social challenges of the day.[12]

A great crisis came in India in 1857. In the wake of the failed rebellion of both Hindu and Muslim sepoys against British rule, the Raj began marginalizing Muslims in its army and administration out of a fear that extremist violence was an irrepressible Muslim trait. Sir Sayyid Ahmad Khan, an Islamic modernist who believed that Islam must be reformed in order to survive, argued that Muslims under British rule were, in fact, forbidden from rebelling against their British rulers. He understood the Qur'an's commands to wage war as applicable only in response to religious persecution. It did not mandate a blanket offensive against non-Muslims, even those who ruled over Muslim populations. To prove this, he cited a well-respected Hadith that, when the Prophet was set to engage in battle with a tribe, he would wait until the morning to hear if the call to prayer rang out in the enemy camp. If he heard this proof of Muslims practicing their religion among the enemy host, he would not make war on them. The British regime allowed India's Muslims to practice their religion freely, Khan assessed, and Muslims must therefore accept colonial rule.[13]

European criticisms of Islam as an ideology that preached holy war concerned many ulama in the Mediterranean world, such as 'Abduh and Rida, as well. They argued that the true, original doctrine of jihad in the Prophet's time was a call to defend against aggression or religious persecution only, and that all the wars fought by Muhammad had been defensive in nature. Rida was able to break away from the traditional Shariah consensus on jihad and ignore the more bellicose Hadiths because of his reformist methodology. He argued that Islam and the Shariah are known only through the Qur'an, the few 'widely and diffusely transmitted' Hadiths and the 'living Sunna' of universal Muslim practice. In a broadly published and translated defense of the Qur'an as legitimate scripture, he argued that Islam called for peaceful relations between nations, each allowed to live and practice its religion in peace. The early Islamic conquest of Arabia was an exception to this, the singular creation of a necessary cradle and safe space for Islam to flourish.

This reformist interpretation of the Qur'an and Hadiths inverted the classical doctrine of jihad, reading the Qur'an's passages on warfare in their contexts instead of using the 'Sword Verses' to abrogate the revelation's principles of proportionality, mercy and the desirability of peace. Writing after the European system had revealed its own bloodthirstiness in the First World War, Rida remarked that it was European nationalism and German warmongering that were the true culprits in fomenting global violence.[14]

This rereading of scripture on jihad resulted in a doctrine comparable to the Western tradition of just war theory. It proved most appealing to Muslim rulers in states like Egypt, which were attempting to modernize first under colonial rule and then within the Atlantic system of international law. The Egyptian government from the 1940s onward consistently promoted the general ethos of 'Abduh's approach to Islam, appointing proponents of this reformist vision to the highest religious offices.

Many readers, however, are more familiar with the jihad narrative created by those actors who have worked *against* these modernizing states and *outside* the international system that they had accepted. The extratextual realities of a new balance of power and modern statecraft led reformists like Rida to reread scripture and overhaul pre-modern discourse on jihad accordingly. But for Osama Bin Laden and the jihadist movements of the last forty years, the reality of the modern world was not 'real' enough to overwhelm the scripture-centered worldview of classical jihad doctrine. Instead, for jihadists, modern realities only sharpened classical understandings of the Qur'an and Hadiths. Their reading of scripture against global politics telescoped time and transposed the medieval into the modern world. In their view, the standing of Muslims in modern geopolitics mapped perfectly onto the circumstances of Muhammad's original call to jihad.

This extremist doctrine of jihad found scriptural footing in a raw, unmediated reading of the Qur'an and Hadiths. God permitted Muhammad's followers to fight those who 'drove them from their homes' or attacked them. Was it then not legitimate to raise arms against the Israeli expulsion of Muslims from their homes in Palestine, or following the Soviet and then American invasions of Muslim lands? On the basis of strong Hadith evidence, classical jihad doctrine had uniformly prohibited the intentional killing of civilians (some scholars like Malik and Awza'i even disallowed 'collateral damage'), but Bin Laden considered the Pentagon a military target and the World Trade Center a vitally symbolic organ of the capitalist imperial system that oppressed Muslims. Moreover, if Muslims were permitted to fight those unbelievers who victimized them for their religion, then what of supposedly Muslim governments that cast aside Shariah law for Western legal codes and consumerism, who imprisoned and executed pious Muslims?[15]

The extremist doctrine of jihad articulated by Bin Laden and others was a warped but recognizable descendant of the militant revivalism that burgeoned in the Wahhabi and Sokoto movements. They too had justified their expansionist jihads (mostly against Muslims they declared apostates) not by artful interpretation of scripture but by imagining themselves in the original contexts of that scripture itself, the pioneering monotheists purifying a heartland for Islam. They created black-and-white schemas that justified endless expansion when applied to the world around them. Callously caulking the theoretical technicalities of Shariah law onto the realities of a thorny world allowed them to attack lapsed Muslims and polytheist infidels alike. In the eyes of these militant revival movements, those who aided the enemy became legitimate targets as well.[16]

In the mid-twentieth century, this militant revivalism found a new, more abstract and politicized expression in the novel and influential reading of Islam's scriptures by Sayyid Qutb, the Egyptian liberal literary critic turned Islamist. After an alleged Muslim Brotherhood assassination attempt against Egypt's new president, Gamal Abd al-Nasser, in 1954 Qutb found himself in prison along with many other Muslim Brothers. Lingering in jail for over a decade, suffering from consumption and subjected to torture, Qutb scrawled ruminations on the Qur'an that would one day be published as the most widely read commentary on the Qur'an in the Arab world. Where classical Qur'anic commentaries were scholastic and concatenated, weighed down by dry grammatical analysis, occasions of revelation and scholarly opinions, *In the Shade of the Qur'an* was an intimate plunge into the holy book, fluid and experiential. It was an inhalation of the Qur'an's ethos of radical monotheism and a revolutionary critique of the modern world order, calling the reader not to earthly barricades for upheaval but to an internal inversion of spirit. In the new world Qutb envisioned, man would be honored and freed through total submission to God.

Where Qutb's commentary on the Qur'an was too profound to be mere political propaganda, the radical manifestos he produced in the years before his execution in 1966 were politically catalyzing. In his seminal set of essays, first circulated secretly and later published together as *Milestones*, the immediacy of his reading of the Qur'an and Hadiths recasts the modern world as one in which the pre-Islamic 'Age of Ignorance' and idolatry once again reigns. The West and its dictator stooges rule through exploitative systems that subjugate man to man. The Qur'anic message is a call to liberation through submission to God, and jihad is the holistic struggle to overturn the idols of human despotism, injustice and the denial of God.

The crux of Qutb's interpretation is the Qur'an's verses on God's absolute sovereignty, 'Rule is God's alone' and 'Those who ruled by other than what God has revealed, they are the unbelievers' (12:40, 67). He had been strongly influenced by the Islamist thought of the Indian (later Pakistani) ideologue Abul Ala Mawdudi, and like him read these declarations as condemnations of secularization and the subordination of the Shariah to fickle, man-made regimes.[17]

For the vast majority of Egyptian (and other Arab) Muslims who pored through Qutb's *Shade* and *Milestones* as they flew off presses in Beirut and Cairo (after their unbanning in Egypt in 1975), his voice was a poetic call to a more deeply Islamic society, reconstituted and empowered. His jihad and denunciations of unbelief (*kufr*) were metaphors for overcoming Muslims' oppression through all-encompassing faith.

For a small minority, Qutb's writings, especially his condemnation of 'rule by other than God's law,' transformed the urge for Islamic revival into a radical political ideology. A return to the Qur'an and the Prophet's teachings took on the new dimension of a jihad against secular regimes in the Muslim world and their unbelieving sponsors in the West. The reverberations of Qutb's thought in the ideologies of jihadist groups such as Al-Qaeda are palpable.[18] A worldview of battling against Crusader foes and so-called Muslim regimes that refuse to rule purely by the Shariah framed Osama Bin Laden's missives and interviews. 'What goes for us is whatever is found in the Book of God and the *hadith* of the Prophet,' he wrote, peppering his speeches with the Sword Verses in exhortation to jihad.[19]

Bin Laden's use of the Qur'an and Hadiths to justify his path would require a book-length study in its own right. His 'first' jihad, however, is an illustrative example of how an artless mapping of scripture onto his perception of global geopolitics resulted in the gross oversimplification of Islam's rich interpretive heritage. Many ulama from within the conservative religious establishment of Saudi Arabia had criticized the kingdom's ruling family for liberal living, allowing Western mores to penetrate Saudi society and for their close partnership with the United States, Israel's indispensable protector. But Bin Laden had been particularly severe and open in his criticism of the Saudi government for allowing US troops onto Saudi soil. Their number had peaked at half a million after the Saudis had requested US military protection against Saddam Hussein in 1990. He was also accused of crossing the threshold into violence in 1996, when explosions rocked the US military mission in Riyadh and a US military housing complex in Khobar, on the kingdom's east coast.

The outrage of many Saudi ulama about the presence of US troops on their country's soil is not difficult to understand. They were angered by their government's alliance with the US and its allowing non-Muslim troops to use their country as a base for attacks on fellow Muslims from the First Gulf War onward. It is simplistic and naive to explain jihadism merely as an inevitable growth from Islam's 'violent' scripture, or as no more than a miscarried interpretation triggered solely by some tragic misreading. It cannot be separated from economic discontent, the enveloping context of US global power, America's influence and military actions in the Muslim world and, most of all, the gaping sore of the Israel–Palestine conflict. Bin Laden, however, grounded his immediate objection to US and Saudi policy in Islamic scripture and what he considered the Saudi government's egregious transgression of clear Shariah law. He begins his 1996 'Declaration of Jihad against the Americans Occupying the Land of the Two Holy Sanctuaries' with a Hadith from *Sahih Bukhari*: part of the Prophet's deathbed testament was the instruction to 'Expel the polytheists from the Peninsula of the Arabs.'[20]

Bin Laden was no stranger to the classical tradition of Islamic scholarship. He occasionally draws on the authority of medieval Hanbalis such as Ibn Taymiyya and Ibn Qudama in his speeches and interviews. The prophetic command he cited was well established, and its order of expulsion was not limited to pagan Arabs alone. In another authenticated Hadith, Muhammad declared: 'Indeed I will expel the Jews and the Christians from the Peninsula of the Arabs so that I leave only Muslims.' This was not accomplished until the reign of the second caliph, Umar, who acted on the Prophet's order and expelled the Jews of the oasis of Khaybar, north of Medina, from the Hejaz.

The Islamic justification for Bin Laden's early jihad becomes much murkier when one investigates how even the earliest Muslim scholars had interpreted the details of the Prophet's order. The 'Peninsula of the Arabs' may seem an obvious geographical unit on maps today, but its medieval definition was narrower and its Shariah status contested. Bukhari notes that it was the area of the twin shrine cities of Mecca and Medina, extending south to the mountains of Yemen and east across the craggy ridges of the Hejaz to the central Arabian oases of Yamama (near present-day Riyadh). Hence Malik had concluded that Umar had not expelled the Jews of the Tayma oasis in the northern Hejaz because it was not considered part of 'the Peninsula of the Arabs.' In later centuries Christian merchants would even accompany Hajj caravans from Syria down into the Hejaz until they were within three days' travel of Medina. Furthermore, medieval ulama recognized that the 'Peninsula of the Arabs' could not include Yemen, since Jewish communities had flourished there since the beginning of Islam.[21]

There was also notable disagreement among the Sunni schools of law on the rules governing the exclusive 'Peninsula' zone. The caliph Umar had allowed Christians, Jews and Zoroastrians three days every year to buy and sell from the markets of Medina. The Shafi'i school of law thus held that no unbeliever could settle in the region between Mecca, Medina and Yamama, but they could enter with permission for up to three days on diplomatic duties or if bearing vital goods. They were only prohibited from entering the sacred Haram Mosque of Mecca, where the Kaaba stands. Most Hanafis, by contrast, had allowed unbelievers, even those from outside the 'Abode of Islam,' to live in the Hejaz and enter the Haram of Mecca and stay there as a traveler, provided they did not settle. Individuals could even be allowed to enter the Kaaba.[22] Crucially, the very 'Peninsula of the Arabs' that Bin Laden claimed the Prophet ordered to be cleansed of non-Muslims actually hosted very few of them. Prior to the 1996 bombings of US installations, most American forces were near the east coast of the country, far from the prohibited enclave.

While Bin Laden and the Al-Qaeda leadership were tailoring their readings of the Qur'an and Hadiths to legitimize their involvement in geopolitical conflicts, other jihadists were realizing how superficial these readings were. The heavy-handed suppression of the Muslim Brotherhood in Egypt under the Arab nationalist state of the 1960s had crushed the organization there. Then, concerned about increased communist appeal in Egypt during the 1970s, President Anwar Sadat began allowing Islamist activism as an ideological counterweight. The university students who formed the energetic 'Islamic societies' in the newfound freedom of the 1970s were shocked when protests against government economic and political policies revealed the limits of Sadat's tolerance.

Arrested by Egypt's security forces and often brutalized in prison, leading members of one Islamist group in particular, the *Jama'a Islamiyya*, turned back to the writings of Sayyid Qutb with a new perspective. His characterization of Egypt's government as a resurrection of pre-Islamic paganism rang prophetically when prison interrogators tortured the young activists for what the victims could only assume was their sincere faith in Islam. When prisoners called out to God during torture, the guards mocked them with barbs like, 'Bring your God and we'll put him in a cell too.' The *Jama'a* activists concluded that they were indeed facing pure enemies of God just as the Prophet had.[23] They and other Islamist groups turned to violence against the infidel state. The *Jama'a Islamiyya* and another small cadre called the *Jama't Jihad* cooperated in assassinating Sadat and a failed uprising against the government in Upper Egypt in 1981. Locked in a destructive tit-for-tat with the Egyptian security services, through the late 1990s *Jama'a Islamiyya* militants carried out sporadic and horrific attacks on state interests and tourist sites.

Imprisoned for almost twenty years, however, the leadership of the *Jama'a Islamiyya* passed their time in group study, reading works of classical Hanbali law and the books of Ibn Taymiyya. In light of the classical ulama's interpretations, they came to re-evaluate the rhetorical reading of the Qur'an and Hadiths that characterized Qutb's writings. Eager to end their destructive and futile conflict with the state, in 2002 the imprisoned *Jama'a* members negotiated a ceasefire with the Egyptian government in return for better prison conditions, and in 2006 most were released.

While still in prison, in 2004 leading thinkers in the organization produced a set of concise, accessible booklets entitled the 'Series for Correcting Understandings,' which condemned violent extremism on the basis of sound interpretation of scripture. The reformed *Jama'a* members warned that a main cause of religious extremism was the literal reading of the Qur'an and Hadiths, without qualified ulama as guides or an understanding of the overarching principles of the Shariah.

Most crucially, these booklets took on the main justification for jihadist attacks on other Muslims. According to those who adopted the jihadist perspective, those states and even those Muslim peoples who were not implementing or living by the Shariah, thus 'ruling by other than what God has revealed,' were declaring themselves apostates – with lethal consequences. The *Jama'a* booklets countered this extremist understanding by turning to the interpretations noted by Tirmidhi over a millennium earlier. The 'unbelief' of not ruling by God's law or even persecuting other Muslims was a rhetorical condemnation of impiety and iniquity, not an expulsion from the Muslim fold – 'an unbelief other than [true] unbelief.'* Drawing on the works of Ibn Taymiyya and his disciples – flawless pedigree among Salafis and militants – they explained how *kufr* (unbelief) takes both greater and lesser form. The former truly removes one from Islam as an apostate. Yet it comes only from denying something 'known essentially as part of the religion,' namely a core tenet that has been communicated by a scriptural text certain in both its attestation and indication, agreed upon by the consensus of the ulama and uniformly well known among the Muslim masses. Denying the requirement to pray five times a day, for example, would constitute such an act. Simply not praying out of laziness would not. The lesser form of unbelief is merely a sin, not a crime worthy of death.[24]

The repentant jihadists found that the leading Salafi scholars of the 1980s and 1990s had been preaching against the warped literalism of extremists for decades. Rooted in the Hadith-based teachings of early Sunnis like Ibn Hanbal, these Salafi shaykhs were political quietists who rejected vigilantism and rebellion against the state. Exemplified by the Syrian Hadith scholar Nasir al-Din Albani, they believed that Muslims should focus on purifying their beliefs and practice and that, in time, God would bring victory over the forces of falsehood and unbelief. They affirmed completely

* Less conciliatory Islamists such as Ahmad Shakir, the leadership of Egypt's Salafi Call movement and (earlier in his career) Salman Auda have objected to using this interpretation by Ibn Abbas as a license for accepting non-Shariah law. They argue that Ibn Abbas meant that a judge who erred in a ruling was not guilty of ruling by 'other than what God had revealed,' not that Muslims could accept a legal system as better than the Shariah.

the classical jihad doctrine, but this doctrine only allowed a jihad to be declared and led by the ruler of a Muslim polity. It was not a personal mission taken up by angry individuals or non-state actors. Non-Muslim visitors in Muslim lands, even members of foreign militaries, could not be harmed because they had received permission from the state to be there.[25]

Fiery youths attending the lectures of Salafi scholars like Albani often objected that the Prophet had taught that, 'Whoever among you sees something reprehensible, let him change it with his hand, and if not that, then with this tongue, and if not that, then with his heart, but this is the weakest of faith.' Should believing Muslims not then lift their hands to end the injustices and iniquities around them – by force? The shaykhs replied with a standard medieval interpretation of this Hadith. As Nawawi had explained, such passages of scripture had to be interpreted in accordance with established Shariah principles, such as the state's sole prerogative in declaring jihad. 'Changing the reprehensible by hand,' or by compulsion, was the purview of the state alone. 'Changing with the tongue' was the right of the ulama. Ordinary, individual Muslims should only reject the reprehensible with their hearts.[26]

WOMEN CANNOT LEAD: HISTORICIZING SCRIPTURE VERSUS GOD'S INSCRUTABLE LAW

A mad admixture of political campaigning and revolutionary tension, the fall of 2011 and the spring of 2012 found Egyptians of every political stripe in febrile preparation for their country's first free democratic election of a leader. Ever. Islamists, liberals and supporters of the ancien régime vied furiously for the attention of the electorate. The powerful newcomer in Egypt's political arena was none other than the Salafi movement, whose bearded scholars (many of them students of Albani) had spent thirty years avoiding the worst of state crackdowns on Islamists by preaching the medieval, politically quietist version of Ibn Taymiyya's conservative, Hadith-based revivalism. They had built up an unrealized mass of followers in the mosques of Cairo and Egypt's Delta. Salafi scholars and preachers were now tasked with mobilizing their flocks for politics.

In a cheap paperback booklet entitled *How to Choose the President of the Republic*, for sale outside many mosques, the popular Salafi scholar Raghib Sirgani outlined the conservative Islamist criteria for Egypt's future head of state. The essential requirement was that the candidate be Muslim and committed to applying the Shariah, 'or else the country will fall into a state of enmity with God.' Another important requirement was that the president be a man, since the Prophet had said in an authenticated Hadith that 'A community that entrusts its affairs to a woman will not flourish.'[27]

In the West, calls for the Shariah are viewed with confusion and fear, accompanied by media flashes of bearded rage and reviving receded memories of medieval inquisitions. Polls demonstrate that for Egyptians, conversely, the 'Shariah' is associated with notions of political, social and gender justice. In 2011, 80 to 87 percent of Egyptians polled wanted the Shariah to be a source of law in the country. Even amid the political chaos in early 2013, a full 58 percent of Egyptians still said that the country's laws should strictly follow the Qur'an.[28] Few Egyptians, even Islamist politicians, could explain exactly what that would mean. The place of the Shariah in their consciousness seems oddly similar to the Constitution for Americans; all venerate it, but few have read it in its entirety. No one knows what applying it always means.

Calls for the Shariah in Egypt and other Muslim countries emanate from a deep recess in people's souls. The cry for the Shariah is a surrogate expression for a longing for dignity, independence, justice and control over one's destiny in a world seemingly controlled by outsiders and outside agendas. It goes far back.

In 1950, a female graduate of Cairo's law faculty wrote the Minister of Justice complaining that, as a woman, she was not permitted the opportunity to serve as a public prosecutor – and eventually a judge – in Egypt's by then European-inspired civil law judiciary. She complained that this was no way to understand a religion birthed by women like Aisha, who was one of the leading transmitters of Hadiths from the Prophet and who was sought out by her male comrades as a teacher. The minister directed the complaint to Egypt's ulama. The letter provoked an enduring controversy over whether or not women could hold offices of public responsibility and ultimately if they could serve as the leader of the government. It was a controversy that again brought Islamic scripture and its proper interpretation to the fore.

One figure who responded to the letter was Ahmad Shakir, an Al-Azhar cleric and a judge in Cairo's family courts, the last bastion of Shariah law in Egypt's judiciary. Shakir was an important link between the Egyptian ulama and the Wahhabi scholars of Saudi Arabia, where the revivalist thought of Ibn Taymiyya was undergoing a renaissance. Shakir, in fact, was a founding figure of the Salafi movement in Egypt. In a journal article responding to the letter, he acknowledged the diversity of Shariah opinion on women serving as judges; Hanafis allowed them to do so on financial matters, and other early jurists had allowed them overall. But this was not the crux of the matter at hand, Shakir insisted. The choice that truly faced Egypt was whether it would be a Muslim polity ruled by Shariah law or if it would accept the Western separation of religion from the state and legal system. The demands of feminist activists like the letter's author simply revealed this moment of choice plainly.

Shakir knew that his species, the classically trained cleric working in a Shariah court, was already endangered. Until the First World War, Egypt remained nominally part of the Ottoman Empire. The land of the Nile, however, had gained effective independence under an Albanian dynasty that often outpaced their titular masters in Istanbul in military, social and legal reform. Caught in the heady rush of modernization and under recent British military occupation, in 1883 the Egyptian government had ordered the hasty promulgation of a civil law code based on European models and drawing on the French Napoleonic Code (in fact, it was first drafted in French and then translated into Arabic). The new 'National Courts' system even hired many of its judges from Europe. The Shariah courts that had administered justice in Egypt for centuries continued to exist and were allowed to hear any cases brought before them. The ulama nursed hopes that this European law code would be temporary pending the adoption of a Shariah-based code. But the transition away from ulama applying God's law to European-trained jurists applying secular law codes had begun.[29]

The uniform, statist character of the French civil law code supported the concerted will of states like Egypt and the Ottoman Empire to achieve greater centralization. The Shariah courts and the decentralized legal tradition they applied did not. Since the medieval period, in some areas of the Islamic world courts for all four schools of Shariah law coexisted. Even in less legally diverse areas like the Maghreb, senior judges could draw upon Islamic law to offer the most equitable ruling. Unlike this often varied and fluid Shariah system, the nineteenth-century Ottoman world witnessed a move toward more standardization. This occurred first in the Shariah courts, where sole reliance on the 'official' Hanafi ruling in any case became the norm. But it was still the ulama who acted as judges.

Moreover, the plurality of Hanafi law books, each with its own opinion on what constituted the 'official' ruling, still allowed these judges flexibility in deciding a case. More importantly, the ulama were still the maintainers of this realm, charged with developing the law as times changed. With the new, formalized civil code, drafted by European-trained lawyers for application by European-trained judges, this would all change. The code laid out strict, non-Shariah guidelines for how any crime was punished or case decided, and changing it would be the work of legislators and parliaments.

As the twentieth century dawned and it became clear that legal reforms were as much about secularization as centralization, Egypt's ulama began objecting loudly. They not only believed that the rule of Shariah law – even if reigning only in theory – was *the* essential feature of a Muslim state, but manning the Shariah courts or at least training the judges was a main avenue for their employment. The objections of the ulama had little effect on the Egyptian government or its British masters, however. The National Courts applied the French-inspired code, and each court had at least one European judge in it. Only family law, covering areas like marriage, divorce and inheritance, as well as homicide cases, was still adjudicated in Shariah courts or by classically trained ulama.[30]

After the Second World War, the Egyptian government tried to create a new, unified law code that was both modern and Islamically legitimate. It turned to 'Abd al-Razzaq Sanhuri, a brilliant French-trained Egyptian jurist who cultivated Islamic modernist sensibilities and had pioneered a novel drafting of Islamic law. The Shariah, he argued, consisted of a core of unchanging rules and values, which had always formed the unifying nexus of the disparate Sunni schools of law. This core of principles is what any Muslim polity must preserve in its legal system in order to remain true to the Shariah's aims. These unchanging principles might manifest themselves differently at different times and in different contexts. It did not matter what precise shape they took or what specific rules they put in place, as long as they were the driving force in a particular legal code. After deducing these unchanging principles, Sanhuri created a new set of laws that he felt promoted them.

This was totally different from the ulama's practice of either following the main opinion of one school of law, choosing its most equitable offering or selecting an appropriate or convenient ruling from the diverse menu of laws found in the four Sunni schools. Sanhuri was creating a *new* body of laws out of whole cloth that he claimed embodied the spirit and aims of the

Shariah. Since the actual origin of any of the particular rules in question was not important, only their fidelity to the Shariah's values, Sanhuri felt free to take many of them directly from European law codes. Prominent ulama and the Muslim Brotherhood protested this new law code vehemently. Some called for a complete return to the Shariah tradition and others, at the very least, for a code composed only of rules chosen from the Shariah schools. But Sanhuri, who was the Minister of Education at the time, proved too powerful and convincing, and the Egyptian parliament passed the law.[31]

For Shakir and others like him, this was a devilish and insidious development. The Shariah was not just a set of values or aims to be promoted. It rested on a core of concrete, eternal rulings, not principles. At its heart were the *Hudud*, or 'boundaries' set by God and the Prophet, like the Qur'anic punishments for adultery and certain types of theft, as well as other fixed rules, such as those governing inheritance. These could not be changed, regardless of circumstance. In a plea to his fellow Egyptian Muslims, Shakir compared Egypt's choice to the precarious and vulnerable position of the Muslim *Umma* when the heathen Mongols occupied its heartlands in the thirteenth century. But whereas the Muslims of that bygone age had confidently drawn their Mongol rulers into the fold of Islam as initiates, convincing them of the wisdom of ruling by their new God's law, the Muslims of the twentieth century were so enamored of Western ways that they were gladly abandoning their faith and the system that protected it.

Shakir wanted to pull away the veil from what he saw as the increasing 'Western occupation' of Egypt's culture and religion. The women's rights movement, he wrote, was simply another avenue for Western penetration into the Muslim world. Feminist activists and their supporters just wanted to enlighten Egypt, he mocked, 'yes, with the light of Europe! So that the Western masters will be pleased!' Islam had always encouraged the education of women, he affirmed. But the Shariah also gave Muslims clear rules that could not be changed simply because some foreign siren beckoned to Progress. All the schools of the Shariah held that women could not lead men in prayer and certainly not legitimately rule a country (though, always practical, pre-modern Sunni scholars had nonetheless required Muslims to obey a woman who usurped power). This was not subject to debate, Shakir stated, citing as insurmountable evidence the Prophet's declaration: 'A community that entrusts its affairs to a woman will not flourish.'[32]

In Shakir's day, many conservatives saw the forces struggling for the soul of Egypt and, he felt, the future of Islam, very clearly. On one side was the colonial, imperial, godless and morally bankrupt West. On the other was the autochthonous moral and spiritual anchor of the Qur'an, the Hadiths and Shariah law. In this sense, Shakir and Kevseri were kin. But as much as they both hated modernist reformers, Shakir and Kevseri despised each other's schools of thought just as much. Salafis like Shakir condemned as heresy popular Sufi practices like grave visitation, the tradition of loyalty to one school of law and the scholastics of Ash'ari theology. These were the very air that Kevseri breathed, and he composed countless articles condemning Salafis and their Wahhabi sponsors as arrogant and moronic literalists who deigned to correct the centuries of accumulated truth embodied in the Sunni tradition.

In his Salafi belief that Muslims had gone astray from the pure, unadulterated and powerful Islam of the *Umma*'s first generations, Shakir shared more with Westernizing, modernist reformers like 'Abduh than one might think. In fact, he praised the embattled 'Abduh for reviving the focused study of the Qur'an in Al-Azhar. Unlike Kevseri, for whom the glory of the Islamic past lived up until the cusp of the present, both 'Abduh and Shakir looked back into the well of early Islamic history and saw the pure Islam they wanted to renew. 'Abduh had seen a reflection of the West, a fantasy of order and progress where he had encountered 'Islam without Muslims.' Salafis like Shakir saw the dream of Ibn Taymiyya and the eighteenth-century revivalists, a classic Arabian Islam cleansed of the dross of superstition and foreign influence.

In the decades between 'Abduh's death in 1905 and Shakir's angry writings, a hybrid strand of ulama had emerged that combined both their visions. Often supported by an Egyptian state eager for an Islamically kosher modernity, they were among the most prominent Islamic voices in Egypt and the Muslim world. One of 'Abduh's students (who had cared for his neglected widow when he died), Mustafa Maraghi, became the Rector of the Al-Azhar Mosque and presided over its transformation into a modern university. 'Bring me anything that benefits the people,' he famously declared, 'and I'll show you a basis for it in the Shariah.' His loyal supporter and later Al-Azhar rector, Mahmud Shaltut, shored up the reformist doctrine of jihad with rigorous scholarship and wrote the earliest fatwas prohibiting female circumcision. Where these middle-ground reformists and the Salafis overlapped was in their contempt for popular

Sufi practices like saint veneration, dancing or group liturgies. Both also believed that Shariah law was the legal system favored by God, however far from application it had become.

At the heart of this middle-ground reformist vision was an abiding desire to fend off an epistemological break in the religious lives of Muslims. Scholars like Maraghi and Shaltut championed the canon of Islamic scripture out of fear that it and the religious culture around it would recede into history. They developed an understanding of Islam as a streamlined and unchanging core built on the certitudes of the Qur'an and agreed upon, uncontested Hadiths, confirmed by a few undisputed tenets of scholarly consensus. Muslims could believe in the flourishes of popular religion or law outside this core, but they could not insist that they were integral parts of Islam, and no one could be called an unbeliever for rejecting them.[33] In a sense, they took the classical doctrine requiring that, as a minimum, Muslims embrace those tenets 'known essentially as part of the religion' and made it public to the masses. Torn between tradition and Western modernity, Muslims would know the basic core of Islam from which no more concessions to modernity could be chipped.

Western power and the allure of its model was an undeniable reality for the middle-ground reformists, however much they resented its looming presence. They clung tightly to the foundational scriptures of Islam, especially the Qur'an, as the mooring of Islamic identity. Like 'Abduh, they hoped to construct an Islamic modernism that matched the West, but they were committed not to fall into the orbit of its epistemological worldview.

In Egypt of the late twentieth century, the figure who strove hardest and most successfully to accomplish this was Muhammad Ghazali, an Al-Azhar scholar and a disciple of Shaltut. His countless books on every aspect of Islam and reviving its proper understanding, with titles like *Our Intellectual Heritage*, *Renew Your Life* and *Islam and Women's Issues*, still sell briskly at Cairo's impromptu sidewalk bookstalls. Through the decades of his prolific writing and serving as an imam in Cairo's leading mosques, Ghazali picked many fights and earned even more admirers.

The constant of his mission never changed. He labored to construct a modern Islamic revival that would push back the tide of foreign encroachment, however it shifted form over the decades. He aimed to restore Muslims' pride in their religion. Ghazali railed in his sermons, books and articles against secular Arab socialism during its acme in the 1960s and against Sadat's capitalist opening to the West in the 1970s. The scholar was widely loved. When the editor of Egypt's state newspaper of record, *Al-Ahram*, published caricatures mocking Ghazali for publicly speaking against Nasser's socialism in 1962, an angry crowd of protesters marched from the Al-Azhar Mosque after Friday prayers to swarm the paper's offices and defend the shaykh.[34]

Again and again in his long career, Ghazali turned to the question of women's rights and improving them within a framework indigenous to the Islamic tradition. As the decades passed, his thought developed and he became ever more convinced of the need for dramatic change in how observant Muslims viewed a woman's place in society. A Hanafi jurist by training, he leveraged that school's qualitative distinction between the standing of the Qur'an and that of the Hadiths, as well as its unique perspective on germane issues, into a pioneering methodology for reform.

Especially during his years spent teaching in Saudi Arabia in the 1970s, and during the blooming of Salafi activity in Egypt in the 1980s, Ghazali directed his writings toward countering those who used literalist readings of Hadiths to exacerbate Egypt's already conservative gender mores. But to challenge this reliance on scripture without signaling treason to the Hadith canon would be a difficult task. Where earlier reformists like Sidqi had sought to rescue Islam by casting aside Hadiths altogether, Ghazali understood instinctively that threatening the canon of scripture would alienate the wider Muslim public. Where 'Abduh's reformist gravitas had been dragged down by his proximity to Western gender norms, Ghazali's unbending opposition to aping either Eastern bloc socialism or the West strengthened his credibility. One of Ghazali's last, and certainly his most controversial, books would confront the Salafi reliance on Hadiths and Egypt's gender conservatism head-on.

Of the many issues that Ghazali took up in *The Prophetic Sunna: Between the Jurists and the Hadith Scholars*, the question of women assuming positions of leadership was the thorniest. His negotiation of the Hadith Against Women Ruling illustrates perfectly the challenge of balancing the truth of scripture with extratextual realities in an era when the very culture in which texts were read was so contested.

Like medieval ulama reading the Hadith of the Sun Prostrating, Ghazali felt that empirical experience plainly contradicted the prediction that 'A community that entrusts its affairs to a woman will not flourish.' A woman, Golda Meir, he remarked in a jab at a generation of failed, 'mustachioed' Arab leaders, had led Israel to victory over her country's enemies. Indira

Gandhi and, in particular, Margaret Thatcher were two more female leaders widely respected both at home and abroad. Aware that 'flourishing' might well be a question of the Hereafter more than of earthly success, Ghazali invoked a Qur'anic example as well. The Hadith, he asserted, blatantly contradicted the holy book. In the Qur'anic pericope of King Solomon and the Queen of Sheba, the queen rules over a prosperous and powerful kingdom that errantly worships the sun instead of the one God. When Solomon convinces her by way of miraculous signs to abandon her idolatry, she professes, 'I submit before God, along with Solomon, to the Lord of all the worlds' (27:23–44). Here, Ghazali concludes, was a woman leader who not only ruled over a flourishing realm but also guided it from religious error to the straight path of Islam. Ghazali asks his reader, 'Would a nation led by this rare type of woman fail?'[35]

The Hadith warning against women leaders, however, was found in the illustrious *Sahih Bukhari*, just like the Hadith of the Fly. Dismissing it as a forgery or error would invite the same fate as Sidqi had suffered. Instead, Ghazali contextualized the Hadith as a specific statement, not a general command. He described how this Hadith was narrated from the Prophet by a Companion who recalled that, 'When it reached the Prophet that the Persians had placed the daughter of [their former king] Chosroes on the throne, he said, "A country that entrusts its affairs to a woman will not flourish."' The Prophet was merely remarking on the dismal condition of the Persian Empire's ruling family, which, in fact, was plagued with a cycle of no less than eight hapless emperors in the four years between 628 and 632. These included two daughters from the royal family, neither of whom had any experience with command. Ghazali concluded that medieval Muslim scholars had incorrectly interpreted this specific assessment as a universal declaration.[36]

By implying strongly that women could lead a Muslim polity, Ghazali was effectively in uncharted Shariah territory. Bypassing the great warehouse of medieval Islamic thought, which had understood this Hadith as prohibiting women rulers, and returning to the Qur'an opened the door for him to take even more dramatic positions. Margaret Thatcher's prominence on the world stage had an enduring impact on Ghazali in his later years, even after his controversial *Prophetic Sunna* was published. In the 1990s he found himself questioning the basis for many of the Shariah laws on women's role in society, such as the Shariah rules governing women acting as witnesses in court.

The Qur'an had instructed Muslims engaged in making loans or commercial transactions to have their contracts witnessed 'by two men, or by a man and two women, so that if one of them forgets, the other may remind her' (2:282). While the majority of Sunni schools understood this as meaning that women could *only* bear witness in cases concerning financial transactions, and even then carrying only half the evidentiary value of a man, the Hanafi school held that they were fundamentally sound witnesses and could thus testify in other matters such as marriage, divorce, inheritance and even manslaughter. Ghazali stepped even further than his Hanafi school on this matter. Acting on the same principle invoked by medieval Hanafis in the case of *Zakat* categories, Ghazali deemed the reasons for which God had treated female witnesses differently than males to be obsolete. He understood the Qur'an's commandment on witnessing to be premised on a world where women had little commercial experience. In the modern world, in which women ran corporations, the reason behind the Qur'anic laws no longer applied.

Ghazali touched still more sensitive chords. He caused tremors in the audience when, speaking on a panel, he addressed the question of women leading men in prayer. He brought up the possibility of Dr. Aisha 'Abd al-Rahman, an esteemed and pious Egyptian scholar of Islam, having to pray behind some unaccomplished, junior scholar. Was this really appropriate, he demanded of the stunned audience?[37]

By the time of his death in 1996, this tireless reformist certainly had many critics. Salafi opponents and more conservative Al-Azhar clerics accused Ghazali of assigning more weight to extratextual morality and perceived welfare than to clear prescriptions from the Qur'an and authentic Hadiths. In the eyes of Salafis like Albani or Shakir, the accomplishments of a leader like Thatcher were ephemeral and carried no weight when put up against the West's rejection of Islam's religious and social message. Whether or not a nation seemed to prosper under Golda Meir or Thatcher did not alter the Prophet's guidance or the immutability of the Shariah. Conservative critics often dismissed Ghazali and others preaching such reforms as 'imitators of the West.'[38]

Even Ghazali's close friend and admirer for almost half a century, a man who would emerge as the most influential global Sunni scholar of the early twenty-first century, Yusuf Qaradawi, could not second an approach to the Qur'an and Hadiths that subordinated their decrees so definitively to our own assessments of how and why they were revealed. Yet he defended his late friend and teacher as best he could. In a paean to Ghazali, Qaradawi pointed out that, behind all the controversy, Ghazali almost always had some precedent for his stances, even if obscure, especially in the byzantine law books of the Hanafi school.* Phrasing his critique as delicately as possible, Qaradawi recognized that allowing a woman to lead the Muslim *Umma* was an exception. It had no basis and was an inconceivable and anomalous stance innovated by Ghazali.[39] A scholar referred to by some as 'the global mufti,' Qaradawi has always been more conservative, less sanguine and less emotive than his friend. Certainly, the Shariah allows for changes according to time, place and culture, Qaradawi has acknowledged. Local custom can define how much dower a husband pays a bride, or when a sales transaction is concluded. But no matter how far women advanced in education and employment, this could not change an unambiguous edict laid down by God and His Messenger.[40] Epitomizing the converse of Ghazali's approach, one scholar of Mecca had written that, even if the Prophet's wife Aisha herself came to bear witness in court, her sole testimony would not be accepted. This despite the fact that many of the rulings of the Shariah itself were established by Hadiths that Aisha alone narrated from the Prophet. Any inconsistency that we sense in such matters comes merely from our inability to grasp the 'divine secrets' of God's justice, the Meccan scholar wrote.[41]

The debate sparked over six decades ago with a female law graduate's petition to apply for a judgeship continues in Egypt and elsewhere to this day. Though little more than a pamphlet, Sirgani's directions on choosing Egypt's president nevertheless grant ample space to rebutting Ghazali's historicization of the Hadith Against Women Ruling. 'The Hadith is general in application,' Sirgani argues, Ghazali clearly in his sights, 'and those who claim it is specified must provide some evidence for that.' He points to a version of the Hadith in the *Sahih Bukhari* that Ghazali had not mentioned. The Companion who transmitted the Hadith from the Prophet recalled that, when the civil wars broke out in the years after Muhammad's death, he had inclined toward joining an army led by Aisha. Then he remembered the Prophet's prediction and realized this would be an error. Even the Companions, Sirgani concludes, understood that the Hadith was a general warning for the future as well.[42]

* Ibn Taymiyya and his disciple Ibn Qayyim had argued that the Qur'anic equation of two women to one man pertained only to notarizing a loan, not bearing witness in court. There a woman of sound mind and character was equal to a man.

SEX WITH LITTLE GIRLS: INTERPRETING SCRIPTURE AMID CHANGING NORMS

Contemporary norms in the West commonly disapprove of marriages between couples with large age differences. Cursory glances at Western media catch on headlines like 'She's twenty-three. He's sixty-nine. What gives?' The media are particularly attuned to reports of such marriages in the Muslim world, perhaps part of the enduring Western fear and fascination with the Muslim man's supposed predatory sexuality and the fate of his young victim. Similar objections appear regularly in liberal-leaning media in the Arab world as well, which gawk at announcements such as 'Shaykh Qaradawi marries a Moroccan woman thirty-seven years his junior.'

Disapproval becomes moral outrage, however, in cases of child marriage (defined by UNICEF as the marriage of a person under eighteen). One need wait only a few weeks to find anger expressed online under banner stories such as 'British child brides: mosque leaders agree to marry girls as young as twelve... as long as parents don't tell anyone.'[43]

Sentiments about the appropriate ages for men and women to marry (read, engage in approved sexual activity) have fueled consuming controversy in recent decades. In great part, this is because these sentiments carry an instinctual moral gravity that suggests they are much more concrete and universally recognized than is actually the case. For many in Western, developed nations, it is inconceivable that the guttural revulsion felt at an adult man marrying a young girl would not be felt by people everywhere. Those who approve of such a match must thus be barbarians.[44]

The turpitude of marriage to underage girls has featured prominently in polemics over Islam and gender in Egypt and elsewhere in the Muslim world in recent decades. Headlines like 'Top Saudi cleric: OK for young girls to wed' appear commonly.[45] In reality, those working internationally to combat child marriage have concluded that its roots are primarily economic and unrelated to any specific religion. Most common in South Asia and Sub-Saharan Africa, regardless of religion, child marriage generally hinges on one of two opposing economic pressures: the premium on high birth rates in agricultural communities, or a desire to marry off daughters as soon as possible to minimize the number of mouths to feed in a household.

Even so, Islam seems to present a particular problem. In Islamic discourse, child marriage and efforts to restrict it run up against the canonical power of scripture and the desire of many Muslims to protect the boundaries of the Shariah and religious authenticity against the perceived encroachment of Western development norms.

When the Grand Mufti of Saudi Arabia was asked if girls under fifteen could marry, he replied that Islam did not prohibit it. In terms of Shariah evidence, the basis for his statement could not be stronger: an authenticated Hadith from the *Sahih Bukhari* and other canonical Hadith collections quotes the Prophet's wife Aisha reporting that he had consummated his marriage with her when she was nine years old. And the Prophet of God cannot sin.[46]

Questions of minimum marriage age for women and issues of consent in the Islamic legal tradition have centered primarily on a woman's physical maturity and sexual status, and the crucial legal moments involved were the marriage contract and the actual consummation. As in the case of Aisha, whose marriage contract was concluded two or three years before the consummation, these two events could be separated by a lengthy period. In all Sunni schools of law except the Hanafi, a female needs the permission of her male guardian (usually her father) to marry, though this could be a pro forma requirement. In the Maliki school, for example, a 'mature and discriminating virgin' was considered capable of choosing her spouse, and if her male guardian objected without valid reason she could appeal to the court for permission.[47]

This was not a license for forced marriage. Well-known Hadiths explained that any woman who had reached puberty must give her consent for marriage, though if she was a virgin who remained silent the Prophet explained that 'her silence is her consent.' This applied to girls who had reached maturity, which occurred when they began menstruating or reached fifteen years old, whichever came first (Maliki scholars alone allowed that eighteen was the oldest possible age by which puberty occurs). All four Sunni schools, however, permitted a father to *contract* a marriage for his *underage* virgin daughter, no matter how young she was, *without* her consent, which had no weight due to her minority.[48] Hanafis alone allowed a girl in such a case to ask a judge to annul a marriage contract previously arranged by her guardian once she reached puberty.

Consummation was a separate matter. The age of the female that primarily concerned pre-modern ulama was the age at which the marriage contract took place. They did not devote a great deal of attention to the minimum age for sex. In part this was due to the Prophet's well-known precedent with Aisha. Nine years old is a young age for sex by the standards of any culture, and his precedent thus set a very low threshold for a minimum age for intercourse. More importantly, the medieval ulama considered the point at which a girl was fit for intercourse to be too varied to be firmly legislated for. It was most appropriate for the bride, groom and the bride's guardian to determine the appropriate age for intercourse.

The norm that the ulama did come to consensus on was only a general guideline: they prohibited sexual intercourse for girls 'not able to undergo it,' on the basis that otherwise sex could be physically harmful. If the groom and his wife or her guardian disagreed about her capacity for sex, a Shariah court judge would decide, perhaps after a female expert witness examined her.[49] This was also based on the Prophet's marriage to Aisha. The couple had concluded the marriage contract when Aisha was only six but had waited to consummate the marriage until she reached physical maturity. In the case of the Hanbali tradition followed by the Mufti of Saudi Arabia, sex was allowed when the bride was 'at the age at which others like her have intercourse,' specifying nine as the norm for suitability for sex on the basis of Aisha's Hadith. A Scottish physician resident in Aleppo in the mid 1700s noted how families endeavored to marry their children off (i.e., complete the marriage contract) at a young age but that they would not consummate the marriage until the girl 'had come of age.' Historical evidence from nineteenth-century Ottoman Palestine suggests that husbands having sexual intercourse with wives before they reached puberty did sometimes occur. But it was rare, condemned socially and censured by Shariah court judges. Shariah courts in French Algeria in the 1850s considered it equally despicable, although colonial officials seemed unable to grasp the crucial difference between contracting a marriage and consummating it.[50]

Although recent research has shown that medical reforms in mid-nineteenth-century Egypt had identified child marriage as a health concern, it was modern Western opprobrium that brought the problematic precedent of the Prophet's marriage with Aisha to the fore.[51] The Prophet's sexuality and married life had been a lurid magnet for criticism even during his own lifetime, and it has remained the most consistent theme in Christian/Western polemics against Islam ever since. His marriage to Aisha did feature in these polemics from the early Islamic period, but what exposed him as a 'sex fiend' (*scortum*), in the words of a seventeenth-century Italian priest, was not Aisha's age but the Prophet's supposed uncontrollable desire for her. He had seen her in a dream, it was said, and become physically infatuated with her (see Appendix I).[52]

Yet I have found no instance of anyone criticizing the Prophet's marriage due to Aisha's age or accusing him of pedophilia until the early twentieth century. Even in the nineteenth century, British, German and French orientalists mostly passed over the matter in silence. Others assumed a Montesquieu-like sense of climatic determinism. In the 1830s the British ethnographer and lexicographer E. W. Lane prefaced his observation that Egyptian women married as young as ten (only a few remained single by age sixteen) with the remark that they 'tend to arrive at puberty much earlier than the natives of colder climates.' The first condemnatory note comes in *Mohammad and the Rise of Islam* (1905) by the British orientalist David Margoliouth. He calls Muhammad's marriage to Aisha an 'ill-assorted union... for as such we must characterise the marriage of a man of fifty-three to a child of nine.'[53]

The lack of Christian and Western vituperation against Aisha's age prior to 1905 is not surprising. And Margoliouth's pioneering disapproval was very English. Even as late as the nineteenth century, societies in which the vast majority of the population worked the land in small agricultural communities ('peasant' societies) were generally characterized by marriage ages that we would consider extremely young. Whether in India, China or Eastern Europe, in the pre-industrial period (and in many areas, even today) marriage age for women tended to be in the mid-teens, immediately after puberty. Shah Wali Allah married at fourteen, and when a scholar in fifteenth-century Damascus raised eyebrows by becoming a father at eleven it was because folk at the time were impressed, not outraged. In some US states, such as Georgia, the legal age of consent for women was as low as ten well into the twentieth century. In all these areas, this was probably due to the need for as many hands as possible to work the fields, hence a premium on high birth rates, as well as a relatively short life expectancy and a need to start families early.[54]

Britain was a bizarre exception even in the medieval period. The 'Wife of Bath' in the *Canterbury Tales* may have married at the 'twelf yeer of age,' but Britain and, to a lesser extent, most of northwest Europe differed from the pre-modern pattern of early marriage. Marriage age tended to be later, in the mid-twenties. In England, available data suggest that this was the case as far back as the fourteenth century.[55]

Britain's unusual marriage pattern was reflected in its law. It is not surprising that English common law was the first to establish statutory rape laws and ages of consent for marriage in Europe. As early as the Statute of Westminster in 1275, sex with an underage girl (meaning under either twelve or fourteen, it is unclear which) regardless of consent was criminalized. In 1576 the age was reduced to ten.

Law was an imperial export. The mission to rescue 'native' women from their backward cultures was a prominent theme in British portrayals of the empire's colonial activities. In the late 1800s and early 1900s Britain moved to bring marriage customs in India into line with her imperial values, and a series of laws introduced age restrictions for Hindu and Muslim girls marrying.[56]

Yet Egypt's experience with modernization and British rule was often counterintuitive when it came to gender. When the British occupied Egypt in 1882, the High Commissioner, Lord Cromer, was eager to trim the country's budget and recoup Egyptian debt. He defunded many of the modernizing reforms instituted just decades earlier by the ruling dynasty of Mehmet Ali. Cromer, for example, withdrew support for training women doctors and midwives, a flagship of Egypt's indigenous, pre-colonial medical reforms. This new class of state-trained midwives had actually started bringing the health concerns of child marriage to light. Yet Cromer professed himself shocked by Islam's apparently barbaric and unamendable treatment of women (ironically, he was a founding member of the Men's League for Opposing Women's Suffrage back in England).[57]

The first decades of the twentieth century brought tremendous change to Egypt: the population burgeoned, and family structures in rural areas fell apart as peasants flocked to the cities. With educational reforms, literacy rates improved dramatically. By the 1920s, exposure to Western norms and modernization efforts had changed how marriage and appropriate marriage ages were viewed within sections of Egyptian society, particularly the newly created urban middle class. Censuses in 1907 and 1917 showed that less than ten percent of Egyptian women were marrying before the age of twenty. 1923 proved a landmark year for reform. After attending a conference of the International Women's Alliance in Rome, longtime women's rights activist Huda Sharawi led the formation of the Egyptian Feminist Union. In the same year, the organization's lobbying efforts for a variety of women's rights issues helped convince Egypt's parliament to pass a law setting the minimum marriage age for women at sixteen (men at eighteen).[58]

Since the late 1800s reformist ulama like 'Abduh had been employing Islamic legal and scriptural arguments for advancing women's rights, in particular for increasing female education and calling for laws restricting polygamy. Although the Qur'an permitted men to marry up to four women, it discouraged this if the husband could not treat each one fairly. Medieval jurists, however, did not conclude that this condition meant any active restriction on polygamy. 'Abduh disagreed. Citing the Qur'anic verse that tells men, 'You will not be able to be fair between women' (4:3, 129), he reasoned that this entailed an effective prohibition on polygamy except when circumstances like war or massive gender disparity required it. Like St. Augustine, 'Abduh argued along Islamic scriptural lines that polygamy had been allowed in the ancient Near East due to the conditions of the time but that it was not the Qur'an's ideal for marriage. The true model for Muslim marriage was the Prophet's twenty-four-year monogamous marriage to his beloved first wife and partner Khadija.[59]

It would be much harder to extricate Islamic reformist ideals from the tangle of Muhammad's marriage to Aisha. Yet by the 1950s there was clearly growing discomfort among upper-class Egyptians over Margoliouth's 'ill-assorted' marriage and what other Europeans were referring to as sexual deviance. The person who rose to challenge 'what the orientalists say about Aisha marrying when she was a child' was one of the most popular Egyptian authors of the twentieth century.

Abbas 'Aqqad was an accomplished and prolific Arabic prose stylist, poet and a member of the Arabic Language Academy. Although modernist and cosmopolitan, he was also a lifelong anti-imperialist who keenly understood that reviving Egypt's confidence in its Islamic and Arab heritage was essential for achieving independence and parity with the West. His numerous books on early Islamic history sought to remind Egyptians of their religion's founding greatness and the creative genius of its early generations. Works such as *The Genius of Muhammad* and *The Genius of Umar* were consciously modeled on Carlyle's 'great man' view of history, efforts to bolster the assurance of Arabs and Muslims who wanted to believe in the legitimacy of their civilization but needed that proven in terms convincing to Europeans. Yet like 'Abduh, Rida and Khan, 'Aqqad's reimagination of Islam's original genius was not too far from the expectations of modernity. Revealingly, Sanhuri wrote him a letter remarking how his jurist's legal mind and the littérateur's books converged on a single enlightened path leading to the 'face of God, the face of truth.'[60]

'Aqqad exemplifies how history and, in this case, the scripture of Hadiths can be reread in consonance with compelling social forces. He was certainly no feminist, but his readable encomium on Aisha rightfully highlighted her role as a crucial transmitter of the Prophet's legacy, a respected early teacher of his religion and even a leading political actor in the violent upheavals that followed her husband's death. He demurs masterfully and tactically, however, on Aisha's marriage age. His modest hesitance evinces respect for the classical Islamic tradition of Hadith criticism while constructing an argument against its consensus on the issue. Historical reports differ on Aisha's age, he explains, going on to argue that she was actually between thirteen and fifteen years old when her marriage was consummated.* Such disparities are normal, he reminds the reader, with a people who had no written records at the time and who could be vague about exactly when they were born. Drawing on an early work of Sunni history and Hadith collection by the ninth-century scholar Ibn Sa'd, 'Aqqad explains how Aisha had already been engaged to another man before her marriage to the Prophet. Since the normal age of engagement was no younger than nine, he claims, and since historical reports agree on the passage of a few years between the marriage contract and its consummation, Aisha must have been in her early teens when her married life began.

'Aqqad cleverly skirts the authenticated Hadith found in *Sahih Bukhari* in which Aisha herself reports that she was nine at the time, addressing it only obliquely by suggesting that Aisha was fond of emphasizing her childhood spent in the nascent days of Islam and how young she was during the faith's formative days. 'Aqqad thus allows his readers to reconcile their faith in the Prophet's complete rectitude and even in Islam's collective historical corpus with what many had come to accept as the 'natural' and ideal norms for marriage.[61]

More conservative Muslim scholars objected to this rereading of the Prophet's life. They sensed the epistemological turnover behind 'Aqqad's defense of Islam. Not only did it upturn the hierarchy of authority within the Sunni scriptural canon by ignoring a clear text contained in Bukhari's august *Sahih*, it also broke with the Shariah consensus on marriage age. No member of Egypt's religious establishment showed more displeasure with 'Aqqad than Ahmad Shakir. In the spring of 1944 he penned a number of

* Several prominent Sunni ulama today, like Ali Gomaa and Taha Jabir Alwani, have concluded that Aisha was in her late teens based on arguments similar to 'Aqqad's.

popular journal articles excoriating the famous wordsmith's book on the Prophet's most active wife.

At the heart of Shakir's criticism was the question of the proper locus of truth in Muslim life. He states and restates that Aisha's recollection of her own marriage age is the lynchpin of historical and scriptural truth on this issue. Her report was categorically authenticated by the great Hadith critics of the classical era and sealed by the consensus of the medieval jurists. 'Aqqad's insinuation that she exaggerated her youth was thus tantamount to calling the Prophet's wife a liar. Against Aisha's own authenticated testimony, moreover, 'Aqqad brought nothing more than a flimsily cobbled-together argument, which Shakir contends rested on flawed premises. For example, there was no 'normal' engagement age for Arabs of the era.

As in the case of women judges, Shakir feels that the specifics of the debate mask the true contention at hand. 'Aqqad had admitted that his argument about Aisha's marriage age was intended as a rebuttal against the moral disapproval of orientalists. But in revising the received Muslim position on Aisha's marriage age, 'Aqqad was implicitly admitting that Western norms and criticisms of Islam and the Prophet were valid. Muslims, Shakir believes, are supposed to derive their laws and sensibilities from the Islamic heritage, not from Europe. He minces no words. Aisha's marriage to the Prophet at the age of nine was historically correct and the basis for the Shariah ruling that marrying an underage woman was permissible. There were to be no apologies for this.[62]

THE ULAMA, THE STATE AND SHARIAH AUTHENTICITY WITHOUT SCRIPTURE

Recourse to the scriptures of the Qur'an and Hadiths was not the only means to make normative claims in the Shariah tradition. The ancestors of Kevseri, 'Abduh and Shakir among the ulama of the great Ottoman metropolises of Istanbul, Damascus and Cairo in the late medieval period were truly, as the Hadith said, 'the inheritors of the prophets.' The book of God and the precedent of Muhammad were the wellsprings of their authority and tradition, but the scholars themselves were the living vessels from which interpretations of Islam's message issued. Masters of the illuminated page and joined through apprenticeship to chains of sages extending back to the Lawgiver, they understood themselves to be the medium of interface between God's law and the temporal realities of society.

The interpretive authority of the scholars eclipsed the evident meaning of Hadiths or Qur'anic verses. Ulama such as Nawawi and Khattabi regularly interpreted individual passages in accordance with the legal or theological principles that had come to be established within Sunni thought. Moreover, by the twelfth century, the Sunni ulama had come to see the diversity of opinion within and between their schools of law as not only an acceptable reality but also a useful one. Late medieval scholars in many regions of the Abode of Islam had treated this vast pool of opinion as a source to be drawn on, using procedural maxims such as 'Hardship requires easing' to select the ruling they felt best promoted justice for those who came to their Shariah courts (even in regions where one school reigned, like the Maliki-dominated Maghreb, experienced judges chose from within the school's varied opinions on a case).

For modernist ulama like 'Abduh and his disciples, the great toolbox of the classical tradition and the legitimizing power of the legal maxims offered an ideal means for reform. They allowed the ulama to reshape the Shariah according to new needs while remaining within its authentic vocabulary. The concept of *Maslaha* (public interest and welfare) had played a minor role in medieval Shariah lawmaking; in the absence of other evidence, it involved a scholar formulating a rule according 'to what reason deems acceptable as long as no explicit text from the Qur'an or Hadiths contradicts it.' Maliki scholars thus deemed marriage to be required for individuals with powerful libidos not because of some scriptural basis or even analogy, but based on promoting society's best interests. 'Abduh, however, made *Maslaha* a centerpiece of his legal thought. From his early days as a reformist scholar writing for Egypt's government journal in the 1880s, 'Abduh had employed the protection of the best interests of the Muslim family to argue that it was permissible Islamically to restrict men's marriage rights and prohibit polygamy.

Also crucial to 'Abduh's argument against multiple wives was the procedural maxim 'The rare case has no value in ruling.' In other words, a jurist must derive Shariah laws based on the plurality of occurrences, not rare exceptions. The Qur'an, 'Abduh argued, allowed a man to marry more than one woman provided that he could treat them all equally and justly. The men of Egypt were clearly no longer able to meet this condition, he observed, and 'even if one in a million did,' this could not be a basis for the law.[63]

Kevseri was 'Abduh's mirror image on the debate over polygamy, and he employed the same ulama toolkit to opposite ends. He rejected placing so much faith in notions of utility and interest outside the scriptural sources of the Shariah. He furiously denounced those scholars who 'had drunk from the brackish waters of the West' and now called for restricting a Muslim man's right to marry up to four wives. It was the ulama's duty to draw on the rich assortment of the Shariah's rules to best meet the needs of the day, but this meant a strict reliance on the venerable treasuries of the past. *Maslaha* could only be resorted to in the total absence of scriptural evidence on a matter, not to innovate new notions of propriety when God's law was clear. As for marriage, God knew what was in the best interests of His creation when he ordered them to 'marry what is goodly for you of women, two or three or four' (4:3) and when He guided countless generations of Muslim scholars to consensus on the permissibility of polygamy. Our flawed reason, Kevseri argued, cannot determine our true best interests in this world and the next, 'since reason often deems a harmful thing to be in our interest, unlike the holy law.'

One of 'Abduh's disciples, Mustafa Maraghi, was appointed the Rector of Al-Azhar and began pursuing legal reforms to equalize divorce rights. He did so by attempting to restrict men's Shariah right to divorce their wives unilaterally and suggested that the power to declare divorces be placed solely in the hands of family court judges. Kevseri again attacked. Maraghi argued in a public lecture that Egyptian men had proven themselves incompetent in their misuse of their ability to divorce their wives without oversight, to the point that a whole genre of jokes revolved around their idiocy. Kevseri turned the same maxim used by 'Abduh against the modernist's acolyte. Hyperbolic claims about some idiocy endemic among the population, made on the basis of jokes, was not enough to affect Muslims' understanding of God's law. For 'general legislation is not built on anomalous, rare cases.'[64]

Yet the true nature of Islam and the machinations of the West, both so vividly conceived in Kevseri's mind, were not so starkly separable to other ulama. The avuncular and beloved 'Abd al-Halim Mahmud (d. 1978) demonstrates how intermingled 'Islam,' the 'West,' authentic and inauthentic could become. A graduate of the Al-Azhar madrasa and a student of Maraghi, he also completed a doctorate in France before returning to rise through the ranks of Egypt's scholarly religious establishment. Eventually he was appointed to its supreme post, held earlier by his teacher, that of Rector of Al-Azhar.

Despite a long career working for the Egyptian state, Mahmud consistently lobbied for the removal of its civil law code and a return to Shariah law. Cutting off the hand of a thief – subject to rigorous Shariah procedure and conditions, of course – was a punishment ordained by God. He claimed that Ibn Saud, the founder of Saudi Arabia, had brought law and order to his realm by implementing such laws. Theft had virtually vanished in the kingdom, Mahmud claimed, though the gruesome punishment had been carried out no more than seven times.

Yet in his capacity as a senior Islamic jurist for the Egyptian government, Mahmud had issued a Shariah opinion supporting the minimum marriage age of sixteen for girls. He acknowledged that the Shariah tradition had never specified an exact age, requiring only that the bride be physically developed enough to engage in intercourse. This did not mean, however, that administrative laws could not be put in place to encourage or protect family integrity. In light of the responsibilities that a wife must bear both in her marriage and as the mother of children, Mahmud felt that only a mature person should marry. 'Developed societies,' he concluded, 'have set the age of marriage at sixteen, and this is appropriate.' Mahmud was a diehard advocate of a return to Shariah law, but he nonetheless affirmed the ulama's – and the state's – right to modify the law even if it restricted a choice made by the Prophet of God.[65] If rule by Shariah law was so essential in the ulama's eyes, how could Mahmud's decision be explained?

Since the days of the Umayyad dynasty in the 700s, the ulama had cultivated and endured a complicated relationship with Muslim rulers. By the mid-800s, a clear arrangement had been reached. Sunni scholars would remain silent on politics and uphold the legitimacy of any ruler who could advance even an iota of Muslim identity, and in return the rulers would cede the realm of law and social norms to the ulama, even providing them with police power to enforce Shariah court rulings.

By the twelfth century, Sunni legal scholars were also increasingly appreciative of a realm of law reserved for the ruler outside the normal boundaries of the Shariah. In fact, the ulama of the Iraqi city of Mosul in the mid-1100s had begged their new sultan, the mentor of Saladin, to implement harsh punishments to stem the wave of thefts that had overtaken the city. They could find no effective deterrent in the practices of the Shariah courts because the evidentiary standards needed to amputate a thief's hand were so strict that this punishment was unrealistic, and the discretionary punishment (*ta'zir*) that Shariah judges would usually mete out instead were limited by Hadiths to only ten lashes.[66] Even during the early caliphate, the caliphs had maintained the rights to hold their own ad hoc courts of law, called *Mazalim* (injustices) courts, to hear subjects' complaints of wrongs they had suffered. But such extra-Shariah justice was impromptu, based on the ruler's fiat, and its legitimacy untheorized. In any case, *Mazalim* courts were normally either staffed by ulama or held with ulama in attendance as advisors. There was no concept of law that held any widely recognized legitimacy outside God's Shariah. Even when a ruler intervened to deal severely with crimes like a heinous murder or threats to public security, many ulama saw this as falling under the *Hudud* crime of banditry (*hiraba*), which allowed the ruler much greater leeway in determining punishment.

With the Mongol conquests in the Middle East, the new law of a new god arrived. This was the Mongol law of Genghis Khan, whom the universal sky god of the steppes had favored with the mandate for universal empire. From the thirteenth century onward, from the Turko-Mongol sultanates of Delhi to Kevseri's Ottoman Turks themselves (who all bore the regnal title '*khan*' or 'lord' in Turko-Mongol tongues), there was now a type of dynastic law, rooted in the traditions and edicts of the sultans, that existed alongside the Shariah. These rulers did not share the ulama's vision of an all-encompassing Shariah. Now it had its own delimited sphere. When the fourteenth-century traveler Ibn Battuta was making his way across the mountains of Central Asia from the Muslim Khanate of the Golden Horde to the Delhi Sultanate, he saw how Muslim Turkic warlords adjudicated complaints in their courts of law. The sultan sat with two bodies of judges seated before him. Cases they determined to fall within the Shariah were decided by the ulama; all others went to the second group, a committee of Turkic elders. Ibn Battuta encountered a similar phenomenon in the court of the significantly fatter sultan of Mogadishu, then a huge and prosperous commercial hub. Cases were shared out between the city's chief Shariah judge and the sultan's primary viziers, the former taking only those cases that the viziers felt fell under Shariah law.[67] Sometimes the law courts held by sultans and their top officials were misused. In the Cairo of Ibn Battuta's time, the chamberlains of the Mamluk sultans were notorious for convening a court and dragging rich merchants in to extort money from them.[68]

Although in more sophisticated realms such as the Ottoman Empire this new dynastic law generally dealt with sensitive areas like sedition or crucial ones like tax collection and military administration, it also influenced Shariah adjudication. The Ottoman sultans justified their involvement in Shariah matters by phrasing their power prerogative within a Shariah framework. God had, after all, commanded Muslims to 'obey God and obey His Messenger and those in authority among you' (4:59). They thus considered it their right as rulers under God's law to select which of the ulama's opinions to make the law of the land or even to create laws where none existed. The looming presence of dynastic law in turn led the ulama to grant the Ottoman sultans more discretionary leeway in legislating for their Muslim subjects. Sometimes this was procedural. In the 1550s, for example, the Ottoman sultan issued an edict placing a statute of limitations of fifteen years on all claims brought before Shariah courts.[69] It could also be substantive. When coffee became popular in the Ottoman realm in the sixteenth century, the ulama were initially split over its permissibility (was it licit, or an intoxicant and a magnet for vice?). While a consensus emerged allowing coffee, the great eighteenth-century Damascus jurist 'Abd al-Ghani Nabulusi insisted that it was well within the ruler's right to outlaw substances like coffee or tobacco if he deemed it pursuant to God's law and in the best interests of his people (a sultan's ban on tobacco in Istanbul in the 1630s proved short-lived, however).[70]

The Ottomans and their Turkic cousins, the Mughal dynasty in India, made the most of this executive authority. Both ordered compilations of Shariah law codes aimed at reducing the unwieldy diversity of even one school of law, with its numerous parallel stances and mainstay reference books, to a manageable, regular set of rules. Committees of scholars in the centralized religious establishments of these two empires drafted law codes to routinize the official Hanafi school. As a result, this drew the ulama further under the aegis of the state. Though rewarded with secure employment in expanded judicial bureaucracies, the ulama would eventually find that their power to channel the Shariah as scholar-judges had been lost to simplified legal codes that a judge would apply by rote in court.

Shah Wali Allah's father participated in compiling the Mughal dynasty's code, the *Fatawa Alamgiri*, along with almost fifty other ulama. They spent eight years carrying out the task commissioned by the Mughal emperor Aurangzeb in 1667: to compile one book identifying the standard rulings of the Hanafi school on *all* points of law. The emperor hoped to create a new, solitary reference for empire-wide application. It would overcome the challenge that, aside from any one *madhhab* almost always listing several positions on a single point of law, there was no one book that could serve as an exhaustive and comprehensive source for all of that *madhhab*'s rulings. Even a large compendium of law might omit a legal issue that a smaller book dealt with at length.[71]

But by then dusk had fallen for the Mughals, and the *Fatawa Alamgiri* met with only limited success in their moribund state. A much more lasting legacy came from the Ottomans, who compiled several law codes between 1870 and 1917 regulating areas from trade to marriage law. A world removed from the traditionalist Mughal compilation, these were modeled in form after European codes but were based in content on Shariah rulings. Although the first law code, which addressed mostly commercial issues, was drawn almost solely from the Hanafi school of law, the 1917 Ottoman Family Law Code drew on more eclectic sources in pursuit of its reformist agenda. It set the lowest age for a girl to even engage in a marriage *contract* (let alone consummate it) at nine years old – a level of restriction unknown in any Islamic school of law.

Following a course similar to its nominal Ottoman suzerain, Egypt's legal reforms of the late nineteenth century eventually left the Shariah in place only in family law, including areas like marriage and divorce, but codified it according to what were deemed the official positions of the Hanafi school. The Egyptian parliament's 1923 decision to set the minimum marriage age for women at sixteen was justified Islamically through recourse to the right of the ruler's discretion in Shariah matters acknowledged by ulama like Nabulusi. Egypt's legislature was not denying God's sole right to dictate law or morals, supporters of the marriage law argued. Marriage contracts drawn up privately according to Shariah law were still valid in the eyes of God. The state was merely exercising its Shariah right in 'restricting judicial procedure' in its Shariah courts by only allowing women aged sixteen or older to register their marriages and only allowing complaints regarding marriages to be heard in court if they had been properly registered. Presumably only a fool would allow his daughter to marry without the documented protection of the law.[72]

In the wake of the Ottoman defeat in the First World War, the newly created state of Syria (under French control) took Egypt's code a step further. Formerly part of the Ottoman domain, Syria inherited the Ottoman Family Law Code and its minimum age of marriage (nine). Then in 1953, the Syrian government introduced a reformed personal status law that overhauled rules on marriage. Women could not marry until they were eighteen, though the judge could grant permission for those as young as thirteen if he felt the circumstances were appropriate.

Although this new law code was a clear effort at Europeanized reform, it offered Shariah arguments for its provisions. The justification for introducing a later marriage age was a tour de force in utilizing the tremendous depth and breadth of the Shariah heritage. The Syrian code cites the opinion of a little-known contemporary of Abu Hanifa in Kufa, Ibn Shubruma, who did not allow any girl to enter into a marriage contract (and thus also not to consummate her marriage) until she reached maturity. The new Syrian law code introduced even more dramatic and unprecedented age restrictions. It gave the judge the right to forestall any marriage in which the couple was 'not suited to each other in regard to their ages.' Unlike the new minimum marriage age, however, the code gave no evidence for this law from the heritage of the Shariah. It merely referred to the vague 'lack of stability in married life' and 'moral corruption' that large age gaps cause.[73]

Most Egyptian and Syrian ulama, even very conservative ones, approved of the move to codify Shariah law in the late nineteenth and early twentieth centuries. Many even accepted secular codes (i.e., those not based directly in form and content on the classical *madhhab*s) as long as they either drew on significantly or did not contradict the Shariah. At least the Shariah would remain relevant. Many ulama also assumed (wrongly, in the end) that they would find continued employment as the main pool of judges and would be in charge of future legal reforms.

Others were less optimistic, and ulama reactions to laws restricting marriage age differed greatly. The memoirs of one of the ulama who worked in Syria's family law courts in the mid-twentieth century depicts the troubled process of coming to terms with a modern, Western-shaped law while maintaining a commitment to the canon of the Qur'an and Sunna. It was acceptable, wrote Ali Tantawi, for the ruler or state to introduce administrative laws and restrictions in the best interests of the people. This was allowed under the Shariah not only within the original, narrow window of public interest (*Maslaha*) but also because God orders Muslims to obey 'those in authority among you.' He was thus content to preside over marriage after marriage in his Damascus courtroom while observing the age requirement of eighteen.

What Tantawi could not abide was to endow this law with any moral or religious weight. At best it was a sensible policy for promoting health and welfare; at worst, bureaucratic red tape to be grudgingly endured. Underage couples who married with a private Shariah contract undocumented by the state were still married in the eyes of God. Tantawi also frequently granted exceptions for brides as young as thirteen, as the new law allowed. He recalled how often he had stood next to such girls and found that they were taller than he was and were fully physically mature. 'So it's not simply a matter of age,' he wrote, 'as those who hastily and mistakenly speak without knowledge or understanding about the marriage of the Messenger of God, may God's peace and blessings be upon him, the best of mankind, the fairest and most just, about his marriage to Aisha when she was nine years old.' Had those outraged by this act actually *seen* Aisha? She could well have been like the girls who came before him in court, especially, he wrote, since girls in hot climes can become mature as young as nine or ten.[74]

It was not the passage of laws or restrictions that might benefit Muslims that Tantawi considered illegitimate. It was declaring the Prophet's deeds depraved or questioning the legitimacy of his precedent in God's eyes that the judge could not accept. In 1941, over a decade before the new age restrictions were introduced, Tantawi had angrily lectured both the outgoing and incoming Syrian ministers of justice about the profanity of the Ottoman Family Law Code (then still in effect). 'It took a position not taken by any scholar ever before,' he thundered, 'considering the marriage contract of a girl under nine to be *invalid*.' This contradicted the established Sunna of the Prophet, who had contracted his marriage with Aisha when she was six or seven. 'Was his marriage to her invalid?!' he ended in a roar of disbelief.[75]

As a young student, Tantawi had met Kevseri. He would recall later, 'After I met him, I followed after no one else.' An Egyptian Shariah scholar who had also pored through Kevseri's writings and finally caught up to him and greeted him meekly on a Cairo street later went on to head the study of Shariah at Cairo's Faculty of Law, write over a dozen books and serve on Al-Azhar's fatwa committee. Hulking and jovial, Muhammad Abu Zahra was adored by his students and widely respected in Egypt. In 1958, freshly retired from heading the faculty, Abu Zahra found himself confronted with Egypt's conflicted marriage norms while sitting to write his column for a popular Al-Azhar journal.

A member of the public had written a spirited objection to marriages with 'inappropriate' age differences and suggesting that Egypt pass a law prohibiting them, as Syria had. Abu Zahra replied as delicately as he could, explaining that the Islamic legal tradition places no restriction on marriage due to age difference. Answering a question that clearly came from a questioner more comfortable with secular state law than with the Shariah, he argued that one cannot restrict people's freedom to contract marriages without some clear proof that some harm is being caused. If the state were to ban marriages with large age gaps, people would no doubt continue to engage in them according to religious law (as Tantawi knew) but without registering them with the state. The result – undocumented marriages and spouses with no basis to claim their rights before a state court – would be a clear social harm. The Syrian law, he explained, was not only harmful but also absurd. If a young woman finds herself in need of an older man, for whatever reason, and an older man finds himself in some need of a younger woman, what is the harm in them marrying? Pious judges in Syria had not even acted on this novel law. When a judge in Damascus tried to stop such a marriage, it caused a public outcry and a campaign to repeal the law.

To hammer home his argument, Abu Zahra finally refers to the Shariah tradition itself. Prohibiting age gaps would be an 'unprecedented, heretical innovation' in Islamic law, since no ulama had ever done so and since the Prophet and his Companions had freely engaged in such marriages. The Prophet had married his daughter Fatima to Ali instead of other suitors in part because the couple were of similar age. But this was a matter of choice, not a legal restriction.[76] Amid all the controversy over Aisha, it was often forgotten that Muhammad's first wife was fifteen years his senior.

THE COURT MUST NOT BE POLITICAL – MORALITY AND TRUTH IN A RUPTURED WORLD

Kevseri's Ottoman world had perished in an agony of war, famine and social chaos that engulfed the remnants of the Empire. Between 1912 and 1923, war in the Balkans, the First World War and war with Greece left one-fifth of the population of Anatolia dead.[77] Ataturk and his comrades built the state of Turkey from the wasteland of Ottoman Anatolia and cleared the slate of Islam completely and brutally. In its place they engineered a secular, westernized nation state whose diverse citizenry would now be Turks first and foremost and who would be forced to accept a modern national destiny. By 1926 the caliphate, Shariah law courts, Sufi brotherhoods, even the Arabic call to prayer, had all been abolished. Students in the new Turkish Republic attended universities where headscarves were taboo or banned outright, and the country's elites allowed no place for religion in public (for many, even private) life.

Life and worldviews in the smaller cities and the Anatolian heartland, however, were more inert than in Istanbul and the new Turkish capital of Ankara. At rallies for short-lived Islamist parties in the 1990s and at times of particularly heightened sensitivity, such as Israel's capture of Jerusalem in 1967, crowds have called for a return to Shariah law. But such extreme calls for a return to the past have proven rare and politically dangerous (advocating for the Shariah is illegal in Turkey).[78] As more conservative and religious segments of the population regain ground from dogmatic secularists, Islamist political parties have exerted more influence. Far from calling for Shariah law, though, since the late 1990s Turkey's Islamist parties have lobbied only for reforms granting practicing Muslims parity in Turkish society. Under the rule of the popularly elected, and re-elected, AK party, since 2009 the lecture halls of Turkish universities bob with stylishly veiled heads often more eager to learn than their male classmates. The largest Islamic movement in the country, following the preacher Fethullah Gulen, boasts tightly organized branches not only throughout Turkey but also around the world devoted to interfaith dialogue, schooling and cultivating non-threatening Islamic piety. In Istanbul's Fatih Mosque small and hesitant study circles meet after the dawn prayer to hear from a few surviving links to an Ottoman Islamic past that seems newly within reach of memory.

How do you retain faith in transcendent scripture and its commandments when many in the world declare them barbaric relics? When the disapproving gazes and piques of contempt issue from colonial masters or an overbearing West, it is easy to understand why many Muslims cling to the canons of tradition and an idealized past more strongly than ever, turning vindictively on others who let them go. How do you read the Qur'an and Hadiths 'authentically' when the foreign-made backdrops enveloping your scriptural world become as real as the scripture itself? In centuries past no one denied that sometimes the month of Ramadan 'falls short,' or that the Abode of Islam must expand so that 'the word of God is supreme.' But now what to some is as self-evident as the evils of holy war or pedophilia seems to others like foreign hypocrisy or capricious imposition.

For modernizers like ʿAbduh, ʿAqqad and Sanhuri, the new world of the modern West was the mold into which Muslims' understanding of their religion had to be fit, and they repurposed the tools of the classical Shariah tradition to do this while remaining within the canonical fold. For conservatives like Kevseri, Qutb and Shakir, the West and its superior, tightly tailored and ordered power were at best baseless illusions tempting Muslims away from God and His Prophet. At worst, for Bin Laden, they were infernal foes to be bloodied in a battle recasting the primal defense of Islam. For all these men, compromising either the principles or the details of God's law in the face of the enemy was sure folly.

Those in between the conservatives and the modernists were pulled between the two poles of religious truth and worldly reality. Muhammad Ghazali was committed to defending Islam and Muslim identity, but modern realities convinced him that Islam was not properly understood, and he reread Islam's scriptures accordingly and courageously. But which master did he serve, scripture or the seductive pressures of the present? Could both be heeded faithfully, or was one the true face and the other the mask placed over it?

Some conservative ulama seem to have found a sort of peace amid the epistemological chaos. The secret of their compromise with modern realities lies in returning to the political quietism of medieval Sunni Islam and ceding even to a modern secular state the legal rights of the Muslim ruler. It was not Western pressure or the pull of a contemporary lifestyle that led to the *Jamaʿa Islamiyya*'s recantation of violence. Its leadership had spent decades in grueling prison conditions without regretting their deeds or pleading for release. Only when their studies led them to understand how they had misunderstood the classical Shariah relationship between individuals in a Muslim society and between the state and its subjects did they seek to redress their errors. Mahmud and Tantawi, two state-employed ulama in modernizing Muslim countries, never questioned the value of the pre-modern Shariah tradition. But part of its heritage was the legal prerogatives of the ruler, and as long as he did not contradict the core rulings of the Shariah, they accepted the modern legal restrictions imposed by a secularized state.

Ironically, with all the weight and meaning that a canonical community invests in its scriptures, it is the interpreters who always matter the most. Whether by reading scripture to accord with itself internally or with extratextual truths, the ulama are the indispensable medium between God's revelation and the shifting needs of its earthly believers. They adjust the interpretive heritage built on the Qur'an and Hadiths against the rough terrain of the present day until a fit is found.

But what is the source of their guidance? What is the truth by which morals and law must conform? Starting with 'Abduh, between 1900 and 2002 the successive Grand Muftis of Egypt have declared collecting interest on bank deposits and loans permissible, prohibited, permissible, prohibited and then permissible again.[79] A justice on the United States Supreme Court, ruling on whether the court should overturn its own controversial ruling on that most divisive of American issues, abortion, wrote of the 'terrible price' that this canonical body would pay if the public lost confidence in it and saw it as just another reed blowing in the political winds of the day.[80] How much greater a price would the ulama pay as representatives of a religion?

Sitting in the Fatih Mosque in the lesson given by Kevseri's last surviving student, I listen to him explain the meaning of Hadiths. They are not controversial ones. I wonder how he would interpret Hadiths on jihad or Aisha's marriage age. The warmth of the Turkish students around me staves off, just enough, Istanbul's predawn chill. They sit as their teacher reacquaints them with Islam's scriptures, unsure of what they will mean. It is so hard to know whence truth comes in a fractured age. What does one cling to and what does one tear up in a world that does not endure?

5

Muslim Martin Luthers and the Paradox of Tradition

THE PARADOX OF INTERPRETIVE CONTROL

It is a quirk of history that, while Christianity has had only one Martin Luther, Islam has had at least six in the last twenty years.[1] So far none has stuck with the tenacity of the great Saxon monk. Still, hope lives on in the press that some Muslim scholar or intellectual will emerge, break the chains of tradition and free Muslims from the Shariah and the parochial dictates of the ulama. Regular readers need wait only a few months for *The Economist* to raise the prospect of another Luther or Luther-like force on the horizon. Heralding the impact of online sources explicating Islam to Muslim populations, the magazine wrote recently: 'For the first time, lay people can easily separate religious commands from tradition by looking at holy texts and scholarship rather than relying on their local preachers.' A Sudanese Muslim blogger pre-canonized by the publication 'even thinks that digital media will be to Islam what the printing press was to Christianity – and ultimately lead to a Reformation.' 'We're still in the early stages,' explains the blogger, 'but we're going to see many eclectic versions of Islam.'[2]

The original Reformation did indeed usher many new and eclectic forms of Christianity onto the European stage. Martin Luther had called Christians to penetrate the decadent 'Tradition' of the Church's teachings, which obscured the Bible's pages, and return to the text of 'scripture alone.' It was solely scripture that conveyed Christ's message, which could be grasped by any good Christian who read the Bible when illuminated by the Holy Spirit. For a remarkably spirited sect of Anabaptist zealots who occupied the city of Münster in 1534 and declared a short-lived theocracy, scripture meant establishing God's law, taking multiple wives, executing anyone who even questioned polygamy and awaiting eagerly the return of Christ.[3] The reforms of the scholarly Socinian movement were just as drastic, if much less dramatic. It abandoned the divine nature of Jesus and the Trinity altogether. Holding that one should believe only what was explicitly contained in the text of the Bible, the Socinians found insufficient basis for both tenets (in time, the Socinians morphed into the modern Unitarian movement).[4] At the opposite end of the Protestants' magisterial spectrum, a Quaker reformer concluded that the Bible was unimportant. The light and inspirational guidance of the Holy Spirit could never be confined to its narrow pages, which were anyway 'corrupted, vitiated, altered and adulterated.' No longer subject to the cultic veneration of the Bible, early Quakers helped pioneer the uncovering of the historical limitations of its text.[5]

Luther's Church opponents had warned of the chaos that results from tearing down interpretive hierarchies. If, as Luther argued, for fourteen centuries the Church and the papacy had erred so glaringly in their interpretation of Jesus' message, how could anyone be sure that Luther was not erring as well? (Thomas More observed with sardonic ebullience that everything Luther believed happened to be in the scriptures, while everything his opponents claimed was not).[6] How could anyone know whose inspired reading of the Bible was correct? As if the guiding light of the Holy Spirit could win a debate or serve as evidence, they objected, 'as if scripture contains no equivocal or analogous passages.'[7] As Johannes Tetzel, one of Luther's earliest opponents, wrote, the people 'will never now believe the preachers and the doctors. Everyone will interpret Scripture as takes his fancy. And all sacred Christendom must come into great spiritual danger when each individual believes what pleases him most.'[8] The *Traditio*, that accumulated body of biblical interpretation and teachings articulated over centuries by the Church, was just as much a brake on Christians' excesses as it might be a barrier to their faith.

Tradition is the scholarly structure built on scripture through interpretation, both systematizing its teachings and controlling its authority, deciding its meaning and making it plain while limiting those who can access scripture directly. Tradition is constructed of parchment, countless fascicules and seas of ink. It is built by generations of devout scholars, who shape it to fit or fight the world of their day, their learned wraiths incorporated into its edifice.

Luther's Catholic opponents were not the first to offer such warnings. Medieval rabbis had long before concluded that sincerity, inspiration and zeal were no guarantors of right guidance. Explaining the grave error of the Karaite Jews, a Babylonian sect who had called for the rejection of the Oral Torah tradition by which rabbis explained the written books of Moses, the Andalusian rabbi Judah HaLevi noted that sincerity of intention is useless. 'For that which appears plain in the Torah is yet obscure, and much more so are the obscure passages.'[9]

And yet tradition is rarely a match for the charisma of scripture. Even centuries after the warnings of figures as distinguished as Thomas More and many bloody wars of religion, Luther's call still rings with understandable allure. What believer does not want to return to the root of faith, to read revelation from the pages of prophets and stand in that place where the divine voice first pierced the fog of our earthly world? Who would want to have their contact with the divine mediated by clergy, voluminous books or the encrusted build-up of centuries of convention?

Such appeal has always masked great danger. It is difficult to know whether to heed the pure tone of the revealed voice, since it has often proved to be the sirens' call. Whenever the spirit of God has appeared in the world, or the books of God have been opened by believers, the custodians of religion have found both voice and letter dangerous and hard to control.

Concerning the written word, its hazards were known as far back as Plato. Writing may seem a 'sure receipt for memory and wisdom,' warned the Athenian, but it is only a 'shadow' of real knowledge. Written knowledge is passive before the reader and unable to defend itself against misunderstanding. People read into books only what they already believe, and books cannot correct them. Only living teachers can. For the disciple seeking knowledge, it is the master who passes on true, sound wisdom, not the book.[10] Left to their own devices, the uninitiated may choose their texts poorly. When dealing with claims of prophetic revelation, only the master knows the difference between the written words of God and the forgeries of Satan.

Of course, democrats do not feel anxiety over the dangers of the written word. Its perils only concern those who believe strongly that knowledge and wisdom are matters of correct understanding. They must be preserved against misreading and misuse. This is the anxiety of a clerical elite or an interpretive guardian class, who worry that those who stumble unassisted onto written tomes cannot grasp what truly lies within, that they cannot see what they are supposed to see. More cynically, they might not see what they *have to* see for words inscribed ages earlier to remain true in the demanding light of changing times. The Jews of antiquity clung to the revealed wisdom in the five books of the Torah, but the Pharisees of first-century Palestine believed that the laws of Moses could only be understood properly when explained by the Pharisees' living teachings. How else could Jews know that the books, which make no explicit mention of the rewards of the Afterlife, did in fact contain encoded within their pages that germane and appealing teaching of hope for a blissful life after death?

Books are meant to linger. The voice is not. Yet too often prophecy overstays its welcome and dies hard. The guardian class of living teachers who inherit the messages of the prophets of yesteryear may find themselves challenged by upstarts claiming their own stirrings and divine inspiration. The rabbis of first-century Palestine found the worship of the God of Abraham redefined by an exceptional young rabbi who preached love of God before all else, the coming Kingdom of God and the Holy Spirit until his mission was brought to an abrupt end. The teachings passed on from those who heard the sermons of Jesus cited the same Jewish scriptures as the Pharisees. Instead of reading them through the Oral Torah, however, the Christians read the Old Testament scriptures through the focused lens of God sending His only son to suffer and die to redeem humankind's sins. The living teachings of early Christians claimed to unlock the true meanings of Isaiah's prophecy that 'A virgin shall conceive and bear a son' (Isaiah 7:14) and the Psalmist's song of the tormentors who would cast lots for the clothing, pierce the hands and feet of one who would 'lie down, sleep and rise up again...' (Psalms 22:16–18; 3:5).[11] As Paul and the Apostles preached the newly revealed meaning of the Old Testament, Christians too understood how essential the living words of teachers were for protecting scripture from misreading. In his *The Sayings of the Lord Explained*, the early Church Father Papias recorded Christ's teachings from the mouths of those elders who had met the Apostles themselves. 'I did not imagine that things out of books would help me as much as the utterances of a living and abiding voice,' he wrote.[12]

Dueling over the true understanding of the Old Testament scriptures, both Jews and Christians realized that their readings had to be cemented in written form if they were to triumph or even survive.[13] As the second century drew to a close, the rabbi Judah the Patriarch and others set down the oral explanation of the Torah in the *Mishna*, while Mark, Luke, Papias and a myriad other followers of Christ confined to written pages their manifold and varied versions of his life and teachings.

But divine inspiration did not cease, and Church Fathers like Papias heard of wandering prophets who drew crowds from Europe to Asia Minor, claiming to be the awaited Paraclete mentioned in John's Gospel, bringing the final apocalyptic chapter of Jesus' message.[14] Others, such as the Christian Gnostics, preached from their own gospel works or claimed to have secret oral teachings that alone contained the keys to salvation. What emerged from this struggle as mainstream Christianity was built on foundations that subdued and controlled both the written word and lived teaching, binding the two together. Irenaeus, a Church Father and bishop in second-century France, wrote that, just as there were only four directions on the compass, there could be no more or less than four Gospels. Each contained the true teachings of Christ. But these teachings could only be accessed and explained by those who read the Gospels according to the 'Rule of Faith,' not twisting away from the evident meaning of their texts unless the inherited teachings of God's true Church instructed it.

Irenaeus and others who would be looked back on as heroes of orthodox Christianity stressed that God's Church preserved Christ's teachings unified and infallible. It was made up of the body of the believers, represented by the bishops, whose authority stretched back in succession to the Apostles.[15] By the seventh century, in Western Europe it was the Bishop of Rome who stood out among them. Over the centuries the power to define Christ's teachings would shift from Church councils to the Pope, but always it was this Catholic Church that determined which books made up the Bible and how they should be understood. This was the tradition of the Church that controlled and perpetuated Christian teachings.

Interpretive traditions are thus presented with a dilemma. Whether in Judaism, Christianity or Islam, writing is essential for preserving inspired wisdom. Even Chinese Zen Buddhism, which claimed to preserve the original teachings of the Buddha so faithfully that it had no need to 'posit words,' had found by the ninth century that setting down this tradition in profuse written form was necessary.[16] Inspired wisdom, however, can never be captured entirely by the written word, so it can never be left to the unlearned to read in the absence of its living inheritors. So revelation is set down in writing by scribes and explicated by prophets. In time, the teachings of the prophets are preserved in writing by scholars, but those books must still be controlled by generations of scholars to come. Books cannot be allowed to be read alone. Even after the *Mishna* had been written down, Rabbi Yohanan bin Nappaha (d. 279) and other rabbis in Galilee still claimed that the tradition of Moses could only be known and passed on orally.[17]

The tradition built to explain revelation becomes the ether in which the cleric thrives, passing on to him the authority of the ancients and regimenting him within the guild of orthodoxy at the same time. Learning the tradition at the feet of scholars creates interpretive authority and preserves interpretive control. Students of St. Anselm were outraged when the overconfident cleric Peter Abelard dared to hold classes explicating books of the Bible using his own knowledge and not by following the interpretations of the elders. Medieval rabbis and bishops sat before their students and performed orally the knowledge they had learned from their masters and memorized from books, maintaining and passing on what a cinematized 1970s Harvard law student sneaking a glance at his professor's own student notes still recognized as 'the unbroken chain... the ageless passing of wisdom' (*The Paper Chase*, 1973).

In Islam, the edifice built by the ulama was equally invested in the living word of knowledge, certain of its indispensability and wary of the dangers of reading unassisted. Like the Oral Torah and Christ's teachings, early Muslim scholars believed that the prophetic wisdom needed to unlock the Qur'an's written message should not be consigned to the written word. Even the Qur'an was only promulgated in written form after worries emerged that too many of the Companions who had memorized it by heart had died. In part, fear of the written word was practical. The Arabic script in the first decades of Islam was still primitive and incomplete, making texts perilous ground for misreading and misunderstanding if not elucidated by a teacher. Written in this ambiguous script, the scrolls and codices in which early scholars like Hasan Basri or Zuhri recorded Hadiths were meant only as skeletal reminders to jog the memory, which alone was the true abode of living, sacred knowledge. '*'Ilm* is not taken from someone who relies on written pages,' was a common early mantra.[18] Some ulama of the eighth century were still instructing their children to burn their books upon their death so that no one would misconstrue notes illegible to the unguided heart.

Parallel to this practical concern was the same valuation of the 'ageless passing of wisdom.' Even in the eleventh century, long after voluminous Hadith compilations had become the norm and a mainstay of ulama life, leading Sunni scholars still wrote manifestos against reliance on the written word. Even today, when most Hadith books are available online, Muslim scholars stress that *'ilm* is a living link of knowledge acquired before a master. One warned in a poem:

> Indeed seeking knowledge without a teacher is like trying to light a lamp when one has no oil.[19]

Ulama opponents of the modern Salafi movement have accused it of advocating autodidactism and encouraging ordinary Muslims to pore over the Qur'an and Hadiths directly. This impetus has certainly come to the surface in the Salafi movement, but even Salafi scholars prize *talaqqi* (the transmission of living knowledge through reading books with a shaykh). Though some notable Salafi scholars, like the late Saudi ascetic Ibn 'Uthaymin, recommend studying at the hands of shaykhs more as a method of accelerating learning than guaranteeing its rectitude, others like the influential Saudi Salman 'Awda continue to emphasize how the ineffable passing of wisdom and authority between master and disciple not only ensures an accurate understanding of Islamic law and theology, which is impossible to achieve with books alone, but also grants access to the blessing (*baraka*) and pious example of the senior ulama.[20]

As Luther had so stridently objected, however, tradition does not just preserve. The carriers of tradition are also its subtle sculptors, shaping it to fit the needs of changing times and inevitably gathering up into its folds the tacit assumptions of community and culture. As bearers of tradition, licensed by the rite of receiving it, rabbis, ulama and modern common-law justices alike are the living face of a canonical heritage, allowing it to survive and maintaining its adherents' faith in its claim to timeless truth by adjusting it just enough to address the present without breaking the link with the past.

In time, as successive generations of the guardian interpreters build upon their predecessors' work, their assumptions of value and culture become built into the tradition that defines their religion – and into the religion itself. Tradition is thus an essential but double-edged sword. As Catholics like More and Tetzel argued, it was necessary to control religious interpretation and prevent chaos and lunacy from engulfing the Christian world. As Luther countered, tradition elevated flawed human interpretations to the level of divine command when Christianity was supposedly built on Jesus' original words. Since the death of Muhammad, Islam has wrestled with the same paradox. The tradition of Islamic legal and theological interpretation is essential for the proper understanding of God's word, but it is also a prism in which divine inspiration and human fallibility mix all too easily.

THE RULE OF INTERPRETATION IN THE CONFLICT BETWEEN SUNNI AND SHIITE ISLAM

Although he had once relished the Ottoman scourge that God sent against the Antichrist Papacy, Luther despised Islam as much as any bishop he condemned. If the Saxon monk had ever managed a visit to Istanbul or Damascus he would have met with a mixed reaction among his Muslim counterparts. His rejection of highly derivative papal canon law, the scholastic theology of Aquinas (with its adoption of pagan Greek logic) and his conviction that Church tradition had departed from the original scripture of the Bible would have endeared him to proto-Salafi contemporaries like the Ottoman iconoclast Shaykh Mehmet Birgili or the followers of Ibn Taymiyya. But the corollary that tradition should be jettisoned and that each believer should return to the original scriptures of the Old and New Testaments would have provoked roars of laughter.

Until the collision with the modern West, no Muslim scholar of any consequence ever advocated that the Qur'an be read alone. They might dispute on all else, but the varied sects of Islam all agreed that Muslims should under no circumstances read the Qur'an in a vacuum. Islam's sects shared two foundational principles: that the Sunna of the Prophet rules over and interprets the Qur'an, and that the Prophet's interpretive authority had been passed on to those authorities who were to lead the community after his death. Where sects diverged was over how and by whom this Sunna was known and who had the authority to speak in the Prophet's name. For Sunnis it was transmitted and known by the Muslim community as a whole, borne via the twin routes of the Hadiths, which recorded the Prophet's words, and the inherited teachings of the early Muslim generations, spoken for by the community's often cacophonous body of ulama. Taken together, this was the Sunni tradition, in which the authority of God and His Prophet could coalesce from the riot of stentorian voices and express itself fully in instances of consensus (*ijma'*). Shiites believed that the Prophet's teachings were inherited by particular lines of his descendants. The esoteric knowledge of the religion and the ability to interpret infallibly the Qur'an's layers of hidden meaning passed from father to designated son like bloodlines. Those descendants designated in succession as Imams spoke with the authority of the Prophet. Further sectarian splintering into Imami (Twelver) and Ismaili (Sevener) schools followed disagreements over which line transmitted this hidden *'ilm*.

Sunni scholars read the Qur'an in the light of their tradition of sacred knowledge. Like Irenaeus and his 'Rule of Faith,' they broke with the evident meanings of the Qur'an or the secondary scripture of the Hadiths (and also ignored the opinions of early scholars) whenever a literal reading seemed to contradict Islam's coherent message as they understood it. The thirteenth-century Sufi master of Baghdad, Suhrawardi, explained this process of interpretation (*Ta'wil*) as a scholar shifting the literal reading of the text 'to another potential meaning that he sees as according with the Book of God and the Sunna.' *Ta'wil* was thus necessarily subjective, admits Suhrawardi, potentially differing from scholar to scholar.[21]

In order to constrain and minimalize an activity that was inherently dangerous – since it undeniably involved muddying the waters of revelation with human judgment – medieval Sunni scholars developed 'The Rule of *Ta'wil*.' It stated that the evident meaning of a scriptural passage could not be abandoned without convincing evidence that this was necessary. As no less than the founder of the Ash'ari school of theology himself explained, Muslims should read scripture 'according to its evident, external meaning (*zahir*), except if some proof is established that it should be read according to a meaning other than its evident one.'[22]

The Sunni trepidation over arbitrary departures from the evident meaning of the Quran and Hadiths was truly born of and exacerbated by a very real threat. Just as Irenaeus championed his 'Rule of Faith' to exclude the heretical interpretations of roving Gnostics riffing on John's Gospel, Sunnis stressed the centrality of literal readings to counter the attractive esoteric interpretations offered by their Shiite competitors.

Especially as it emerged in the second half of the ninth century, Shiism was the bête noire of Sunni ulama. Dispersed throughout the Middle East but especially numerous in Iraq and northern Iran, scattered communities of Muslims continued to believe that the right to lead the Muslims and articulate the true teachings of Islam lay with the Prophet's family, specifically with his descendants through his daughter Fatima and his son-in-law, the fourth caliph, Ali. By the mid-800s, the most revered surviving line of descent from this couple, the succession of Shiite Imams, lived as prisoners in the Abbasid court and tended to die young. With the death of the eleventh representative descendant in this line in 874, the Shiite communities faced a crisis. He had no heir.

One segment of the Shiite community, however, believed that the eleventh Imam had, in fact, produced a son. Hidden away from the Abbasid rulers in the city of Samarra north of Baghdad, the infant twelfth Imam withdrew from the sick and unjust world and went into hiding. Moving unbeknown among the people, performing Hajj annually as he matured, he communicated with his followers through a select series of 'ambassadors.' In 941, the dying last ambassador announced that the 'Hidden Imam' was withdrawing from the world altogether. He would leave his community and communicate no more, trusting his followers to the Shiite ulama. Eventually the Hidden Imam would return to 'fill the world with justice as it was full of injustice.' He was thus also the 'Awaited Imam' and the promised messianic figure of the Mahdi. The group that continues to await him has grown to be the largest Shiite sect, known as Imami or Ithna'ashari (Twelver) Shiites, and forms the majority of the populations of Iraq and Iran, as well as a plurality in Lebanon.

Imami Shiism is based on the belief that Ali, as the first Imam, and the eleven Imams who followed him inherited the Prophet's infallible understanding of the message that God revealed in the Qur'an. Although they did not claim to receive revelation in the same way as the Prophet did, the Imams were angelically guided and each was bequeathed a mystical capacity to access the infinite wisdom of the Qur'an. Imami law and dogma was built on the Qur'an, as explicated by the Imams, on the Hadiths of the Prophet as transmitted by the Imams and on the Hadiths of the Imams themselves (standing in the place of the Prophet, their rulings and teachings are just as authoritative as Muhammad's own).

The principal objection raised by Sunnis to Imami Shiite claims, however, was that a reading of the Qur'an does not seem to support any of them. The holy book never mentions Ali, Fatima, the twelve Imams or even any essential leadership role for the Prophet's descendants. Imami Shiites have answered this objection by asserting that, if the Qur'an is read properly, it

FIGURE 1
Part of the walls of the Mughal Empire's massive Red Fort in Delhi (2012).

FIGURE 2
The Al-Azhar Mosque at sunset. Cairo (2007).

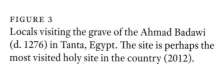

FIGURE 3
Locals visiting the grave of the Ahmad Badawi (d. 1276) in Tanta, Egypt. The site is perhaps the most visited holy site in the country (2012).

FIGURE 4
Crowds gather at the shrine of the famous Sufi Nizam Al-Din Awliya (d. 1325) in Delhi on the Prophet's birthday (2012).

FIGURE 5
Tawfiq Sidqi (photo provided by Umar Ryad).

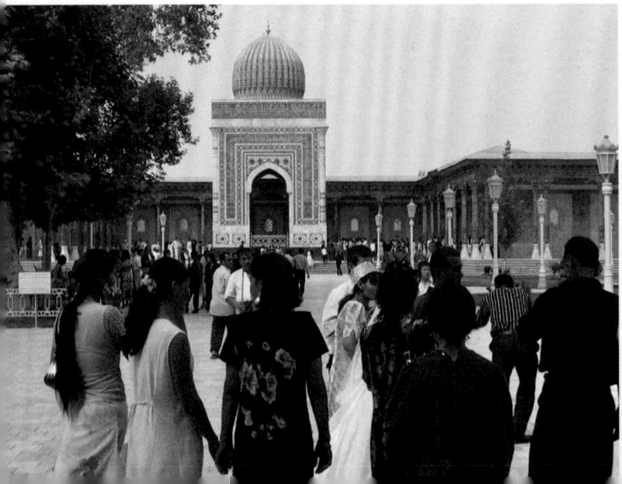

FIGURE 6
Bukhari's tomb outside of Samarqand, Uzbekistan. The site's baraka (blessing) has made a visit de rigeur for newlyweds (2006).

FIGURE 7
Muhammad Zahid Kevseri (d. 1952)

FIGURE 8
A man reads the Quran near the pulpit of the Fatih Mosque in Istanbul (2013).

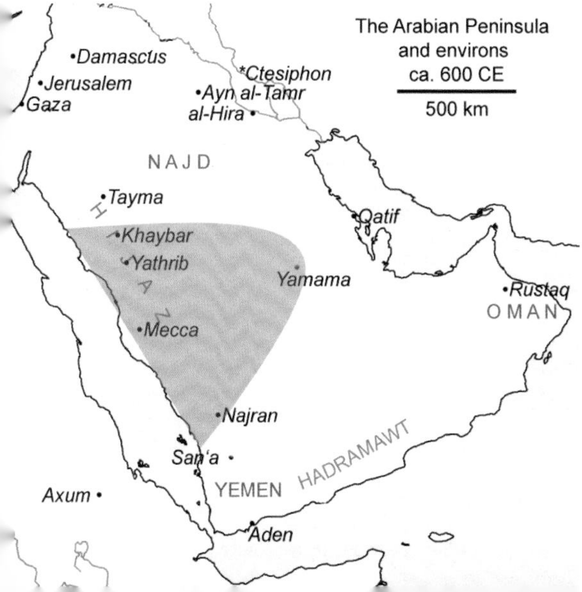

FIGURE 9
The shaded area approximates what early Muslim scholars understood by 'The Peninsula of the Arabs (Jazirat al-'Arab)'. Based on a map by Fred M. Donner.

الإسلام والفكر الإسلامى.. هل هما سواء؟!

د. ناجح إبراهيم

n.ibrahem@youm7.com

فالفكر الإنسانى لا قدسية له.. أما القدسية فهى للكتاب والسنة

معصوم أو حجة على أحد.. ولم يقل أحد من علماء الإسلام قديمًا أو حديثًا إن أقوال المجتهدين غير معصومة.. رغم أن الأصولى والمجتهد أكثر علمًا بالشريعة من المفكر.

فالفكر الإنسانى لا قدسية له.. أما القدسية فهى للكتاب والسنة.. وأحكام الإسلام القطعية المجمع عليها منهما، والخطأ فى الفكر الإسلامى ينتج عادة عن ثلاثة أسباب:

1 - الخطأ فى قراءة وفهم النص الشرعى من الكتاب والسنة.

2 - الخطأ فى قراءة الواقع الذى سيطبق عليه هذا النص الشرعى.

3 - الخطأ فى إنزال النص الشرعى على الواقع.. وهذا ما يسميه الأصوليون «تحقيق المناط».

ومن أهم أمثلة الخطأ فى تحقيق المناط هو ظن بعض السلفيين أن التكييف الفقهى لثورة 25 يناير هو خروج على الحاكم.. بينما تحقيق المناط الصحيح لها يدل على أنها تندرج تحت باب النهى عن المنكر وقولة الحق عند الحاكم الظالم ورغم أن الفكر الإسلامى الحديث فى القرن العشرين أثرى الحياة الفكرية عمومًا.. إلا أنه فى المقابل وقع فى أخطاء كثيرة نتج معظمها من الخطأ فى تحقيق المناط أو قراءة الواقع قراءة صحيحة.

FIGURE 10
A summer 2011 newspaper op-ed by Dr. Nageh Ebrahim, a leader of Egypt's Jama'a Islamiyya and a chief author of its Series for Correcting Understandings. The piece emphasizes the difference between Islam and humans' inevitably flawed interpretations of it.

FIGURE 11
A young Muhammad Ghazali (d. 1996) wearing the robes and fez turban of Al-Azhar. Photo provided by his family.

FIGURE 12
An older Ghazali leading prayer. Photo provided by his family.

FIGURE 13
Shaykh Ali Gomaa as Egypt's Grand Mufti (circa 2005). Photo provided by Tarek Elgawhary.

FIGURE 14
The Salafi Shaykh Yasir Burhami on the cover of Egypt's long running, secular leaning weekly magazine Rose Al-Yousef from Jan. 21, 2011. Published just days before the protests that toppled Mubarak began, the cover story describes Burhami as 'The most dangerous man for Egypt.'

FIGURE 15
Students and teachers in the courtyard of the Jenderami Pondok outside of Kuala Lumpur, Malaysia (2009).

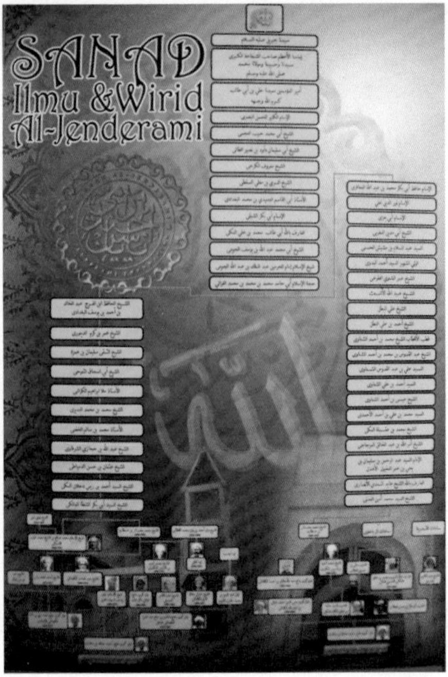

FIGURE 16
The display of the Jenderami school's Isnad for Islamic law and Sufi Learning, starting at the top with God and the Prophet and ending with the school's founders. There is an undisclosed break in the chain between the eleventh and twelfth boxes down from the top in the middle column (2009).

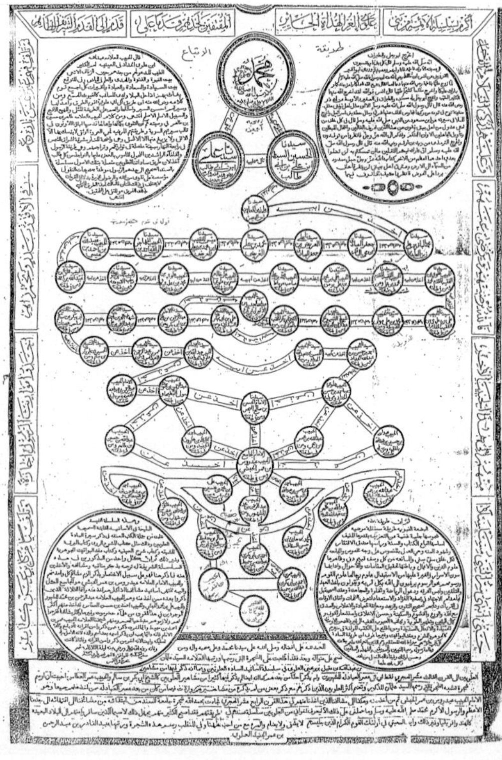

FIGURE 17
A certificate showing the chain of sacred knowledge for the Ba'alawi Sufis. Beginning with Muhammad at the top, it ends with Habib Hamid bin Sumayt and then the author at the bottom.

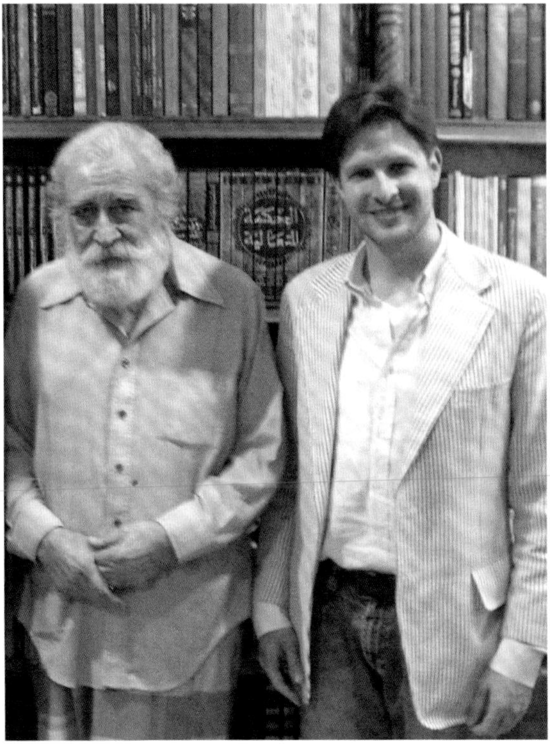

FIGURE 18
Sayyid Naqib Al-Attas and the author in Kuala Lumpur (2009).

FIGURE 19
The stunning city of Hajrayn in the Hadramawt Valley of Yemen (2007).

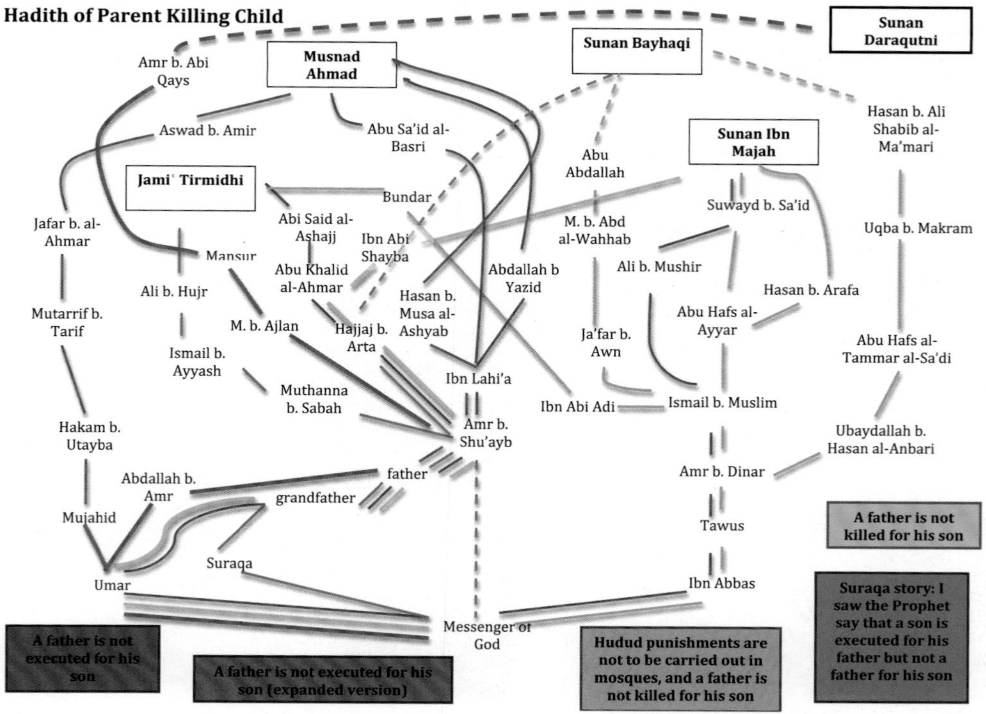

FIGURE 20

A map of the principal narrations/versions of the Hadith of a Parent Killing a Child. Hadith compilations are boxed in bold; dashed lines represent broken or abbreviated chains of transmission.

is nothing less than a complete discourse on the virtue and station of the Prophet's family and the duty to obey the Imams. When the Qur'an refers to the 'truthful ones' whom Muslims should seek out as companions (9:119), the holy book is referring to the Imams. They are 'Those in authority among you,' whom the Qur'an orders Muslims to follow along with God and His Messenger (4:59). 'Those firmly established in knowledge,' who know the true meaning of the Qur'an's ambiguous verses, are none other than the Imams according to the Shiite reading (3:7).[23]

What Imami Shiites claim as the correct, esoteric reading of the Qur'an is known through the recorded teachings attributed to the Imams. These teachings and the Shiite body of prophetic Hadiths, which overlaps in part with Sunni Hadith collections but which contains a whole swath of separate material, provide the key to this totally alternative reading of the Qur'an. The Hadiths of the Imams explain that the holy book's poetic verses pronouncing 'By the fig tree and the olive, and by Mount Sinai, and by this inviolable land! Verily We have created man in the best of forms' (95:1–4) should be understood as meaning, 'By the Prophet, and Ali, and Hasan and Husayn (Ali's sons, the second and third Imams), and by the Imams, they were created in the best of forms...' Verses that at first glance speak of God ordaining that the Tribes of Israel would 'twice cause great strife in the land,' with God sending against them 'strong and powerful servants of Ours' (17:4–5) really refer to the two original failures of Sunni Islam. First, the majority of the Prophet's Companions failed to recognize Ali's true right to succeed Muhammad. Second, the Companions and later Sunnis denied the Imams' true standing as caliphs. The powerful servants of God sent against these foes refer to Ali and his defeat of Aisha and her forces during the First Civil War.[24]

As Ayatollah Khomeini noted, Sunnism and Imami Shiism have much more in common than not.[25] Aside from the paramount place of the Imams, the details of Imami Shiite law and theology do not differ tremendously from the internally heterogeneous system of their Sunni counterparts. Imami Shiites combine their daily prayers and perform them three times a day instead of five. They forbid eating most shellfish (not shrimp) and grant daughters a greater share of inheritance at the expense of non-immediate male relatives. But most Sunni schools also allow combining prayers when traveling, and Hanafis also forbid shellfish. Unlike Sunnism, Imami Shiism adopted the Mutazilite school of rational theology. But the teachings of the Imams confirmed many of the tenets that the Mutazila had rejected because they were not mentioned in the Qur'an and that had earlier formed such a divide between them and Sunnis, such as belief in the Punishment of the Grave and in the Mahdi. Moreover, both Sunni and Imami Shiite ulama fall along an interpretive spectrum between those advocating more reliance on the Qur'an, guiding legal principles and analogy as opposed to those who favor a conservative adherence to the texts of the Hadiths. The late seventeenth and eighteenth centuries saw a Hadith-based revival movement among the Shiite scholars of southern Iraq and Bahrain similar to the contemporaneous revival movements sweeping the Sunni world. Most importantly, like Sunni Islam, Imami Shiism was politically quietist, devoting its attention primarily to developing a comprehensive system of law and belief from the Qur'an and Sunna as conceived by the Imami Shiite ulama.

Another Shiite movement emerging alongside the Imamis in the 870s was not so docile. At its most extreme, it represented a complete break from the Muslim mainstream. Imami Shiites believed that the twelfth Imam had vanished into supernatural hiding, to return at the end of time as the Mahdi, the 'Rightly Guided' one who would bring God's justice to the whole earth. But he was not the only messianic contender. In this same decade, a mysterious figure in Syria began propagating the message that he was the grandson of the fifth Imam. Thought to have died, this grandson had actually vanished from the world but had now returned as the Imam-cum-Mahdi to usher in an apocalyptic end time. This mysterious puppetmaster sent missionaries far and wide, and soon armed bodies of his followers gathered and built camps and redoubts on the plains of southern Iraq, on the Arab Gulf coast, in Yemen, northern Iran and in modern-day Tunisia. Soon the troops of this Fatimid movement, as it became known due to the Mahdi's claimed descent from Fatima, began ravaging the peasant communities of Iraq and Syria, even laying siege to Damascus in 902. When adversity forced the self-proclaimed Mahdi to move from Syria to North Africa, the Fatimid caliphate, the 'State of Truth,' was proclaimed in 910. Within decades the Fatimids would conquer Egypt and Syria, build the great capital metropolis of Cairo and even briefly occupy Baghdad. The Fatimid armies threatened the Abbasid caliphate's borders, its extensive network of recruiters and propagandists penetrated the great Sunni strongholds of Iraq and coreligionists installed in the impregnable mountain fortresses of Syria and northern Iran sent their supposedly hashish-crazed *Hashishiyin* ('Assassins,' coining the term) to cut down Sunni and Crusader

Christian princes alike. The Fatimids and their sect of Shiism, known as Ismaili Shiism, were the most dominant and feared force in the Middle East until Saladin put an end to the Fatimid state in 1171.

Like the Imamis, the Ismaili Shiism of the Fatimids was based on an 'inner' (*batini*) reading of the Qur'an. Ismaili teachings, however, grew out of the legacy of Plotinus and Gnostic notions of the inherent corruption of the material world, a world that had been born out of sin and rebellion against God. Human souls were imprisoned in this matter and yearn for release into the divine realm. They can achieve this redemption only after being granted the secret, saving knowledge brought by prophets. Ismaili teachings held that history has seen a series of six of these prophets, each one a 'Speaker' bringing a new law: Adam, Noah, Abraham, Moses, Jesus and Muhammad. At the side of each 'Speaker' came an 'Inheritor.' These were more laconic figures like Aaron, Peter and, in Muhammad's case, Ali. While the shape and details of each prophet's law created distinct religions that differed outwardly, the 'Inheritors' carried the secret, true and unified teaching. It revealed to the elect initiates that behind all these exoteric religions was the one 'Religion of Truth.' Each 'Speaker' is followed by seven Imams, the last of whom begins the cycle again. Then, in this last cycle of Muhammad and Ali, the seventh Imam will be the messianic Mahdi who inaugurates the glorious and open rule of the Religion of Truth. When he comes, all religious laws, the Shariah included, will be swept aside and humankind will live by the pure Edenic religion of Adam once again. The Ismailis preached that this was all contained in the Qur'anic scripture and the true teachings of Muhammad, but only the Fatimid Imam's teachings could decode this hidden message.[26]

The Fatimid Imam was the living prophetic presence on earth. Ismaili scholars argued with Sunni delegations that the Qur'anic verse that declared Muhammad to be 'the Messenger of God and the Seal of the Prophets' (33:40) actually referred to two separate individuals. Muhammad was the Messenger of God, but it was the Fatimid Imam who was the 'Seal,' ending prophecy and ushering in the end of days. Indeed, the Imam's appearance could have signaled the immediate end of the Shariah, but the Fatimid state continued to rule by Shariah law like all Muslim states. Although modern Ismaili followers of the Agha Khan practice a religion markedly different from other Muslims, the original Ismaili law school was based on much of the same Hadiths recorded from the early Shiite Imams and found in Imami law, and Imami and medieval Ismaili law overlapped to a great extent. The Fatimid state instituted the Shiite version of the call to prayer (which adds the phrase 'Ali is the inheritor from God'), banned the optional nightly communal prayers held at mosques during Ramadan (a custom introduced by Umar, a vile figure for Shiites) and (oddly, like Salafis) banned the visitation of saints' graves. They generally left the Sunni population of North Africa unmolested, with the most contentious issue of practice being the Ismaili custom of fasting Ramadan for thirty days without variation, while Sunnis might fast only twenty-nine days if the new moon was sighted early.[27]

But a splinter group of Ismailis in southern Iraq, the east coast of Arabia and even in Yemen, who had broken away from the Fatimid claimant to the imamship, took a radically different approach to the Shariah. Identifying their own local, true, returned Imam, whom they considered to be God incarnate, they declared the age of religious law terminated. Between 912 and 951, these communities of Qarmatians, as they were known, banned Islam's daily prayers, destroyed mosques in eastern Arabia, ate pork and drank wine openly in daylight during Ramadan. They repeatedly robbed and slaughtered caravans of pilgrims headed to Hajj and, in 930, they committed the unprecedented abomination of sacking the holy sanctuary of Mecca as pilgrims performed their Hajj, massacring countless innocents. The Qarmatian leader Abu Tahir wrenched the sacred Black Stone from the Kaaba and returned with it to eastern Arabia. There he broke it in half and installed it as steps to his latrine, while his followers contented themselves with wiping their anuses with pages ripped from copies of the Qur'an (the stone's return was negotiated twenty-two years later).[28]

Several prominent Sunni ulama perished in the Qarmatian attack on Mecca, and one scholar who survived recalled that even amid the carnage questions of misinterpreting scripture rose to the fore. As the Qarmatian warriors slaughtered pilgrims in the sanctuary around the Kaaba, the scholar described how the Qarmatian leader mocked the Qur'anic verse in which God describes Mecca as the first sanctuary appointed for humankind and that 'whoever enters it is safe' (3:96). 'What sort of safety is this!' the Qarmatian scoffed. He had not understood, the Sunni scholar realized, that the verse was not a description but rather a prescription. It was a command to assure the safety of anyone who entered the sanctuary.[29]

These monstrous deeds (even the Fatimids in Egypt renounced the Qarmatian Ismailis), the military success of the Fatimid state and the threat of the Ismaili Assassins sent the Sunni political and scholarly elite into paroxysms of fear. The allure of the Ismaili message, which offered initiation to the privileged and elite 'Friends of God' who would learn the true, hidden meaning behind the Qur'an, was deeply threatening to the Sunni ulama. It offered a totally alternative interpretive path and presented the Imam as an infallible and living source of certainty as opposed to the contentious disunity of Sunni law and dogma, a tradition that the Fatimid Imams accused of turning the Qur'an 'into lies.'[30] It has been plausibly argued that the institutionalization of Sunnism in the eleventh century was a defensive reaction to the multilevel Fatimid threat.[31]

Imami Shiism was equally threatened by its close relative. Fervently denying any link to the Ismailis, throughout the eleventh and twelfth centuries Imami scholars accused them of using *Ta'wil* perversely. The Ismailis assigned supposedly hidden meanings to Qur'anic verses that had no relation to their original intentions, argued Imamis, for 'corrupt purposes, to delude the people and to call to their false school of thought.'[32] Imami Shiism read esoteric meanings behind the surface of the Qur'an (as Sunni Sufis did as well), but this hidden wisdom only added to the outward letter of the revelation. It could never invalidate or contradict it. For Imamis, there might be numerous levels of meaning behind the verse declaring Muhammad 'the Messenger of God and the Seal of the Prophets,' accessible only to the Imams. But they would not dare question its fundamental, outer teaching: that prophecy was sealed and ended with Muhammad. Responding to and rebutting Ismaili arguments thus became a chief priority of Sunni and Imami Shiite scholars alike. In 1011, in fact, the Sunni caliph in Baghdad and the Iranian Shiite military junta that was exercising effective control over Iraq and Iran issued a rare joint manifesto. It was a condemnation of the Fatimid state and Ismailism.

TRADITION AS GOVERNOR, SCRIPTURE AS SUBJECT

Whenever he could, St. Augustine answered questions with scripture. On several occasions, however, the peerless Church Father was asked about the validity of Christian practices that had no basis in the Bible. Augustine responded that, if the practice was widespread enough, it needed no such justification. 'In those things concerning which the divine Scriptures have laid down no definite rule, the custom of the people of God, or the practices instituted by their fathers, are to be held as the law of the Church.'[33]

Beyond carrying the weight of God's law, the 'custom of the people of God' could sometimes bestow on otherwise earthly writings the status of words inspired by God. A century before Augustine, the Bishop of Caesarea in Palestine had taken up the relation of custom and scripture. Like his teacher Origen, Eusebius was a thorough collector and scholar of texts. His *History of the Church* provides one of the earliest listings of which writings Christians (or at least those who shared Eusebius' near-orthodox Christology) considered canonical. Eusebius describes his criteria for distinguishing true Gospel writings from false. Books that embodied the authentic teachings of the Apostles could be traced back to their putative authors, reflected their particular writing styles and conformed to the true teachings of the Church. Spurious books forged by some malfeasant or mistakenly attributed to an Apostolic figure were betrayed by their inconsistent writing styles, their heretical contents or because they were books to which no 'churchman of any generation has ever seen fit to refer in his writings.'[34]

There was also a middle tier of 'Disputed' writings, whose textual authenticity and attribution to their authors were suspect but which were nonetheless accepted as scripture. These included such books, familiar to modern readers of the New Testament, as the Epistles of James and Jude and the Second Epistle of Peter. Eusebius accepted these dubious writings as scripture inspired by God and compelling for Christians because they 'have been regularly used in very many churches.'[35] The custom of the people of God had validated them.

The methods that Eusebius and Origen had used to authenticate writings attributed to the Apostles foreshadowed the Islamic science of Hadith criticism, but the depth and breadth of the ulama's accomplishments dwarfed those of the Church Fathers. The endless volumes of Hadith transmitter criticism, of examinations of the chains of transmission for breaks or corroboration had no precedent in scale or complexity in either Christianity of Judaism, on indeed in any heritage. The great canonical Hadith collections of the ninth century stand as monuments to Sunni Islam, expressions of that sect's resounding commitment to basing both action and belief on the rigorously authenticated precedent of the Prophet. The Sunni obsession with Hadiths and grounding law directly in the Qur'an and Sunna was a hallmark of the movement, eclipsing in rhetoric if not always in reality those schools that held that Muhammad's precedent was best preserved in principles of problem-solving or sacred custom.

Reality fell short of this rhetoric, however, and during the first four centuries of Islam, the religious practice and legal customs affirmed by the ulama continued to play a central role in determining Sunni law and dogma, often above or despite scripture. As in the case of Eusebius, custom could *create* scripture and, like Eusebius, the ulama acknowledged this. During the crucial period of Islamic religious scholarship in the ninth century, Sunni scholars otherwise committed to deriving laws and beliefs from Hadiths often admitted that an otherwise inadmissible Hadith was just a fig leaf, corporealizing custom in the legitimate form of the Prophet's words.

It would take a cosmic level of cynicism to accuse Muslim scholars of feigning entirely their commitment to preserving the Prophet's Sunna and concocting the vast body of Hadiths out of whole cloth to justify received practice. This was, of course, precisely the level of cynicism exhibited by several generations of Western scholars of Islam, many of whom claimed that all of early Islamic history was an illusion conjured up by Sunni orthodoxy in the 800s. The most recent Western scholarship on Hadiths has shown that such wide-scale forgery was highly improbable. Textual analysis and archeological evidence can take us back reliably to within a century of the Prophet's death, and as far back as that horizon the Sunni science of Hadith transmission and law seems to have been an honest if hotly contested undertaking. As for the first crucial century of Islam, beyond its broad outlines, it lies out of historical sight. For those who ponder it, the contents of its veiled chamber are determined by presupposition, whether belief in Islam or skepticism about religion, whether Sunni or Shiite. Only scattered epigraphic evidence and the unique artifact of the Qur'an shed a narrow archival light on this period, a mission that the existence of the very trenchant disagreements in question proves the holy book was never meant to fulfill.

As Muslim scholars themselves admitted, Hadith forgery in the generations after the Prophet was widespread, and many Hadiths were certainly concocted for political or sectarian causes or in an effort to help make exegetical sense of the Qur'an. But we are justified in granting individual Hadiths the historical benefit of the doubt until given some reason to think otherwise. It is not unlikely that many Hadiths really can be traced back to the generation of the Companions and represent their personal recollections of Muhammad's teachings.[36] When looking at the lengthy and unexciting chapters on ablution, prayer or inheritance in mainstay

Hadith collections, it seems more plausible that the Prophet actually made many of these statements than that each Hadith was made up to suit some boring purpose.

Though they may have occasionally forged scriptural evidence and frequently engaged in great artistry or gymnastics to twist evidence to their liking, Muslim scholars could also abandon cherished positions when confronted with compelling arguments. Daraqutni, the leading Sunni Hadith scholar of tenth-century Baghdad, espoused the virulent anti-Shiite sentiments typical of Sunnis in a period in which Ismaili and Imami Shiism were triumphant. When he heard the Hadith supposedly said by the Prophet that 'Hasan and Husayn (the two sons of Ali, the second and third Imams) are the two lords of the youths in Heaven,' he dismissed it as a forgery by one Suwayd bin Sa'id. Daraqutni recalled that he clung to this opinion for years, thinking that 'Suwayd had committed a great crime in narrating this Hadith,' until he traveled to Egypt and found the Hadith corroborated by another, reliable chain of transmission. Regardless of its pro-Shiite flavor, Daraqutni accepted the Hadith as sound and cleared Suwayd's name.[37]

On occasion we can perceive clearly the role of pious custom in elevating to scriptural status some item from the commonplace utterances of early saintly teachers and scholars. In Islam, as in Judaism and even more so in Zoroastrianism, menstruation or vaginal bleeding places a woman in a state of ritual impurity. As a result, she abstains from her daily prayers until the bleeding ceases. In the case of menstruation, a woman does not pray for the normal duration of her menses. If a woman experiences incessant light bleeding apart from her normal period, she simply performs normal ablutions and prays as usual.

The bleeding that a woman experiences after childbirth, known as *Nifas*, is more irregular and difficult to chart. Early Muslim scholars were asked how long a woman should skip her prayers after delivering a child. Finding no evident scriptural ruling on the subject, they used best judgment. Malik felt that a woman should ask other women around her how long her bleeding might last and abstain for that time. Most early scholars, including Shafi'i and Ibn Hanbal, felt that she should stop her prayers until her bleeding ceased. If the period exceeded forty days, then the period of *Nifas* had ritually ended even if some bleeding continued. Hasan Basri, for his part, felt that *Nifas* could last fifty days. Eventually all four Sunni schools converged on the position that the period of *Nifas* was forty days, with no fixed minimum. After that, the new mother would resume her daily prayers whether her bleeding had stopped or not.[38]

There was no reliable Hadith anywhere on this topic. Yet we find chapters devoted to the issue in the canonical Hadith collections of the mid-ninth century, which feature several Hadiths on *Nifas*. These Hadiths then repeatedly appear as evidence in subsequent books of Shariah law. The main Hadith quotes the Prophet's wife Umm Salama recalling that women in the Prophet's time observed a forty-day break from prayers after childbirth. But none of these Hadiths in any way met even the lowest bar of reliability according to the Sunni science of transmission criticism. After including this Hadith in his canonical Hadith collection, Tirmidhi admits its unreliability. But he is quick to add that 'scholars had come to consensus on this ruling.'[39] The Hadiths that set a forty-day period for *Nifas* thus entered into the body of Islamic scripture not because they could be reliably traced back to the Prophet, but because they manifested in compelling scriptural form the amorphous collective custom of Muslim legal culture. Similarly, Muslim scholars from all four Sunni schools of law agreed that a person paid no charity tax on green vegetables they grew. Tirmidhi provides a Hadith in which the Prophet is quoted to that effect but notes that it is unreliable as well. 'And there is nothing sound on this topic coming from the Prophet,' he concludes, 'but it is the practice of the scholars.'[40]

KILLING ONE'S CHILDREN: TRADITION BETRAYING SCRIPTURE

In 1947, in the Muslim north of British-ruled Nigeria, the colonial appeals court overturned a death sentence handed down by a local Shariah court in the case of a man who had murdered his wife's lover. Unlike the Shariah court, the British judges decided that the cuckolded killer had been provoked and should be spared due to mitigating circumstances.[41]

Along with quips about camels and hummus, 'honor killing' is among the first phrases that average folk in the West associate with Islam. As intimated by the British court's decision, this does not reflect the reality of the Shariah tradition. Violence committed against women for perceived compromises of family honor is a product of patriarchal societies suffering from economic underdevelopment. The phenomenon is found across religions and from Brazil to India. Ironically, those Arab countries with legal provisions that treat honor crimes more lightly than comparable offenses all draw these laws from the Ottoman Criminal Code of 1858. It, in turn, translated this provision directly from the French Legal Code of 1810.[42]

Questions about honor killings have regularly found their way into the inboxes of leading muftis like Yusuf Qaradawi or the late Lebanese Shiite scholar Muhammad Husayn Fadlallah. Their responses reflect a rare consensus. No Muslim scholar of any note, either medieval or modern, has sanctioned a man killing his wife or sister for tarnishing her or the family's honor. If a woman or man found together were to deserve the death penalty for fornication, this would have to be established by the evidence required by the Qur'an: either a confession or the testimony of four male witnesses, all upstanding in the eyes of the court, who actually saw penetration occur. In great part, this uniform condemnation results from the Prophet having clearly affirmed that even killing someone found in the act of adultery would be punished as murder, unless four males happened to be present to witness penetration and testify that adultery had occurred. But in his strong condemnation of honor killing as foreign to the Shariah, Qaradawi has to note one exception to the normal punishment a murderer could expect. 'A father is not executed for killing his child,' he notes, 'which is the position of the Muslim jurists.'[43]

Questions such as the duration of *Nifas* or tax on green vegetables are innocuous. On other topics, however, legal custom could create scripture in a way that would seriously affect the lives of Muslims. It is assuring that, in these controversial cases, claims of universal agreement tend to dissolve upon inspection. One finds a minority who objects to the primacy of custom over revealed scripture. Just as Augustine had to qualify his empowerment of the 'custom of the people of God' with the condition that this custom be one 'observed throughout the whole world,' so Muslim claims about the consensus of jurists lose their force if they prove less than unanimous.

In the Shariah, offenses were divided into those against God and those against man. Crimes against God violated His *Hudud*, or 'boundaries,' and were offenses whose punishments were specified by the Qur'an and, in some cases, the Hadiths, such as the punishment of certain kinds of theft by amputating a hand, punishing adultery by stoning and sexual slander by lashing. Because these offenses were affronts against a merciful God, the evidentiary standards were often impossibly high (such as the four witnesses to sexual penetration required to prove adultery). Moreover, the Prophet ordered Muslim judges to 'ward off the *Hudud* [punishments] by ambiguities.' The severe *Hudud* punishments were meant to convey the gravity of those offenses against God and to deter, not to be carried out. If a thief refused to confess, or if a confessed adulterer retracted his confession, the *Hudud* punishments would be waived.

This did not entail that the culprit escaped justice. Circumstantial evidence, such as a witness to the theft or finding the stolen good in the thief's possession, could lead the judge to find him guilty of wrongful appropriation (*ghasb*). The wronged party could reclaim their possession or receive compensation for its value plus damages entailed. This coexistence of two legal wrongs identical in fact but subject to two very different standards of evidence and punishment is analogous to the relationship between the crime of theft and the tort of conversion in common law. While the first requires evidence of guilt beyond a reasonable doubt and can be punished with prison, the second only needs a preponderance of evidence and carries monetary damages. In cases that fell below the *Hudud* category in the Shariah, judges regularly assigned lesser punishments such as a beating, prison or public humiliation.

Shariah judges did not perceive applying lighter punishments as compensation for a design flaw in God's law. Rather, they felt they were obeying the Prophet's infallible command to find some means to move a crime from the harsh realm of the *Hudud* to the lower level of offenses that a judge could punish at his discretion. This was a priority for the ulama. In fifteenth-century Cairo, when the Mamluk sultan's men caught a royal administrator 'embracing' a mistress, and the couple confessed to fornicating, the sultan himself took an interest in the impending execution. When the couple then retracted their confession, the senior Shariah judge in Cairo was sent into exile for insisting – correctly, other ulama affirmed – that the couple's sentence had to be commuted and that 'whoever executes them should be executed in turn.'[44]

Offenses against man included murder, manslaughter, injuring someone intentionally or accidentally or damaging property. These were not necessarily less serious than offenses against God in terms of the harm they caused; murder is arguably more grievous than slander, yet the latter is a *Hudud* offense and the former is not. God could forgive wrongs against Himself, but offenses against man involved a person whose rights had been infringed. Earthly torts must be redressed. In the adjudication of injuries, victims or their kin won either the right to request retaliatory punishment against the perpetrator (a murderer would be executed by the court) or, more often, financial compensation from the perpetrator (the family of a murder victim received one thousand gold coins, for example). If an injured party did not want to accept monetary compensation for their injury, he could request that the court inflict an 'eye for an eye' punishment on the offender.

In this light, why would a parent not forfeit their life for taking the life of their child? To be sure, the parent was still liable for lesser punishments and for paying compensation money. Yet the message sent by exempting a parent from the possibility of facing death for murdering their child nonetheless seems an unjust undervaluation of the child's life. The Qur'an, after all, ordains 'a life for a life' and declares, 'O you who believe, death as retaliatory punishment has been ordained for you in the case of those killed...' How could the exception for a parent exist?

The answer lies in the Hadith 'A father is not killed as punishment for [killing] his child,' which all Sunni schools except the Malikis took as qualifying the Qur'an. The precedent was purportedly first set by the caliph Umar when the Hadith led him not to execute a father who had killed his son. This Hadith, however, was only attested by unreliable chains of transmission (see Appendix II). Early scholars from Shafi'i to Tirmidhi admitted that it was unreliable but replied that a large number of early scholars had nonetheless acted on it. Invoking the power of judicial custom, the prolific author and Shariah judge in eleventh-century Lisbon, Ibn 'Abd al-Barr, defended the Hadith by claiming it 'is so well known among the jurists of all climes, so widely spread and acted on that a chain of transmission is unnecessary.'[45]

Yet contrary to Qaradawi and Ibn 'Abd al-Barr, only three of the four Sunni schools of law held that a father cannot be executed for killing his child (Hanbalis and Hanafis apply this to the mother as well). There was never some universal custom that could empower an otherwise feeble Hadith. Ibn Mundhir, a tenth-century scholar who collated the many and varied opinions of Muslim scholars to determine when consensus had actually occurred, rejected the claim of consensus on filicide (a parent killing their non-infant child). A number of leading scholars, he noted, held that the father was treated like any other person based on the evident meaning of the Qur'anic verses as well as the Hadith that 'The believers are equal to one another in their blood.' He added that he had heard no reliable Hadiths to exempt the father from this ruling. The entire Maliki *madhhab* had rejected the unreliable Hadith in question as evidence for abandoning the Qur'anic principle of 'a life for a life.' Malik understood the report of Umar's ruling in the case of the father and son to mean that, in the case of a father committing the *unintentional* manslaughter of his child, the parent should not face death but only pay compensation. If a parent committed the premeditated murder of a child or did so in cold blood, the Malikis concluded, then he would face death like anyone else.[46]

What could explain this bizarre exception to what otherwise seemed a clear Qur'anic principle, as well as one of broader equity, that a life answers for a life? One of the most influential parts of the legal heritage of the Near East before Islam, which formed the context in which the Shariah was articulated, was Roman law. Throughout the eastern empire and over a span of centuries, this important heritage was shaped in each Roman province as the edicts of emperors and the judgments of local Roman prefects alternately asserted Roman values and affirmed local practices.

Famous in its own time and notorious for some time since, the Roman principle of *patria potestas* was a hallmark of the Eternal City's law. 'The power of the father' was *vitae necisque potestas*, 'the power over life and death' for all members of his household. It granted the patriarch the right to kill a child with impunity. In time, this godlike authority sat uneasily with an increasingly Christian empire. Among Roman Christian writers, the idea of the father as the holder of the power over life and death was more suitably transposed onto God the Father.[47] And by Constantine's time, the crime of filicide was listed under the category of *parracidium*, punishable by chastisement. The skilled imperial jurists compiling the self-assertively Christian law code of the emperor Justinian found a more assertive solution. They located a legal ruling by the pagan emperor Hadrian that sentenced a father who had killed his son to exile on an island.[*]

Christian sentiment seems to have tempered *patria potestas* markedly by the time Islam arrived in the eastern provinces. But evidence indicates that the Roman father's power over life and death had always been an 'abstract definition of power,' to quote Yan Thomas, and not a reality in daily life. The authority of the father as the center of the family was the primordial

* That Justinian's legal experts were scraping hard for a condemnation of filicide is evident in the details of Hadrian's law. The father was being punished not because he killed his son but because he killed his son in anger, forgetting the parental obligation of mercy (*Digest*, 48:9:5).

bedrock on which Roman law was built and the idiom in which power was conceived. It had to be absolute. The rare instances in which *patria potestas* was invoked in its fullest sense come from Rome's semi-mythic past, such as the legendary character of Lucius Junius Brutus putting his son to death for a conspiracy against the Republic. The actual references to *patria potestas* in later, functioning Roman law suggests that it was a hyperbolic device used to characterize the core ideals of filial loyalty. It was an ancient and reaffirmed testament to the belief that, ultimately, family and the authority of the father over the son trumped the man-made institutions of the state and even the law itself.[48]

Several European scholars have argued that Islamic law adopted much of Roman provincial law, notably as passed through Jewish law. The Shariah tradition certainly mirrors the principle of *patria potestas* in noticeable ways, but this could have indigenous roots as well. Like its Roman precursor, the Shariah's effective confirmation of *patria potestas* seems more a reflection of the deep logic of law and society than a common court ruling. Like the ancient familial origins of Roman society, the Arabian world of the Qur'an was based on the family and tribe, and patrilineal descent was its organizing principle. A product of this stateless world, the Qur'an conceived of murder as a wrong committed against the victim's kin, not against 'the state.' The father was the font and axis of his progeny's entire legal existence and rights to protection in the tribal system. How could he be punished for killing one of them?

Yet the Qur'an also created a system of values above and outside its tribal context, encouraging mercy. The holy book allowed the family of a murdered individual a choice: insist on the murderer's execution, accept monetary compensation (or wergild, *diya* in Arabic) instead, or pardon the killer altogether. The majority of Muslim scholars held that those relatives who had the prerogative of pardoning the murderer or receiving the compensation payment were the very same relatives who would inherit from the victim.

The Qur'an vitiates the patriarchy of Arab society in its schema for dividing inheritance, granting shares to males and females, patrilineal and matrilineal. If the dead person has children and surviving parents, then the (grand)father and the (grand)mother each receives a sixth of the wealth. But the ancient agnatic (agnates here being one's patrilineal relatives) framework of Arabia remains in the Qur'an. A son receives twice the inheritance portion of a daughter. If the deceased had no children but was survived by his parents, then the father receives two thirds of the estate and the mother only one third (4:11). Sunni ulama affirmed the agnatic underpinnings of inheritance when elaborating further details of the law. Of non-agnates, only the deceased's wife, mother, grandmother, sister and daughter inherited. Eligible agnates were much more numerous: paternal uncles and cousins as well as grandchildren through sons can all inherit, with any remainder going to other agnates.[49] The Maliki school, moreover, grants the victim's agnates, such as the father and paternal uncles, priority in deciding whether to pardon a killer or receive the monetary compensation.

All Muslim scholars agreed that a murderer cannot inherit from his victim, nor can the killer pardon himself if he is a relative of the victim.[50] Nonetheless, when a father kills his child, the obstruction in the deep logic of the law is still felt. How can the father be killed in retaliation for his son when he is the axis of the patriarchal structure that still, despite Qur'anic mitigations, manages punishment and resolution? In a way, the father is the keystone of the legal structure. The law cannot remove him from its own vault.

The contradictions in the deep legal logic of the Shariah or the vestigial patriarchy of its foundations were not enough to convince some medieval ulama. The Qur'an had, after all, condemned with great pathos the Arabian practice of burying unwanted female infants alive. It was not just the Maliki school of law that rejected exempting a father from death for murdering his child. The question troubled a leading Shafi'i scholar of the twelfth century as well. Lecturing at the preeminent Nizamiyya Madrasa in Baghdad, not far from the pontoon bridges that spanned the Tigris at the heart of the city, Fakhr al-Islam Shashi told his students that jurists had based their ruling in this question on a false Hadith and then blindly imitated each other for generations. The reasoning behind not putting a father to death for killing his child, Shashi explained, was ostensibly that the father was an essential cause in the child's existence, so how could the child be the cause of the father's non-existence? Shashi found this laughable. If the father fornicated with his own daughter, he would be stoned to death even though he was the cause of his daughter's existence as well. 'And anyway, what understanding of law comes from this?!' he objected in exasperation. Why could the child's murder not be the reason for the father's death, 'when the father had disobeyed God most high?'[51]

RECONSIDERING THE PENALTY FOR APOSTASY: TRADITION REDEEMING SCRIPTURE

According to all the theories of language elaborated by Muslim legal scholars, the Qur'anic proclamation that 'There is no compulsion in religion. The right path has been distinguished from error' is as absolute and universal a statement as one finds. The truth had been made clear, and now, 'Whoever wants, let him believe, and whoever wants, let him disbelieve,' the holy book continues (2:256, 18:29).

Why then do all four Sunni schools of law agree that a Muslim man who leaves Islam is killed if he refuses to recant (the Hanafis only punish a woman with imprisonment)? The ruling is based on a number of Hadiths considered totally reliable by Sunni scholars, such as 'Whoever changes his religion, kill him' and another specifying that a Muslim's life is only taken for three crimes: murder, adultery and apostasy.[52]

Most Western polities have placed religious choice in the realm of private life, which became possible once the significant structures and identities of states were sufficiently detached from religion. Spinoza praised the religious freedom of the new Dutch Republic, and he contrasted it with ancient Israel. There, the Jewish religion had been coterminous with the Hebrew polity. Anyone who defected from the worship of Yahweh was a traitor to the state and ceased to be a citizen.[53] The *Umma* that germinated from the Muslim community in Medina quickly became too vast and diverse to be politically centralized, but it remained unified as a confessional polity in which Islam undergirded the regnant order. Other religious communities, global minorities like Jews or regional majorities like Hindus, fit as protected minorities within the *Umma*. If a Christian, Hindu or Jew wanted to move into the Islamic community, this was welcomed. A Muslim leaving the fold, however, was undermining the religious order of the *Umma*. This vital dimension of communal loyalty is alluded to in the Hadith laying out the three capital crimes for Muslims. The Prophet describes the apostate as 'one leaving his religion, *forsaking the community*.'

This mode of thinking about religion as a political and communal identity as opposed to a mere matter of conscience went unchallenged until the modern period, when Muslims encountered the Western model. The ulama had always been exceedingly patient with potential apostates, granting them the chance to explain any problematic religious statements they may have made. 'The speaker is to be asked about his intended meaning' was a standard procedural principle. When asked about an unthinkable slander overheard in the literary salons of Cairo in 1902, that people were 'mocking' the Sunna of the Prophet, the conservative Grand Mufti of Egypt ruled that the person who said this could not be declared an unbeliever until he was asked if he was mocking a specific practice that he thought was unworthy of the Prophet, or if he was really insulting the Prophet himself. In the first case, the man might only be mistaken but otherwise sincere in his Islam.

Consensus on the severity of apostasy held strong well into the twentieth century. Even reformists like the tireless Rector of Al-Azhar, Mahmud Shaltut, affirmed the basic rule that leaving Islam was a death-penalty offense. It was not until the 1990s that more contemporary Egyptian ulama tackled the problem of apostasy and religious freedom in the modern world. Two scholars in particular have stood out. The son of a successful lawyer, Ali Gomaa was recognized for his exceptional talents while he was firmly ensconced within Al-Azhar's anti-Salafi and politically quietist mainstream. In 2003 he was elevated to the position of state Grand Mufti. Also an Al-Azhar-trained Egyptian, the village-born Yusuf Qaradawi felt the other end of the state's pike along with thousands of other Muslim Brothers summarily dumped in prison. Later, as a darling of the Qatari royal family, he combined the rich heritage of the Al-Azhar tradition with a mild Salafi leaning. He rose to prominence through his prolific writing and pioneering appearances on pan-Arab satellite media.

Both scholars arrived at the same conclusions regarding apostasy, and both took the legal custom of Muslims as more determinative of the Prophet's teachings than Hadiths themselves. Gomaa and Qaradawi affirmed that, at the level of personal conscience and private religion, the freedom of belief was absolute. The Qur'an had clearly mandated this. But neither scholar questioned the authenticity of the *sahih* Hadiths that declared leaving Islam a death-penalty offense. To do so would be to cut too deeply into the flesh of tradition. Instead, the two scholars bypassed the Hadiths by subordinating them to the actual case-by-case rulings of Muhammad and the early caliphs on apostates. Gomaa provides a lengthy list of instances in which the Prophet overlooked blatant unbelief among the Medinan 'Hypocrites' and even pardoned such career reprobates as Ibn Abi Sarh, a Meccan who had converted to Islam and joined Muhammad as one of his scribes in Medina, only to cast off the new faith and seek fortune anew back in Mecca as a satirist insulting the Prophet in poetry.* Both Gomaa and Qaradawi cite the ruling made by Umar, who as caliph stated his preference for offering apostates another chance to believe before imprisoning them if they refused. The legal custom of the Prophet and early caliphs therefore prove that the Hadiths ordering execution for apostasy cannot be taken as definitive. It must be understood within some specified context.

Gomaa compares the apostasy condemned by the Hadiths as closer to high treason, namely a betrayal of the Muslim state and polity. Qaradawi distinguishes this severe form of apostasy, which he labels 'Apostasy of Transgression,' from the lesser apostasy of an individual making the personal choice to privately change his or her religious beliefs. This lesser form was not punishable under the Shariah. Transgressive apostasy, such as public ridicule of Islam or calling others to apostatize, however, amounted to an attack on the religious structures of society and was indeed punishable by death. Furthermore, Qaradawi interprets Umar's lenient statement on apostasy as evidence that the gruff second caliph understood the Prophet's severe condemnations of leaving Islam as a ceiling of punishment and not a strict rule. Like the case of forbidding tobacco and coffee, treatment of apostates fell to the ruler's discretion.[54]

Dyed-in-the-wool traditionalists like Gomaa and Qaradawi could not justify ignoring authenticated Hadiths by invoking modern values. They had concluded that the evidence, in this case communal practice, trumped the Hadiths. They explained this by recourse to the epistemological hierarchy of Islamic legal theory. Even the soundest Hadiths were rarely transmitted widely enough to meet the grade of massively diffuse and parallel transmission (*tawatur*), like that of the Qur'an. As a result, they only yielded strong probability, not certainty, that the Prophet had made the statements attributed to him in the Hadiths. Qur'anic principles like religious freedom, by contrast, were certainties, and any Hadiths that touched on such principles would have to be understood in light of them.

This strategy for bypassing authentic Hadiths was not a modern innovation. For centuries, Sunni scholars have dismissed a *sahih* Hadith in which the Prophet states that his father, who died before he was born, was in Hellfire. Although the Hadith is found in the authoritative *Sahih Muslim*

* In fact, after converting to Islam a second time, he was eventually appointed governor of Egypt.

collection, it is narrated through only one chain of transmission for three generations and thus cannot supersede the agreed-upon theological position that people who die in times and places unreached by prophecy cannot be held accountable for not embracing God's true religion.[55]

WOMEN LEADING PRAYER: SHOULD SCRIPTURE TRUMP TRADITION?

In March 2005, web traffic and media in the Muslim world convulsed with new controversy. Its source was unusual. Muslims in America rarely contribute to the regular flow of scandals or outrageous fatwas that provide standard media fodder. In New York, a collection of Muslim activists along with the organization MuslimWakeUp.com had helped organize what they described as the 'first public Juma prayer of its kind' in the history of Islam. It would be led by a woman, who would deliver the Friday sermon before leading the congregation in prayer.

The Manhattan prayer received premier attention in the US media. Motives were mixed among the organizers. For many, asserting a woman's right to lead men or a mixed-gender group in communal prayer and deliver a Friday sermon was a necessary step toward reclaiming Muslim women's parity with men and their legitimate role in Islam's public religious life. For the American Muslim scholar and activist who was asked to lead the prayer, Dr. Amina Wadud, it was the continuation of her own spiritual struggle to realize Islam's liberation of all people, an outgrowth of the African-American struggle for equality. For author and media activist Asra Nomani, who buzzed around the event coordinating publicity for an upcoming book, it was a step in her ongoing public cry for reform in Islam (she had some days earlier taped '99 [sic] Precepts' to the door of her local mosque in West Virginia).[56]

Reactions to the woman-led prayer came immediately, vehement and polarizing. Western Muslim supporters of MuslimWakeUp.com's message applauded the act as courageous and overdue. Some Muslims in the US and Canada worried that, regardless of the Shariah ruling on such a prayer, the event would only sharpen divisions within the community without advancing women's rights. Ultimately, its Shariah legitimacy would hinge on three questions: could a woman lead a mixed congregation in prayer? If so, could she lead them in one of the five daily required prayers or only in extra prayers? Finally, could a woman lead the required Friday communal prayer, a duty that included giving the Friday sermon?

Ulama condemned the act. From prominent American Muslim scholars to the towering figures of Yusuf Qaradawi and Ali Gomaa, the response was clear: the infallible consensus of the *Umma* prohibited women from leading mixed groups in any of the required daily prayers. Moreover, a woman delivering the Friday sermon was inconceivable and unheard of in Islamic history. As Gomaa wrote in a representative fatwa, these prohibitions had been agreed upon by 'the people of knowledge from the four schools of law, nay the eight schools of law,' referring to the four Sunni schools, the two Shiite, the Zahiri and the Ibadi Kharijite schools.[57]

But even Gomaa's fatwa tacitly acknowledged the dearth of any real scriptural evidence against woman-led prayer. This lay behind the decision by the epochal Sufi sage Ibn Arabi to actually affirm women's categorical right to lead prayers. Ibn Arabi was no lackluster jurist and Hadith scholar, and he noted that none of the ulama who prohibited woman-led prayer had any scriptural proof (*nass*) to support their views. Thus, 'they should not be listened to.'[58] Indeed, the Qur'an is silent on the question of woman-led prayer, and the only Hadith cited directly in classical and modern discussions, which quotes the Prophet as ordering, 'A woman will not lead a man in prayer, nor a Bedouin a townsman, nor an iniquitous man a believer,' has never been upheld as reliable at all. Rather, it has always been rated as 'weak' or even 'feeble.'[59]

Much of the verbiage on the prohibition of woman-led prayer in classical works of Shariah law consists of derivative arguments. Each leaves ample opening for objection. In a sophistic inversion of the a fortiori argument, Bayhaqi puts forth as his strongest evidence the tangentially related Hadith that 'A community that entrusts its affairs to a woman will not flourish.' One could object that not allowing a woman to serve as the ruler of a state in no way necessitates disqualifying her from the significantly lesser charge of leading the men in her family in a daily prayer at home. Another standard argument, that women lack the spiritual and intellectual faculties to lead prayer, is dispensed with summarily by Ibn Arabi. At various points in history, he explains, women have been affirmed by revelation as leaders and bearers of prophecy. Women are, as such, no different as a class than men regarding the capacity to lead religious rituals. Certainly, specific women lack the knowledge or piety required to lead a prayer. But men with those failings would also not be allowed to lead prayer. Protests against someone unqualified leading prayer should therefore be directed against specific individuals, not an entire sex.[60]

Hanafi jurists denied the possibility of woman-led mixed prayer because the Prophet had supposedly commanded Muslims to 'move them (females) back to where God moved them' in the order of prayer lines. But they had to admit that this was not a Hadith at all but merely a Companion's opinion. The great Cordoban judge Ibn Rushd (best known in the West as the philosopher Averroes) repeats the a fortiori argument that, since numerous undisputed Hadiths state that women must line up *behind* men in prayer, a woman cannot conceivably be *in front* of them leading.[61]

But what if, as some Hanbali scholars suggested, a woman leading the prayers stood behind the men (admittedly, these scholars only meant this in the case of the optional night prayers in Ramadan)? Some ulama rightly objected that standing in front of the congregation was a basic requirement of leading prayer. A woman would thus have to lead from in front of the men and could not stand behind their ranks. The guidelines for how various groups in the congregation line up to pray, however, do not necessarily apply to the prayer leader. It is agreed that slaves should pray behind freemen, youths behind elders, but many jurists allowed a youth to lead elders in prayer and most schools allowed slaves to lead prayers with freemen in the congregation on the basis of a report from Aisha.[62] Why then could a woman, who would usually line up behind the men, not stand in the unique position of imam in front of them?

The main reason that men do not pray behind women in Islam is easily understood: a woman bowing and prostrating on the floor in front of men, her posterior raised in the air, could hamper concentration for both parties. A female prayer leader, however, could be shielded by a screen: the Shafi'i and the Hanbali schools considered the prayer of a member of the congregation valid even if he was separated from the leader by a wall, barrier or street. What mattered was being able to hear the commands of the prayer. This ruling rested on sound Hadiths and lay behind the inventive argument by the traditionalist Moroccan cleric Ahmad Ghumari that villagers could follow a Friday prayer broadcast by radio provided that the imam leading the prayer was spatially somewhere between the village and Mecca.[63]

For many ulama, it was the homily that precedes the Friday prayer and the idea of a woman speaking before the crowd that proved most problematic. Qaradawi makes explicit the long-assumed wisdom behind disallowing women's public religious leadership. Seeing a woman speak or hearing her voice, even her recitation of the Qur'an, would excite the uncheckable male appetites in the audience and result in social strife (*fitna*). According to this logic, whether reading the Qur'an aloud in prayer or delivering a sermon, by speaking aloud before men a woman is essentially exposing part of her nudity (*'awra*) and tempting men.

This claim falls flat, however. Two of the five daily prayers are led in silence. Even in the case of a woman delivering a sermon or leading a prayer aloud, there is nothing impermissible about hearing a woman's voice. Women in the Prophet's time spoke openly to unrelated men. The Prophet sought the counsel of women in Medina, and the Companions turned to his wives, like Aisha, for guidance on the proper understanding of their religion. Even the most conservative medieval ulama explained that the legal dictum 'A woman's voice is part of her nudity' was not literal; it merely conveyed the teaching in the Maliki, Hanbali and Shafi'i schools that it was 'discouraged' for women to raise their voices unnecessarily around unrelated, potentially intrigued men in public. For the Ḥanafi school, it would only apply to her voice in prayer.[64] Opponents of woman-led prayer or sermons might reply that women speaking in public or reciting the Qur'an may be permissible, but it is not necessary and thus presents a needless, if slight, provocation of men's desires. But the male Companions who learned about Islam and transmitted thousands of Hadiths from Aisha did not *need* to have direct contact with her either. They could have asked their sisters to act as intermediaries, for example. Necessity has never been part of this question. Gomaa himself notes that the Shariah has no problem with women reciting the Qur'an aloud in public.[65]

Aside from the questions surrounding the sermon, the specifics of leading the Friday prayer are otherwise moot. Leading it is no different than leading a regular daily prayer in the mosque. The requirement that the Friday preacher be male stems from the broader prohibition on women leading men or mixed congregations. And it is precisely this prohibition that the 2005 New York prayer contested.

The appeals to consensus in the responses of Gomaa, Qaradawi and the many other ulama who spoke out against the Manhattan prayer also ring hollow. They noted, as had the prayer organizers, that the great tenth-century jurist Tabari (d. 923) had allowed women to lead prayer categorically, as had two of Shafi'i's leading students, Muzani (d. 878) and Abu Thawr (d. 854). We have already mentioned Ibn Arabi's position. A cadre of Hanbali scholars had allowed women to lead men and women in the optional nightly prayers in Ramadan (*Tarawih*) if the women in question were learned in the Qur'an and all the available males ignorant (and also provided the woman stood out of the men's sight, behind them).[66]

This was no mean gaggle of supporters. Tabari was so respected a jurist in Baghdad and beyond that a *madhhab* formed around his teachings. Although it eventually became extinct, Tabari's *madhhab* flourished among Sunni ulama for two centuries after his death. Just decades after the scholar died, a leading intellectual historian of the age counted his school among the eight *madhhab*s recognized at the time. Abu Thawr also constituted his own *madhhab*, which attracted numerous adherents in Azerbaijan and Armenia. Muzani was one of the main disciples of Shafi'i, and his abridgement of Shafi'i's teachings became the basis for all later books of substantive law in the Shafi'i school.

The claim of consensus made by Gomaa and others is unconvincing in light of this dissent. For consensus to be binding, the vast majority of classical Sunni legal theorists allowed no difference of opinion among the qualified scholars of an era, a position to which Gomaa himself subscribes. Making a claim of consensus when three of the most famous legal scholars of a generation disagreed is thus problematic.[67] Gomaa and others may be referring to the common Shariah principle that an early diversity of opinion is erased and replaced when later scholars come to consensus, but even this is hardly agreed upon. Even those who insist on such late-round consensus must recognize, as the fourteenth-century luminary of Cairo, Zarkashi, reminds us, that it is not the rock-solid consensus that quashes all objection. It is only a 'probable consensus.' More importantly, a lengthy roster of the greatest medieval legal theorists denied that consensus wipes out the dissent of earlier scholars, for their arguments remain valid, as if the dissenting scholar himself still sat in debate. As Shafi'i himself once said, '*madhhab*s do not die with the death of their practitioners.'[68] Dismissing early diversity of opinion is especially ironic today, since the restriction on marriage age in Egyptian law as well as a crucial argument for Shariah-compliant mortgages, both supported by Al-Azhar scholars for decades, rest on this principle. Both derived Shariah legitimacy chiefly by resuscitating the defunct and anomalous ancient opinions of Ibn Shubruma.

Some of the ulama responses to the 2005 prayer reflected the weakness of the mainstream prohibition. While they all prohibited women leading public mixed-gender prayers and giving the Friday sermon, Qaradawi did allow a qualified woman to lead daily prayers in her own household, since all the men were family. Zaid Shakir, a respected African-American Muslim scholar and cofounder of America's first Muslim college, also wrote that women are allowed to lead their family in prayer if no male is qualified.[69]

Scriptural evidence for and against women leading prayers was slim, but once again Hadiths have played a determinative role. The proponents of women leading prayer, including the MuslimWakeUp.com organizers, cited as proof the Hadith of the female Companion Umm Waraqa. In this Hadith, the Prophet instructs Umm Waraqa to lead her household in prayer, even assigning an old man to act as her muezzin and perform the call to prayer. Even the medieval scholars most opposed to woman-led prayer acknowledged that the word 'household' (*dar*) used in the Hadith should be assumed to include men and women.[70]

Much better attested than the previous Hadith banning woman-led prayer, the Hadith of Umm Waraqa has been deemed 'sound' (*sahih*) by respected medieval scholars such as Ibn Khuzayma and Hakim Naysaburi, and the ultra-conservative modern Salafi Hadith critic Albani rated it as 'good' (*hasan*), the status of most Hadiths used in law.[71] In the case of Umm Waraqa's Hadith, the incredible detail and labyrinthine channels of Hadith criticism have proven crucial, as critics of woman-led prayer argue that the correct version of this Hadith only describes Umm Waraqa leading the *women* of her household in prayer as opposed to a mixed congregation.

All narrations of the Hadith of Umm Waraqa pass through the eighth-century scholar Walid bin 'Abdallah bin Jumay'. There are two widely transmitted versions, both telling how the Prophet instructed Umm Waraqa to recite the Qur'an in her home, to lead her house in prayer and assigning her a muezzin (one narration emphasized how she had memorized all of the Qur'an revealed until that time). There is also one isolated, uncorroborated transmission of the Hadith that appears only in the *Sunan* of the tenth-century Baghdad scholar Daraqutni. It includes the added phrase that she should lead 'the women of her home in prayer.' Daraqutni also includes the gender-unspecified version in his *Sunan*.[72]

In total, five transmitters narrated the gender-neutral version from Walid, with only one person passing onward the version specifying women only. Here the fossilization of scholarly trends within the science of Sunni Hadith criticism rears its head. The change to Umm Waraqa's Hadith introduced by the one minority narration is a textbook example of a phenomenon that ulama termed the 'Addition of the Trustworthy Transmitter' (*Ziyadat al-Thiqa*).

Among the founding generations of Sunni Hadith criticism during the ninth and tenth centuries, Hadith critics authenticated material based on the preponderance of evidence. After gathering all the narrations of a particular Hadith, the critic would select as the most reliable whichever one enjoyed the strongest evidence, both in terms of the raw number of narrations and the quality and status of the authorities who transmitted them. Daraqutni, the scholar in whose collection the minority version is preserved, stood on the cusp of a slide away from this early critical rigor. After him, fewer and fewer Sunni jurists acquired the expertise in Hadiths needed to wade into the details of authenticating reports. The Hadith study circles of Baghdad's mosques thinned as students flocked to the stipends and lodging of the newly established madrasas. They churned out ulama trained in the intricacies of applying law but with limited interest in Hadiths. Jurists wanted to increase the number and diversity of scriptural proof texts available to support their arguments, which made the categorical acceptance of any 'Addition of a Trustworthy Transmitter' attractive. By the mid-eleventh century this had become the norm. As a result, as long as the transmitter providing the version of the Hadith with an addition could be argued as meeting the 'trustworthy' rating, the addition was accepted. It became the received, authentic version of the Hadith regardless of the greater number or superior accuracy of contradictory narrations. In the case of Umm Waraqa's Hadith, jurists have used the rule of the 'Addition of a Trustworthy Transmitter' to advance the isolated, women-only version found in Daraqutni's *Sunan* as the only version worthy of consideration.[73]

Examined more closely, however, Umm Waraqa's Hadith should not fall under this rule. Daraqutni included both the majority and minority versions of the Hadith in his *Sunan* collection. Both versions come from Walid via his student Abu Ahmad Zubayri, a well-respected Sunni scholar and Hadith transmitter. The majority non-gender-specifying version is transmitted from Zubayri by one Ahmad bin Mansur Ramadi, while the solitary women-only version comes from Zubayri via Umar bin Shamma. These two alternative links in the chain are quite comparable to one another; both were very well-respected Sunni scholars lauded as being trustworthy narrators of Hadiths by a range of critics. Daraqutni, himself considered the last of the great early Hadith critics, rated both men as 'trustworthy.'[74]

So far nothing raises alarm, but at this point the two versions of the Hadith diverge in a slight but crucial way. The majority version continues on via one of Daraqutni's most respected teachers, Abu Bakr Naysaburi, while the minority one goes through a much less well-known source used by Daraqutni, Abu Hasan Baghawi (d. 934). Daraqutni called Baghawi 'trustworthy,' but his praise for Naysaburi was lengthy and glowing. It befitted such a renowned scholar. Indeed, Abu Bakr Naysaburi was one of the leading Hadith scholars and Shafi'i jurists of Iraq in his day. Daraqutni said of him, 'I have never seen anyone with a better command of Hadiths.' More tellingly, Daraqutni expressly appreciated Naysaburi's mastery of 'additional phrases and wording in the contents of Hadith.'[75] Baghawi, by contrast and ironically, is known to posterity in great part because of an unusual addition he made in one Hadith's chain of transmission. In fact, it is none other than Daraqutni who noticed this oddity. Baghawi was praised for his piety and even referred to as 'the Sufi,' but otherwise Daraqutni's mention of his flawed, isolated addition to an *Isnad* is all that historical sources noted about him.

Rarely in Islamic legal discourse does a ruling hinge on a single datum. Rarely in Hadith criticism does an evalution hinge on a single comparison. The case of women leading prayer is thus doubly rare. With no Qur'anic verses, other Hadiths or compelling analogical evidence, one is left with the Hadith of Umm Waraqa in its two versions. All depends on the choice between them. On the one hand, there is the widely attested majority version of the Hadith affirmed by a master scholar renowned for his expertise in additions to the texts of Hadiths. On the other, there is the isolated, uncorroborated version vouched for by an accepted but obscure scholar known for little more than making an unusual addition to a Hadith. If we were to follow the more critically rigorous methods of the early Muslim Hadith scholars like Daraqutni, before they succumbed to the allure of maximizing evidence, the correct choice of which version of the Hadith to accept would be obvious at many points in the calculation: the majority version. Even if we follow the later, lax methodology, which accepts the 'Addition of a Trustworthy Transmitter,' the majority version should still emerge victorious. Although Baghawi was rated as reliable by Daraqutni, he is recorded as having a questionable record in additions to Hadiths. It would be difficult to argue that the limited accreditation he received could really qualify him as reliable when addition is the question at hand. As a result, whatever the motivations of the Manhattan prayer organizers, they had some sound precedent in the Hadith of Umm Waraqa. It is not surprising that some of the greatest Sunni scholars of Islamic civilization's halcyon days came to the conclusion that a woman could lead mixed-gender prayers.

Among the many controversies and fierce debates swirling inside the global *Umma*, and amid the societal tensions that entangle the unavoidable, hypostatized orbs of 'Western reform' and 'Islamic tradition,' the 2005 Manhattan prayer has been one of the loudest. The reason is not hard to guess. The motif of the European knight/gentleman rescuing the oppressed oriental maiden from her harem prison remains a well-watered one. The native 'oriental's' preservation of his 'authentic' tradition has sprung up in response. Taking the iconic example of Hindu widow self-immolation (*satti*, banned by the British in India in 1829), Gayatri Spivak notes the discourse that spirals destructively between the colonialist impulse of 'white men saving brown women from brown men' and its inevitable epiphenomenon, the 'brown men's' response that 'the women actually wanted to die.'[76]

At no point has the woman's voice been heard. How can it be when whatever she says will either be 'delusional' (from the perspective of the white man) or 'selling out' (from that of the brown man)? The same dilemma applies to Muslim scholars opining on woman-led prayer. No fatwa can be neutral or claim to stand on scholarly merit alone. All is sucked into the black hole of contest over identity and power. From the British Raj to the US invasion of Afghanistan, calling for the liberation of oppressed 'brown women' has been a mainstay in justifying cultural or military imperialism.[77] As such, scholars like Gomaa and Qaradawi are understandably suspicious of Western Muslims trying to enlighten them. As with *satti*, whether fetishized as victims to justify condemning the non-Western Other or subjected to a reinforced or imagined authentic 'tradition,' women's bodies and rights are the ground on which power is contested.

It is capitally naive to imagine that the Qur'an and Sunna are gender blind. No amount of charitable rereading can mold them to conform to what are touted as modern, 'universal values.' It is equally naive to assume that, beyond the gender roles and distinctions clearly mandated by God's Messenger, the patriarchal societies of the pre-modern Near East and South Asia in which the Shariah was elaborated added nothing else to the mixture. Patriarchy could bend the law to its will. Abu Hanifa had concluded that women did not need a male guardian's permission to marry, and this became the main stance on this issue in the Hanafi school. But when employing their sultanic right to pick which legal opinion to make state law, the Ottomans had opted for an obscure opinion from a solitary early Hanafi scholar who did require a woman to secure her guardian's approval.[78] From its dawn, Islamic law granted women full financial personhood, but the wealthy women of metropolises like Damascus and Istanbul often had to rely on male agents to carry out their transactions. The public world belonged to men. Noblewomen should only leave the home for 'a licit necessity,' concluded a stern but representative fourteenth-century Cairene scholar.[79]

It is a bizarre irony of history that the *physical* consigning of women to the private space of the home, so ubiquitous in the Shariah heritage that flourished with classical Islamic civilization, clashes so discordantly with the decidedly open and active role that the Prophet's wives and other Arab women played in the Arabian cradle of Islam. A woman once rose up and interrupted the caliph Umar while he was addressing the congregation from the pulpit of the Prophets' mosque. Far from silencing her, he admitted the mistake she had pointed out.[80] Aisha's prominence in the life of the Prophet and the early Muslim community, ranging from a senior bearer of the religion's teachings to the head of a faction in Islam's first civil war (whatever her regrets), cannot be denied. During the vulnerable early days of Muhammad's community, Umm Fadl, the wife of his uncle, killed one of the leading enemies of Islam in their home by crushing his skull with a tent pole after he beat a Muslim slave. When the Prophet was surrounded by enemy warriors at the Battle of Uhud, and the bulk of the Muslims had abandoned hope, a woman who had been tending the wounded, Nusayba bint Ka'b, fought beside him to guard her Prophet from sword blows and arrows. Later, she accompanied the Muslim campaign into central Arabia to avenge her fallen son, returning to Medina with twelve wounds. At the Battle of Yarmouk against the Byzantines, another Muslim woman, Asma' bint Yazid, killed nine enemy soldiers with her tent pole.[81] Umm Waraqa, in fact, had originally approached the Prophet because she wanted to die as a martyr in battle herself. But instead the Prophet instructed her to remain at home and lead her household, men and women, in prayer.

Women have always been present among the ranks of the ulama, but their role has almost always been invisible. Of the inestimable library of books produced by scholars of the Shariah before the twentieth century, no more than a handful issue from the hands of women. As one fourteenth-century (male) jurist observed with more pride than disapproval, it was surely the Shariah's emphasis on female modesty and protecting women's honor that prevented them from a greater role in scholarship, though he notes that many of the greatest scholars would issue fatwas with their learned wives' or daughters' signatures attached in approval.[82] Women won respect as Sufi ascetics, and continue to be sought out as transmitters of Hadiths and the Qur'an to this day. But the urge to keep them from the pulpit has only grown stronger as Muslim communities and Islam's global religious universe feel ever more encroached upon by outsiders. Muslims seek instinctively to guard a sense of authentic tradition by staking out the ground of women's bodies and voices.

Clearly, woman-led, mixed-congregation prayers are not established practice in the Islamic tradition. But they are not unprecedented or as controversial as many think. The Hadith of Umm Waraqa proves that the Prophet commanded at least one woman to lead a mixed congregation in prayer. A woman-led Friday prayer, with the sermon delivered by a woman, is clearly a novelty. But none of the ulama's objections to it rest on any firm, direct scriptural evidence, and solutions exist to the concerns they raise. Muslims today thus find themselves faced with a question: in the absence of opposing evidence from scripture, does simply adhering to how things have always been done justify denying half of the population the right to public religious leadership? It is revealingly plain that if this issue did not involve the knot of gender and power, the evidence for permitting it would carry the day without controversy.

That fact casts light on a dark and unworthy place in the male conscience. A humbling reminder of this is found in the life of Ibn Taymiyya, a learned and conservative Hanbali don but also an iconoclast unintimidated by mainstream censure. He used to admit how impressed he was by one Fatima bint Abbas (d. 1315), a female Hanbali scholar who had mastered the greatest works of law and took to the pulpits of Damascus mosques to harangue and inspire a sinful public with her preaching. Despite his respect for her, Ibn Taymiyya recalled that he had marked reservations about her speaking in the mosque pulpit. He intended to put a stop to it. Then the Prophet came to him in a dream. 'This is a righteous woman,' the Messenger of God counseled him. The inimitable scholar, who had stood unperturbed before sultans and had smashed idols, held his tongue.[83]

THE 'QUR'AN ONLY' MOVEMENT

Casting off tradition altogether has been a common theme in the calls of Muslim Martin Luthers for over a century. A response has been the emergence of an Islamic modernist school of thought often dubbed the 'Qur'an Only' movement. In Egypt, Tawfiq Sidqi had argued for understanding Islam through the Qur'an alone, calling himself 'one of the Qur'anists,' but he quickly recanted. His contemporaries in British India fared better. A movement known as the Partisans of the Qur'an (*Ahl-e Quran*) emerged in literary salons and new Urdu-language journals from the 1890s onward. Centered particularly in the Punjab region of North India, several generations of Indian Muslim intellectuals, many educated in missionary schools, became disillusioned with Hadiths after coming across reports like that of the Hadith of the Fly or the Devil Farting.

The Partisans of the Qur'an movement was exemplified by intellectuals such as Ahmad Din Amritsari, Mistri Muhammad Ramadan and, most famously, the senior Pakistani civil servant Ghulam Ahmad Parwez (d. 1985) and his 'Tulu-e Islam' (Islamic Dawn) organization. The early articulators of the Partisans of the Qur'an argued that the details of how to perform daily prayers and other basics of Islamic law could actually be derived from the Qur'an without recourse to the Hadiths. These derivations involved extremely tenuous gymnastics, and later figures like Parwez abandoned the idea of a comprehensive Shariah in favor of a pared-down version. Muslims were only intended to conform their lives to the basic 'moral law' in the Qur'an, grasped and applied by reason. Like Sidqi, they believed that the Hadith corpus was fatally unreliable and that the Sunna could thus not be normative. Parwez and other like-minded authors penned voluminous commentaries on the Qur'an based on the central principle that the sacred text was a self-contained missive that could be understood without external supplements, with even its odd or ambiguous verses explained by reference to other parts of the book.

Descended from the Indian reformist movement of Sir Sayyid Ahmad Khan, the Partisans of the Qur'an ultimately sought to create a religious and cultural space for the South Asian Muslim elite, produced and employed by the infrastructure of British rule. Defined more by their erstwhile role as the comprador to the colonial power than by wealth, more a cultural group than a class, this elite body both opposed the complete integration of an imported Western identity and also deeply disliked the traditional, extremely conservative Islam controlled and propagated by the ulama. Parwez's Islamic Dawn movement resonated among Pakistan's bureaucratic and military elite. For Parwez and his followers, the Qur'an brought a message that was rational (miracles were metaphors, angels were forces of nature), 'civilized' (*Hudud* punishments were meant as mere ceilings for punishment, which should normally be proportional to the crime) and spiritually fulfilling. It preached above all an orientation toward God and a moral law (monogamy was ideal, and men and women were equal, though the latter's proper place was in the home). The principles of this moral law were contained entirely in the holy Qur'an: freedom, tolerance, justice, responsibility and the limiting of sex to marriage.[84] The ritual pillars of Islam, like prayer and fasting, were passed on from generation to generation by living practice. The obscurantist corpus of Hadiths and the Sunna more broadly were manifestations of man's constant urge to trammel God's liberating message with human custom and desire for control. The Sunna was the symptom of a disease that metastasized into the barbaric ulama and their backward clericalism.

Parwez's thought has never attracted a popular following. A product of a sociocultural group stranded by the end of empire, the general message of Parwez and the Partisans of the Qur'an has had a marked and lasting, if circumscribed, influence on the Pakistani upper class. It has also carried disproportionate influence in Pakistani law. When the country's Federal Shariat Court decided in 1981 that stoning could not be required as an Islamic punishment, two of the judges in the majority based their arguments on Parwez's ideas as well as those of Abu Rayya.[85]

Pakistan produced a more ingenious Islamic thinker in Fazlur Rahman (d. 1988), who in 1968 was forced to flee his country due to controversies about his writings and eventually settled as a professor at the University of Chicago. He articulated a new vision for reading the Qur'an and understanding the Sunna that would echo among Islamic modernists for decades, one that rejected the classical Sunni (and Shiite) assumption that an authoritative reading of the Qur'an and its teachings had been locked in place by the rules and practices of an idealized prophetic community.

Like the Partisans of the Qur'an, Rahman accepted the conclusions advanced by Western historians: the Hadiths were historically unreliable and largely forgeries. But Rahman did not conclude that the Sunna was invalid or unnecessary. Instead, he redefined it. The Sunna was never supposed to be fixed rulings transmitted from the Prophet. It was a moving frontier, the constantly evolving effort of Muslim scholars to apply the message of the Qur'an to the challenges of human life and society. The forgery of Hadiths had not been an act of intentional deception on the part of the ulama. Rather, they had put their own legal or doctrinal rulings into the mouth of their Prophet because they were acting as the living implementers of his authority, speaking with his voice. It was only the excessive textualist zeal of the early Sunnis, such as Shafi'i, that petrified this living and adaptable Sunna by setting it down in unchanging Hadiths in authoritative collections. Rahman's solution was that the Hadith corpus needed to be re-examined critically according to modern historical criticism. Once this was done, Muslims could pick up where the earliest Muslim scholars had left off when the Sunna was frozen in the ninth century. They could redefine the Sunna: 'whose very life blood was free and progressive interpretation.'[86]

For understanding the core message of Islam, Rahman turned to the Qur'an. Instead of reading the book verse by verse, each section locked within the interpretation of the Hadiths and 'occasions of revelation,' the Qur'an should be read as a unified whole. It is its own best commentary. Today Muslims must understand the intent *behind* Qur'anic verses and the commands they issue. The Qur'an was revealed at various moments in the Prophet's career to address specific historical realities. What modern Muslims must do is undertake a 'double movement' in which they first identify the moral reason or ethical goal behind a Qur'anic verse, and then see how that intent and goal should be realized in the present day. The Shariah was not supposed to be a set of unchanging rulings. It must be redefined in changing times to accomplish the basic message of the Qur'an, namely 'socioeconomic justice and essential human egalitarianism.'[87]

Rahman's theories have been echoed prolixly by a number of Muslim intellectuals contributing to the genre of postmodernist textual analysis. In a series of dense tomes, the late Egyptian literary scholar Nasr Hamid Abu Zayd and the Syrian engineer and solo intellectual Muhammad Shahrur have proved to be two of the most controversial and widely published advocates of the Qur'an Only approach. They build their calls for reform on the precept that neither language nor texts have fixed meaning but are instead constantly redefined through the act of communication between text, context and reader.

For Abu Zayd, this meant that trying to force the Qur'an literally onto the landscape of modern life and thought breaks the original unity between the revelation and its pre-Islamic Arabian context, effectively imprisoning the holy book with faulty expectations of timelessness. By fixing the interpretation of the Qur'an with the forged shackles of Hadiths, classical Muslim scholars made it anachronistic and inapplicable in any future world. To repair this, modern Muslims must liberate the Qur'an by historicizing it and reading it within its original context, using reason and the book's linguistic content to comprehend the lofty *principles* it originally advanced. Only then can we determine which aspects of its message are specific to its original audience and which can be generalized and applied to later contexts. These latter aspects form the core, eternal message of the Qur'an. Since no group of readers can claim that their reading of a text is any more inspired or authoritative than any other group's, Abu Zayd concluded that all readings of the Qur'an are equally human. The interpretation of God's message among the early Muslim community, which served as the foundation of the Shariah, was no exception. The Shariah was thus 'a man-made production' with 'nothing divine about it.' Its specific rules and references do not deserve the sacred authority claimed by the ulama. What Muslims need today is a 'democratic and open hermeneutics,' asserted Abu Zayd, which relies on reason to read the Qur'an.[88]

The Qur'an Only trend has sprung up in the work of individual scholars and local journals from Arizona to Cape Town. It has had strong influence in Turkey, where it has found a degree of acceptance in the country's secularized public sphere. Although it has not generated an organized religious movement, public intellectuals like the preacher Mustafa Islamoğlu and the former theology professor and one-time Turkish parliament member Yaşar Nuri Öztürk have produced popular Turkish translations of the Qur'an strongly informed by the Qur'an Only ethos. The approach's most productive advocate in recent years has been a Turkish-American community college professor in Arizona named Edip Yüksel. Along with several like-minded colleagues, Yüksel has published a translation of the Qur'an, *The Quran: A Reformist Translation* (2011). They promise a 'non-sexist' rendering that relies only on 'logic and the language of the Qur'an itself,' eschewing the 'all-male scholarly and political hierarchies' that are expressed in the Hadiths.[89] When confronted with unique or bizarre Qur'anic phrases, Yüksel's translation cleverly scans the meaning of other words in the Qur'an derived from the same Arabic root to approximate a translation. Instead of turning to Hadiths or the *Tafsir* tradition to explain otherwise ambiguous references in the Qur'an, the *Reformist Translation* leaves them – honestly – unexplained. Elsewhere, Yüksel and his team interpret liberally in the tradition-less vacuum. The Qur'an's declaration 'Indeed We have sent it down on the Night of Power' is explained uniformly by the *Tafsir* literature as describing the night on which the Qur'an was first revealed. By Yüksel's guess (he renders it 'Night of Decree'), it refers arbitrarily to the night that comes in the life of 'every appreciative person' in which 'they decide to dedicate themselves to God alone by fully using their intellectual faculties.'

NO ESCAPING TRADITION

Spinoza did not believe for a moment the rabbis' claim to command a tradition with an unbroken chain back to Moses, or the Pope's contention that inspired Apostolic succession guaranteed the Church's teachings. He called for a reading of the Bible that looked only at what the text 'said,' not what its generations of rabbinical interpreters claimed it meant when decoded through the prism of tradition. The revolutionary thinker quickly ran up against the limits of his own mission, however. Even if he could cast off the tradition of the Oral Torah that the rabbis had foisted upon the text, he could not rid himself of the language in which it had been written. How could one read the Hebrew Bible free of tradition when the very grammar and lexicon of biblical Hebrew itself had been defined and passed down by the same rabbis? The archaic language was a heritage of the past and was subject to all the same historical skepticism as rabbinic tradition. Though he submitted that changing the meaning of words is much harder than altering religious teachings, Spinoza had to admit that even biblical Hebrew was under the power of the rabbis. Just like Arabic, the Hebrew script was incomplete (lacking short vowels) and its early grammar fluid. One had to know what it meant to read it. Even the meanings of many biblical words were known only through the teachings of the rabbis. Because Spinoza was committed to a method of interpreting the Bible that drew on the Bible alone, he had to accept that if the text did not yield clear answers on its own, 'we must simply give up' on the point in question. Ultimately, core matters necessary for salvation and happiness would be clear, since Spinoza believed they were universal anyway.[90]

Qur'an Only intellectuals like Parwez had 'given up' on the earlier Partisans of the Qur'an attempts to preserve the detailed Shariah. Neither the specifics of prayer nor any real comprehensive body of law was possible without Hadiths and the tradition borne by the ulama. Even after disposing of this burden, one unacknowledged obstacle remained insuperable. With its archaic language and elliptical style, the Qur'an is either inaccessible or incomprehensible outside of its context. Parwez and the Partisans of the Qur'an believed that the Sunna was unnecessary and insufficiently reliable for elaborating Islamic law and theology, but Parwez nonetheless draws on the details provided by Hadiths to describe the Prophet's model of marriage to Khadija and many other aspects of his life. He also needs to refer to detailed events in Medina in order to understand the elliptical references in the holy book.[91] In the same way, Rahman's and Abu Zayd's proposed methodologies for understanding the Qur'an's ethical message are also premised on being able to grasp in detail the historical realities of Medina in the Prophet's time.

The rub is that those historical particularities were recorded by the same Muslim scholars via the same chains of transmission and affirmed by the same overall critical method as the Hadiths that these modernist intellectuals dismissed as forgeries. Of the Islamic modernist school of thought, Rahman retains the strongest attachment to the tradition of the Sunna, acknowledging that calling for a complete rejection of all Hadiths would be tantamount to burning down Islam's entire structure, leaving 'a yawning chasm of fourteen centuries between us and the Prophet' and making interpretation of the Qur'an impossible. He only wishes for a critical re-examination of the Hadith corpus and the details of the Shariah, not a rejection of the pillars of Islamic faith and practice. In fact, he insists that these pillars have been preserved in the living tradition of the Muslim community. Yet Rahman himself admits the lack of a clear demarcation between the body of fossilizing Hadiths he believes were forged and those authentic ones communicating central concepts of the Shariah or preserving the necessary context for reading the Qur'an. There is no way to prove that these had not also been forged. At times, it seems as if Rahman's skepticism is restrained not by methodology but by a sentimental unwillingness to sacrifice the core of his religion.[92]

Yüksel's *Reformist Translation* of the Qur'an makes a more consistent break with the past. When faced with the lexical rarities and elliptical references of the holy book, the *Reformist Translation* just renders them literally or offers footnotes with suggested interpretations. But, like Rahman and Abu Zayd, this work still relies on the complex description of Arabian religion, law and society that the ulama produced as part of their exegesis of God's message. Points where Spinoza might have called for 'giving up,' the *Reformist Translation* is seduced into a disguised reliance on the tradition it claims not to need. A set of Qur'anic verses enshrining the idiosyncratic Arabic custom of *Zihaar* is a fine example. It is singularly impenetrable and yields coherent meaning only if placed against its ancient backdrop. Defined by Hadiths as a man renouncing his wife by declaring 'You are like the back (*zahr*) of my mother to me,' *Zihaar* was a form of pre-Islamic unilateral divorce. Yüksel renders the standard understanding of these verses, in which the Qur'an rejects the validity of the practice: 'Nor did He make your wives whom you estrange to be as your mothers...' (33:4, also 58:3–4). This use of the verb *zaahara*, however, is unique. It appears nowhere else in the Qur'an. In all other instances in the text, the verb means 'to offer aid or assistance' (33:26, 60:9, 9:4). By the *Reformist Translation*'s stated methodology, the verse should be read, awkwardly if at all, 'He did not make your wives to whom you granted aid from as your mothers...'

Oddly, the *Reformist Translation* never cites its lexical or grammatical sources for translating the Qur'an's archaic Arabic (it makes one desultory reference to the famous fourteenth-century *Lisan al-'Arab* dictionary of Ibn Manzur). Yet the association of *Zihaar* with 'estrangement from one's wife by declaring her like one's mother' comes *only* from the classical Arabic dictionaries compiled by the ulama. They note this rare usage as coming *only* from this Qur'anic context, which is explained by *Tafsir* reports transmitted from scholarly forefathers of the early eighth century, like Mujahid bin Jabr and Qatada bin Di'ama, and recorded in exactly the same works and by exactly the same authors as composed the Hadith corpus.[93]

The Qur'an Only approach is, in the end, not a solution to the prison of tradition. It is only a selective reliance on it. None of these intellectuals has achieved a systematic break with the past or reread the Qur'an apart from it. This may well be impossible. Deeply anticlerical, inspired by the Mutazila rationalists of the ninth century and committed to broad Qur'anic principles rather than a concrete and detailed Shariah, the general Qur'an Only trend is an expression of a desire for an Islam compliant with modern rationalism and Western sensibilities. It is the product of how a particular segment of society wants religion to be.

THE PRICE OF REFORMATION

The religious instruction offered by Egyptian cab drivers comes gladly and free of charge. In the decades of stasis that preceded the Egyptian revolution, foreign passengers could also expect spirited testimonials about the confessional harmony that reigned between Muslims and Egypt's Coptic Christian minority. 'We are all brothers. There are no problems between us,' was a predictable refrain. 'A neighbor has rights, you see, whatever their religion.' One driver delved into unusual detail as he peeled through the streets of Mubarak's Cairo. 'The Messenger of God, peace be upon him, taught that a neighbor who is Muslim and your relative has three rights: the right of Islam, the right of family and the right of a neighbor. A neighbor who is a relative and not Muslim has two rights: the right of family and the right of a neighbor. A neighbor who is not Muslim and not family still has one right: the right of a neighbor. You see?'[94]

After Mubarak's fall, routine bromides would no longer suffice. Communal tensions broke to the surface with unusual virulence. In December 2011, a year into Egypt's dangerous but exhilarating 'transition,' Shaykh Yasir Burhami was awoken in his Alexandria apartment by an assistant.[95] The leading Salafi scholar was being attacked on the popular evening talk show, *Egypt Chooses*, by one of the studio guests, a Coptic priest who accused him of inciting hatred against Christians. Specifically, the priest lambasted Burhami for instructing his followers 'not to love' Christians and for referring to them as unbelievers. This had become a leitmotif on Egyptian television during the previous months, with a number of prominent Salafi scholars taking to the air on the many Salafi satellite channels to deliver expositions on interfaith relations or appearing as guests on workhorse talk shows to respond to callers outraged by Salafi sound bites, many of them Copts or '*librali*' Muslims. A recurring point of contention was Islam's implied intolerance, often illustrated by referencing the Qur'anic verse commonly translated as, 'O you who believe, do not take Jews or Christians as friends; they are but friends of each other, and whosoever takes them as friends he is one of them...' (5:51).[96]

Calling in to defend himself, Burhami explained on air that anybody who opened the Qur'an would see immediately that those who reject Muhammad's prophethood, let alone those who believe in the divinity of Jesus, are indeed branded as 'unbelievers' (*kuffar*). But this did not entail that Muslims should harm them or even disrespect them. 'God does not forbid you from dealing kindly and fairly with those who have not fought you in your religion or driven you from your homes,' counsels the Qur'an (60:9). Differences in belief should not be glossed over, Burhami continued, but Muslims had been commanded to treat others with politeness and compassion even if they did not share their faith. Another studio guest, the avuncular septuagenarian Kamal Hilbawi, who had served as the Muslim Brotherhood's spokesman in Europe during an exile in Britain, spoke up to assist. The great medieval scholar Ibn Qudama, he explained, had written that a Muslim must grant neighbors their rights whether they are Muslim or not. The Prophet had explained this clearly in Hadiths.[97]

Medieval ulama had indeed elaborated at great length on the definition of 'neighbor' and the precise rights that a neighbor enjoyed. The Hadith that Hilbawi and, eight centuries earlier, Ibn Qudama had relied on lays them out:

> The Messenger of God said: The rights of a neighbor are that, if he falls sick you visit him, if he dies you follow his funeral procession, if he asks you for a loan you lend to him, if he is in need you assist him, if good befalls him you congratulate him, if misfortune befalls him you console him, that you not build your house up above his, blocking out the breeze, and that you not afflict him with the aroma of your cooking pot without offering him some.[98]

The definition of neighbor varied, but in all cases it extended far beyond those living immediately next door and attached no importance to religious identity. One definition, reported from Aisha, defines a neighbor as anyone living within forty houses in every direction. Ali explained that a neighbor is anyone who hears the call to prayer from the same mosque, including Muslims and non-Muslims of all sorts.[99]

The tension on display that evening on *Egypt Chooses* resulted from the disconnect between two competing discourses on national identity and social cohesion. The host of the show, his Coptic guest and the concerned callers subscribed to a secular, nationalist conception of society in which cohesion and comity were phrased in the idiom of a love that transcended confessional bounds. This school of Egyptian-ness, upheld by the state since the early twentieth century, coalesced out of the milieu of French nationalism. It was informed by ideals like Rousseau's Civil Religion, an expectation that faiths should prohibit intolerance ('It is impossible to live at peace with those we regard as damned,' Rousseau wrote). This ideal of a unified Egyptian nation was infused with the influential Progressivism of Auguste Comte, in which a rational and ordered society was held together by 'universal love.'[100] The nation state was bonded and propelled by love of itself and fraternity among its citizens, and religions must be stripped of confessional thorns.

National unity had to be cultivated on an emotional level for its reality to be achieved and preserved. When Burhami explained on air that 'love' was unrelated to external actions and that Muslims could 'hate' a Christian for their heretical beliefs yet still treat them with kindness, the Coptic priest exclaimed, 'That's a contradiction!' A French nationalist ideologue could not have agreed more. The contrasting vision proposed by Burhami was an Islamic nationalism and a Shariah conception of polity: an Ottoman realm of confessional pluralism with no secular 'national' destiny in sight. Its citizens moved and interacted in an order of regimented rights and obligations on which abstract emotions like love and a belief in the salvific validity of all faiths had no effect.

The most influential Egyptian Salafi shaykh, Burhami and other conservative Islamists regularly expressed this social vision in writings and sermons, particularly on the infamous topic of *wala' wa bara'*, or 'loyalty' to Muslims and 'disavowal' of unbelievers. They pointed out that considering non-Muslims 'unbelievers' had little effect on the routine interactions that make up daily life. Muslims can buy from, sell to and engage in business partnerships with non-Muslims. They can seek the aid of non-Muslim specialists in mundane matters such as doctor's visits and in dramatic matters like warfare. On *Egypt Chooses*, Burhami proudly recounted to his Coptic accuser and the show's viewers that, during the chaos of January 2011, Salafis in Alexandria had protected a local church when the police had vanished. Salafi scholars were particularly fond of the Hadith recounting how the Prophet even let a delegation of Christians perform their prayers in his mosque in Medina.[101]

Unfortunately for Burhami, the alarm generated by Qur'anic verses and Hadiths on interfaith relations had long ago overflowed all efforts to contain it. As a Somali refugee newly settled in the Netherlands, Ayaan Hirsi Ali (an avid Spinoza admirer) had 'picked up the Qur'an' and found in it verses such as 'do not take the Jews and Christians as friends' (her translation). They convinced her that the terrorism of Al-Qaeda was not unrelated to Islam. In truth, it was only a symptom of the hostility and religious intolerance explicit in Islam's holy book.[102] In the Arab world, the fevered airtime devoted to Islamists responding to concerns about this verse from the public or offering prophylactic lessons on it illustrates the dangerous friction between the verse and many segments of society.

Read through the lens of the Hadiths, *Tafsir* reports and biographies of the Prophet that constituted the first layers of Islam's tradition, however, this verse was easily explained and misunderstandings easily defused. The word commonly misunderstood in modern colloquial Arabic and by Hirsi Ali as 'friends' (*awliya'*) actually meant 'patrons' or those to whom one has some commitment, either as a protector or a subordinate. The verse thus warns Muslims against taking the side of unbelievers against fellow Muslims in conflicts, since these other groups 'are but allies of themselves,' the Qur'an explains.

The basic lexical disconnect between modern native Arabic speakers and the ancient text of the Qur'an poses a serious challenge to the post-modernist school of Qur'anic interpretation, which subjects the text to the authority of the reader, the changing landscape of epistemological eras and discourse communities. Abu Zayd dismissed the Shariah as an obsolete human creation and called for 'a democratic and open hermeneutics' to read the Qur'an. Was not the new, (mis)understanding of 'friends' in the above Qur'anic verse an example of democratic interpretation in action? Abu Zayd had objected to Islamists like Sayyid Qutb dumping raw Qur'anic discourse onto the twentieth century, acting as if the Qur'an speaks for itself and directly to us, ignoring the chasm of language and context that separates us from seventh-century Arabia.[103] Ironically, in his criticism of Qutb, Abu Zayd becomes a great defender of tradition. The interpretive mediation that he faults Qutb and conservative Islamists for missing is precisely what tradition provides. Whether performed by docile state ulama in Al-Azhar or outsider Islamist scholars like Burhami, the mediation between scripture and society that Abu Zayd called for is none other than the tradition he accused of retarding Muslim society. Abu Zayd, in fact, praised tradition. The Qur'an's many commands to fight the Arab polytheists until they embraced Islam were the products of a context in which these 'unbelievers' posed an existential threat to Muhammad's new religion. From the time of the Companions onward, Abu Zayd observed, the classical ulama had understood this. As the immediate danger faded amid Muslim military triumph, the ulama immediately admitted Zoroastrian dualists and the polytheist pagans of India as protected 'People of the Book' with the right to practice their religions freely.

According to the critiques launched by Abu Zayd and a legion of other Islamic modernists, the descendants of these medieval ulama, today's bearers of tradition, have lost the ability to apply the message of Islam to new situations. Instead they have reified and paralyzed Islamic interpretation. Whereas their more dynamic and capable predecessors would be calling for religious equality in today's world, asserted Abu Zayd, modern conservative ulama threaten to level the *jizya* tax on Egypt's Christians.[104] Abu Zayd's disappointment with the ulama was therefore not ultimately a disapproval of tradition per se. It was a disapproval of how the traditional ulama understood Islam and the Shariah at the turn of the twenty-first century.

This same fundamental disagreement over the proper conception of religion has been clearly exhibited in Egypt since the 2011 revolution, as have the awkward and resentful steps that 'Islamists' and 'liberals' have taken toward the fragile possibility of a shared future. The liberal television host Wael Abrashi channeled this angst in an interview with Burhami seven months after Mubarak's fall, the conversation lightened by the Egyptian humor that bubbles up even in the most contentious moments. Would the newly empowered Salafis push for levying the *jizya* on Christians, prohibit them from positions of authority or destroy public statues, Abrashi asked? Burhami tried to reassure the journalist. The *jizya* was only one of numerous options that the Prophet had employed in his relation with Christian subjects, and these other issues would be discussed with the broader political community and consensus sought.[105]

Hannah Arendt's diagnosis of crisis in the West could be applied equally well (mutatis mutandis) to Egypt and much of the Islamic world. In the West, for centuries the present was made sense of and the future imagined through the language and conceptual vocabulary of the tradition that was born and reigned in the shadow of Rome. 'That this tradition has worn thinner and thinner as the modern age progressed is a secret to nobody,' Arendt wrote. Eventually the thread broke, and what had previously been the bookish interest of intellectuals alone then 'became a tangible reality and perplexity for all.' It became a political dilemma.[106] The loss of tradition had become political because, phrased differently, if the accepted framework around a discussion is removed, any claim that then assumes the presence of a framework is in actuality imposing it. This act is of political consequence in that it seeks to compel. And it is sure to be contested.

The universal 'Reason' touted by Western natural-law philosophers was an early casualty of the snapping of tradition's last threads. Born in the rubble of postmodernity, contemporary critics of liberalism note that Reason cannot be the judge that rules impartially from outside discourse. It is part of the discourse, and any transcendent throne claimed for it is a stealthy grab for power. Stanley Fish observed that Reason(s) 'always come from somewhere,' and it is clear that once you have stepped outside of a tradition or leveled its authority, you cannot in fairness invoke 'Reason' without admitting its aims and assumptions and convincing others to accept them – precisely the unifying role that tradition used to perform.[107]

New, post-tradition frameworks for Reason in the West sometimes surface. But more often they are vestigial, with Reason wandering through discourse like an orphan imposing itself far and wide with a deluded sense of independence but knowing only what it learned in its ancestral home. In liberal discourse it is now axiomatic that sex is acceptable as long as it occurs between consenting adults. Yet even among segments of Western societies that embrace same-sex marriage, polygamy is still considered repugnant, as are other sexual relationships. Even the pro-gay rights liberals of New York web sardonics reacted with shock and disgust to an American advice columnist who, true to the new framework principle that harmless sex between consenting adults should be licit, approved of the sexual relationship between identical twin brothers.[108]

Western demands that other people act 'reasonably' because that is what 'reasonable people' should do still smell of British colonial efforts to bring native customs into accord with 'good conscience.' Especially in its avatar of 'common sense,' Reason in global discourse today carries its ancestry barely concealed: the early modern British ideal of unifying, upper-middle-class values, a relaxed but assumed Anglo-Saxon Christian temperament, French anticlericalism and Jefferson's democracy-justifying yeoman wisdom.[109] Muslim protests over French cartoons mocking the Prophet in 2011 were rebuffed in the West with indignant referrals to the freedom of expression, a right self-evident to those possessed of 'Reason' and 'common sense.' A year earlier, however, the UK's Advertising Standards Authority had banned an advert featuring a pregnant nun as a 'serious offense' to Catholics.[110] A young Egyptian web entrepreneur and self-proclaimed 'liberal' advocating the motto, 'You are free as long as you do no harm' betrayed the cultural boundaries of his own Reason. Discussing freedom of expression in a talk-show dialogue with a conservative Sufi shaykh, he immediately agreed that, 'of course, insulting Muhammad could not be allowed. It harms his followers.'

Yet 'Reason' was precisely the hermeneutic lens through which Abu Zayd called for a new democratic and open interpretation of the Qur'an. Speaking at a university in Washington, D.C. in the late 1990s, Abu Zayd devoted his entire lecture to recounting recent fatwas issued by Egyptian ulama. 'Can I undress in front of my dog?' one woman had asked. Yes, though it is preferable not to if it is a male dog. Abu Zayd knew well that, for his audience, these were 'unreasonable' and laughable manifestations of religion. And laugh the audience did. Indeed, for many in Abu Zayd's native Egypt such fatwas are enraging as well. This is not only true for many upper- and upper-middle-class Egyptians, who reject unanimous positions of the Shariah tradition such as the requirement that women cover their hair. It also applies for many conservative, observant Muslims born out of the post-1960s Muslim Brotherhood awakening, who often view the ulama of Al-Azhar as disappointments politically and such fatwas as encouraging 'great superficiality and the annulment of reason.'[111]

But taken out of these milieux, what was really so 'unreasonable' in the fatwa mocked by Abu Zayd? The scholar issuing it had not solicited the question any more than the advice columnist had with the Gemini lovers, nor did he impose any requirement on the woman asking it or constrain her freedom in any way. His fatwa was confined to the 'recommended' grade of Shariah rulings. The fatwa's only fault is that it applied religion where some do not approve. But if it is 'unreasonable' that religion should be brought to bear on such banal matters, then Islam's guilt runs far deeper than some modern stagnation. As far back in Islamic history as textual evidence can take us, the ulama envisioned the Shariah as a total and comprehensive system that could and should assign a ruling to any conceivable act. Moreover, if twin-brother gay lovers are seeking the public assistance of advice columnists about broader public approval, it is impossible to know the potential utility of even the most seemingly absurd speculations. Especially in the Hanafi school of law, hypothetical casuistry was always seen as an important exercise in legal reasoning. Even in the medieval era, some jurists were mocked by others for hypotheticals that were 'impossible,' like the question 'Can a person pray holding a bag full of flatus?' (i.e., does it violate the person's state of ritual purity).[112] Today

Muslim scholars are faced with the very real and traumatic question of how individuals with colostomy bags should negotiate the requirements of the ritual purity needed to pray. Who can predict what future use the fatwa that Abu Zayd mocked might have?

THE GUIDE OF TRADITION: A NECESSARY BUT THANKLESS JOB

Martin Luther was never as contemptuous of Catholic *Traditio* as his opponents liked to believe. He was as mortified by the Anabaptist Kingdom of Münster as any Catholic, and he understood well that flocks need shepherds. Touring the German parishes where his reading of the gospel was being taught, Luther was grieved by the ignorance he encountered. He penned a pair of catechisms to set out clearly Christ's teachings and to guide folk in their reading of the Bible (newly translated into German by Luther himself). He was further troubled by the arrogance of many who claimed that, since the scriptures were now easily accessible, there was no further need for pastors or preachers. There is some irony in the predictability of his subsequent plea. Pastors and nobles alike must not 'imagine that they know everything,' Luther upbraided, but should continuously study his Large Catechism, which was 'a summary of all the holy scriptures.'[113]

Appointed Grand Mufti of Egypt, Shaykh Ali Gomaa compiled a short collection of fatwas that resembled a modern catechism: *Elucidating What's Troubling People's Minds*. The fatwas were clear, efficient responses to questions that commonly vexed Muslims in Egypt, and the book was printed in cheap, pocket-sized paperback form. Gomaa was the state official charged as the contemporary voice of the living tradition through which the present interfaces with the authoritative sources of religion. Before his appointment, clerics-in-training and engaged laymen had long flocked to his lessons in the Al-Azhar Mosque because he helped them understand their religion in the present, because he inspired them by blending the longed-for authenticity of the past into the unavoidable demands of the modern day. Though appointed by the Mubarak regime, Gomaa was not at heart a political operator. But in the tradition-imperiled space of Egypt's public life, his rulings were inevitably political. No, bank interest was not prohibited, because fiat currency has no inherent value and cannot be subject to the rulings of *Riba*. Conventional banks applauded. Almost all specialists in the Islamic finance industry expressed shock. Yes, the Prophet Muhammad will marry the Virgin Mary in Heaven, on the basis of a sound Hadith that states this. Coptic representatives were outraged. Muslims were surprised to know the Hadith existed.[114] When the protests against Mubarak intensified in 2011, Gomaa called on Egyptians to stay home. He was roundly excoriated for not supporting the revolution. When the Muslim Brotherhood and supporters of Egypt's first democratically elected president formed sit-ins to protest the military coup that ousted him in 2013, Gomaa called on them to go home as well. Again, he was concerned for their safety. Many Egyptians cheered him. Many were disgusted. Like centuries of Sunni ulama before him, Gomaa supported military strongmen because stability was all that mattered, the sine qua non of religious life.

Many of the fatwas included in Gomaa's booklet enjoyed unanimous support among the ulama across the ideological spectrum, from supple Sufis to conservative Salafis, and even the population at large. No, women could not lead Friday prayers, and acting on the anomalous opinions of classical scholars who allowed it was to insult the *Umma* 'of early and latter days.' Yes, Muslims can visit and exchange gifts with non-Muslims. All schools of law agree that the Prophet gave presents to and received them from non-Muslims, so doing the same today is actually a laudable act of imitating the Prophet's Sunna. The great scholars of classical Islam allowed Muslims to host and visit non-Muslims, and it was indeed permissible to tell Egypt's Christians 'May God grant you life' on holidays, just as one would do with Muslims.[115] Being the state's official voice of tradition was a thankless job. 'There are some scholars who know the Tradition' (*turath*), he explained one day to his students, 'and some who understand present realities. But there are very few who know how to fit the two together.'

6

Lying about the Prophet of God

Even among the colossal glass high-rises and tightly winding motorways of Malaysia's capital, the lush verdancy of the jungle is always within arm's reach – an oblong face of exposed rock shaded by creepers; the odd gargantuan and gnarled jejawi tree. Outside of the city in Jenderami, the dark ribbon of freshly tarred road weaves a serene path through the hills of green palms and sedate roadside shops.

The Jenderami Pondok is a model of calm and good order. Not only does the immaculate mosque and madrasa complex house students, it boasts a supermarket, an orphanage and a home for the elderly and retired. The institution of the *pondok*, or 'lodge' madrasa, first appeared in the Southeast Asian world in the sixteenth century. The ulama of 'Javan' Islam (as the region's scholarly tradition came to be known), who had acquired their learning across the Indian Ocean trade routes in Yemen or Mecca, built schools in villages and remote jungle clearings. Children seeking knowledge flocked to them, and soon their families joined them. Pondoks became entire villages centered around Islamic learning.

The ancestral chain tracing the authenticity of the Jenderami Pondok's sacred knowledge stretches back along the seaways and polyglot coastal enclaves of Islam's Indian Ocean world, with its telltale signs of the sarong and stunning cuisine as unmistakable in Yemeni ports as in Sumatra. The intimate connections and interminglings of these distant lands reveal themselves in the ambiguity of phenotypes and in smooth, blended facial features. They are heard daily in Hindi loanwords in Gulf Arabic and in Arabic's lexical largesse to Malay, and in the cases filed unrelentingly in Singapore courts by some cousin suing some relative for control of some decayed family property near Aden.

The Hadramawt valley of Yemen is the spiritual heart of this world. The Jenderami Pondok is connected there through its heritage of *'ilm* and the days its ulama spent as students there. Even today the relationship is as much a lively circuit of visiting scholars and shared Sufi festivals as it is an umbilical cord connecting the Southeast Asian world to the Arabian heartland of Islam. The chain of tradition is laid out before you as you step into the main reception hall at Jenderami: a wide wall hanging leads your eye from tiny photos of late local Malay masters, back before the photograph to the early modern scholars of Yemen and the Hijaz, further back to Egypt and Baghdad and finally, across fourteen centuries, to Medina and the Messenger of God. As a prominent sign reads, this is 'The Chain of Jenderami's Knowledge of Islamic Law and Sufism.' It is the credentials of Jenderami's teachers and the fount of the school's *Baraka*, or blessings, the palpable substance of faith that draws in the faithful.

In the midst of the reserved students and elderly widows milling around the Pondok's central courtyard, a busload of visitors from Malaysia's state-owned oil company dismounts to enjoy the peace and spiritual ambience. Jenderami has wealthy donors. Malaysia's petrochemical and palm-oil production swamps the country's economy with annual, if uneven, plenty. The palatial shopping malls of Kuala Lumpur have few equals in the West, and the football-field-sized food courts are, to my knowledge, unique in the world.

Malaysia has been a pioneer in Islamic finance, or the business of effectively funneling surplus wealth in ways that observe the Shariah's prohibitions on *Riba* (interest) and *Gharar* (excessive risk). The centrality of routine interest in the modern world economy has, not surprisingly, made finding an Islamic alternative highly desirable. Islamic finance has grown to a $1.3 trillion annual industry globally, with Malaysia as a central hub. Fully one-fifth of the country's banking sector is Shariah-compliant, and it issued more than 80 percent of global Islamic bond notes in 2012.

Of course, religious observance is not uniform. It is difficult to approximate how many Muslims observe the Shariah rules on modern finance, which are highly contested to begin with. Recent estimates run from 12 percent of Muslims using Shariah-compliant financial products to an approximation that two-thirds of Muslims would like to if it were feasible.[1]

Convincing average Muslims of the sinfulness of dealing in interest has always been a challenge for the ulama, and never more so than with rulers eager to borrow and influential merchants eager to lend. In the late eleventh century, the Seljuq sultan of Baghdad expelled a hugely popular scholar from the city for urging his large audiences to heed the Shariah's ban on *Riba*. It seems he threatened too much the gears of commerce. By the late sixteenth century, the Ottoman religious establishment had come to accept that interest was regularly being charged. Despite fierce resistance by purist ulama, their more pragmatic colleagues employed in the Ottoman administration recognized that such practices had become a thread running inextricably through the empire's economy. They sought only to prevent exploitatively high rates.[2] Yet the campaign to stomp interest out completely has never ceased, with preachers to this day reiterating to the faithful the severe condemnation of *Riba* in the Qur'an and Hadiths. One modern Malaysian cleric begins a concise online primer on the severity of *Riba* with a startling Hadith: the Prophet declared that '*Riba* is of seventy types, the least severe is like a man having sex with his mother.'[3]

This Hadith often strikes Muslims as odd. How could it be that receiving five percent interest on a savings account is tantamount to an unnatural sexual act? Some ulama offer explanations emphasizing that it is God who assigns the moral weight of actions, not man. Rulings from the Qur'an and Hadiths are sometimes arational, like the Qur'an's prohibition on pork, and inaccessible to the mortal mind if unassisted by revelation. Other ulama argue that mild *Riba* only *seems* a petty sin because daily life has desensitized our moral compass. If we really grasped the effect of financial interest on society, we would see its perfidy clearly. With the exception of the spiritually aware, however, we are veiled from the reality of God and the true nature of our actions by the shroud of this earthly life. All will be laid bare on Judgment Day. Sayyid Naquib Al-Attas, Malaysia's most famous Islamic intellectual and educational reformer, often speaks about the fog that obscures our moral vision and our inability to grasp the true nature of our actions or the realities of the Afterlife. He cites the Hadith of the Prophet, 'People are asleep, and when they die they awaken.'

THE TRUTH, WHAT'S THAT?

One surprising feature unites the Jenderami chain of tradition, the Hadith equating mild *Riba* with incest and the Hadith about humankind's earthly somnolence: none of them is technically 'true.' Put differently, none of them corresponds to the historical reality that each claims to represent.

A crucial link in the Jenderami chain relies on the Basran Sufi Abu Talib Makki receiving the knowledge of Islamic law and Sufism from Abu Bakr Shibli, a saint of Baghdad. But the two never met, and the chain of the school's *'ilm* is thus broken.[4] The Hadith equating the slightest form of *Riba* with incest has been widely considered unreliable or even a blatant forgery by Muslim Hadith scholars, and the Hadith quoted by Al-Attas was never said by the Prophet but rather by the caliph Ali bin Abi Talib.[5]

What does it mean that something is true, or to speak the truth? For Aristotle and the intellectual worlds he so profoundly influenced, the truth of things is their essential nature. Speaking the truth is, as Aristotle asserts in his *Metaphysics*, 'to say of what is that it is, and of what is not that it is not' – it is a proposition that corresponds to external reality.[6] Modern Western philosophers have labeled this predominant perspective on truth the Correspondence Theory of Truth. Islamic civilization adopted the Aristotelian definition almost word for word. For Muslim legal theorists, a true proposition was one 'that corresponds to reality.' A falsehood, by contrast, is a proposition that 'does not correspond to reality.'

For Aristotle and his Muslim and Western heirs, the reality to which our speech must correspond in order to be true was not in doubt. It was eminently graspable by the senses and perceivable by man's faculty of reason. As the pillars of the West's medieval philosophical edifice crumbled one by one in the Renaissance and early modern periods, however, philosophers articulated new understandings of truth and how it should be expressed. Nietzsche, that great idol smasher, took his hammer to the fragile claim that language has the capacity to represent reality, undermining our claim to grasp it. Just as language is no more than an invented convention created and affirmed by our human communities for our own convenience, he insisted, so the 'truth' that language claims to describe is no more than a convention agreed upon to create hope for an inconsequential species in a vast world. Truth, Nietzsche revealed, is just a necessary lie – a drug – that we need for our comfort and sanity. Within the sphere of our great global lie, what people truly object to when they condemn quotidian falsehoods is not untruth per se but the act of fraud, deceptively claiming that something unreal is real for some improper motive.[7]

Over the last two centuries, as the sense that reality is of humankind's own making has gained increasing acceptance, some philosophers have articulated what has become known as the Coherence Theory of Truth. This holds that propositions or beliefs are true when they fit into consistent systems of belief or worldviews. In contrast to the Correspondence Theory, the Coherence Theory does not hold out some external reality as a measure of truth. Since we cannot escape the axiomatic nature of our basic beliefs, the restrictions of language or even the subjectivity of our own sense perception, there is no external, objective proof that something is true. The very backgrounds against which we compare claims of truth are themselves no more than claims. However obvious or deeply rooted a truth seems, then, the only guarantor of the truth of any one claim is a greater system of claims.[8] If that system is based in a certain belief in some immeasurable metaphysical reality, like God and revelation, then anything that accords within the structures of that system is true.

The American philosopher and pioneer psychologist William James proposed a theory of truth that could be seen as a middle ground. Known as the Pragmatic Theory, it shuns dogmatic definitions of truth in favor of something more practical. Propositions are true when people believe they are true. Certainly, this is constrained in empirical questions. The Pragmatic approach conceives of truth as correspondence with reality in questions relating to the material world. In terms of ideas, beliefs or metaphysical claims, however, an individual finds truth when they feel that an idea makes sense and fits into their own subjective reality.[9] Speaking truth about the empirically measurable world around us means describing it as it is, but claims about higher realities are true if they bring the speaker solace.

NOBLE LIES AND PROFOUND TRUTHS

At one lecture given by Sayyid Naquib Al-Attas, an audience member who specialized in the study of Hadiths rose and objected to his attributing Ali's saying 'People are asleep, and when they die they awaken' to the Prophet. Al-Attas replied, 'Why should we not use this, when it is an important principle (*asl*) in our religion?'

Even those who subscribe wholeheartedly to the Correspondence Theory of Truth and believe that an external reality is the measure of truthful speech face a quandary. Is 'reality' one-dimensional and made up only of the superficial facts that compose the perceptible surfaces of our world, as materialists like Aristotle believed? Or is reality possessed of depth and layers, with more profound dimensions of reality existing behind and above the material world we perceive, as Plato held? Was

Al-Attas misrepresenting truth – as surface fact – when he attributed this saying to Muhammad, or was he accurately invoking truth – as profound reality – when he placed an inherently true statement in the mouth of the Prophet whom Muslims revere as 'The Truthful One, Believed in Truth'?

How one answers this question informs how one defines lying and conveying 'truth' to others. As Aeneas flees the burning streets of Troy in the *Aeneid,* inconsolable over the ruthless massacre of his countrymen, Virgil summons into the fray the hero's mother, the goddess Aphrodite. She reveals the reality behind the patina of horrific events engulfing Troy. The clouds of perception are swept away, and for a moment Aeneas sees the gods themselves destroying the great city. He understands the divine will behind his human suffering.

Which, then, is the better description of reality, literal truth or the profound realities behind it? Are the events of the past better served by a historian who recounts facts, or by an epic poet who conveys deeper truths? The Renaissance poet Petrarch begs the question as he ruminates on Virgil's scene: 'It is in this way that truth abides in the fictions of the poets, and one perceives it shining out through the crevices of their thought.'[10]

The archetype of advancing profound truth at the expense of superficial falsehood is the 'Noble Lie' described by Plato in his *Republic.* Speaking through his avatar, Socrates, Plato charts his plan for an ideal state, where justice is achieved and maintained through each organ of society's body performing its proper function. This ideal state will consist of three classes performing different tasks, with children moved from one to another if they are better suited for it than the class into which they were born. They will accept their assignment without objection and however base it be because they will be told a 'Noble Lie' from a young age. It is a myth that teaches that people originally all sprang from the earth. The gods mixed gold into the constitutions of some individuals, silver into others and finally lead or brass into the last group. If each person is not placed within his caste, the myth warns, ruin will befall the state (*Republic* III:414–15).

Lying for noble purposes has long crossed civilizational lines. The Mahayana Buddhist text known as the *Lotus Sutra,* dating from as early as the third century CE, affords an example of the Buddhist teaching device of 'Skillful Means,' or shaping the Buddha's teachings to what is appropriate for each audience and sometimes even deviating from the strictures of Buddhist practice. The *Lotus Sutra* tells of a rich man whose house is aflame but whose children are too distracted by play to answer his cries to evacuate. He eventually lures them out by promising them beautiful gifts. They rush out and, unbeknown to them, are saved from the fire. But they find their father has lied about the gifts. Then, in the place of his false promises, he gives each of them a more stunning gift: an orange chariot drawn by a white bull. In the allegory of the *Lotus Sutra*, the burning house was the prison of desire and the false gifts were the Buddha's teachings that bring the children out into the world of Enlightenment. Associating Buddhist teachings with lies was morally fraught, though, and there was debate among early Buddhist masters about whether the father had told a falsehood. It was concluded that he had done no wrong. His was a Noble Lie. Like the quest for civil justice in the *Republic*, Enlightenment was the objective in the Mahayana Buddhist tradition. As with Plato, there was a degree of flexibility in the means used to attain it.[11]

Plato's Noble Lie and the *Lotus Sutra*'s allegory of the burning house are falsehoods that literally misrepresent reality. Humankind is not born of the earth and alloyed with metals. There were no toys outside the house for the children as the father described. But, like Petrarch's 'fictions of the poets,' both lies are true as metaphor. All people are not born with equal talents, so some *are* arguably made of better metal than others and more suited for specific tasks. The children of the burning house were granted rewards much greater than mere toys.

These Noble Lies require more than just a particular conception of truth and reality for justification. They are inseparable from a vision of society that assumes the leadership of an elite possessed of superior wisdom and authority. Plato's lie is not called 'Noble' simply because the philosopher's intentions were commendable. In Greek it is 'noble' (*gennaion*) in the sense of being a 'well-born' lie, one born of aristocratic stock. The cerebrum of Plato's body politic is the class of the Guardians, the true Philosophers (Lovers of Wisdom) who attain wisdom and, like Aeneas, have seen behind the veil of the material world. The Philosopher is justified in lying to his subjects because he knows it is in their own best interests. Similarly, the Buddha is described as a physician who knows how and when to dispense cures. Like doctors tricking a patient into taking medicine, the Philosopher or Enlightened Teacher can engage in falsehood because it is harmless compared to the great good achieved. The Noble Lie is justified because it works and is used by those who know how to use it.

When he was not occupied with his work as a Shariah court judge in Cordoba or writing manuals of Islamic law, Averroes (Ibn Rushd) wrote precious commentaries on the works of Plato and Aristotle. Discussing the *Republic* and the Noble Lie, Ibn Rushd remarks: 'There is no lawgiver who does not employ fictitious tales, because this is necessary for the masses if they are to attain happiness.'[12] Like his philosophical paragon Aristotle, Ibn Rushd believed that different audiences should be addressed with different types of proof or methods of argumentation. When it came to the masses, the ulama should address them not with demonstrations of the truth or complex argument but with compelling rhetoric. In this way they might be urged toward what helps them and steered away from what harms them.[13]

The man the Latin West would come to revere as Averroes was not the first Muslim scholar to have adopted this Aristotelian model of a gradated set of proofs or the Platonic model of the Guardian class. As far back as Shafiʿi, the ulama had considered themselves the 'Elect' whose job it was to ruminate on and derive the details of Islamic law and dogma in order to properly guide the 'Masses,' whose only duty was to follow their scholarly instruction. Beneath the ulama's stormy debates over schools of law and theology, their view of the masses was uniform: 'the layperson has no *madhhab*.' This did not mean that he or she was not subject to the order of some school of law. It meant that the laity was not even qualified to think about Islam at the level of contrasting schools of thought. They simply followed whatever *madhhab* the local ulama instructed them on.

Early works of Islamic law and theology are replete with the maxim that 'We have been commanded to speak to people according to their minds' abilities.'[14] The Prophet had once instructed one of his Companions not to tell the masses of his followers that God would protect from Hellfire anyone who professed that there is only one God and that Muhammad is His Prophet. He feared that such a guarantee might encourage laxity in his followers' practice. In his definitive commentary on Bukhari's collection, the fifteenth-century Cairene scholar Ibn Hajar notes that it was desirable to refrain from telling mass audiences any Ḥadith that might, at face value, mislead listeners into heresy or incite rebellion against the state.[15]

THE ULAMA AS GUARDIANS

'It is said,' a sixteenth-century text on the lives of Sufi saints reports, that the Egyptian Sufi master 'Abd al-Ghaffar Qusi was once eating squash when his son remarked, 'Verily, the Messenger of God, may God's peace be upon him, loved eating squash.' The master replied angrily, 'That's nonsense!' unsheathed his sword and struck off his son's head. 'He put the aim of the Lawmaker before the fruit of his own heart,' concludes the scholar writing Qusi's biography.[16] The biographer, himself a great jurist and Sufi, was not at all certain that this dramatic rebuke of Hadith forgery had really occurred. But, in any case, it was a striking story that left no ambiguity in the reader's mind about the horrendous sin of 'lying about the Prophet of God.'

Lying, even Noble Lying, was considered an unmitigated sin in Sunni Islam. Ulama had inveighed against it since the earliest days of the Muslim community. Of course, there were situations in which lying was allowed and even encouraged, but these had been delimited by the Prophet in a well-known Hadith: 'Lying is not permitted except in three instances: a man speaking to his wife and trying to make her happy, deception in warfare and lying to help reconcile people.'[17] This was a very narrow window, however, with one ninth-century book devoted to condemning lying including a Hadith in which the Prophet – with due respect to the *Lotus Sutra* – even forbade tricking a child with a false offer.[18] This aversion to lying was due in great part to the cult of authenticity and preservation of truth that permeated the Sunni science of Hadith criticism. The most widely transmitted Hadith was the Prophet's dire warning, 'Whoever misrepresents me intentionally, let him prepare for himself a seat in Hellfire.' This became the mantra of Sunni scholarly culture. When the greatest Hadith scholar of eleventh-century Baghdad died, the huge crowd of mourners accompanying his body to the cemetery cried out, 'Make way! Make way for him who fended off lies from the Messenger of God!' Without exception, Sunni scholars across the centuries absolutely condemned the intentional forgery of Hadiths, even for good causes.

If uttering 'propositions that contradict reality' was forbidden in Islam, speaking truth could be flexible and left many avenues open for Skillful Means. Generalization, omission and creative phrasing were all accepted by Muslim scholars as tools of pedagogy and rhetoric. 'For every situation there is a thing to say,' went a famous Arabic aphorism embraced by the ulama; 'If a layperson comes to me off the street and asks me if there are mistakes in the Two Authentic Collections (*Sahihayn*) of Bukhari and Muslim,' admitted one modern Egyptian Hadith scholar privately, 'I'd tell them no. But among the ulama,' he added, 'we all acknowledge that the two books have errors – there is no perfect book but the Book of God.'

More importantly, the Sunni science of Hadith criticism rated the reliability of attributions to the Prophet along a spectrum. The optimum rating for a Hadith was 'widely and diffusely transmitted' (*mutawatir*) – a report so well established that it could not possibly be a forgery. This level was followed by the 'sound' (*sahih*) rating, the level of many of the Hadiths in the canonical Sunni collections. Toward the other end of the spectrum were 'weak' (*da'if*) Hadiths, those with interrupted chains of transmission, limited corroboration and/or unreliable narrators reporting them. Finally there were egregious, 'baseless forgeries' (*mawdu'*). The ulama acknowledged that using blatantly forged Hadiths as evidence for anything was off limits, but Hadiths rated merely as 'weak' were a different matter. Although a Hadith critic might not find reliable chains of transmission establishing that Muhammad had said those particular words, this was an absence of evidence more than evidence of absence. It might well be that the Prophet had made the statement but that all traces of it had been lost. As the Lisbon judge and Hadith virtuoso Ibn 'Abd al-Barr observed in the eleventh century, 'How many Hadiths there are with a weak chain of transmission but a sound meaning.'

The ulama who undertook intensive Hadith study often maintained stricter standards in their craft. They sat hunched over volumes of transmissions, tracing and evaluating the minute details of words attributed to Muhammad. Such committed scholars insisted over the centuries that preserving the Prophet's legacy in its true form meant only attaching the noble phrase 'The Prophet of God said…' to statements with established chains of transmission.

For other ulama, however, like jurists deriving details of obscure rulings, local imams mounting the pulpit to deliver Friday sermons or Sufis describing mystical encounters with God, less rigor would suffice. Even the paragon of adhering to the authentic Sunna, Ibn Hanbal, had included hundreds of 'weak' Hadiths in his voluminous *Musnad* because he believed they might serve some use in a legal issue or assist Muslims in their manners.[19] By the eleventh century it had become routine for ulama compiling their vast Hadith collections (the largest would fill 180 printed volumes today) to include countless patent forgeries, excusing this by declaring that they had provided the chains of transmission for each Hadith appearing in the book. They had thus done their due diligence, they argued, and left the expert reader with all the evidence needed to evaluate the Hadith. Jurists penning legal commentaries or preachers admonishing a congregation would invoke the Prophet's authority with a weak Hadith by introducing it ambiguously as 'It has been reported that the Messenger of God said...' or 'It was narrated from him that...': modes of citation that were acknowledged in manuals of Hadith study to indicate uncertainty about the Hadith's status. Hence the phrasing of the hyperbolic vignette about Qusi. 'It is said,' wrote his biographer, that the Sufi decapitated his own son for lying about God's Messenger. Its authenticity neatly sidestepped, the story was cited and the point made.

The utility afforded by unreliable Hadiths conveniently tailored for public sermons made employing them too difficult to resist. Street-side haranguers or preachers occupying a perch in a mosque made the most use of them, frequently inciting the ire of more erudite ulama. Ibn Hanbal was torn between disapproval of the preachers and an appreciation for the positive influence they could have. 'How useful they are to the masses,' he once said as he passed by a preacher, 'even though the mass of what they say is false.' The lower rung of ulama who manned the local neighborhood mosques of Islamdom might take advantage of prepackaged booklets of mostly forged Hadiths fabricated specifically for homilies. One perennially popular book consisted of forty Hadiths supposedly taken from the Prophet's own Friday sermons, including concocted spiritual bromides like, 'O people! The world is an abode of affliction, a site of transience and distress. The souls of felicitous folk are removed from it, while it is stripped forcefully from the hands of those bound for perdition...'[20] Occasionally a pious forger was unmasked. Ghulam Khalil was a venerated Sufi saint of Baghdad and was so beloved that when he died in 889 the markets of the city shut down in mourning. Yet once, when he had been questioned about some dubious Hadiths he narrated concerning righteous behavior, Ghulam Khalil had replied, 'We forged these so that we could soften and improve the hearts of the people.'[21]

With the efflorescence of Sufism in the thirteenth century, the use of unreliable or baseless Hadiths entered a baroque phase. Vulgar forgery was no longer required. In the absence of *Isnad* evidence, ulama of mystical inclination could claim the authenticity of an otherwise unattested Hadith by more dignified means. The paradigmatic mystic Ibn Arabi declared himself able to verify Hadiths that had no chains of transmission whatsoever on the basis of 'unveiling (*kashf*)', or inspiration from God that took the place of more earthly evidence. A respected cleric discussing the authenticity of a Hadith before his students in a madrasa was interrupted by a Sufi dervish who ejaculated: 'That Hadith is false!' The dervish explained that he knew this because, at that very moment, he could see the Prophet standing over the cleric's shoulder signaling his disapproval.[22] Even as late as the early twentieth century, revivalist Sufis like the Moroccan 'Abd al-Kabir Kattani (d. 1910) received the wording of new Sufi liturgies directly from the Prophet in dream encounters or even in waking visions.

As with the case of the man who claimed the Prophet had appeared to him and granted him a tax exemption, in principle authenticating Hadiths by 'unveiling' could not affect the duties and prohibitions of the sacred law. Yet this principle was often obscured amid the thriving pietistic culture that characterized the religious space in which most Muslims from Morocco to India lived. In the fourteenth century a famous Egyptian scholar came across a Hadith that warned Muslims not to cut their fingernails on Wednesdays because it caused leprosy. The Hadith struck the scholar as odd, and when he investigated its transmission he concluded it was decidedly unreliable. Having cut his fingernails on a Wednesday, he awoke the next morning afflicted with leprosy. When the Prophet appeared to the ailing cleric in a dream, the scholar pleaded that he had analyzed the Hadith and concluded that it was weak. 'It should suffice you to have heard it,' the Prophet said. The scholar repented and was miraculously cured.[23] While studying in Cairo's Al-Azhar Mosque in the 1920s, a Moroccan Sufi scholar committed to a more disciplined approach to Hadiths found himself receiving embarrassed apologies from senior scholars, including a master from his own Sufi order, after he had alerted them to the abundant number of Hadiths well established as forgeries that peppered their writings and lessons. 'But the ulama have all agreed that the aim of narrating Hadiths is to act on them whether they are sound or forged,' one of the senior scholars objected incorrectly, prompting the young Moroccan to retort that no Sunni scholar had ever condoned forging lies about the Prophet.[24]

Whether in Cairo or Delhi, from the thirteenth century onward Muslim religious devotion centered on the veneration of living Sufi saints, congregating at the shrines of departed ones and, most intensely, revering the Prophet Muhammad as a cosmic reality rather than a mere man. Ironically, it was in the celebration of Muhammad himself that the indulgence of forged Hadiths reached its acme. The Prophet had said that he was 'the best of mankind,' and the Qur'an had commanded Muslims to 'call

God's peace and blessings down ever' upon the man who was their 'most goodly exemplar.' In the mystical thought of Ibn Arabi and other Sufis, Muhammad was far more than an earthly being. Behind the flesh of his mortal life was an eternal reality, the perfect reflection of God's wondrous unity. By the fifteenth century, meditating on the person of the Prophet and his attributes had become a centerpiece of Sufi devotion and popular religion, and invoking God's blessings upon him became a mainstay ritual activity for groups and individuals. So widespread and moving was love for the Prophet that in eighteenth-century Egypt a book entitled *The Signs of the Good* (*Dala'il al-Khayrat*), which included a weekly regimen of poems praising the Prophet and prayers for him, was the most commonly owned book after the Qur'an.[25] Even today, books written for public reading and poems sung in the Prophet's praise are ubiquitous during celebrations of his birthday in Egypt's Nile Valley cities and the verdant farming hamlets of the Delta.

These books and poems brim with concocted Hadiths and descriptions of Muhammad's perfection. Of the roughly twenty-five Hadiths in the introductory chapter of *The Signs of the Good*, which provides a selection describing the virtues and rewards of praying for Muhammad, one-fifth are not only 'weak' (a rating that ulama could frequently disagree on) but also totally untraceable, unknown in any other Hadith collection or even in the catalogs of forged Hadiths. One such baseless report tells that the Prophet proclaimed that anytime a Muslim prayed for him, God would transform that prayer into a bird soaring across land and sea on 'seventy thousand wings, each wing with seventy thousand feathers, each feather with seventy thousand heads, each head with seventy thousand faces, each face with seventy thousand mouths, each mouth with seventy thousand tongues, each tongue praising God in seventy thousand words,' and God rewarding him for each one.[26]

Sometimes profound love for the Prophet could overcome the scruples of even cognizant ulama. Since the time of Ibn Arabi, a number of Sufi works on the Prophet's status had featured a Hadith in which he told his Companion Jabir that 'The first thing that your Lord created was the light of your Prophet, O Jabir...' proving that Muhammad was an eternal light that preceded the creation of the world. Yet even those medieval Hadith critics known for their laxity could find no evidence that the Prophet had ever said this. Belief in its truth persisted, however, especially among Sufi scholars. Some claimed that the Hadith of Jabir had been verified in an early ninth-century Hadith collection written in the Yemeni city of Sanaa but that those crucial pages of the book had been lost. The young Moroccan Sufi who had corrected his elders' use of forged Hadiths went to Sanaa to search for the missing pages, to no avail, and his equally driven younger brother later wrote a definitive treatise on the falsehood of that particular Hadith. Nonetheless, in 2005 a Muslim scholar in Dubai claimed to have received the vanished fascicule from an Indian colleague who had come across it in an obscure manuscript library. Replete with anachronistic errors, written in the modern Indian style of Arabic script and published under dubious circumstances, evidence for the long-lost Hadith of Jabir met with near-unanimous skepticism among Sunni ulama. Asked to produce the supposedly ancient pages for modern scientific study, the publisher claimed they had been lost in a fire.[27]

APPEALING TO THE FLESH: USING UNRELIABLE HADITHS IN SUNNI ISLAM

Once a sought-after beauty, Lady Montagu's face had been scarred by smallpox by the time she began her travels in 1717. Reflecting in wonder on the masterpieces of classical perfection she saw in Naples and Florence, she wrote that no letter home could communicate the magnificence of a statue's face or figure. An image conjured by words could not provide 'a true idea; it only gratifies the imagination with a fantastic one, until the real one is seen...' Intellectually voracious, a noted prose stylist and enamored of Newton's new science, Lady Montagu accompanied her husband on his diplomatic posting to Istanbul. Along with a remarkable set of observations about Ottoman society, she introduced its lifesaving practice of smallpox inoculation to Britain upon her return.[28]

Had he met Lady Montagu, her Neapolitan contemporary Giambattista Vico would have admitted himself appropriately impressed by her scientific discoveries and by the multiplying body of 'facts' in their new, modern world. But he also understood well that, since the birth of myths among ancient peoples, the truest stories have often been the ones that made sense of the world even if they later fell short of facts. The professor of rhetoric could not bring himself to endorse the new fad of reconfiguring ethics, language and education through the same scientific lens of mathematics and measurement. The world of human experience was too immense and clouded in the miasma of man's own invented cultures to be measured so exactly. Poetry, not arid prose, was man's original language, the common-sense probabilities of alert living his best guide, and rhetorical flourishes, not dry accuracy, his most convincing moments.

In an inaugural address given before the University of Naples in 1708, Vico vented his disapproval. In public speaking, he observed, enthusiasts of the mathematical philosophy of Descartes might assume that nothing sways an audience like reasoned truth. While wise men might be so convinced, Vico objected, 'the multitude, the *vulgus*,' are in the end only carried by 'corporeal images' and carnal appeals to their fears and appetites. If 'modern' philosophers thirsted after truth, they were better off consulting the 'invented examples' of the poets than some cold review of observed facts. They would find a 'loftier sense of reality.' Surely this explained why the ancient pagans of Athens and Rome tolerated poets spinning elaborate myths and concocted tales of the gods and heroes. They encouraged this because it meant 'the masses were imbued with a more grandiose opinion of the might of their deities.' Only in the rituals and sacrifices that were the concrete and public manifestations of religion did Greek and Roman rulers enforce exactness and accurate details. Only then did they punish deviation from superficial truths.[29]

As far back as textual evidence can take us in Islamic civilization, the ulama understood Vico's point well. As Ibn Rushd and Aristotle before him insisted, rhetoric was the tool that the elect employed to move the masses toward what benefited them and away from what harmed them. To dissuade the *vulgus* from a sin like usury, what could shame them into cringing reconsideration more than the Prophet of God himself equating the least collection of interest with mounting one's own mother? By positive contrast, a tired mosque imam, perhaps not as eloquent as he had once hoped, might find great utility in a book of forty homiletic quotes, each rhetorically refined and packaged with the authority of the Messenger of God.

One genre of Hadiths that the ulama found useful in this regard was Hadiths of 'exhortation and warning' (*targhib wa tarhib*). These either described the fantastic rewards that believers could expect in the Afterlife for performing some deed, such as extra prayers, or alternatively warned of dreadful punishments in Hellfire for transgressions. This genre was also replete with forgeries and material of dubious authenticity.

To justify acting on or disseminating patently unreliable Hadiths of exhortation and warning, the ulama often cited a Hadith in which the

Prophet promises, 'Whoever comes across a report from God (and his Prophet) about the virtue of some act and then acts on it, believing it and hoping for that reward, God will grant him the reward even if the report was not true.' Ironically, this Hadith itself was of dubious origin.[30] By far the most persistent defense for employing unreliable Hadiths, however, was not a justification at all. Rather, it was a simple statement about the ulama's distinction between areas of their religion that merited a strict regime of accuracy and those where such a regime might constrict benefits. Ibn Hanbal drew on the words of one of his teachers when he stated, 'If Hadiths are related to us from the Prophet concerning rulings of the Shariah and what is licit and prohibited, we are rigorous with the chains of transmission.' 'But if we are told Hadiths dealing with the virtues of actions, their rewards and punishments [in the Afterlife], permissible things or pious invocations,' Ibn Hanbal qualified, 'we are lax with the chains of transmission.' Generation after generation of the titans of Sunni scholarship, from Nawawi to Suyuti, from the last Ottoman Shariah court judge of Beirut to the founder of the first Muslim college in America, have upheld this principle: provided they are not clearly forgeries (in any case a subjective judgment), unreliable Hadiths could be used to describe the moral weight of actions in God's eyes and the punishments or rewards they carry in the Afterlife. They could also be cited in sermons and invoked to inculcate good manners. Among scholars of the Hanafi school of law, unreliable Hadiths even sufficed as legal evidence in categorizing things as 'recommended' or 'disliked.'

Some ulama sensed a contradiction between this strategy and the stated Sunni disavowal of 'lying about the Prophet of God.' In the fifteenth century a clique of stricter Hadith scholars in Cairo proposed the requirement that an unreliable Hadith could be invoked or acted on only if it fit under some established principle of the Shariah, and also provided the person hearing it did not actually believe that the Prophet had said it. Yet such measures only highlighted the dissonance in the ulama's use of weak Hadiths. Why would an illiterate grocer, for example, perched against the column of a Cairo mosque be moved one way or another by a Hadith he heard in a Friday sermon if he did not believe Muhammad had actually said it? The metropolis' leading Hadith scholar of the 1490s, Shams al-Din Sakhawi, replied to these objections with atypical academic obtuseness. His answer belied the underlying inconsistency between the ulama's valorization of textual authenticity in theory and their use of pseudo-scripture in practice. We assume, he explained, that someone citing, hearing or acting on an unreliable Hadith only believes that the Hadith is 'in all probability' authentic, not necessarily that it can be attributed word for word to the Prophet with absolute certainty.[31]

This was a contorted and unconvincing defense. Not even the vast majority of the Hadiths that Muslim scholars had actually authenticated as *sahih* (sound), which filled the pages of the canonical Hadith collections and played so crucial a role in the interpretation of Islamic law, were judged to be reliable with absolute certainty. Muslim scholars had centuries earlier integrated their collection of Hadiths into the greater Aristotelian system of knowledge by acknowledging that, with at most a few dozen massively transmitted exceptions, even Hadiths rated as *sahih* were only 'most probably' the words of the Prophet. They were not transmitted widely and diffusely enough to meet the philosopher's standard for certainty. How could this same scheme be used to excuse using 'weak' Hadiths, which no one could claim were 'probably' the words of the Prophet at all? Sakhawi's thin defense illustrates how the guardians of the Prophet's authentic legacy were reaching the outer limits of justification for their habitual use of unreliable Hadiths.

So why had rigorous clerics, who believed earnestly that 'lying about the Prophet of God' was a mortal sin, strayed so far into the gray land between truth and falsehood? As Vico recognized in his study of ancient Greece and Rome, the answer lies in their understanding of what constituted the core of religion. Ibn Hanbal had specified that Hadiths establishing firm Shariah rulings such as 'obligatory' or 'forbidden' were verified with strict scrutiny. The details and requirements of prayer, ritual purity, fasting, marriage contracts and inheritance distribution – these were the foundations and framework of Muslims' duties to God and each other. Other topics were of secondary importance. Ibn Hanbal and Sunni scholars across the spectra of time and temperament considered reports about the early history and campaigns of Muhammad's community to be too obscure and unreliably preserved to stand up to much historical criticism. Ultimately, this material had limited use for understanding God's law. Similarly indistinct in their chaotic detail but looming in the future as opposed to the past, Hadiths in which the Prophet described the traumas and triumphs that would befall the world of men and bring about its apocalyptic finale were also outside the core areas of religion. Reports in which Muhammad lauded the virtues of his Companions and early Muslim heroes were likewise seen as too harmless to merit serious criticism. One of the pillars of Sunni Islam had been that all Muslims who had met the Prophet were 'upright' exemplars of Muslim practice. It was assumed that all the Companions merited praise, so the details of each one's virtues mattered little. Finally, Hadiths of exhortation and warning, as well as those promoting etiquette and good morals, posed no threat even if they could not ultimately be substantiated. If a scholar could not find evidence to authenticate a report of Muhammad laying out the heavenly rewards that await those who treat their parents with mercy and respect, what harm could come from releasing it to a public audience nonetheless? The Qur'an already commanded Muslims to honor their parents, so the duty was well established. Even in the eyes of the Sunni ulama, steeped as they were in the resolve to 'fend off lies from the Messenger of God,' it did not seem necessary to demand critical rigor in authenticating Hadiths in the peripheral areas of etiquette, exhortation, history and the end of the world. Hadiths used in these areas either served to promote already established truths or provided details deemed useful but unessential to religious life.

A FAMILIAR HABIT: ASSISTING TRUTH IN WESTERN SCRIPTURE AND HISTORIOGRAPHY

Sunni ulama across the centuries considered consciously forging a Hadith of the Prophet to be an egregious and unjustifiable sin. But they offered up theoretical justifications for a long-standing practice of copying, absorbing, publishing and distributing Hadiths and other material they *knew* were either distinctly unreliable or completely fabricated. This seems so glaring a contradiction that it is tempting to ascribe it to the cognitive inadequacies of a medieval tradition that lacked the sophistication of the West and the Greco-Roman patrimony that rescued it from the Dark Ages.

Yet the inconsistency born of the tension between accuracy and utility is not as foreign as one might think. It has appeared century after century in the Western tradition of scriptural study and historical writing. The textual accuracy of the Bible knew no greater advocate in the sixteenth century than Desiderius Erasmus, forgery no greater foe. As he worked to produce an edition of the New Testament based not on the Church's derivative Latin translation but on the earliest available manuscripts of the book's original Greek, Erasmus made a stunning discovery. The only verse that explicitly references the doctrine of the trinity (1 John 5:7) was not an authentic part of the biblical text. Yet this same crusader against forgery chose to overlook the same problem in the case of the moving pericope of the woman accused of adultery ('Let him who is without sin cast the first stone,' John 8:1–11). Erasmus knew that many of the early manuscripts of the New Testament garbled the story or lacked it entirely. St. Jerome had concluded that the story lacked evidence, and Eusebius had felt it was apocryphal. But Erasmus nonetheless included the section because it conveyed a good message. Like Origen and Eusebius over a millennium earlier, Erasmus acknowledged that stylistic indicators left little doubt that Paul was not the author of the Letter to the Hebrews, as it was widely believed. But, like those Church Fathers, Erasmus included the letter in the New Testament canon because, even if Paul had not written it, it embodied the spirit of his teachings.[32]

Herodotus, the 'Father of History' in the Western tradition, set out the discipline's twin goals: studying the causes of great conflicts and preserving the epic deeds (*kleos*) of men for later generations. His younger contemporary Isocrates incorporated the study of history into his program for training effective and conscientious citizens, and it soon became the predominant school of Attic education. This pedagogical use of the past would have its most lasting impact in the work of Roman historians, who wrote history first and foremost as 'the best medicine for a sick mind,' as Livy phrased it. Reading about exempla from the past would be the narrative equivalent of Romans gazing upon the funerary portrait masks of their great ancestors, which the Roman historian Sallust noted had always inspired heroic deeds in younger generations.[33]

Ever since Herodotus, Western historians have consistently confirmed that writing 'history' is a scholarly endeavor defined as describing and explaining *true* events in the past. Aristotle said clearly that the difference between a writer of history and a poet is that the first concerns himself with particulars and 'relates actual events', while the second sings of more universal things that might or might not have actually occurred. Cicero wrote that 'history's first law is that an author must not dare tell anything but the truth.' He was following on the heels of the pioneering second-century BCE historian of Rome's rise, Polybius, who exclaimed that 'when truth is removed from history the remainder turns out to be a useless tale.' He excoriated an earlier historian for recreating a leader's speech based on 'what he thinks he ought to have said' instead of adhering to fact. 'If the account is not true, it ought not even to be called history,' affirmed the sixteenth-century French Renaissance scholar Jean Bodin in his seminal treatise on how to write in the genre.[34]

Modern readers of history share these sentiments. They expect no less than a truthful observance of fact or, at the very least, an honest admission of ignorance. Perhaps the individual most identified with modern history writing, the German Leopold Von Ranke, wrote that the historian 'seeks only to show what actually happened.' When the modern consumer of history reads the speech of a historical person, they expect that the speech was actually delivered as is.[35]

Yet all these great historians of antiquity took liberty with facts when utility required it, particularly in recounting speeches that could never have been recorded word for word. Despite being the father of archival research, Thucydides offered a famous caveat in the introduction of his *Peloponnesian War*. It would be too hard to recall verbatim all the speeches he includes in the work, he admitted, 'so my habit has been to make the speakers say what was in my opinion demanded of them by the various occasions.' Polybius' own *History of Rome* was, ironically, punctuated with impossibly detailed reproductions of speeches given by generals decades earlier on remote fields of battle.

Furthermore, if ancient historians viewed history first and foremost as a storehouse of edifying exempla, then they could find themselves torn between accuracy and affect. Isocrates used the books of Herodotus and Thucydides in his pedagogy, but he was unconcerned with the truth or accuracy of their facts. What interested him was their effectiveness as moral exempla. Cicero admitted an exception to his 'first rule of history' when he affirmed the rhetorician's (in whose hands the writing of histories properly belongs, he believed) right to artistic license. When referring to the past in speeches or compositions, Cicero wrote, 'the privilege is conceded to rhetoricians to distort history in order to give more point to their narrative.'[36]

Some modern scholars of the classics have argued that the luminaries of Greco-Roman historiography such as Livy and Plutarch understood truth and fact differently from modern audiences, focusing more on what plausibly conveyed the desired story than on correspondence to reality. Scholars like C. B. R. Pelling, however, have shown that they were more like modern historians than not. The greatest classical historians were, in general, fastidious about sourcing, accuracy and truthfulness. They strayed into fancy or falsehood not on the substantial facts of history, which they understood to be the dramas of politics, war and the great men who made them, but when dealing with the distant or mythical past, where fancy was inevitable ('All antiquity is, of course, obscure,' Tacitus concluded of what lay in his own distant past), or when presenting supplementary material that cast insight on the character of a historical personality.[37] Did the fabulously wealthy Crassus really make his sole traveling companion return the cloak he would lend him for trips as soon as they arrived home? Perhaps not, but Plutarch felt there was clear evidence that Crassus was remarkably stingy, and this vignette drove that point home. Plutarch acknowledged how many scholars had questioned the veracity of Solon's famous exchange with Croesus because of chronological disparities. But he insisted that the episode was so famous and 'consistent with Solon's character, so worthy of his wisdom and magnanimity,' that he could not help including it in his *Life*.[38] As Pelling explains, historians and biographers like Plutarch were not 'presenting a false picture, just helping his truth on a little.'[39]

Von Ranke and his modern ideal of the historian as providing a record of the past, factual in its composition and objective in its evaluations, claimed to abandon the temptation to favor utility over accuracy. 'History has had assigned to it the office of judging the past and of instructing the present for the benefit of the future ages,' von Ranke wrote disapprovingly. In his opinion, that was not the historian's proper job. Yet not only has the Western reading public continued to browse the 'History' section of bookstores first and foremost for learning the lessons of the past (lest they be condemned to repeat it), but professional historians have continued to meet this demand.

The awareness that the historian is always part of society – as bard and moralizer – contributed to the battering that claims of presenting objective history and historical truth have taken in the Western academy since the 1970s. Scholars of historiography like Hayden White have exposed how historians construct their narratives according to the same themes of tragedy, satire, redemption, and so on, as are used by less meticulous storytellers. This critical re-evaluation of Western historiography proposed that the conception of truth operative in the genre was less that of Correspondence than that of Coherence. There was no account of history that corresponded to what really happened. There were only narratives, told from perspectives and only as true as they could be nestled into the worldviews of the communities that recounted them. More conservative and confident defenders of history as a discipline argue that, like the Pragmatic Theory of Truth, while interpretation and even many areas of fact are relativistic, there is a 'factual bedrock' of undeniable historical truths, such as Nazi atrocities during the Second World War, that cannot be declared untrue simply through a change of perspective.[40] Such a bedrock *must* exist, many contend, because denying it would have the same impact as denying the common-sense reality of our sense perception and leave us stranded, disoriented in time.[41]

While academic historians wrangle over the possibility of objectively representing the past and how much accuracy their guild can lay claim to, there remains the ancient tension between the implicit claim to truth made in presenting 'history' and amending the past to facilitate its telling. This tension still burdens the modern-day mass purveyors of historical epic. Americans are invested in the notion that 'history' as a scholarly endeavor is, as described by the French historian Paul Veyne, 'a truthful story, nothing else.'[42] But Hollywood audiences routinely accept factual embellishments in the cause of conveying the real truth perceived at the heart of the story. The final episode of the critically acclaimed HBO series *John Adams* offers a metacritical nod to this dissonance. In the finale, the aged former president stands in the Capitol building staring at the gigantic (and actual) painting that depicts the signing of the Declaration of Independence. The painting may be compelling, Adams blusters, but 'It is very bad history!' The signers had never gathered in one room at one time to calmly and nobly affix their signatures to the document, as the painting depicts. When the stunned artist insists on his artistic rights, Adams rebukes him. 'Do not let our posterity be deluded by fictions under the guise of some poetic or graphic license!'[43]

A twenty-first century successor to the heroic portrait painter, American filmmaker Martin Scorsese acknowledges the factual liberties taken in making a period film recounting historical events. 'It's the truth wrapped in a package of lies,' he explains. As demonstrated in the controversy surrounding the 2012 Oscar-nominated film *Zero Dark Thirty*, which offers a realistic and ostensibly accurate depiction of the hunt for Osama Bin Laden, the film-as-history is a fraught, problematic but ultimately deeply desired way of making sense of the past in modern America. The film opens with the somber titles 'Based on firsthand accounts of actual events,' yet even senior US government officials remarked that it includes profound historical inaccuracies such as the claim that information extracted by torture led to locating Bin Laden. Despite the film's style of verisimilitude and its claim to veracity, the film's screenwriter defended its inaccuracies by insisting that 'It's a movie, not a documentary.'[44]

What seems jarringly inconsistent in the ways of others somehow becomes natural and unremarkable when pointed out in ourselves. Whether in scripture or in the high and low registers of writing history, the Western tradition has often inclined toward utility at the expense of fact without a sense of having betrayed a commitment to truth. Similarly, the Malaysian mufti warning about the dangers of *Riba* by citing an unreliable Hadith equating it with incest and the Jenderami Pondok's broken chain of knowledge were not expressions of contempt for truth. The Qur'an made clear that *Riba* was a vile sin; the Hadith comparing it to incest merely communicated this to a distracted audience in an unforgettable way. The ulama of Jenderami had without a doubt received their training in Islamic law and Sufism in respected madrasas and from teachers who, via their own pedigrees of learning, enjoyed convoluted but unbroken chains of scholars back to the classical period of Islam. The chain of transmission on the school's wall simply encapsulated this in a convenient and appealing form. Neither falsehood was tampering with the core areas of Islam or its history in the eyes of the ulama who produced them. They were 'just helping truth along.'

SEVENTY-TWO VIRGINS: PRAGMATIC TRUTH AND THE HEAVENLY REWARD OF MARTYRS

Osama Bin Laden's missives left Western publics much more familiar with Hadiths of exhortation and warning than one might suppose. American fans of the television comedy *Family Guy*, late-night talk-show hosts and Danish newspaper readers have all chuckled nervously at the 'seventy-two virgins' that the late Al-Qaeda leader promised Muslim martyrs in Heaven. Often mistakenly cited as coming from the Qur'an, the promise of seventy-two huris, or 'dark-eyed heavenly beauties,' for each martyr is actually found in a problematic and unreliable Hadith of exhortation.

The Qur'an certainly contains elaborate descriptions of Heaven. The book frequently speaks of 'Gardens under which rivers flow,' promised for those 'who believe and do good deeds.' They abound with 'gushing springs,' and those blessed with this abode recline on 'couches raised' and silken carpets with silver goblets and all the foods and fruits they could desire. They are paired with the huris (Arabic singular, *hur al-'in*), as well as with their earthly spouses. They never taste pain or death, and they are greeted with the call of peace. The Gardens of Paradise are an abode where space, wonder and pleasure are infinite, but time is collapsed into one eternal moment of bliss, when longing and fulfillment coexist in an unending oscillation between anticipation and achievement. Martyrs merit special reward. The Qur'an praises again and again those who fight and die 'in the path of God,' promising that they are not dead but rather 'alive, given sustenance with their Lord' (3:169).[45]

From the time of their earliest polemics against Islam, Christians in the Near East and later the inheritors of the Western Roman Empire have been fascinated and disturbed by Islam's sexuality, in both its supposed excesses and its perceived perversions. As an eighth-century Byzantine emperor wrote, the Qur'an's alluring images of a 'Paradise' (like the Bible, the Qur'an uses the old Persian word *firdaws*) and 'Blessed Garden' abounding with rivers of milk and pure wine, brocaded couches, vines heavy with fruit and sexual mates could only suit a religion that sanctioned sexual excess in this earthly world as well. Later Western fascination with the carnal rewards of Islam's Paradise was an extension of Christian disgust with Muhammad's own sexuality and the sometimes licentious ways of the Ottoman sultans. For Europeans, Islam's Paradise was a heavenly harem to condemn with the same voyeuristic outrage as its earthly counterparts. Montesquieu could not resist mention of the love-slaves who awaited both male and female believers (indeed, ulama stated that women who had no husbands will have male huris created for them). The often prudish Gibbon interrupted his *Decline and Fall* to note how Muhammad had lured the Arabs of the desert into his faith with promises of 'seventy-two Houris, or black-eyed girls, of resplendent beauty, blooming youth, virgin purity, and exquisite sensibility...' Voltaire, in a more sympathetic moment, reminds us that promises of a carnal Afterlife were common in the ancient world.[46]

Whether Achilles, the Spartans standing at Thermopylae (retold most recently in the 2006 film *300*), Beowulf (a 2007 feature film), the masterless samurai avenging their slain lord in the *Treasury of the Loyal Retainers* (*Chushingura*) or Will Farrell's accountant in the film *Stranger Than Fiction* (2006), throughout history men have sought what one of the three hundred Spartans calls 'a beautiful death' in order to find immortality in shared memory. In a secular age of nationalism, death for one's country, family or a just cause is deemed its own reward, though films eulogizing heroes usually provide a denouement that assures the audience that fallen protagonists receive the public attention needed to guarantee the remembrance of their deeds. This may be a neo-pagan vestige of the ancient Greeks and Romans, for whom an afterlife in the shades of the underworld offered little comfort. Truly surviving death came from dying heroically and living on in the memory of generations of the living through 'the lords of song and story,' as Pindar sang. 'Even in death your name will never die,' Agamemnon confesses jealously in the underworld to Achilles, even as both of them rest in the disappointing gloom of the Elysian Fields. 'Great glory is yours, Achilles, for all time, in the eyes of all mankind.'[47]

Islam's idiom of commercial quid pro quo for describing the martyr's rewards (the Qur'an calls believers to 'lend God a goodly loan' with their lives and resources, to be repaid with beatific interest, 2:245, et al.) seems venal and selfish to many in the West. The Classical thirst for immortality through glory, however, was equally self-involved. The wise woman Diotama administers an elixir of realism in Plato's *Symposium*: 'Do you think that Achilles would have died for Patroclus... if [he] hadn't expected the memory of their virtue – which we still hold in honor – to be immortal?' Far from Troy's ruins, Aeneas finds fuel to inspire his men and urge them forward into further dangers. Stumbling across heroic images of themselves carved in temple reliefs that preserved in stone the already epic tale of the Trojan War, Aeneas tells them, 'This fame ensures some kind of refuge.'[48]

The Qur'an and Hadiths leave no doubt about Islam's paramount praise for martyrs and the rewards due to 'those who are killed in the path of God,' a cause that the Prophet defines as 'fighting so that the word of God might be supreme.' A bevy of Hadiths extended the category of martyr far beyond those who died in war. They list other causes of death that earn an individual the status of martyr: death from plague; stomach illness (like diarrhea); an abscess; tuberculosis; drowning; structure collapse; childbirth and its aftermath; someone killed for their money, their family or religion; someone who speaks truth to an unjust ruler and is killed or dies in prison; as well as anyone who stands alone for truth in corrupted times.[49]

The Hadith of the Seventy-Two Huris is one of many prophetic reports enumerating in tantalizing detail the pleasures awaiting martyrs in Heaven. Muhammad explains:

> The martyr receives six special rewards with God: he is immediately forgiven his sins; he sees his seat in Paradise; he is protected from the torment of the grave and the greatest terror of the Resurrection; he is given the crown of honor, whose ruby is greater than the world and all in it; he is given seventy-two huris as wives and allowed to intercede on behalf of seventy of his relatives.

In light of the centuries of disapproval that this Hadith has elicited from Western critics, it seems supremely ironic that it is not reliable at all according to leading Sunni Hadith scholars (see Appendix IV).

Like the Hadith equating the least form of *Riba* with incest, the Hadith of the Seventy-Two Huris functioned to urge Muslims toward a goal already established firmly in the foundations of the Shariah. Along with dozens of other Hadiths enumerating the martyrs' many prizes, it often appeared in books on the virtues of jihad written during periods of heated conflict with non-Muslims on the frontiers, like the ninth-century raids and counter-raids between Byzantium and the Abbasid caliphate, or the height of the Crusades in the late twelfth and thirteenth centuries. As with the threat against engaging in *Riba*, the fact that the ulama lacked strong evidence tracing the Hadith of the Seventy-Two Huris to its supposed prophetic source provoked little concern. The Qur'an had already made clear the praiseworthiness of martyrdom and the existence of heavenly beauties, so what harm would come about if this particular Hadith and the additional details it offered proved to be untrue? As one Muslim cleric explained, it is like a merchant who undertakes a venture expecting to make a large profit but then makes only a modest one. No true harm has been done.

Moreover, even if the Hadith of the Seventy-Two Huris were untrue, the heavenly rewards it listed represented only a fraction of the myriad blessings awaiting those who are accepted into the Gardens of Paradise, whether martyrs or not. One particularly carnal Hadith might seem less dignified than others, but it provides a glimpse into the frank exposition of Paradise's pleasures. The Prophet states, 'Indeed a man from those granted the Garden is given the potency of one hundred men for eating, drinking, sexual union and desire.' A Jew asked Muhammad, 'Does one who eats and drinks not feel the need [to use the bathroom]?' The Prophet replies, 'It leaves his body as sweat after his stomach has taken it in.' Hadiths overflow with hyperbolic imagery of the huris' otherworldly beauty. Their liquid dark eyes beckon in inviting contrast to their near-reflective white skin, which is softer than the membrane separating egg white from its shell and so fine as to be almost translucent.[50]

Indeed, Hadiths enumerate so diverse and rich a list of rewards awaiting *all* believers in Heaven that the martyr seems to lose his or her premium. Even the least worthy denizens of Paradise will receive seventy-two wives, states a Hadith appearing only a few chapters after the Hadith of the Seventy-Two Huris in one canonical Sunni Hadith collection. This Hadith goes on to promise that this lowest class in Paradise will also receive 'eighty thousand servants... and a pavilion of mother-of-pearl, emerald and ruby.'[51] The most reliable Hadith on rewards in Heaven according to Sunni Hadith scholars states that, of the foremost to enter Heaven, each man will have two wives, with an alternate and equally credible version adding that 'they do not urinate, defecate, wipe their noses or spit; their combs are of gold, their sweat of musk and the coals of their braziers are of Indian incense, and their wives are from among the huris...'

Evaluating the reliability of all these Hadiths and reconciling them proved a lasting challenge for the ulama. The most encyclopedic Hadith scholar of the late medieval era, Ibn Hajar, noted all the various Hadiths on this subject (the most extravagant, which he warns has a very weak *Isnad*, gives each man in Heaven five hundred huris in addition to four thousand earthly virgins and eight thousand earthly non-virgins). He reconciles and distills all these reports to reach a composite conclusion: each man has at least two wives drawn from the earthly believing women who enter Paradise along with him, with whatever remaining number of partners he receives being Heaven-created huris. At some point in the early centuries of Islam a purported Hadith appeared to assure Muslim women that they would be superior to any huri competitor due to their faith and the good deeds they had done in their earthly lives.[52]

Christian audiences were not the only ones disconcerted by the carnal descriptions of Heaven in the Qur'an and Hadiths. Medieval Muslim thinkers deeply influenced by the Near Eastern heritage of Aristotle and Plotinus rejected them because they believed such images fell far short of accurately describing the loftiness of heavenly bliss. Muslim 'Philosophers' (*falasifa*) such as the famous physician Ibn Sina believed that the prize attained by the righteous and enlightened after death was the soul's rejoining the divine realm. Those souls that had purified themselves in life through right action and acquiring wisdom would bask in the presence of divine beauty without the body's constraints, while those who had become attached to the appetites of their earthly bodies would suffer their deprivation. The pleasures of the Afterlife would be ethereal and intellectual. In fact, resurrection on Judgment Day would exclude the body altogether. Of course, Muslim Philosophers believed heartily that the Qur'an was a revealed message from God. But it used corporeal language to describe Paradise not because it was accurate, insisted Ibn Sina, but because that was the only idiom that the masses would find appealing.[53]

The Islamic Philosophers were an elite group whose works and thought remained consistently controversial for the mainstream of Sunni Islam. Unlike the Sunni ulama, they did not hold obedience to God's law as an absolute command and the basic foundation of any Muslim's life. For Philosophers like Ibn Sina, the Shariah existed to guide the masses toward Aristotle's Golden Mean of virtuous behavior so that they might purify their souls. For those who had attained true understanding of the nature of reality, said Ibn Sina to his students, the letter of the law did not apply. Ibn Sina himself could and did drink wine because he had disciplined his soul, while the masses clearly must follow the Shariah prohibition on intoxicants.[54]

The most celebrated attack on those Muslim intellectuals who had adopted the cosmologies of Aristotle and Plotinus came from an eleventh-century Sunni scholar from Iran named Abu Hamid Ghazali (the namesake for the twentieth-century Egyptian reformist), who was so influential that he became known as Hujjat Al-Islam (The Proof of Islam). He listed among the Philosophers' most severe sins their suggestion that the duties of worship and the Shariah restrictions that applied to all Muslims did not apply to them (Ibn Sina might have struck too close to home – Lady Montagu would later hear her Ottoman ulama interlocutors excuse their own wine indulgence with the claim that 'the Prophet never designed to confine those that knew how to use it with moderation').[55]

Even more egregious, however, was their denial of bodily resurrection. Hujjat Al-Islam condemns specifically their denial that Hellfire and the Garden of Heaven were realities, along with such heavenly rewards as the huris. Ibn Sina and his cadre had no right, Hujjat Al-Islam objected, to limit the rewards and pleasures that God could grant His righteous servants merely because the Philosophers considered them unbefitting. More importantly, the Qur'an and authentic Hadiths had made it abundantly clear that Judgment Day would involve the resurrection of both the body and soul. The Philosophers' argument that these descriptions must be interpreted figuratively, like Qur'anic verses on God's 'eyes' and 'hands,' was horribly flawed, Hujjat Al-Islam argued. First, unlike God's attributes, there is nothing rationally impossible about God creating *real* Gardens and *real* heavenly mates for the believers in the Afterlife. Second, unlike phrases such as 'hand' and 'eye' that had a long history of metaphoric meaning in the Arabic language, the meticulous details provided about the Garden and Hellfire suggest no figurative meaning. Taken with their opinion that God had employed these supposedly false corporeal descriptions only to lure the masses to believing in Islam, Hujjat Al-Islam concluded that the Philosophers were accusing God of nothing short of lying. It might be a Noble Lie, but any suggestion that God's revelation contained falsehood or manipulation was ascribing to the Divinity a heinous imperfection far below Him.[56]

At the root of the Sunni rejection of reading a concealed truth behind the Qur'an's depictions of the Afterlife was the looming terror of the Ismaili Shiites and their 'Inner' (*Batini*) reading of Islam's scriptures. Their sectarian and military threat to the Sunni caliphate was ever present in the many writings that Hujjat Al-Islam penned as a star professor in the vaulted halls of the Baghdad and Nishapur Nizamiyya madrasas, where he taught during his illustrious career. His own patron, the vizier Nizam Al-Mulk, fell before the dagger of an Ismaili Assassin. The threat was still palpable two centuries later in the many pages that Ibn Taymiyya devoted to rebutting Ismaili thought. It lay behind his vehement rejection of the distinction between an exoteric and esoteric reading of scripture as well as his denouncing Ibn Rushd's implication that the Prophet revealed varied levels of truth to different audiences.[57] Denying the literal reality of Heaven and Hell as portrayed in the Qur'an and Hadiths and instead claiming that they were superficial falsehoods tailored for the masses dovetailed dangerously with the Ismaili claim that the exoteric reading of the revelation obscured the 'Religion of Truth' known only to the Ismaili Imam and taught to his elect followers. If it were accepted that the evident meaning of scripture could be set aside for an elite, inner sense on topics such as the nature of the Afterlife, the door to the Ismaili reading of scripture would be opened wide.

Ironically, though they championed vigorously the Hadiths describing the pleasures and agonies of Heaven and Hell, Sunni scholars admitted that not even the clear texts of the Qur'an and Hadiths could convey any immediate understanding of these unseen realms. What the ulama insisted on was that believers affirm the truth of what God and the Prophet had revealed about the world to come. Its actual nature could never really be known in this life. Ultimately, the ulama admitted to an agnosticism about the actual nature of the 'Gardens under which rivers flow.' Al-Attas had come across the pseudo-Hadith that humans are asleep and only awaken upon death while reading the books of his beloved Hujjat Al-Islam Ghazali. The saying is one of the prime pieces of scriptural evidence that the great Persian divine had cited in his defense of the Islamic conception of the Afterlife against the Philosophers' cynicism about its carnal imagery. Hujjat Al-Islam, a towering jurist and theologian but not known for his accurate knowledge of Hadiths, used the report to prove that 'it is not conceivable to explain the heavenly realm while in this earthly domain except by expounding parables (*amthal*).'[58] Like Lady Montagu's statues, words could never convey such images to those whose eyes had never beheld them.

Even the basic realities about the world to come proved difficult to pin down. At one point after Muhammad's death, a group of men and women in Medina came to the Companion Abu Hurayra to resolve a debate: would there be more women in Heaven or more men? Abu Hurayra replied that there would be more women, citing as his evidence the Hadith that each man in Heaven would have two wives.[59] In subsequent centuries, many prominent ulama would uphold this same opinion, such as the Cordoban judge Qadi Iyad and the Damascus madrasa professor Nawawi. Another school of thought hesitated on the point due to another Hadith considered supremely reliable in which the Prophet said that the majority of the people of Heaven were the poor, while the majority of the people in Hellfire were women. This was not a hard problem to solve, explained Qadi Iyad: 'What emerges from all of this is that women are the majority of humankind.' Hence they can be the majorities in both abodes.[60]

Ibn Hajar responded to a more serious flaw in the position that more women entered Heaven than men. In another authentic Hadith, the Prophet states that 'I gazed into the Garden and saw that the least group of its inhabitants was women.' Ibn Hajar offers an explanation. It might well be that one of the narrators of this Hadith allowed his own understanding to shape what he transmitted. He might have assumed that the above Hadith stating that the majority of the people in Hellfire are women meant that women must be the *minority* in Heaven. Of course, he replies, if women are the majority of the human race, then 'their greater number in Hellfire does not necessarily exclude their greater number in Heaven.'[61]

In a sense, it was overly ambitious to demand concrete answers to such questions. How could minds that know only the earthly world parse descriptions that were no more than crutches for imagining an unknowable realm? Only through metaphor could scripture constrained by human language and its lexicon of imagery convey glimpses of the unseen. Sunni discussions of the Afterlife thus frequently quote a report of God declaring, 'I have prepared for my righteous servants what no eye has seen nor any ear heard nor what has ever occurred to a mortal heart,' and their affirmations of the ultimate truth of Heavenly rewards might end with the Companion Ibn Abbas' agnostic admission that 'There is nothing common between this world and the Afterlife but words.'[62] Whether martyrs received exactly seventy-two huris, or if the same reward awaited even the meanest believer, Hujjat Al-Islam explained that the Afterlife held countless echelons of reward and punishment to suit perfectly each person's faith and the deeds they did in life. The Qur'an had promised that 'for each and all there will be levels from what they had done, so that He might recompense them for their deeds. And none will be wronged' (46:19).

In this light it is easier to make sense of the seventy-thousand-winged bird into which a prayer for the Prophet would transmute according to the (baseless) Hadith in *The Signs of the Good*. In a famous commentary on the biography of the Prophet, the twelfth-century Andalusian scholar Suhayli offered an important clarification about the scriptural description of angels and their wings. In the context of otherworldly beings, features like wings cannot be understood literally. 'They are not what comes first to one's mind as the wings of a bird with feathers.' Instead they are metaphors for grandeur and ennoblement by God, 'angelic features that cannot be understood except by seeing them face to face.' This explains the Qur'anic verses describing angels 'with two wings, three or four' (35:1). 'How could they be like the wings of birds when no bird has been seen with three wings, or four, let alone six hundred, as Gabriel is described as having.' 'So this demonstrates that they are features whose modality cannot be grasped by the mind,' Suhayli concluded. 'No report [from the Prophet] appeared clarifying them. We are required to believe in them, but exercising our thought by speculating about their nature is of no use. At any rate, we are all close to seeing them in person.'[63]

THE COST OF NOBLE LYING

'Abraham told only three lies,' the Prophet said in an authenticated Hadith. When he was called to worship the idols of his people he claimed he was sick. When he finally destroyed those idols, leaving the largest one intact, he told his interrogators sardonically that the biggest idol had done it. Traveling to Egypt with his beautiful wife, he told the lustful Pharaoh, who might kill a husband for such a woman, that she was his sister. Muslim theologians exhausted themselves defusing the theoretical charge of a prophet lying. Abraham actually *was* sick – spiritually sick – because of his polytheist surroundings, some proffered. His accusation that the biggest idol had smashed the others was meant to be an absurd statement predicated on the absurd premise that idols can act, others proposed. Sarah was his sister in God's true religion. Truth has many registers.

Sensitivity about the human mediums of God's revelation speaking falsehoods was understandable. But lying is hard to avoid completely. Muhammad had allowed deception in warfare and also permitted the white lies needed between spouses and for mending social fabric. Indeed, it is hard to make the argument that speaking falsehoods is always wrong. Many morally conscientious people hold that being truthful is the best policy, unless lying seems necessary to promote an unquestionably greater good or if the lie is of the minor, white variety. Both of these species are, in effect, Noble Lies. They are falsehoods told for a greater good, whether they are serious lies told for the preservation of life and property or insignificant ones used as social lubricant.

Yet, as David Nyberg points out, the tradition of championing the absolute duty to speak the truth and condemning lies categorically has been a regular theme in Western moral philosophy. It has resurfaced in the post-philosophical field of psychiatry, where 'denial' and being 'out of touch with reality' are destructive or symptoms of illness while honesty to oneself and others is 'healthy.'[64]

Important figures in Western moral philosophy (and probably many psychiatrists) have rejected the claim that Noble Lying causes no appreciable harm and have refused to excuse falsehood through euphemism and mental gymnastics. One objection to the Noble Lie holds that intentional deception is inherently evil and inexcusable regardless of what good is sought. Another objection finds nothing prohibitively wrong with speaking falsehood in and of itself. But it doubts whether any short-term good achieved through lying can outweigh the long-term damage to truth and trust that lying causes.

It is easiest to insist that lying is always wrong and never excusable if one acknowledges metaphysical absolutes. Belief in a god who forbids lying and declares that 'the mouth that belieth slayeth the soul' (Wisdom of Solomon 1:11) made Augustine adamant that lying could never be condoned, even to save an innocent life. The transitory goods of this world mean nothing next to the love of God and a Christian's fate in the life to come. Since 'eternal life is lost by lying,' Augustine wrote, 'a lie may never be told for the preservation of the temporal life of another.' Surely one should not steal or commit adultery merely because it would extend one's life for a few moments.

Augustine wrote his treatise on lying before he was a bishop in order to rebut those who claimed that Paul's public rebuke of Peter in Galatians II was not part of a real disagreement but rather an affected public performance meant to instruct their followers on the correct attitude toward gentiles – a Noble Lie. Augustine could not accept this. Falsehood and deception could never be part of true religious instruction. Nothing of this world was ever good enough to justify disobeying God, and the true worship of God could never be promoted with lies.[65]

Augustine's confident theism could not sustain a categorical prohibition on lying in the face of the agnosticism and skepticism of the Enlightenment. Immanuel Kant, however, effectively replicated Augustine's argument through the secular prism of reason and duty. Kant asserted that to be truthful in all one's declarations is 'a sacred and unconditionally commanding law of reason that admits of no expediency whatsoever.' Applied to lying, his famous Categorical Imperative would lead to the conclusion that no individual can lie because if everyone in society were to do so the very eternal duty of truthfulness, on which all duties and social relations themselves are founded, would crumble. Critics mobbed Kant for being so dogmatic that he would, conceivably, not allow the owner of a house to lie to a murderer who had come to kill an innocent man who had taken refuge there. But this seemingly obvious excuse for lying is based on nothing more than our fallible suppositions about promoting good, Kant responded, and it neglects the absolute interests being damaged. The owner of the house could lie to the murderer and tell him that his intended victim was not inside. The murderer could leave and walk away, only to run straight into the victim, who might have fled out the back door of the house and into the street. A falsehood would have been uttered and the harm still not averted. The results and ramifications of our actions are often beyond our ken, while the duty to be truthful is fundamental and obvious to all who ponder it.[66]

The Noble Lie could never be justified for Kant because he rejected the essential premises needed to justify it. For him, humankind's world consisted of the material reality he perceived through the senses and the inner world of cognition. There was no more profound reality for the Noble Lie to promote. And there was no loftier ethical truth that could justifiably constrain human freedom than the Categorical Imperative that had already proven lying inexcusable. It is fitting (and probably not a coincidence) that Kant also rejected with unvitiated scorn the very notion of a Guardian class empowered to tell the Noble Lie. The Guardians of European society had long kept their flocks shrouded in ignorance and superstition in order to render them placid and malleable, Kant observed. The future Enlightenment he dreamed of was nothing less than 'man's release from his self-incurred tutelage.' Individuals and communities may be imperfect and prone to error, but they must stumble forward in the quest for progress. A human being is a flawed creature who requires rules and structure in order to attain his own happiness and safeguard those around him, but any class of Guardians that claimed the right to oversee this structure would be just as flawed.[67]

Another objection to the Noble Lie is expressed in the Utilitarianism of John Stuart Mill. The British intellectual was irked by his opponents' assumption that Utilitarian ethics, which seek to promote the greatest amount of good for the greatest number of people, would lead to rampant lying as each person pursued his own benefit. This is the consequence, opponents argued, of a philosophy that places expediency over principle. Mill responded by reiterating that truly comprehending the benefit or harm done by an action requires looking beyond any short-term gains. The immediate, short-term good sought by a liar would, in fact, most likely not lead a Utilitarian to condone lying. Quite the contrary: what is expedient often threatens a rule or habit that promotes a much greater good in society. Mill gave telling a lie to save oneself from embarrassment as an example. It might seem expedient and beneficial to escape a moment of shame, but cultivating a respect for veracity brings far more good. It is, in fact, one of the greatest goods an individual can pursue, and weakening that respect for truthfulness is one of the greatest harms he can do. Beyond the scope of the individual, Mill explained that lying enfeebles 'the trustworthiness of human assertion,' an essential building block in relationships and a crucial ingredient for the existence of human civilization itself. There may well be instances in which telling a lie truly promotes greater good than telling the truth, but in that situation the benefit of the lie in question would have to be so great as to outweigh whatever damage it could do to the long-term sense of trust in society.[68]

The long-term harm that lying inflicts on the shared conventions of truthfulness necessary in society is the common thread running through the various criticisms of the Noble Lie. 'All heroic virtue rests on truth,' sang the poet Pindar with profound economy. Plutarch recounts that Solon sat through a new Athenian tragedy only to disapprove of the many lies represented in the plot. When the playwright replied that lies in such unimportant matters counted for little, the Athenian lawgiver retorted, 'If we encourage such jesting as this, we shall quickly find it in our contracts and agreements.'[69] This same theme underlies Augustine's metaphysical commitment to the idea of an absolute truth and is the silent premise in the enthymeme behind Kant's application of the Categorical Imperative: we cannot will for all people to lie because the resulting world would be unbearable. Augustine warns that, 'When regard for truth has been broken down or even slightly weakened, all things will remain doubtful.' Kant observes that, though it might not be intended to harm, a lie always harms others or humanity in general 'inasmuch as it vitiates the very source of right.'

Indulging in falsehoods about the past does similar damage to the integrity of history as a genre. In his second-century treatise on how to write history, Lucian of Samosata lambasted historians of his age for their sycophancy and transparent efforts to win patronage by flattering the powerful in their works. Not only does he find the historians he critiqued guilty of betraying a discipline whose 'only goddess is truth,' but he also predicts that they will be reviled 'by future generations for making all historical activity suspect by their exaggerations.' Francis Bacon phrased this objection pithily. Lies are like alloys in coins, he wrote, 'which may make the Metall worke the better, but it embaseth it.'[70]

MUSLIM OBJECTIONS TO THE NOBLE LIE

Visiting Baghdad on his way back from Hajj in the year 1184, an Andalusian traveler attended a sermon of the most famous preacher of the day, held every Saturday near the caliph's palace. As Ibn Jawzi mounted the pulpit, twenty Qur'an reciters, arrayed before the audience, began singing choice verses of the holy book, each group of two or three calling out and responding to each other's recitations in antiphon rhythm. Then Ibn Jawzi rose to speak. As he began, he invoked the passages of the revelation that still echoed in the vaulted hall. Gradually he wove them together toward a crescendo of exhortation, threading them with the Prophet's words and his own prodigious learning. 'Hearts were struck with longing,' the visitor recalled, 'spirits melted with ardour, and the sobs of weeping resounded. The penitent raised loud their voices and fell on him like moths on a lamp.' Ibn Jawzi would recall later in life that thousands had repented at his hands, and thousands more had converted to Islam.[71]

Known as 'The Knight of the Pulpit' in his own time, history has remembered Ibn Jawzi not as a preacher but as one of the most accomplished and learned of the medieval ulama, a prolific Hanbali jurist, Sufi, Hadith scholar and historian. He was also an influential critic of the excesses of Sufism and popular religion. As a preacher, he was well aware of the advantages of employing Hadiths of exhortation and warning, but he was the most vocal opponent of what he saw as the rampant use of baseless fables and forged Hadiths by popular preachers. In fact, he wrote one of the earliest and most capacious reference books documenting forged Hadiths as well as a manual for those giving homilies and lessons.

Although the large-scale acceptance of unreliable Hadiths was the dominant position among Sunni scholars, prominent opponents from within the ranks of the ulama objected, especially a cadre of conservative Hanbali and Shafi'i scholars rooted in the Hadith study circles of Baghdad and Damascus from the twelfth to the fourteenth centuries. Some of them, like 'the Sultan of the Ulama,' Ibn 'Abd al-Salam, and his student Abu Shama, focused their energies on the alarming consequences of circulating dubious or baseless Hadiths. Principally, they were being used to justify religious innovations that many ulama considered heretical, such as a special prayer known as the Prayer of Things Desired (*Salat al-Ragha'ib*). According to weak Hadiths, a Muslim who performed this prayer in the Islamic month of Rajab would be granted any wish.

In addition to their attacks on specific heretical practices, the ulama who rejected the use of weak Hadiths also articulated principled objections. These matched familiar notes among critics of Noble Lying elsewhere. They did not question the ulama's role as a Guardian class tasked with guiding the Muslim masses toward felicity in this life and the next. Rather, these critical ulama reiterated that part of this obligation was the preservation and propagation of the Prophet's authentic Sunna. The author of one of the two most revered Hadith collections in Sunni Islam, the ninth-century scholar Muslim bin Hajjaj of Nishapur, had written his famous *Sahih* because he had seen too many Hadith scholars obsessed with the quantity or rarity of the material they collected, boastfully reading it out to students or to mosque audiences with no concern for its authenticity. Muslim bin Hajjaj explains the dangerous crime committed by the collector of Hadiths who knows that material he is attributing to the Prophet suffers from some flaw in its chain of transmission and yet still presents it. 'He is sinning in that act, cheating the masses of Muslims, since it is not certain that some of those who heard these reports would not act on them.'[72]

Other opponents of using unreliable Hadiths reminded their colleagues that it was the absolute duty of the ulama to preserve the Prophet's words and precedent exactly as they were, not to offer to the masses whatever seemed helpful or appealing. The tremendous sin of 'lying about the Prophet of God' could not be euphemized. Scholars could propose all sorts of excuses that they were only using 'weak' Hadiths and not clear forgeries, but they had to consider the greater scope of the enterprise they were promoting. In a debate in Damascus over using unreliable Hadiths to justify the popular Prayer of Things Desired, Ibn 'Abd al-Salam reminded his opponents that 'being a means to lying about the Messenger of God, may God's peace be upon him, is not permitted.'[73]

One of the last great Muslim scholars of Andalusia, living in the surviving Muslim mountain kingdom of Granada, pointed out the contradiction inherent in using unreliable Hadiths. The commitment to 'warding off lies from the Messenger of God' had been the raison d'être for the Sunni science of Hadith authentication to begin with. If Muslim scholars were open to using Hadiths regardless of their unreliability, then what was the purpose of the intricate and highly developed system they had constructed over the centuries? 'For the heart of the matter is that it be established as reliable and doubtless that the Prophet, may God's blessings be upon him, actually said that Hadith,' wrote the Grenadine cleric. If Muslim scholars felt the need to invoke other sources of authority, whether compelling maxims or moving stories, they could certainly do so. But they could not quote the Prophet as their source. Ibn Taymiyya reminded those bent on attributing everything useful to Muhammad that, 'Much speech has sound meaning. But one cannot say "from the Messenger" for what he did not say.'

Ibn Jawzi appreciated these principled objections to using unreliable Hadiths. Walking the lanes of Baghdad, taking in the sight of crowds gathered around mosque preachers and hearing the sincere but misguided petitions of confused laymen, what concerned the scholar most were the social and religious consequences of misrepresenting the Prophet. Sometimes he could not help but laugh at preachers bumbling through their pious forgeries. 'The name of the wolf that ate Joseph was such-and-such,' a jovial preacher had announced once in the mosque. An attendee remarked that Joseph had not been eaten by a wolf. 'Then it is the name of the wolf that didn't eat Joseph,' the preacher replied. Lying about the Prophet, though, was no joking matter. No good could come from lying or exploiting fatuous and false attributions to God's Messenger, wrote Ibn Jawzi in his treatise on weak Hadiths, especially for the purposes of exhortation and warning. Even a good cause is automatically undermined and delegitimized when the forbidden act of lying about the Prophet is committed in its pursuit. Ibn Jawzi observed how the Shariah courts of Baghdad heard cases in which wives complained about their husbands neglecting them after some Hadith promising an outrageous reward for asceticism had led them to wander like a dervish for weeks. When ulama included forgeries in their Hadith collections with the ostensible excuse that a reader could evaluate the chain of transmission himself, they were deluding themselves. This was like using counterfeit coin in the market, Ibn Jawzi explained, on the untenable assumption that ordinary folk would be able to authenticate every coin before accepting it.

Most worrying for Ibn Jawzi was how using weak or forged Hadiths that promise outrageous rewards or punishments for certain actions 'ruins the scales of the significance of actions.' Taking up the Hadith equating the least sort of *Riba* with incest, Ibn Jawzi first demonstrates its unreliability by pointing out the damning flaws in its *Isnad*s. Apart from shortcomings from the perspective of *Isnad* criticism, however, Ibn Jawzi insists that 'what truly refutes the authenticity of the Hadith is that the magnitude of sins is known by their effects.' 'Fornication corrupts lineage and relations,' he explains, 'shifting inheritance to those who do not deserve it.' Did the least severe forms of *Riba* really have this same moral weight or inflict such social harm?[74] Ibn Jawzi beheld the effects of such Hadiths in Baghdad. He cites the specific case of storytellers in the city advocating a special type of prayer, the Prayer of Disputants, which they claimed the Prophet promised would nullify all a person's sins if performed. Now Baghdad was filled with rank-and-file Muslims who thought that stealing was no serious matter since this special prayer would wash them clean of the act.[75]

The Hadith martinets of the Hanbali and Shafi'i schools in Baghdad and Damascus in the thirteenth and fourteenth centuries were forerunners of the revivalist tidal wave of the eighteenth century and the Salafi movements of the twentieth. Ibn 'Abd al-Wahhab, the iconoclastic Yemeni scholar Shawkani and the family of Shah Wali Allah embraced the strict rejection of using unreliable Hadiths. Restricting any reliance on weak or dubious Hadiths became a hallmark of both traditionalist Salafis like Ahmad Shakir and modern reformists like Muhammad 'Abduh. For Salafis in Egypt, Syria and Saudi Arabia, lapsing into an acceptance of unauthenticated attributions to the Prophet had been a disastrous misstep that had led the Muslims astray into popular superstition, like the belief that the rose was created from the sweat of Muhammad, and cultural accretion, like the forged Hadith warning: 'Beware of a flower growing in manure, namely a beautiful woman from a bad family.' For Western-oriented reformists like 'Abduh, shedding the baggage of weak Hadiths held a twofold appeal. It helped delegitimize Sufi 'superstitions,' such as venerating saints and glorifying the Prophet, which so clashed with Protestant and European rationalist sensibilities. It also reduced Islam's overall scriptural exposure and cut down the extent to which the Shariah and pious customs permeated all areas of life.

The Salafi precept that the great ship of Sunni Islam had veered off the scriptural course set by the first generations of Islam, and the modern reformist conviction that modernity was snapping Muslims out of their medieval slumber, enabled a re-evaluation of the mainstream Sunni laxity toward Hadiths in both these ideological camps. As a result, they arrived at many of the same conclusions that Ibn Jawzi had more than seven hundred years earlier.

Yusuf Qaradawi and Muhammad Ghazali, both Muslim Brothers at early stages in their careers, the first with a Salafi inclination, the second with modernist leanings, spoke alike of 'clouds of weak Hadiths obscuring the horizons of Islam' at the expense of the 'purifying truths brought by God's messenger.' Qaradawi recalls with despair how during a sermon given on the occasion of the Prophet's birthday, of all the many Hadiths and stories about Muhammad that various speakers had invoked, only two were reliable. He concludes that, even if the great scholars of the past had not realized it, allowing unreliable Hadiths like the one on *Riba* into Muslim discourse 'ruins the relative status that the all-wise Lawmaker assigned to different obligations and acts.' Every act of worship, good deed or sin, he continues, has its own 'cost' in God's eyes. The proper cost is set forth in the Qur'an and authentic Hadiths, and Muslim communities destroy their own moral compass when they degrade those sources with base fable.[76]

There is in the revivalism and reformism of ulama like Shakir, Qaradawi and Ghazali something strongly reminiscent of the anticlericalism of the English Deists of the seventeenth and eighteenth centuries as well as their Enlightenment successors like Voltaire. These contemporary Egyptian scholars certainly identify themselves as ulama, but their desire for revival or reform is premised on a disappointment with the historical failures of that Guardian class and its manipulation of the masses. Kant observed the clear consequences of the religious impositions of Europe's priestly Guardian class. Terrifying their flocks with sermons about the Afterlife and ushering them through rituals and catechisms, the clergy constructed a unified religious society, but it was one built on manipulation and not on understanding.[77] The eighteenth-century revivalists like Shah Wali Allah and modern-day ulama like Ghazali and Qaradawi write constantly of this same crisis and the need for Muslims to reacquire the power of real faith by returning to the scriptural sources of Islam instead of relying on stagnant tradition. The great eighteenth-century Islamic revival movements were often 'anticlerical' in that they could not challenge practices like seeking intercession at the graves of saints without undermining the authority of the mainstream Sunni ulama who had justified them for centuries. Salafi paragons like Shah Wali Allah's grandson Shah Ismail Shahid used printing presses to direct cheap, accessible attacks on popular 'heresies' directly to the masses, arguing that anyone could understand Islam's simple message of untainted monotheism.

Conversely, it is no surprise that those modern ulama like Ali Gomaa who remain confident in the unbroken, unchanged historical continuity of Sunni Islam stand by the medieval acceptance of unreliable Hadiths. Yusuf Nabhani, a Levantine cleric and a Shariah judge in the Ottoman courts before the empire fell, defended this principle with unprecedented vigor. He devoted five years to compiling a thick tome on the virtues of calling God's blessings down upon Muhammad, listing the sound Hadiths and defending the unsound ones such as those found in *The Signs of the Good*.

Shaykh Ismail Daftar, an Al-Azhar cleric and the imam who preaches the Friday sermon at Cairo's oldest mosque, affirmed the Sunni principle that one cannot firmly attribute an unreliable Hadith to the Prophet. Yet such Hadiths can still be invoked as lessons. Who knows, Daftar insists, what wisdom they might hold? A baseless Hadith that Ibn Hanbal once heard a preacher recite in a mosque quoted the Prophet saying, 'Whoever says "There is no god but God," God creates from that word a bird with a golden beak and feathers of pearl, with seventy thousand tongues, each tongue with seventy thousand words, each invoking God's forgiveness for that person.' Even if no evidence exists for the Hadith's reliability, Daftar explains, we now find that when a person testifies to God's unicity on television his voice might appear on seventy thousand screens in seventy thousand homes.[78]

GENRE VERSUS BOOK: REVIVING AN OLD APPROACH TO AUTHENTICATING HADITHS

Ghazali once recalled that, when he was teaching in Algeria, an alarmed student had asked him if the ulama of the past had really declared authentic the Hadith of the Prophet telling how, when the Angel of Death had come to take Moses' life, the Hebrew prophet had knocked the Angel's eye out. Ghazali told the student that his anxiety over the Hadith was a distraction. Could he not see the real threats to the Muslim *Umma*, that 'the enemies of Islam are encircling us'? In any case, he added, this Hadith did not deal with a tenet of faith or any core element of Islam.[79]

The veteran Egyptian preacher knew well what lay behind the student's query: could a Hadith really be true if it required a Muslim to believe that a prophet of God such as Moses would resist his fate, or that a human could knock out an angel's eye? What did these seemingly absurd beliefs say about the tradition that had declared such Hadiths authentic? Modern ulama and Muslim activists have regularly found themselves in Ghazali's place, trying to ease tensions between Islam's scriptures and modern realities and thus preventing young Muslims from falling into the same trap as skeptics like Sidqi and Abu Rayya. Why are the majority of people in Hellfire women? Why does a Hadith quote Muhammad as saying that 'I'll not leave behind me among you a source of strife more harmful to men than women,' and another that the Day of Judgment will not come before

'You [Muslims] fight the Jews, to the point that a Jew will hide behind a boulder, but that rock will say, "O servant of God, there is a Jew behind me, come kill him!"?'[80]

Ghazali chose to dodge the student's question because the Hadith about Moses and the Angel of Death, along with all the above Hadiths, comes from one of the *Sahihayn*, the two authentic Hadith compilations of Bukhari and Muslim bin Hajjaj that Sunni Islam has long declared the most reliable books after the Qur'an. The standards for examining the chains of transmission and authenticating Hadiths employed by these two authors became the definitive canon of rigor and excellence in the Sunni discipline of Hadith verification. Although for centuries Muslim scholars had freely noted minor flaws in the two books, in the nineteenth century the pervasive anxieties over the validity of Islam in the face of the West catapulted the canon of the *Sahihayn* to the level of the sacred and unimpeachable. Defending the two books against skeptics like Sidqi or the Partisans of the Qur'an was more than just defending a reliance on prophetic scripture over modern and Western sensibilities. It was a desperate defense of the very foundations of the Sunni religious heritage.

It was not that the *Sahihayn* were actually the Hadith sources for Sunni law and dogma – the *madhhab*s had their own bodies of Hadiths that predated the *Sahihayn*. Rather, what was at stake when the two books were criticized was the methods that Bukhari and Muslim bin Hajjaj had used to compile their two books and the ulama consensus that stamped them with canonical standing. The *Sahihayn* exemplified the Sunni science of Hadith criticism, and they were the embodiment of the claim that Sunni Muslims had identified a core body of authentic Hadiths that encapsulated the Prophet's true teachings. This was the very pillar of the Sunni approach to scripture and the key to the sect's authority. Admitting a flaw in the books or, worse, in the methods of their compilers was to call into question the soundness of a religious heritage that was already fighting for its survival. Zaid Shakir, a leading American Muslim imam, recognized this instinctively. 'If you knock out *Sahih Bukhari*, you knock out the Shariah,' he once noted.[81]

Addressing the Algerian student's nervous query in one of his books, Ghazali offered his readers numerous interpretations from medieval ulama for the Hadith of Moses and the Angel of Death (for example, the angel had appeared to Moses in human form, and the prophet mistook him for an ordinary assailant). But what interpretation could plausibly mitigate a

Hadith stating that, as the Day of Judgment draws near, Muslims will fight the Jews until even rocks and trees betray those Jews seeking refuge behind them? Does this not sow seeds of religious hatred and excuse violence?

Whether the Hadith of Moses and the Angel of Death, that of the Seventy-Two Huris or that of the Rocks and the Jews, all of these reports belong to the genres either of Hadiths of exhortation and warning, Hadiths about Endtime or Hadiths about the virtues of famous believers. Even the notorious Hadith of the Devil fleeing flatulently from the sound of the call to prayer is located in the chapters of the *Sahihayn* on the 'Virtues of the Call to Prayer.' Along with the Hadiths about women tempting men and the number of women in Heaven, these Hadiths are all found in the chapters of Hadith collections devoted to 'Good Manners (*Adab*),' 'Niceties of Behavior (*Riqaq*, *Raqa'iq*), 'Temptations and Apocalyptic Strifes (*Fitan*),' or 'Virtues' of prominent believers.

This raises an important possibility that scholars like Ghazali overlooked in their efforts to reconcile authoritative scripture with modern expectations. Sunni scholars have for more than a millennium conceptualized the corpus of Hadiths as being embodied and organized in discrete containers, namely books of Hadiths like the *Sahihayn*. When the ulama of the tenth and eleventh centuries needed manageable and authoritative references for Hadiths, they invested a canon of six respected Hadith books with authority. In the modern period, when the ulama felt their scriptural tradition under unprecedented threat, it was this very same canon of books whose authenticity had to be defended at all costs in order to protect the scriptural integrity of Islam itself. When early skeptics of Hadiths like Abu Rayya attacked specific Hadiths, ulama responded by touting the *Sahihayn*'s stamp of canonical authority; a Hadith could not be criticized because it was in *Sahih Bukhari* and was thus above reproach. Later generations of 'Qur'an only' advocates and Hadith skeptics thus made the Hadith canon itself their target, as the Moroccan intellectual Khadija Battar did in a series of highly critical newspaper articles in 2002 to 2003 (later combined into a controversial book, *On Criticisms of Bukhari: A Man Veiled from the Truth*).[82]

Early scholars like Bukhari, however, had not conceptualized the authenticity of Hadiths in terms of books and authors. They had associated Hadiths with their transmitters, and they determined the degree of critical attention that each Hadith deserved according to its subject matter. Those formative Sunni ulama who had actually sifted through the Hadiths in circulation and compiled the canonical Hadith collections had explained openly that they treated Hadiths differently based on their topics. Hadiths on the virtues of actions or individuals, on the apocalypse, on manners and on exhortation were only subjected to lax authentication. Hadiths on the core areas of Shariah law and explicit tenets of theology were evaluated stringently.

This policy is one of the oldest and best-attested practices in Sunni scholarship. A self-identified Sunni of the ninth century and an author of one of the canonical Hadith collections provides proof of this method in application. Tirmidhi was unique in that he rated each Hadith he included in his collection. We see that Tirmidhi's chapters on subjects that Sunni ulama considered pillars of the Shariah include relatively few reports to which he gives a poor rating, such as might result from a weak narrator or a lack of corroboration. Only 17 percent of the Hadiths in the chapters on tithing (*Zakat*) and the Ramadan fast are rated poorly, and only seven percent in the chapter on inheritance law. Chapters on topics outside the core areas of ritual and legal obligation fare far worse. Tirmidhi points out noticeable flaws in the reliability of 27 percent of the Hadiths in his chapter on etiquette and 35 percent in the chapter on apocalyptic strife presaging the world's end. The percentage exceeds 50 percent in the chapters on the virtues of various early Muslims and pious invocations.

The Hadith of the Rocks and the Jews was attested by the most respected early Hadith narrators, widely transmitted and corroborated at every level of its chains of transmission. From the perspective of Sunni Hadith criticism, it was above reproach. But the fact that it was viewed as a Hadith about the dramas of Endtime means that it might still be unreliable. All available evidence suggests that the earlier Hadith transmitters that a collector like Bukhari relied upon as sources for Hadiths shared the approach of treating reports they heard with two very different critical lenses, depending on their topic. When Bukhari decided a Hadith was sound, it was because it came via a chain of narrators who could be trusted to have passed on information reliably from their sources. But if every link in that chain of reliable narrators each passed on Hadiths on dividing inheritance much more carefully than Hadiths like that of the Rocks and the Jews, then that chain of narrators actually consisted of two separate channels of different quality, one stringent and one lax.

This is not to suggest that an exacting collector such as Bukhari dropped his requirements in certain chapters of his book, as Tirmidhi clearly did. Bukhari's and Muslim's collections attained their paramount status because their authors limited their contents only to Hadiths that each scholar felt met the highest criteria of reliability. There does not seem to be a significant difference in the reputations or dependability of the transmitters that Bukhari relied on in chapters of his collection on the issues that early Sunnis considered core and those that were normally treated in a more relaxed manner.[83] Rather, my suggestion is that the two-tiered system of laxity versus stringency was a systematic feature of Sunni Hadith transmission and criticism. We could draw an analogy to security screening at an airport. In theory, the security staff follow specific rules for checking passengers and their luggage using the same scanners and a unified procedure. But if every member of the security staff, from ID checkers to scanner operators, decided to subject elderly ladies to an absolute minimum of examination, then the passengers passing through the security checkpoint would in reality be moving through two very different levels of scrutiny, one for old ladies and one for everyone else. This would be the case even if, and the analogy here is to Hadith collectors like Bukhari and Muslim, an airport sought to employ only the best scanning equipment and the most competent security personnel.

Judging Hadiths not solely by the reputation of the books that include them but also according to whether their subject matter would have merited rigorous versus lax criticism from classical Hadith scholars could provide enormous benefit today. It could reconcile the traditional methods of Sunni Hadith criticism with many reformist objections to the contents of Hadiths like the Devil Farting and Moses punching the Angel of Death. Because the vast majority of problematic Hadiths like these fall within the genres that the scholars who developed the Sunni method of Hadith criticism did not feel actually warranted its full application, it would be possible to accept most of the critiques leveled by the likes of Sidqi and Abu Rayya without challenging the overall value of the Sunni Hadith tradition.

THE DANGERS OF NOBLE LYING FOR MUSLIMS TODAY

Before he was killed in a Damascus mosque in 2013, Muhammad Sa'id Ramadan Buti was the most famous member of the Syrian ulama. An accomplished Shafi'i jurist, former rector of the Shariah College at the University of Damascus and a strong supporter of Sufism, in an interview he once recalled his own father's death many decades earlier. Buti's father had been an admired Muslim cleric, and after his death Buti recounted how his father suddenly became the center of numerous miracle stories. Legends circulated in the neighborhood about the angelic presences and portents of God's favor that appeared at his father's deathbed. 'When the people love a pious person,' Buti remarked, 'they invent miraculous stories about him.' Buti certainly did not want to contribute to the disenchantment of the world. He acknowledged that such saintly miracles were possible and that tales of them might well nourish religious devotion in some folk. He inclined toward the Hanafi position on such matters: if people wanted to believe random stories of saintly miracles, they could. Disbelieving them, however, was no sin. Yet Buti also recognized the dangers. 'Ultimately,' he concluded, 'the negative consequences of these stories are greater than their positive ones.'[84]

A population that believes stories merely because they are useful or warm the heart places expedience toward an end above a commitment to demonstrable truth as a common reference meaningful to all individuals regardless of their religious beliefs. A community that accepts Noble Lying wholeheartedly is likely to drift into gullibility, uncritical of what it is told and vulnerable to manipulation. Fear of such an eventual fate lay behind much of Ibn Jawzi's disapproval of using unreliable Hadiths. In the Baghdad of his day, pious falsehoods drew people down a slippery slope toward damaging asceticism and manipulation by fraudulent Sufi saints and charlatans. Buti shared such worries in the twenty-first century.

It mattered little that the ulama who purveyed unreliable Hadiths claimed they provided ample warning about the dubious authenticity of the reports. Research on consumer opinion and marketing suggests that Ibn Jawzi was prescient in his analogy to circulating fraudulent coins on the market. Studies on how people pass on information or impressions demonstrate that, while attitudes and opinions are primary beliefs that tend to survive communication from person to person intact, the certainty or doubt about those attitudes or opinions tends to be lost along the way.[85] If one person tells another person, 'It *may be* that this car model performs poorly,' the second person will likely only remember and pass on in turn the impression that 'This car model performs badly.' The more stages of transmission there are, the less nuance survives and the closer what may have originally been a qualified statement comes to being a certainty.

It is tempting to ascribe the absurd credulousness displayed at times in the Muslim world to some feature of Islamic religious culture. In the spring of 2012, for example, as presidential elections loomed in Egypt, Mubarak's loyal lieutenant Omar Suleiman announced his candidacy. Foreshadowing the dumbfoundingly bloody counter revolution that would grip Egypt a year later, when an interviewer asked Suleiman how he had procured the forty thousand signatures needed to enter the race in a mere twenty-four hours, he replied without a hint of irony, 'It was a miracle brought about by divine assistance.'[86] In the summer of 2012, even intelligent and well-informed Egyptians expressed shock at how the Muslim Brotherhood-dominated parliament had proposed a law allowing 'The Farewell Intercourse' – a husband would have the right to have sex with his dead wife up to twelve hours after her death. This was, of course, totally untrue. Parliamentary sessions were all televised, and no such proposal occurred (needless to say, the act would also be prohibited by the Shariah).

Ignorance even among the educated, however, is not the monopoly of any one culture. Americans are prone to equally absurd if less prurient conspiracy theories. In 2012, almost four years after he began his term as President of the United States, and despite his weekly church attendance, fully 17 percent of the American electorate believed Barack Obama was Muslim.[87] Yet the pathways of religion are uniquely perilous in their slippery slopes toward gullibility. Societies in which religion pervades and plays a wide-ranging role can find their fabric laced with dangerous naiveté. The willingness to suspend normal rules of disbelief in the case of matters religious comes from the submission to the supernatural that faith and scripture demand. Describing the difference between Homer's fabrications in his epic poems and the stories of the Bible, Erich Auerbach explains that Homer never requires his audience to believe that any of his fantastic stories of gods intervening crassly in the lives of men are true. In contrast, biblical pericopes like Abraham's sacrifice of Isaac require all involved, from the narrator to the audience, to believe in their utmost truth. Scripture does not 'court us' with the possibility of historical truth, like Homer. Scriptures 'seek to subject us.'[88]

So scripture subjugates. While true scripture might do so rightly, apocryphal scripture is a false idol, sometimes an opiate and at other times a tribulation. Unreliable Hadiths can cause harm at numerous levels in society, from facilitating illegitimate violence to masking its true drivers. The testimonials of Muslim suicide bombers regularly cite the Hadith of the Seventy-Two Huris as a motivation or consoling reward. This feeds the Western stereotype of Islam as carnal, venal and backward. Media and viewing publics pay more attention to the now infamous seventy-two virgins than they do to the substantive political or socioeconomic injustices that the bombers also mention as impetus for their actions.

Many times Muslim university students in the United States have expressed to me the confusion and concern they felt after hearing the imam of their mosque quoting their Prophet equating the lightest form of *Riba* with incest. Sitting in the audience during the Friday-prayer sermon at a prominent African-American mosque in Chicago in 2003, I heard a huff of incredulity from a man seated near me as the imam read out the same Hadith that Shaykh Daftar mentioned about the wondrous, thousand-winged, lingua-feathered birds God purportedly creates out of words of praise for Him. In some distant time and place, this Hadith might have motivated Muslims to improve their faith and practice. But not on that day, in Chicago, with that man. For him, the Hadith sounded absurd and chipped away at his confidence in Islam's scriptural tradition.

Why should that man, or any Muslim, suffer even a moment of anxiety due to a Hadith that none of the ulama has ever labeled as anything other than forged? Dubious Hadiths of admonition and encouragement, along with fanciful prophecies of Endtime, once had a place in Islam's imposing scriptural edifice. In an era characterized by skepticism toward scripture writ large, however, they have become a liability. Even a traditionalist like Kevseri could see the dangers in indulging in the Noble Lie. Those contemporary Muslims who sought to promote or defend Islam with baseless claims and attributions to the Prophet were 'destroying a garrison to build a hut,' he warned.[89] Explaining the Hadith of the Rocks and the Jews, Ibn Hajar suggests that the rocks and trees speaking might be figurative – meaning that the Jews will have no place to hide. But, as in the case of the Hadiths of the Seventy-Two Virgins and *Riba*, why should any interpretive capital be wasted or minds bent in labor to find explanations for what is most likely ersatz scripture?

PRAGMATIC TRUTH AND THE BEAUTY OF NOBLE LYING

In the summer of 2007 I asked one of my teachers, a young Yemeni Sufi master, about ulama citing unreliable Hadiths. 'It may be that they are mentioned to make the point in an appealing way,' he replied. At the time we were sitting over lunch in the lively Indian Ocean port of Mukalla, white thobes stretched over bent knees or purple-and-chocolate-striped sarongs folded between them, eating chilled potato and pineapple salad before piling into the massive SUV to ply the route inland from the Yemeni coast. We followed the road across the lunar landscape from which eons of rain had carved the giant rivulets that converge like tree roots into green, irrigated tributary ravines. The road drops down their banks, shrubs sprouting where biblical frankincense and myrrh were once harvested, to the rocky ravine beds below. There, rainwater scours the valley floors annually before soaking in and making life possible. Eventually these tributary branches, with their scattered ancient villages, lead into the broad Wadi of Hadramawt, so expansive and patched with green farm plots that one forgets that this flood valley and the floods themselves ultimately vanish into the dead yellow sands of Yemen's inland desert.

We passed from town to town along the flood-valley network. From Hajrayn to Shibam, their fantastic mud-brick, medieval skyscrapers jabbing up into the sky from rock promontories perched on the valley walls, to the sprawling settlement of Sayyun and eventually Tarim at the valley's narrow inception. This great valley is the heartland of the Ba'alawi Sufis. It is also their domain. Even as night fell and the Yemeni soldiers at their checkpoints grew more alert and suspicious, they waved our car past when they saw among our party the white turbans of the *Habayib*, the scholars descended from the Prophet who lead the Ba'alawis and who form the religious elite of Hadramawt and Indian Ocean Sufism.

In every town we visited venerable *Habayib* ulama. We were fed and listened to poems praising God and the Prophet before we implored the aged scholars to share some of their *'ilm* with us. 'You are all that remains,' the young Sufi scholar plied the elders over and over, 'those great ones who came before bequeathed their *'ilm* to you before they departed.'

The then nonagenarian Ali bin Muhammad Al-Attas (note the last name) brought out the weathered turban of his teacher, Abdallah bin Umar Shatiri, who taught for fifty years at the Sayyun madrasa and produced so many students that it is said that all the scholars in the Indian Ocean basin from Yemen to Malaysia are either his students or his students' students (the Jenderami ulama included). In the tiny village of Amd we paid our respects to Safiyya, then a woman of 105, who lay diminutive and feeble in a cot in her mud hut, all but her eyes veiled in thin black muslin. We took turns holding her hand through the sheet as she prayed and greeted us, occasionally raising her finger to point up and rasp defiantly, 'In the presence of the Prophet!' Her children had long since died of old age, and she alone remained of those who had heard the guidance of Ba'alawi Sufi saints from three generations ago. She too passed away in 2008.

In Mukalla, Habib Hamid bin Sumayt, himself well over ninety, received us in his home and asked his servants to bring out a tray of dates and water. Each one of us approached him in turn and he placed a date in our mouth and gave us a sip of water. He recounted his chain of sacred knowledge back through Yemen's Ba'alawi masters to Iraq, then to Medina and to the Prophet of God himself. Just as he had given us dates and water, so had he received them from his shaykhs, they from theirs, all the way back to Muhammad. Habib Hamid recited the Hadith repeated by every link in that chain after serving dates and water: the Prophet said, 'Whoever receives a believer as a guest, it is as if he has received Adam as a guest; whoever receives two believers, it is as if he has received Adam and Eve; whoever receives three, it is as if he has received the angels Gabriel, Michael and Israfil...' and so on.

No one in the gathering felt any need to question the authenticity of this living Hadith. It had no relation to the rulings of the Shariah or to Islamic theology. The *Baraka*, or pious blessings, of this smiling old shaykh inspired us and warmed the hearts of his guests. We all felt incorporated into an intimate bond with the Arabian prophet of fourteen centuries past. In time, we will feed dates and water to another generation and recount the chain of connection, brought into the present with our names added on at the end, in turn. No one in the gathering noted or thought to care that this living Hadith was actually forged by an eighth-century figure named 'Abdallah Qaddah. As one medieval Hadith critic explained, 'The telltale signs of forgery are manifest with this Hadith, but the ulama of Hadiths still pass it on out of a desire for blessings and with good intentions.'[90]

Like all 'friends of God,' the Ba'alawi Sufi masters understand that they are His instruments, and that He can work miracles at their hands at any time or place of His choosing. Over the centuries they have sought to observe the fundamental Sufi maxim, most often neglected in Sufism's medieval decadence, that saints should conceal their miracles so that lay folk might not misplace their adoration. The Ba'alawi masters came to Hadramawt from Iraq in the late tenth century and moved on to the distant Indian Ocean lands beyond carrying the message of their Prophet. One of the fourteenth-century *Habayib* would travel from region to region in

Yemen, and wherever he would settle his *Baraka* would bring miraculous rains and productive harvest. The people would come to love Islam, and the saint would move on.[91] From Yemen to Singapore, the gravestones and mausolea of the Ba'alawi saints stand as signposts and loci of the miraculous.

As night fell we at last neared our final destination, Tarim, the narrow valley heart of the Ba'alawi order. The young scholar leading us recounted experiences with his own Sufi master, the late 'Abd al-Qadir Saqqaf. The two had once left a Sufi gathering and, as teacher and disciple were getting into their car, a layman rushed up to 'Abd al-Qadir, closed his door for him and issued a protracted plea for the shaykh to pray for him. 'Abd al-Qadir listened kindly and assented. As the man walked away, the shaykh told his young disciple, 'Can you open the car door for me, the man closed it on my hand.' 'God is most wondrous,' the young Ba'alawi scholar recalled, 'Shaykh 'Abd al-Qadir knew how upset that man would be if he found out he had closed a beloved saint's hand in a car door.' 'At Shaykh 'Abd al-Qadir's hands the supernatural was natural,' he continued fondly, 'but, as we say, consistent righteousness is the greatest miracle.'

Over the centuries it has been common in the Sufi tradition to adduce innumerable miracles to saints. One famous thirteenth-century Egyptian Sufi was said to have lived so supernaturally long that he had prayed behind Shafi'i himself, though the *madhhab* founder had died almost five hundred years earlier. One day, one of the saint's students decided to ask his master the truth about this story. 'Yes, I prayed behind Shafi'i,' he replied, 'when the great mosque of Cairo was just a donkey market and where the city is today was just reeds.' 'Behind *the* Shafi'i?!' the student begged. The master lay back and laughed, 'In a dream, my son, in a dream.'[92]

7

When Scripture Can't Be True

Not lightly should you transport aluminum trays of oily Pakistani food in the back of your mother's car. This was one of many lessons I learned as part of the Muslim Students Association (MSA) in university. Though tragically not reflected in catering, a glorious diversity has generally characterized attendance at MSA events across the varied campuses of North America's colleges and universities: the second-generation children of Hyderabadi physicians suffering toward medical school themselves, well-heeled scions of Syrian engineers from the Midwest on break from serial brunching, African-American Muslims bemused by immigrant angst, occasional pompously coiffed upper-crust Pakistanis expiating sins incurred while clubbing and the odd Saudi exchange student committed to bringing order to this religious soup.

When the Muslim Students Association national organization was created in 1963, its founding members were predominately Iraqi and Lebanese graduate and undergraduate students in the US. They were all confident proponents of the transnational 'Islamic activism' inspired by the Muslim Brotherhood, committed to creating an environment where Muslims could live Islam actively and nurture their faith. Their objective has been tempered by time and circumstance, but it still animates MSA activities today. Whether due to family pressure, a personal attachment to Islam, a desire for familiar surroundings or an admixture of the above, the students who organize and attend MSA events are those who have chosen at one level or another to struggle toward an understanding of what it means to be Muslim in a modern and sometimes hostile West that is often the only home they know.

At Georgetown University in the late 1990s, the MSA met all the needs of Muslim students, from serving sunset meals during Ramadan to organizing Friday prayers and, of course, planning the annual Eid Dinner. Mounds of greasy biryani or shawarma meat, rice and the perennially and inexplicably undressed 'salad' would diminish as lines of Muslim and non-Muslim students passed over them like so many coed ants before settling in folding metal chairs to listen to the annual Eid speaker. Invitees ranged from Muslim and non-Muslim specialists on Islam to respected American and international imams. They usually addressed the controversial issues of the day and the challenges that Muslims faced in the West and worldwide.

THE QUR'AN AND DOMESTIC VIOLENCE

In 1997, a well-known Muslim professor of East African descent was invited to address the issue of Islam and human rights at the Eid Dinner. He championed the compatibility of these two sets of values, which perturbed some of the more conservative students. Universal rights that did not originate in Islamic scripture might contradict it, forcing Muslims to choose one or the other. A student rose to challenge the speaker. Their exchange became heated and quickly crystallized into the clash between the hypostatized forces of 'modern human rights' and 'traditional religion.' It centered on a simple question that epitomized the crisis of scripture in the modern world: did Islam allow husbands to beat their wives? This question struck at the core of how Muslims understand their scriptures, since a passage of the Qur'an addressing the responsibilities of husbands and wives ends with the following commands:

> Thus the righteous women are those devout and obedient ones, guarding what God has commanded them to guard. And those women whose *nushuz* [egregious disrespect and dereliction] you [plural] encounter, admonish them, leave them alone in their beds, *and strike them.* If they then obey you [plural], seek nothing further against them, indeed God is highest and great. If you [plural] fear a breach between the two, then send an arbiter from his family and an arbiter from hers. If the couple wants resolution, God will grant them success in this, for indeed God is most knowledgeable and aware of all things. (4:34–35)

When the student asking the question accused the speaker of granting more weight to modern values than to God's direct commands, the professor could contain his outrage no longer. 'Are you suggesting that, in this day and age, men should beat their wives?!' he thundered at the student. In the awkward pause that followed, a few hardy souls still sipped chai and spooned rice pudding.

A year later, a wholly different speaker addressed the MSA Eid Dinner. Instead of an academic clad in a suit and tie, a young shaykh of Syrian ancestry, dressed in a simple white robe and a white kufi cap, approached the podium. He opened his speech by narrating a Hadith to the audience, tracing at length its entire chain of transmission, scholar by scholar, from himself back to the Prophet. When he had finished, he explained that this painstaking exercise was meant to remind the audience of the unbroken chain of tradition by which the knowledge of God's revelation and the Shariah has come down across the centuries in the hands of the ulama. During the question-and-answer period, this speaker too was asked how Muslims should make sense of what is sometimes simply referred to as 'The Wife Beating Verse.' He replied that, contrary to what is widely believed, the Shariah in no way condoned a husband striking his wife. He pointed out that the Arabic verb taken to mean 'strike' or 'beat' in the verse, *daraba*, had been incorrectly interpreted. God could not have intended this meaning because it would have contradicted the conduct of the Prophet, whom well-known Hadiths described as never having struck any of his wives in any way. *Daraba* was used in numerous other ways in the Qur'an, he continued, some much better suited for the verse. One usage of the word was also found in a Hadith in which the Prophet explains a rule about business partnerships by expounding a parable of passengers together in a boat. A careless person in the lower part of the boat starts to drill a hole in the hull so that he can access water without climbing above deck. The Prophet describes how the other passengers should 'strike upon his hand' to stop him.* As with these imperiled passengers, the young shaykh explained that the verb *daraba* in the Qur'anic verse is thus really an instruction for a husband 'to do whatever is physically necessary to rectify the situation' and save his wife from bringing about the demise of the marriage.[1]

* This Hadith can be found in *Sahih Bukhari* and elsewhere, but I have found no version that uses the verb *daraba*. Rather, all versions use the phrase 'take up their hands' (*akhadhu 'ala aydihim*).

The professor and the shaykh were delivering the same message. Both rejected categorically the evident meaning of Qur'an verse 4:34, refusing to accept that Islam's sacred scripture could condone domestic violence. But the approaches and appeals of the two speakers differed dramatically. The first speaker attacked tradition from outside it, appealing to the authority of 'this day and age.' The second mounted a defense of tradition from within, deriving authority by acting as an indigenous and trusted bearer of sacred knowledge. The first speaker, in effect, defied the text of the Qur'an, restricting it to its pre-modern origins by admitting its anachronism and breaking the yoke of tradition. The second speaker claimed that there was no contradiction between the Qur'an and modern justice. There was no anachronism, just misunderstanding. It was the ulama, the qualified interpreters of God's law, who could point this out and resolve it.

From one perspective, the professor's cry of rage against the failure of scripture to meet modern expectations of justice was emotionally gratifying. But it offered no solution to the quandary of Qur'an 4:34. His audience of Muslim students was left with the choice between a belief that the Qur'an was the infallible, universally relevant and authoritative word of God, or demoting it to being yet another titular 'holy book,' exposed as containing as much shameful anachronism as godly wisdom and finally put in its proper place by the march of progress. The shaykh, by contrast, offered a spirited reconciliation that invigorated the students' hope that the religion they had been taught since childhood was the truth really was and always had been, carried and kept alive by the ulama. He offered them the possibility that there was no contradiction between the justice within revelation and justice outside it as we understand justice today.

Yet the young shaykh's conciliation of scripture and modernity was an illusion. His claim that the Shariah had never allowed a husband to strike his wife was false. It was a desperate attempt to avoid the rub of the crisis, namely that interpreting *daraba* as 'to beat' meant affirming, to one degree or another, that God was validating a husband striking his wife. But it was impossible to choose another meaning for the verb *daraba* without overturning sound Hadiths and over a millennium of interpretation, undermining the very pillars of the scholarly tradition that guaranteed the intactness of Islam as a whole. Unlike the secondary scripture of Hadiths, a Qur'anic verse cannot be dismissed as historically unreliable or overlooked as an isolated anomaly. It is unavoidably the word of God. Qur'an 4:34 is thus the ultimate crisis of scripture in the modern world.

Both the professor and the shaykh had precedents in their efforts to distance Islam from the evident meaning of Qur'an 4:34. A more consistent and better-supported version of the young shaykh's problematic explanation came from the Saudi Islamist intellectual Abd al-Hamid Abu Sulayman in 1998. Removing any validation of spousal abuse from Qur'an 4:34 required breaking completely with the precedent of tradition. Unlike the young shaykh at the Eid Dinner, Abu Sulayman acknowledged this. Centuries of Muslim scholarship on the verse had missed the mark and had to be cast aside entirely. Reconsidering the specifics of how the ulama had interpreted the word *daraba*, however, did not mean rejecting the Shariah. Rather, it meant fulfilling it as a comprehensive set of values, Abu Sulayman insisted. Like Ghazali's arguments about women heads of state, Abu Sulayman based his interpretation of Qur'an 4:34 on Muslims' duty to pursue the 'aims of the Shariah (*Maqasid al-Shariah*)' even if it meant breaking with consensus on the law's details. In the case of family life and marriage, Islam's overarching and abiding objectives were affection and mercy. Violence and intimidation contradicted these, so understanding 4:34 as advocating striking one's wife was impossible.[2]

Seeking a reading of *daraba* that did accord with the themes of affection and mercy, Abu Sulayman identified seventeen meanings in which the verb is used in the holy book. The one that fits best with the context of 4:34 is the meaning of 'withdrawing from, leaving and abandoning.' In other words, if after admonishing his wife and then sleeping in a separate bed, the husband finds that she has still not rectified her behavior, he leaves the marital home entirely. This was, in fact, what Hadiths described the Prophet doing in Medina when his wives' conduct had so disappointed him that he almost divorced them.[3] As for the sound Hadiths in which the Prophet supposedly teaches his followers that husbands can beat their wives but only 'in a light way that leaves no mark' (*ghayr mubarrih*), Abu Sulayman suggests that these reports were corrupted in the process of historical transmission and may actually be the comments of a later scholar, not the words of the Prophet.[4]

The professor's railing against the Shariah status quo, in turn, echoed the position taken by another American Muslim intellectual, none other than the same Dr. Amina Wadud who led the controversial Manhattan prayer in 2005. In a book entitled *The Qur'an and Woman* first published in 1992, Wadud stated her intention clearly. The Qur'an had always been read and interpreted by men, whose interests and patriarchal society had stained the authoritative understanding of the revelation. She proposed breaking with tradition, both the fraught corpus of Hadiths and the commanding consensus of the male ulama, in order to reread the Qur'an from the perspective of a woman who sought liberation through God's religion of mercy. Though she offered no concrete alternative reading for the verse, Wadud proposed that the verb *daraba* had meanings other than 'to strike' that could well apply in Qur'an 4:34.

Writing a second book in the wake of the Manhattan prayer, Wadud staked out a more radical position. She rejected unreservedly any interpretation of Qur'an 4:34 that preserved its evident meaning, in her words, saying 'no' to the sacred text. This was all she could do, Wadud confessed, at those few seemingly insoluble points in Islam's scripture that are 'inadequate or unacceptable' no matter how much interpretive energy is poured into them.[5]

WHO DECIDES WHAT GOD MEANS?

The tragedy of domestic violence against women is far too common worldwide for any one religion or scriptural passage to be its cause. In Nigeria, a country that straddles deep religious and ethnic fault lines, a survey found that 74 percent of Muslim women considered it acceptable for a husband to beat his wife in certain circumstances. But so did 52 percent of Christian women and 64 percent of women adhering to African religions. Social science theories for explaining the global phenomenon of spousal abuse run a wide range, but they converge on socioeconomic factors. Some focus on economic adversity and the challenges it presents to men's status expectations. Others find the roots of violence in women's economic disempowerment and the vulnerable position in which it leaves wives who rely solely on their husbands.[6]

Culture matters a great deal too, especially in societies with strong strains of machismo. In some Muslim societies, there is evidence that some men justify violence against their wives by citing Qur'an 4:34. For many people, then, Islam's scripture shares the blame. Despite efforts to find alternative interpretations of the verse, for these critics its problems are unresolvable because it is as unambiguous as it is repugnant. As Wadud plainly lays out, taken at its prima facie meaning, the verse advocates a practice that she can only describe as 'archaic and barbarian' in our time and according to how we understand justice today. Whatever interpretive gymnastics are performed, the Qur'an *literally* tells a husband to strike his wife. Even if we indulge apologetics that propose some deep alternative meaning for the verse, we are still left with the troubling question of why God would say something whose intended meaning differed so dramatically from its literal one.

Here we must remember, however, that there is no such thing as 'literal meaning' in its usual sense of 'what a text really says.' We often assume that, however much we differ on interpretations, a statement or text has an obvious and objective 'literal' aspect that preserves an unchanging core of meaning and cannot be escaped. We assume that we can isolate this stable, stand-alone meaning using the dictionary definition of its words and by removing it from any context. What we might term the 'dictionary meaning' of a text may indeed exist, but it is neither objective nor universal. As generations of Shakespeare readers have found, the definitions of words are not at all stable. They are shaped and reshaped by the speakers of a language as the language evolves. The bard's 'silly women' in *The Two Gentlemen of Verona* were 'innocent,' not foolish. In a more recent example, when Lauren Bacall asked Charles Boyer 'Are you making love to me?' in a 1945 film, she only meant 'flirting.'[7]

'Literal meaning' is also commonly understood as the meaning that makes sense to us with the least interpretive effort. Put simply, it is the first coherent meaning that comes to mind. Better termed 'evident meaning,' as the Muslim legal theorists called it (*Zahir*, or 'outward'), this is not necessarily the same as the dictionary meaning. When a thief points a gun at you in a dark alley and growls, 'Give me all your money,' your mind immediately passes over the fact that, literally, 'all your money' includes everything in your various bank and investment accounts as well as other liquid assets you might own. You understand instantaneously that he only means the contents of your wallet (and maybe non-money items like your watch as well).

But like the dictionary meaning, evident meaning is also subjective. It is determined by context and by a tradition of symbols and veteran assumptions shared by what Stanley Fish has called the 'interpretive community' to which the reader or hearer belongs.[8] That evident meaning is not universally obvious or undisputed is clear when courts in the US and UK feel the need to refer to how a 'reasonable person' in those societies would understand speech or art in order to determine if it is defamatory or obscene. Unlike minority or idiosyncratic interpretations, this hypothetical 'reasonable person' is imagined as epitomizing the proper thinking of the interpretive community in question. The obliquity of evident meaning has been a boon to comedy writers, as seen in films like *Airplane!* and *The Naked Gun* franchise (Banquet doorman: 'Your coat, sir?' Detective Drebin: 'Yes it is, and I have the receipt to prove it').

The evident meaning of a text seems obvious to those within an interpretive community, but, as Detective Frank Drebin illustrates, moving from the dictionary meaning to the evident one requires significant, if unnoticed, interpretive steps. In evident (i.e., 'literal') meaning, these unnoticed steps are those assumptions that the reader leaves unstated because he or she assumes everyone else shares them. Frank Drebin is so humorous because he is clueless about them. A tough noir cop supposedly ensconced in society and its hard-boiled dialogue, he is comically outside its interpretive community. He is oblivious to the understanding that you should leave your coat at the door at a fancy party; that the doorman is there to serve you; that you will be spoken to according to an etiquette that assumes you are used to being served.

Ironically, the unstated assumptions that many readers today would generally see as encasing the 'literal meaning' of 4:34 were shared by none of the pre-modern ulama. They are, in fact, totally foreign to the Islamic tradition. Reading the verse as an unambiguous legitimization of spousal abuse assumes that the Qur'an should be read in isolation and that duties should be derived from it unmediated. Yet no pre-modern Muslim school of thought ever advocated that (except perhaps the early Kharijite extremists), and Islamic modernists who claim they do this today cannot manage to do so consistently. On the contrary, Muslim sects agreed that the Qur'an had to be read through the prism of the Prophet's teachings as expounded by the ulama, who then disagreed endlessly on what those teachings should be.

The ulama who articulated the Islamic tradition, as Amina Wadud correctly observed, were men. Taken as a whole, however, their reading of Qur'an 4:34 was characterized by neither the interests of patriarchy nor what is sometimes imagined to be an untempered indifference to violence. Rather, the most salient theme in the ulama's writings across the centuries has been one of restricting almost completely the apparent meaning of the verse. This seems to have appeared with the first, infallible interpreter of God's revelation, the Messenger of God himself. Canonical Sunni Hadith collections quote the Prophet at first teaching his followers: 'Do not strike the female servants of God.' Only when his lieutenant Umar complained about Medinan women disrespecting their husbands (as opposed to the more submissive Meccan wives to whom they were accustomed) did the Prophet allow hitting them. The Hadith continues, describing how a wave of seventy (i.e., many) women subsequently came complaining to the Prophet about their husbands. This led him to declare that those men who beat their wives 'are not the best of you,' adding, 'The best of you will not strike them' in some versions of the Hadith.[9]

The canonical Sunni Hadith collections also include recollections of the Prophet's Farewell Sermon, given on Hajj in what would be the final year of his life. One of the parting pieces of wisdom he leaves his followers is the commandment to 'Fear God as concerns your womenfolk, for indeed you took charge of them with God's assurance.' The Prophet further explains that only if a wife allows herself to converse with men against her husband's wishes or, in another version of the Hadith, commits some grievous transgression (*fahisha mubayyina*, a phrase with sexual innuendo) can the husband strike her, and then only 'with a light blow that leaves no mark.'[10] Another sound Hadith has the Prophet further discourage striking one's wife, imploring his followers, 'Would one of you beat his wife like a slave and then sleep with her at the day's end?'[11]

All available evidence of Muhammad's own conduct shows a complete aversion to domestic violence. As recorded in the canonical Hadith collections, Aisha recalled that 'The Messenger of God never struck anything with his hand, not a woman and not a slave, except when making war in the path of God.'[12] One Hadith that lacked any chain of transmission reliable enough to merit inclusion in Hadith collections but that was preserved in Qur'anic commentaries from the ninth century evokes a tension verging on unease over God's command in 4:34. When the Prophet's condemnation of a husband striking his wife is overruled by the revelation of the Qur'anic verse, the Prophet purportedly admits: 'I wanted one thing and God wanted another. And what God wants is best.'[13]

The vast majority of the ulama across the Sunni schools of law inherited the Prophet's unease over domestic violence and placed further restrictions on the evident meaning of the 'Wife Beating Verse.' A leading Meccan scholar from the second generation of Muslims, 'Ata' bin Abi Rabah, counseled a husband not to beat his wife even if she ignored him but rather to express his anger in some other way. Darimi, a teacher of both

Tirmidhi and Muslim bin Hajjaj as well as a leading early scholar in Iran, collected all the Hadiths showing Muhammad's disapproval of beating in a chapter entitled 'The Prohibition on Striking Women.' A thirteenth-century scholar from Granada, Ibn Faras, notes that one camp of ulama had staked out a stance forbidding striking a wife altogether, declaring it contrary to the Prophet's example and denying the authenticity of any Hadiths that seemed to permit beating. Even Ibn Hajar, the pillar of late medieval Sunni Hadith scholarship, concludes that, contrary to what seems to be an explicit command in the Qur'an, the Hadiths of the Prophet leave no doubt that striking one's wife to discipline her actually falls under the Shariah ruling of 'strongly disliked' or 'disliked verging on prohibited.'[14] It became received opinion among Sunni ulama from Iberia to Iran that, though striking one's wife was permitted, other means of discipline and dispute were greatly preferred, more effective and better for the piety of both spouses. As another thirteenth-century Andalusian scholar observed, nowhere in the Qur'an besides 4:34 and in listing the *Hudud* punishments does God command believers to punish a person violently. Just as the *Hudud* punishments were meant more as signs of the grievous nature of certain offenses than as sentences to be enacted, so the command to strike a wife was intended to communicate the severity of her behaving disgracefully towards her husband, not as a license for domestic abuse.[15]

The substantive laws that the Sunni schools of Shariah articulated over the centuries followed this same mitigating course. If a wife exhibited egregious disobedience (*nushuz*) such as uncharacteristically insulting behavior, leaving the house against the husband's will and without a valid excuse or denying her husband sex (without medical grounds), the husband should first admonish her to be conscious of God and proper etiquette. If she did not desist from her behavior, he should cease sleeping with her in their bed. If she still continued in her *nushuz*, he should then strike her to teach her the error of her ways. Shafi'i law only allowed the husband to use his hand or a wound-up handkerchief (*mindil malfuf*), not a whip or stick. All schools of law prohibited striking the wife in the face or in any sensitive area likely to cause injury. All except some Maliki jurists held that the wife could claim compensation payment (*diya*) from the husband for any injury she sustained, and Hanbalis, the later Shafi'i school as well as the Maliki school, allowed a judge to dissolve the marriage at no cost to the wife if harm had been done. In effect, *any* physical harm was grounds for compensation and divorce since the Prophet had limited striking one's wife to 'a light blow that leaves no mark.' Causing any injury thus meant that a husband had exceeded his rights. All schools of law agreed that if the wife died due to a beating, her family could claim her wergild or possibly even have the husband executed.[16]

That Qur'an 4:34 was not understood as a legal license is affirmed by how medieval ulama interpreted a provocative, if poorly attested, Hadith: 'A man is not asked why he beat his wife.' They understood this primarily as part of the etiquette of privacy between men; people should mind their own business. This did not outweigh public duties and legal protections, though, and the principle of not asking was qualified by the phrase 'if there is no need to do so.' The magnet of Shafi'i legal thought in the eastern lands during the thirteenth century, 'Abd al-Karim Rafi'i, remarked that one interpretation of this Hadith was that it referred only to the Day of Judgment. Thus, a man giving an accounting of his deeds before God might not be asked to justify having once struck his wife. This was not God's law on earth, however. In this life the Shariah punishes the husband for his act according to its regulations.[17]

Like the problematic knots of underage marriage and polygamy, Qur'an 4:34 has been a thorn in the side of the ulama since they first felt the condescending gaze of Western critics. They have negotiated a relationship with the verse and the medieval interpretive heritage using a variety of schemes, some venturing further out from the penumbra of tradition than others. Reformists like Abu Sulayman remain bound to tradition only by the elastic threads of 'the aims of the Shariah.' They argue that all Muslim scholars have fundamentally misunderstood the Qur'anic verse and that this misreading went so far as to corrupt their authoritative records of the Sunna as preserved in the Hadith collections. According to them, striking one's wife was simply never intended by God's revelation.

Khaled Abou El Fadl, an Egyptian-American professor trained both in American law and at the hands of ulama, makes an argument similarly rooted in 'the aims of the Shariah.' His is bound more closely to classical Islamic legal theory than Abu Sulayman's, and he uses the framework of *Usul al-Fiqh* to extricate contemporary understandings of Islam from the predicament of 4:34. As in the cases of the Hadiths on killing apostates and the Prophet condemning his own father to Hell, the different grades of epistemological certainty needed to admit a transmitted report as evidence provides a means to bypass even authenticated Hadiths. Abou El Fadl concludes that the Hadiths allowing beating simply do not provide the epistemological heft needed to overrule the Shariah priorities of the preservation of life and honor as well as the Islamic values of mercy and beauty. These are the themes we see exemplified in the Prophet's own treatment of his wives. Abou El Fadl does not deny that Qur'an 4:34 includes an instruction to strike one's wife, but he uses another instance in the Qur'an (4:128) that refers to *nushuz* as well as the Prophet's testimony to his followers during his Farewell Sermon to argue that the only situation in which a husband may hit his wife is if she has committed a *fahisha mubayyina*, a gross act of sexual betrayal.[18]

In contrast to these reformists, the traditionalists who uphold the undiminished relevance of Islam's pre-modern heritage resolve the issue of Qur'an 4:34 by emphasizing the role of the ulama as the guardian class. It is they who should decide how the message of God and the Prophet should be applied in any one place and time, and it is they who must mediate between the Muslim masses and the revelation. Already implicit in the medieval ulama's explanations of 4:34 was the notion that physical violence was just one option for disciplining wives. Not only was it 'disliked' as an action in God's eyes in all but exceptional circumstances, it might also prove ineffective with many women. A twelfth-century Shariah judge in Seville named Ibn Al-Arabi, who had traveled east to study in Baghdad, instructed his students that people are not all the same in how they should be disciplined. 'A slave might be hit with a stick,' the judge noted as an analogy, 'while with a free man it's enough to point it at him.'[19]

Ali Gomaa has built on this theme in a small book of fatwas recently written for women. He took the standard late Shafi'i school position that it is not recommended for a man to strike his wife and that he must pay her compensation for any injury he causes. Men who truly want to follow the model of the Prophet would never beat their wives. Gomaa tries to preempt the question asked by many Muslims today: why would the Qur'an include this dangerous command at all? 'The Qur'an came for all humankind,' Gomaa explains, 'for every time and place, and every kind of people that there will be until the Day of Judgment.' Though unpalatable in the West, there are some cultures, Gomaa contends, where a woman will not heed her husband unless he uses physical force against her – in fact, she sees this as proof of her husband's manliness (Gomaa gives his native Upper Egypt as an example). Ultimately, Gomaa concludes, harmful abuse of women is unacceptable in any situation, and men who seriously abuse their wives are ignorant of Islam's teachings. As they have in the past, Muslims must continue to turn to the ulama for proper instruction about their religious rights and obligations. The learned guardians will take the universal law of the Shariah and adjust it for particular settings so that its overarching aims are achieved. They will also use reminders of the Prophet's example, like 'The best of you [men] will not beat women,' to effect gradual change in cultures where domestic violence is tolerated.[20]

Another crucial point underlies Gomaa's fatwa. It assumes that, though it might be reviled in many cultures and unacceptable in many circumstances, striking one's wife is not *inherently* wrong.[21] What is uniformly condemnable is what transgresses the legal red lines drawn by the Shariah, which apply regardless of the mores of one community or epoch. Causing physical injury to *anyone*, wife or not, is an offense that carries legal consequences.

Two generations before Gomaa began his tenure as Egypt's Grand Mufti, another denizen of the late Ottoman ulama world found himself serving in the religious bureaucracy of a rapidly secularizing state. Muhammad Tahir Ibn 'Ashur served as a judge on several Shariah tribunals in Tunisia after the French pried the colony from weakened Ottoman control. He hailed from a prominent ulama family that had settled in Tunis after fleeing the Spanish Reconquista and was blessed with a remarkably long career, living from 1879 to 1973. Among the many honored posts he held, the scholar served as the senior Maliki Mufti of Tunisia and the Rector of the ancient Zaytuna Madrasa, the country's premier center of Islamic learning.

Ibn 'Ashur was a product of the same bureaucratized Ottoman ulama culture that allowed the state substantial prerogative in shaping the application of the Shariah on issues such as restricting marriage age. He was also inspired by Muhammad 'Abduh's call to construct an Islamic modernity that could compete with the West. It is no surprise that Ibn 'Ashur followed his fellow clerics in Istanbul, Cairo and Damascus in granting religious approval to what turned out to be open-ended legal reforms imported from the West. They culminated in 1957 when Tunisia's Shariah courts were eliminated, ironically not by French colonial rule but by the newly independent country's first president, the militant secularist Habib Bourguiba. Though he bore this assault on the Shariah patiently, like Tantawi and other establishment ulama, Ibn 'Ashur had his limits. National law could not unquestionably contradict the Shariah. In 1960 Bourguiba pushed the venerable scholar too far when he gave a speech calling on Tunisian workers not to fast during Ramadan because it harmed productivity. The president spoke too soon when he claimed that Ibn 'Ashur, along with the senior Hanafi Mufti, would allow this. Instead, the Hanafi Mufti flatly denied this in a published fatwa, and Ibn 'Ashur announced on the radio that 'God has spoken the truth and Bourguiba has spoken falsehood.' Both scholars were dismissed from their posts.

Ibn 'Ashur's interpretation of Qur'an 4:34 uses the discretion and executive role granted to a Muslim state to disarm the verse's dangers. Like his pre-modern predecessors, Ibn 'Ashur understands the verse as providing alternatives suited to the different kinds of societies and individuals that the Qur'an might address. The commands in the verse are thus directed at whatever authority can carry them out most effectively, whether the couple themselves, their families or the Shariah court. In a novel turn, Ibn 'Ashur argues that the sole addressee of 4:34 and 4:35 was the court authorities. In most societies, he explained, no license can be given to husbands to discipline their wives violently. This is clear if one applied Shariah procedure at a family level, for only in exceptional circumstances can a person involved in a case also act as the judge who decides guilt and metes out punishment. In addition, experience shows that husbands cannot be trusted to restrain themselves in private. Even if they are told that they can only use light blows, husbands will inevitably 'quench their anger' and 'in all likelihood transgress the limits.' In urbanized societies and modern states, which enjoy functioning legal systems, Ibn 'Ashur suggests that the whole verse is addressed to the state and the organs of the court. The authorities (*wulat al-umur*) are obligated to announce that any man who beats his wife will be punished and assign the duty of disciplining wives to the courts alone. It is the Shariah court judge who hears complaints of a wife's unacceptable conduct. If she is guilty, the judge admonishes her, separates the couple if necessary and finally orders a beating administered should she refuse to reform.[22]

COURTS HAVE THE FINAL WORD

Of course, some medieval Muslim scholars saw no complication with following the evident meaning of Qur'an 4:34. A minority considered it natural for God to grant husbands the right to beat recalcitrant or disobedient wives. The pugilistic Ibn Faras found striking an unheeding wife far from problematic. He considered it 'recommended,' in fact, because it prevented a wife from falling victim to her own irrational impulses.[23] For a strict Baghdad Hanbali like Ibn Jawzi, legal limitations on striking a wife came only from the Hadith limiting any non-*Hudud* punishment to a maximum of ten lashes with a whip. He limited this even further to between one and three strokes, although he doubted the efficacy of whipping overall, since 'if threats of whipping don't work with someone, actually whipping them won't stop them either.' Contrary to Ibn 'Ashur's court-centered interpretation, the influential thirteenth-century Qur'an commentator Qurtubi, who himself fled the Spanish Reconquista for a safe haven in Egypt, insisted that the right to discipline a wife violently was granted by God to the husband alone.[24]

Yet this severe strain among the ulama appears not to have had any real influence on adjudication. Qurtubi was a luminary of medieval scholarship, but he was not a judge, having opted for a hermetic life of devout erudition in a hamlet in Upper Egypt. Ibn 'Ashur may have come at the tail end of a functioning Shariah judiciary, but he nonetheless worked as a judge inside its living system for two decades. He was first appointed as a Shariah court judge in 1911 in a judiciary that the French colonial administration in Tunisia left relatively free of interference. His explanation of Qur'an 4:34 reveals the insight that the system of rights and obligations set forth in the Qur'an and Hadiths had to solve real problems. Scripture's definitive interpretation often came not in legal textbooks but in the actual application of Shariah law.

Whatever individual scholars like Ibn Faras or Ibn Jawzi might say about the benefits of lashing one's wife, available evidence suggests that Shariah courts in the pre-modern Muslim world were surprisingly receptive to women seeking redress or protection from spousal abuse. If it were established that violence had been done, the wife could expect judicial remedy, and the husband's excuse for why he beat his wife did not matter.

The perspective of Shariah courts on domestic violence and Qur'an 4:34 was one of public dispute resolution rather than opining on private conduct. From the court's perspective, the Qur'an-mandated process of admonishing, sleeping separately and finally striking one's wife was moot. If, for whatever reason, a wife or husband came before the local Shariah court to complain about a spouse's behavior, it was assumed that the process had reached the stage of requiring 'an arbiter from his family and an arbiter from hers' (4:35) to determine who was harming whom. The role of arbiter was played by the court.[25]

Both books of law and their application in Shariah courts assumed an intrinsic link in purpose behind the verse commanding beating and the subsequent command for arbiters to resolve the problem. In the broader context of Shariah law, all marital disputes took place against the background of the husband's unilateral right to end the marriage without any excuse (a type of divorce called *Talaq*). If a wife was innocent of any wrongdoing, the only consequence her husband faced for declaring a *Talaq* was that he forfeited the dower payment he had given her (or, more frequently by the 1800s, still owed her in part) and had to pay spousal maintenance for a period of time. A wife also had the right to exit the marriage through a process known as *Khul'*, by which she disassociated herself from her husband but also forfeited her rights to her dower and spousal maintenance. As Maribel Fierro has observed, the approach that Shariah courts took to instances of abused wives was designed to protect women from a loophole in this system. If a wife's behavior was truly so horrid and unacceptable that a husband had reached the point of striking her, why had he not already divorced her? He could have done so easily and without seeking anyone's permission. That he continued in the marriage meant either that he still wanted to be married to his wife or that he hoped to avoid the financial burden of his unilateral divorce by bullying her into seeking a *Khul'* and leaving at her own expense.[26]

To avoid wives being railroaded into leaving the marriage and surrendering their rights, as soon as a woman reported abuse Shariah courts took up the role of the third party called for by the Qur'an. Instead of appointing arbitrators from the couple's families, by the tenth century the most widespread tactic used by courts from Iran to Andalusia was housing the couple or the wife in the home of a trustworthy neighbor who could prevent further problems and report to the court. If the husband was in fact abusive, under the Maliki school in North Africa and Andalusia judges could terminate the marriage and award the wife compensation. If the wife's behavior was unbearable, the husband could receive a divorce by judicial decree.[27] Although the Hanafi school did not allow a judge to end the marriage because of abuse, a famous tenth-century Hanafi jurist in Rayy (now absorbed into modern-day Tehran) wrote that it is the judge's responsibility to prevent a husband from abusing his wife, both by assigning the wife to live in the house of a trustworthy neighbor and by requiring compensation from the husband for any injury she suffered. Traveling in the fourteenth century through Mardin, near the contemporary Turkey–Syria border,

Ibn Battuta recounts how the city's chief judge had been approached by a woman complaining that her husband had beaten her. The court had closed for the day, but the judge accompanied the woman to the couple's home and calmly spoke with the mortified husband in the presence of a crowd of prying neighbors, instructing him to put his affairs in order and give his wife satisfaction.

Despite the limitations that the empire's official Hanafi school placed on judges in such matters, Ottoman court records suggest a similar receptiveness to wives seeking assistance. The influential sixteenth-century chief of the Ottoman religious establishment, Ebusu'ud Efendi, issued a fatwa that a judge was permitted to use any means possible to prevent a husband from hurting his wife. A leading Shariah consultant (*mufti*) to the courts in seventeenth-century Ottoman Palestine issued a fatwa that a husband who had knocked out three of his wife's teeth had to pay the set compensation sum of one hundred and fifty gold coins. A series of cases from Shariah courts in and around Aleppo in the late 1600s and early 1700s demonstrated another phenomenon: women who had stipulated in their marriage contracts that if their husbands ever struck them they would be divorced immediately, keeping their dower payment and with the husband responsible for spousal maintenance.[28] Ottoman Shariah courts could end up extending their jurisdiction into the non-Muslim minorities in the empire. In 1529, the Ottoman Shariah court in a Greek town heard the complaint of a Christian family whose daughter had been beaten to death by her husband, ultimately awarding them her wergild amount.[29]

Shariah courts that continued under colonial rule and others that continue to function today have taken a similar approach. Women who come before the judge with complaints of abuse and evidence to prove it receive compensation for their injuries and, should they wish, judicially declared divorces and full maintenance rights. If a woman has no witnesses or other evidence that abuse has occurred, the judge might still house her with a neighbor temporarily. Shariah court records from Zanzibar between 1900 and 1950 show that judges would refuse to dissolve the marriages of wives who claimed their husbands abused them but could provide no witnesses, from among the neighbors or family, or other evidence to that effect. If there were any witnesses, the judges immediately housed the wife with a reliable neighbor, dissolved the marriage and fined the husband.[30] In French West Africa in 1911, courts in Kita and Jenne (both in present-day Mali) granted divorces to numerous women who claimed their husbands had beaten them and either brought witnesses to corroborate this or when the husband admitted it. The courts usually awarded the wife compensation from the husband, dissolved the marriage and allowed the wife to keep her dower gift. One case records the husband explaining to the judge why his wife deserved a beating. The court ignored him since, by dint of requiring legal remedy, his actions had exceeded his rights to discipline her.[31] A case from Casablanca in 1917 shows how the classical principles of Shariah procedure were still active. If neighbors claimed they heard a wife screaming but saw nothing (i.e., they could provide no evidence of abuse), the judge would still punish the husband. In the Maliki school it was reasoned that, if the husband had not sought help from anyone when his wife was screaming, it could be assumed that he had been responsible for her distress.[32]

Saudi Arabia presents a fascinating case of a legal system that still relies primarily on Shariah courts. In fact, Saudi Arabia struggles with a judiciary that continues to resist the type of efforts to centralize and routinize the law that were completed in countries like Egypt in the early twentieth century. The founder of the modern Saudi state, Abd al-Aziz Ibn Saud, tried to build on the modernized Ottoman court system that he inherited when his forces won control of the former Ottoman province of the Hejaz in 1926. The ulama serving as Shariah judges in the Saudi state's Najd heartland, however, retained their Salafi aversion to institutional authority. They not only rejected Ibn Saud's efforts to centralize the judicial system, they even refused calls to codify the Hanbali school of law by selecting as definitive one of the school's multiple rulings on every point of law. The Saudi Ministry of Justice has still not succeeded in compelling Shariah judges in the country to abide by precedential rulings or even to limit their choices to the Hanbali school.

In an effort to create a format for regularizing judicial rulings, the Saudi Ministry of Justice has begun publishing yearly compilations of case records that offer examples for how to rule on types of cases. The model for domestic abuse is a 2002 case handled in the Riyadh lower claims court, which heard the case of a woman who accused her husband of beating her and abusing her verbally. Hospital reports confirmed that she had suffered bruises on her back, arms and thighs as well as a black eye. The husband admitted insulting her and that he had hit her 'to discipline her' because she had insulted him foully. The judge deemed that the husband had violated the Qur'anic principle requiring husbands to 'Live with them [wives] according to what is right' (4:19) and, based on the medical reports, ruled that the husband should pay his wife 9,000 riyals (around $2,400) compensation for her injuries and receive thirty lashes for his insulting language. The excuse that the husband gave, that his wife had insulted him, held no weight before the court. Unlike the husband, she had not admitted using abusive language, nor had the husband provided any evidence for his claim.[33]

Available data thus strongly suggest that Shariah courts generally went further than the already very restrictive, mainstream position taken by the Sunni schools of law in their cautious reading of Qur'an 4:34. I have not come across any evidence that the more permissive stances of ulama like Ibn Faras and Ibn Jawzi manifested themselves in court rulings. That the substantive law (*fiqh*) explicated in books could differ from the conduct of the courts that supposedly applied it does not betray some cognitive dissonance between the law as theory and the law as practice. Incongruence often came about because the *madhhab*s were not monolithic and rarely had only one position on an issue. The 'official' position of the *madhhab*, usually the one used in court rulings, often depended on which books of law were in favor during one era or in a particular region. The Hanbali law of Ibn Jawzi in thirteenth-century Baghdad differs greatly from Hanbali law as applied in modern Saudi Arabia, a distinction that appears both in books of law and in court rulings.

This is not to suggest that Shariah courts have offered perfect justice for abused wives. Social prejudice, class and ingrained misogyny exert alarming influence. In cases brought before Egypt's Shariah courts between 1900 and 1955, women suing for divorce based on claims that their husbands had been inflicting harm on them won more than half of the time. But the bar for what constituted a harmful beating was higher for lower-class women than for the elite.[34] Between 1983 and 1995, almost a quarter of the women who came to a court in Yemen's capital seeking a judicial divorce cited domestic violence as the cause. Overall, women tended to be successful litigants before the court. They won the vast majority of their cases. With complaints of domestic abuse, though, only 20 percent of the women received the divorce they sought. This was mostly due to the evidentiary standards held up for poor women – the majority of the litigants – whom the court would only grant divorces if the physical abuse they were suffering qualified as a criminal offense. Upper-class Yemeni women found it much easier to convince a judge with lesser claims.[35]

SAYING 'NO' TO THE TEXT AND THE HERMENEUTICS OF SUSPICION

Amina Wadud states that, when the Qur'an says something 'unmeaningful' or 'unacceptable,' we have two choices. Either we say 'no' to the revealed text, which means either denying its validity or authority, or we find an alternative interpretation.[36] Qur'an 4:34 epitomizes the crises of scripture in the modern world because many feel that the notion of God saying anything like 'strike your wives' is indefensible, and alternative interpretations are either too far-fetched or too costly to the structural integrity of the Islamic tradition. The verse seems tantamount to a modern moment of God commanding Abraham to sacrifice his son, posing a decisive challenge. Either we testify that God's will supersedes all reason and intuitive sense of justice, or we refuse to obey Him. Unlike Abraham, however, we are not ancient Semites hearing the voice of God directly. We are eons away, being presented with a text and told that it contains God's words for us to follow. Reason and justice seem a steep price to pay.

Yet no matter how immediate God's command or how obvious any act of speech might seem, we cannot process their meanings without engaging in the act of interpretation. Abraham did what he *understood* God to have asked. A prophet is in the rare place of receiving corrective instructions from God. Scriptural communities, by contrast, have only the texts left behind by prophets to mine for clarity and the tradition handed down to aid in interpretation. In articulating their understanding of what God meant in Qur'an 4:34, no Muslim scholar has understood the verse as granting a husband unrestricted license to strike his wife. On the contrary, beginning with Muhammad (or what Muslims imagined to be Muhammad), the majority of the ulama strongly discouraged any act of violence against wives. And all schools of law offered the wife protection and required the husband to pay her compensation for injuries. Most allowed a judge to dissolve the marriage without the wife losing any financial rights. If one takes Shariah courts as the primary interpreters of God's law, then they repeatedly said 'no' to the evident meaning of the Qur'anic verse. As defendants before a Shariah court, husbands effectively had *no* legitimate right to strike their wives.

Qur'an 4:34 epitomizes the crisis of scripture in the modern world because the interpretations and explanations advanced by ulama for the verse seem to many like clumsy and futile apologetics. The fact that Muslim unease with the evident meaning of the verse long predates modern sensibilities, extending to the very origins of the Islamic scholarly tradition, raises the possibility that for over a millennium the ulama have been affecting a cover-up for a clear flaw in the holy book. But these are only *our* perceptions of clumsiness, apologetics and affectedness. They are based on our notion that explanations are far-fetched if they are too far removed from the 'literal' meaning of a text. For the Muslim scholars actually interpreting the verse, however, being far-fetched was not a function of distance between the apparent and intended meaning. Rather, all that mattered was that the interpretive distance was justified by sufficient evidence. The ulama's Rule of Interpretation allowed departing from the evident meaning of a text for some other interpretation provided a solid piece of evidence from the Qur'an, Sunna or reason demanded it. In the case of Qur'an 4:34, the ulama restricted significantly the verse's evident meaning in response to the strongest extrinsic evidence in their intellectual world, namely the well-established precedent of the Prophet's treatment of wives and his strong criticism of striking women.

Qur'an 4:34 epitomizes the crisis of scripture in the modern world because it posits a God or a religion would even leave the door open to such an obvious and harmful misunderstanding. Yet no text is immune to misunderstanding, whether ancient or modern, bellicose or pacifist. Jesus' praise for those 'who have made themselves eunuchs for the kingdom of heaven's sake' (Matthew 19:12) led Origen to castrate himself – literally – even though the Church Father was synonymous with a figurative reading of the Bible.[37] Since any set of commands allows for misunderstanding, the written word must be constrained and explained by living tradition. As Ali Gomaa and centuries of ulama before him have reiterated, the Muslim laity should not be deriving conclusions about their rights and obligations from the Qur'an and Hadiths to begin with. This was the job of the ulama. The very elliptical style of the Qur'an and the Hadiths, with their constant interaction with the shifting contexts of the Prophet's surroundings, makes them incomprehensible at times without context. This also leaves them dangerously vulnerable to misreading. Hence the admittedly provocative warning issued by a leading Al-Azhar scholar of the early nineteenth century that acting on the evident meanings of the Qur'an and Hadiths alone is 'one of the sources of unbelief.'[38]

Wadud makes an important point in explaining her comments on Qur'an 4:34. In a practical sense, saying 'no' to the Qur'an was not controversial at all. Muslims had, in effect, said 'no' to the Qur'an and Hadiths innumerable times over the centuries. They had said 'no' to the evident meaning of the Qur'an when it said 'polytheists are naught but filthy,' favoring a figurative interpretation in light of Islam's overall teachings that humans are pure. They had said 'no' to the evident meaning of the Hadith of the Sun Prostrating on the basis of empirical observation, understanding it instead as a personification of the sun's submission to God's will. In effect, the overarching teachings of Islam and empirical realities were more powerful than the specific words of God or the Prophet as contained in a Qur'anic passage or Hadith. But this was phrased as an act of *clarification*, not overruling, of asking 'how' rather than saying 'no.' The distinction in tone made all the difference, as it reflected a willingness to submit to revelation. It was seeking understanding from a just and living Lord, not refusing to obey a suspect patriarch and ossified relic of the old world.

That what appears to be a straightforward command by God could be rendered by the ulama as 'strongly discouraged' in almost all circumstances might be seen as far-fetched interpretation. But it was an ordinary product of the deterrence-based logic of Islam's scriptures. The Qur'an clearly instructs Muslims to cut off the hand of thieves, but Hadiths and the consensus of jurists made this punishment almost impossible to enforce. The Prophet ordered adulterers to be stoned, but the evidentiary standards for the punishment were so high that records show that in Ottoman Istanbul only one instance of stoning ever took place.[39] These terrible punishments were meant to convey the gravity of sin against God, and so strong was the sense of duty to avoid carrying them out that Cairo's senior judge chose exile over agreeing to execute two adulterers.

However, unless one accepts the argument that the basic meaning of *daraba* in Qur'an 4:34 was misunderstood, one *must* accept that a husband using violence to discipline his wife is not inherently, absolutely and categorically wrong. There must be some time, place or situation when it is allowed, or God would not have permitted it. Many today are unwilling to accept this. It is in this sense that saying 'no' to scripture is fatal to its authority and signifies a turnover in epistemological eras. The move from assuming that scripture contains the truth but need only be understood properly to saying 'no' to scripture because it says something unacceptable or impossible is a blow that shatters the vessel of scriptural reverence. It means that some extra-scriptural source of truth has been openly acknowledged as more powerful and compelling than the words of God in scripture. If scripture is read with a hermeneutics of suspicion (borrowing from Paul Ricoeur), then dire problems can appear on every page. If, on the other hand, one believes that a scripture contains true and infallible guidance from the divine, then one will read it with the assumption that it must be consistent internally and with external realities. Sense will be made in light of present challenges as it was made in the past.

Certainly, a scriptural tradition still has its uses even for those who have moved on to believe that truth comes from secular sources. It can be drawn on and quoted to move an audience or bolster ideas rooted elsewhere. But sooner or later, it will clash with secular truths and become a burden. In such cases the scriptural tradition can be reread and picked from selectively to reconcile it with the recognized sources of truth. But it must be substantially reconfigured, as the Qur'an Only movement has done with Islam's scriptures, or else at some point one must say 'no' to the text.

Our world has been for some time one in which secular, extra-scriptural truths reign. It is so hard to avoid the hegemony of 'science,' 'universal values' and 'common sense.' Yet they are not omnipotent. From America to South Africa, hundreds of millions of Christians believe the Bible is the literal word of God and consider belief in scientific 'facts' like evolution to be heresy. But they do protest too much. Affected resistance to extra-scriptural truth only confesses to its power. Galileo was echoing Augustine and Catholic orthodoxy when he asserted that undeniable, empirical observation could not disprove the Bible, it only meant that Christians had been misinterpreting some of its details.[40] Had he not been so prickly at a time of such sectarian tension, his advocacy of the scientific method would have raised no furor. But, as it is, we look back at Galileo as the symbolic proof that one must choose *between* religion and science. This dilemma has been set up by a civilization that, since the late nineteenth century, has reified these two concepts and for the most part placed them at loggerheads. Now those who would defend a scriptural tradition must defend it, right or wrong, in a zero-sum contest. Woman-led prayer must be rejected regardless of evidence. To be free of the tyranny of the extra-scriptural you have to mistrust and perhaps even hate its sources with a vehemence that blinds you to the necessary, natural process of reconciling truth in scripture with truth outside it. Yet in the modern world there does not seem to be any other mode of resistance, since the relationship between scriptural and extra-scriptural truths has been recast permanently as one of mutually exclusive enmity.

If it is possible in this day and age to abide tranquilly in the truth of scripture, I do not know if it can be done via reasoned demonstration. Like the young Syrian shaykh, telegenic ulama and Muslim preachers pop on and drop off satellite channels and conference circuits based on their ability to inspire listeners and convince them, if only for an evening, that they are hearing the true Islam, authentic, unforced, unaffected and also totally suitable for our world. It may be that one such scholar or preacher really does bear that treasure. But how can we tell? If a scholar says women can lead mixed prayers, is he (or she) selling out to Western sensibilities or presenting a sincere opinion about the correct Shariah stance? If the scholar says there are certain circumstances when a husband can strike his wife, is he or she standing firmly by the true teachings of God and the Prophet against the tsunami of globalization or merely being a patriarchal reactionary? For many Muslims today, a strong commitment to gender equality and a revulsion at domestic violence would determine the answer to these two questions, and any 'Islamic' argument to the contrary would wither on the vine. For Muslim students attending an Eid Dinner, then, is what makes a good speaker and a great Muslim scholar a consistent and honest approach to deriving Islam's teachings from scriptural sources? Or is it the ability to make the audience feel that they can be Muslim and modern at the same time, even if that feeling is only temporary? How can Muslims distinguish between the hegemonic values of globalized modernity and 'the true teachings of Islam' when the markers once used to define Islam's boundaries, such as a charitable approach to scripture, the Rule of Interpretation and Consensus, have been laid low by modern disenchantment?

Visiting the famous Dar al-Ulum Deoband madrasa not far from the North Indian town where Shah Wali Allah was born, I heard of a profound experience that one student who had studied there in the early 1900s had recorded in his memoirs.[41] The student had strayed from the madrasa curriculum and submerged himself in books of philosophy and the modernist arguments of Hadith skeptics. Sitting in class at Deoband, the student's mind was flooded with the most profound doubts about the reliability of Hadiths. He even questioned Muhammad's prophethood. Instead of being open to possible explanations for reports like the Hadith of the Fly or the Devil Farting, the student felt he was falling into an abyss of irreverent suspicion. Finally, he went to his teacher, one of India's most saintly and revered ulama. The elderly scholar comforted the student and told him not to worry, that his faith was strong. 'Go now, and never again will you experience doubts of any kind,' he told him. The student never did.

Appendix I

Marracci and Ockley on Aisha's Marriage to the Prophet

Simon Ockley (d. 1720) was a Cambridge scholar who wrote the monumental and influential *History of the Saracens*. His discussion of Muhammad's marriage to Aisha is unusual for its time. It is also misleading, both in the way it portrays Aisha's father, Abu Bakr, replying to the Prophet's offer of marriage and in the subsequent encounter between the future husband and wife. It is based on an inaccurate translation and requires clarification. Ockley writes:

> Ayesha was then but seven years old, and therefore this marriage was not consummated till two years after, when she was nine years old, at which age, we are told, women in that country are ripe for marriage. An Arabian author cited by Maracci, says that Abubeker was very averse to the [sic] giving him his daughter so young, but that Mohammed pretended a divine command for it; whereupon he sent her to him with a basket of dates, and when the girl was alone with him, he stretched out his blessed hand (these are the author's words) [sic], and rudely took hold of her clothes, upon which she looked fiercely at him, and said, 'People call you the faithful man, but your behaviour to me shows you are a perfidious one.' (Ockley, *History of the Saracens*, 19)

Ockley's source, however, had not rendered the original material accurately. Lodovico Marracci was an Italian priest and anti-Islam polemicist who had published a translation of the Qur'an, along with introductory material about the Prophet and a refutation of Islam, in Padua in 1698 (Lewis, *Islam and the West*, pp. 86–88). He quotes as his source on Aisha's marriage the *Sab'iyyāt fī mawā'iẓ al-barriyyāt*, written in 1588 by the Muslim author Abū Naṣr Muḥammad bin 'Abd al-Raḥmān al-Hamadhānī (*Kashf al-ẓunūn*, Beirut, 2:272; Ziriklī, *A'lām*, 6:195). Marracci (inaccurately) paraphrases his source: 'Abu Bakr had resisted for a time, that [his] daughter would not marry Muhammad at such a young age (*AbubaKrum diu restitisse, ne filia in tam parva ætate nuberet Mahumeto*)' (Marracci, 'Prodromus,' 23).

The original Arabic source is very different. It includes an unusual report, which I have not been able to locate in any other source, which is clearly meant more as entertainment than as religious instruction. In a section describing the Prophet's marriages, al-Hamadhānī cites a report (with no source or *Isnād*) of the Prophet having a dream about God sending Gabriel to show him an image of a girl who would be his bride, namely Aisha, and giving her to Muhammad as a wife in Heaven. The Prophet tells his friend Abu Bakr about the vision, asking him to marry his daughter Aisha to him on earth as well. Abu Bakr responds, 'O Messenger of God, she is young, and I do not know if she is suitable (*taṣluḥu*) for you.' The Prophet asks rhetorically how it could be that Aisha might not be suitable for him when God considered her so. Abu Bakr immediately agrees and tells the Prophet he is marrying his daughter to him. Aisha is sent by her father to visit the Prophet, not knowing yet that she has been wed to him, and is shocked when he takes hold of her robe and pulls her toward himself. She upbraids him and leaves to tell her father. Abu Bakr responds by telling her not to think badly of anyone since he had already married her to the Prophet.

In the Arabic original, Abu Bakr's concerns over Aisha's age are not profound or moral. It was not uncommon to reject a suitor due to age issues. A report in the *Sunan al-Nasā'ī* tells of the Prophet rejecting Abu Bakr's proposal to the Prophet's daughter Fatima because she was too young for him (*kitāb al-nikāḥ, bāb tazawwuj al-mar'a mithlahā fī al-sinn*). The word Abu Bakr uses for 'suitable' or 'fitting', *ṣ-l-ḥ*, is often used in the context of marriage to mean 'fit for sexual intercourse.' Aisha was, in fact, not fit for it at the time. Hence, once they agreed on the marriage, all parties involved also agreed to delay the consummation of the marriage for several years. The reader's pleasure of revelation in the vignette comes from the relief from the tension created by Aisha upbraiding the Messenger of God (!), i.e., when she finds that he had been within his rights to touch her because he was already her husband.

Interestingly, there seem to be significant differences between manuscripts of the *Sab'iyyāt*, with at least three disparities in this story alone. When Abu Bakr replies to the Prophet's request, the unnamed manuscript(s) used by Sayyid Ṣiddīq 'Abd al-Fattāḥ in his 2009 Cairo edition (Maktabat al-Madbūlī, p. 195) reads: 'I do not know if she is suitable for your service (*taṣluḥu li-khidmatika*),' while the Ms. of King Saud University in Riyadh (Ms. 1378 of Jāmi'at al-Malik Su'ūd, 92b), which was copied in 1845, reads 'suitable for you (*taṣluḥu laka*).'

Marracci is chiefly interested in depicting Muhammad as a lecher (*scortum*) and a hypocrite, who gropes women who are not his wives and uses his claims of prophecy for carnal ends. His exaggeration of Abu Bakr's hesitance merely provides dramatic effect, suggesting that he also wanted to keep his daughter out of lecherous hands. Ockley adopts this and adds his own layer of interpretation. Perhaps because he is skeptical about the claims that women mature so early in warmer climes, Abu Bakr's original response turns into him being 'very averse' to marrying his daughter off at such a young age.

Appendix II

Hadiths on a Parent Killing His Child

RATINGS OF THE HADITH BY MUSLIM CRITICS

Al-Suyūṭī rates it as *ṣaḥīḥ*, and al-Albānī affirms it as *ḥasan* (*Ṣaḥīḥ al-Jāmiʿ al-ṣaghīr*, 2:1231). Al-Dhahabī considers it possible that it is *ḥasan* (*Mukhtaṣar Sunan al-Bayhaqī*, 6:3125). Ibn ʿAbd al-Barr remarks that the Hadith undergirding the ruling on this issue 'is well known (*mashhūr*) among the jurists of Iraq and the Hejaz, so widespread and acted on (*al-ʿamal bihi*) that an *Isnād* is unnecessary. In fact, providing an *isnād* for it might be excessive' (Ibn ʿAbd al-Barr, *al-Tamhīd*, 23:437). ʿAbd al-Ḥaqq al-Ishbīlī, however, observes that 'all its narrations are flawed (*maʿlūla*) and none are sound' (Ibn Ḥajar, *Talkhīṣ*, 4:1314–15).

EXAMINATION OF INDIVIDUAL NARRATIONS (I HAVE OMITTED REPETITIONS IN LATER SOURCES) *SEE FIGURE IN THE ILLUSTRATION PLATES*

One narration of this tradition comes from the Companions Surāqa bin Mālik, who recalls the Prophet saying that a parent cannot be put to death for killing his or her child. The majority of the narrations of this tradition, though, consist of the caliph ʿUmar recalling the Prophet's ruling on this issue. Both Surāqa's and ʿUmar's narrations come via ʿAmr bin Shuʿayb. Al-Tirmidhī says that these narrations are unresolvably problematic (*muḍṭarib*) but that the Hadith is acted on by jurists. ʿAmr bin Shu'ayb (d. 736) was relied upon extensively as a transmitter in the Four *Sunan* but not in the *Ṣaḥīḥayn* of al-Bukhārī and Muslim. Early Hadith critics agree that, if a Hadith was narrated from him by a trustworthy transmitter (*thiqa*), 'Amr could be used as part of the proof, but not otherwise. Critics like Ibn Maʿīn and Abū Zurʿa al-Rāzī note he made many mistakes due to his relying on a written book of Hadiths he received from his father without proper audition (*samāʿ*) (al-Dhahabī, *Mughnī*, 2:146), and this book seems to be his source for the Hadith in question here. Al-Rāzī adds that many unacceptable (*munkar*) Hadiths are narrated from 'Amr by Ibn Lahīʿa and al-Muthannā bin al-Ṣabbāḥ, both highly problematic transmitters in their own right. Ibn Ḥanbal is of the opinion that 'Amr's Hadiths should only be written for consideration in evaluating other Hadiths, not for use as proofs in law (Ibn Ḥajar, *Tahdhīb*, 8:42–43). None of the transmissions of the Hadith in question from him are via trustworthy transmitters (they include al-Ḥajjāj bin Arṭa, Ibn Lahīʿa, Yaʿqūb bin 'Aṭā' and others) except one found in the *Sunan* of al-Dāraquṭnī (3:140). This *Isnād* presents no problems until it arrives at the segment with 'Amr bin Abī Qays ← Manṣūr bin Muʿtamir ← Muḥammad bin 'Ajlān ← 'Amr bin Shuʿayb. 'Amr bin Abī Qays, though not considered very weak, was known to err in Hadiths. The fact that the only chain of transmission leading back to a reliable transmitter from 'Amr bin Shuʿayb comes to us through a later transmitter who was known to err, and the fact that 'Amr bin Shuʿayb received this Hadith only in written form without proper audition suggests that all the narrations of the Hadith through 'Amr are weak.

We should note here that 'Abd al-Fattāḥ Abū Ghudda argued that the narrations of 'Amr bin Shuʿayb from his father should be considered uniformly reliable. His argument centers on the fact that 'Amr's Hadiths were often acted on by jurists, however, and it is precisely this reliance on tradition to authenticate Hadiths that is at issue here (see Abū Ghudda's appendices to his edition of *Qafw al-athar fī ṣafw 'ulūm al-athar* [Beirut: Dār al-Bashā'ir al-Islāmiyya, 1988], 210–19).

The transmission of the Hadith of the Parent Killing His Child from 'Umar that does *not* pass through 'Amr (found in Ibn Ḥanbal's *Musnad*) includes the problematic link between al-Ḥakam bin 'Utayba ← Mujāhid bin Jabr. Al-Ḥakam was a known *mudallis*, with Shuʿba bin al-Ḥajjāj warning that anything he received from Mujāhid without explicit audition (*samāʿ*) was passed in the form of a book (Ibn Ḥajar, *Tahdhīb*, 2:390). Since this

Hadith comes via the phrase 'from (*'an*),' which does not denote audition, this narration is unreliable.

The transmissions of the Hadith from Ibn 'Abbās all pass via Ismā'īl bin Muslim al-Makkī, who is uniformly panned as a narrator. Al-Bayhaqī and al-Dāraquṭnī have a version that bypasses Ismā'īl bin Muslim by going directly to the respected scholar 'Amr bin Dīnār (al-Bayhaqī, *Sunan*, 8:70), but this version passes through Ḥasan bin 'Alī bin Shabīb al-Ma'marī of Baghdad, who was respected and well known but who made errors like mixing up reports from the Prophet (*raf'*) and versions from Companions and other later folk (*waqf*). Al-Dhahabī correctly observes that this is not a minor flaw at all, since it regularly excludes a transmitter from the category of being reliable (al-Dhahabī, *Siyar*, 13:513). This narration of the Hadith is thus unreliable.

Al-Ḥākim offers a bizarre version via the Meccan scholar Ibn Jurayj that is totally baseless in part due to the presence in the *Isnād* of 'Umar bin 'Īsā, who is either a forger or unknown. Al-Dhahabī dismissed this version, and even Ibn Ḥajar, who usually tries to defend al-Ḥākim from al-Dhahabī's criticism, accepts this critique (Ibn Ḥajar, *Lisān al-mīzān*, 4:320–22; al-Ḥākim, *al-Mustadrak*, 4:369). Al-Ḥākim and al-Ṭabarānī include another insignificant narration via the unknown transmitter 'Ubayd bin Sharīk.

MY EVALUATION OF THE HADITH

Taken together and based on *Isnād* evidence alone, one might conclude that the two main clumps of narrations of the Hadith from 'Umar buttress one another and raise the Hadith to a *ḥasan* rating. Though this is generally reliable enough to justify a legal ruling, the extent to which the Hadith's contents clash with the explicit principles of the protection of innocent life and personal responsibility before the law suggest that this Hadith evidence is not reliable enough.

CITATIONS FOR HADITH OF A FATHER KILLING HIS CHILD

Musnad Aḥmad Ibn Ḥanbal: 1:16, 22, 49; *Jāmi' al-Tirmidhī*: *kitāb al-diyāt, bāb rajul yaqtulu ibnahu yuqādu minhu am lā*; *Sunan Ibn Mājah*: *kitāb al-diyāt, bāb lā yuqtalu al-wālid bi-waladihi*; al-Ṭabarānī, *al-Muʿjam al-kabīr*, 11:5; al-Ḥākim al-Naysābūrī, *al-Mustadrak*, 4:369; al-Bayhaqī, *al-Sunan al-kubrā*, 8:69–70; Abū Nuʿaym al-Iṣbahānī, *Ḥilyat al-awliyāʾ*, 4:18; Ibn ʿAbd al-Barr, *al-Tamhīd*, 23:440–42; Ibn al-Mulaqqin, *al-Badr al-munīr*, 8:372–79; Ibn Ḥajar, *Talkhīṣ al-ḥabīr*, 4:33–34.

Appendix III

The Hadith of *Riba* and Incest

RATINGS BY HADITH CRITICS

This Hadith presents an excellent case study of how Hadiths of admonition and encouragement were treated. Its narrations are all flawed in serious ways. Despite this, prominent Hadith scholars from al-Ḥākim al-Naysābūrī to al-Suyūṭī and al-Albānī have all considered it sound (*ṣaḥīḥ*) (al-Suyūṭī, *al-La'ālī al-maṣnū'a*, 2:129; al-Albānī, *Silsilat al-aḥādīth al-ṣaḥīḥa*, 4:488 ff., no. 1871).

Various narrations of the Hadith were criticized or declared forgeries by early critics. The Hadith as a whole, inclusive of all its narrations, was considered an outright forgery by many scholars as well, including Ibn al-Jawzī, Ibn 'Arrāq and Muḥammad Ṭāhir al-Fatanī. In his abridgement of Ibn al-Jawzī's *Kitāb al-Mawḍū'āt*, al-Dhahabī affirms the author's conclusion that the Hadith is forged (overruling his own youthful affirmation of its reliability in his comments on al-Ḥākim's *Mustadrak*). Al-Sakhāwī provides the most comprehensive analysis of this Hadith in his *Fatāwā*, and he seconds Ibn al-Jawzī's conclusion that *all* the versions comparing *Riba* to incest are unreliable.

For these varied criticisms, see: Abū Ja'far al-'Uqaylī, *Kitāb al-ḍu'afā' al-kabīr*, ed. 'Abd al-Mu'ṭī Amīn Qal'ajī, 4 vols (Beirut: Dār al-Kutub al-'Ilmiyya, 1984), 2:257–58; Ibn Abī Ḥātim al-Rāzī, *'Ilal al-ḥadīth*, ed. Sa'd 'Abdallāh al-Ḥumayyid and Khālid 'Abd al-Raḥmān al-Juraysī (Riyadh: Maṭābi' al-Juraysī, 2006), 3:614 (no. 1132); Ibn al-Jawzī, *Kitāb al-Mawḍū'āt*, 2:245; 'Alī bin Muḥammad Ibn 'Arrāq, *Tanzīh al-sharī'a al-marfū'a 'an al-akhbār al-shanīʿa al-mawḍūʿa*, 2 vols (Cairo: Maktabat al-Qāhira, [1964]), 2:194; Muḥammad Ṭāhir al-Fatanī, *Tadhkirat al-mawḍūʿāt* (Beirut: Amīn Damaj, [1960]), 139; al-Dhahabī, *Tartīb al-Mawḍūʿāt*, ed. Kamāl Basyūnī Zaghlūl (Beirut: Dār al-Kutub al-ʿIlmiyya, 1994), 196–97; Shams al-Dīn al-Sakhāwī, *al-Fatāwā al-ḥadīthiyya*, ed. ʿAlī Riḍā ʿAbdallāh (Beirut: Dār al-Maʾmūn li'l-Turāth, n.d.), 155–59.

MY EVALUATION OF THE HADITH OF *RIBA* AND INCEST

Early transmission of this Hadith was concentrated in Basra, and it appears in several manifestations, some mentioning that there are seventy types of *Riba*, some seventy-one, -two or -three, originating supposedly from the Companions Abū Hurayra, Ibn Masʿūd, Barāʾ bin ʿĀzib, Wahb bin al-Aswab and Ibn ʿAbbās. The main versions are as follows (brackets [ ] indicate sections of the text missing from some narrations):

- Abū Hurayra ← Prophet: *Riba* is seventy types of sin, the least severe is like a man having sex with his mother [And to practice *Riba* is to impinge on the honor of a Muslim].
- Abū Hurayra ← Prophet: *Riba* is of seventy types, the least of which is like someone having sex with his mother.
- Ibn Masʿūd ← Prophet: *Riba* is of seventy-[three] types, [the least severe is like a man having sex with his mother. And to practice *Riba* impinges on the honor of a Muslim man].
- Barāʾ bin ʿĀzib ← Prophet: *Riba* is of seventy-two types, the lowest of them like a man coming to his mother for sex. And, for a man, practicing *Riba* is taking liberties with the honor of his fellow Muslim.

The two versions of Wahb and Ibn ʿAbbās are too weak to merit serious discussion. Ibn Ḥajar notes that the narration from Wahb suffers from several weaknesses in the *Isnād*, including the addition of two weak transmitters according to some versions, and the ninth-century master Hadith critic Abū Zurʿa al-Rāzī dismisses the narration from Ibn ʿAbbās as '*munkar*' (unacceptable).

The main transmission of this Hadith comes from the Companions Abū Hurayra and Barāʾ bin ʿĀzib via the bottleneck of the Basran scholar

'Ikrima bin 'Ammār from his Basran teacher Yaḥyā bin Abī Kathīr. Anything passing via this link in the *Isnād* is unreliable because a number of leading early Hadith experts, from Ibn Ḥanbal, Abū Ḥātim al-Rāzī and 'Alī bin al-Madīnī to Yaḥyā al-Qaṭṭān and al-Bukhārī all felt that 'Ikrima's material from Yaḥyā was riddled with mistakes. In part this was because he had relied on a written book with no oral explanation. There is no other source for this Hadith from Yaḥyā bin Abī Kathīr to corroborate 'Ikrima's narration. Unfortunately, al-Albānī glosses over this serious flaw when authenticating this narration of the Hadith.

Narrations from Abū Hurayra that do not pass via this 'Ikrima ← Yaḥyā link, like the one found in Ibn Mājah's *Sunan*, rely either on the unreliable Abū Ma'shar al-Sindī or on the uniformly avoided (*tarakūhu*, says al-Dhahabī) 'Abdallāh bin Sa'īd al-Maqburī, as in the case of the narrations found in the books of Ibn Abī al-Dunyā.

The narration from the Companion Ibn Mas'ūd in the *Mustadrak* of al-Ḥākim relies on Zayd bin al-Ḥawārī al-'Ammī, an error-prone and very problematic transmitter from Basra about whom Ibn 'Adī says, 'the mass of what he narrates is weak.' The narration through Barā' has a total break in the *Isnād* between him and Isḥāq bin 'Abdallāh, and a later transmitter in the chain, 'Umar bin Rāshid, is widely considered 'weak' (Ibn Ḥajar, *Tahdhīb*, 3:355; 7:227).

From the perspective of Sunni Hadith criticism, the number and variety of Hadiths conveying the message that *Riba* is a serious sin comparable to fornication leave little doubt that this idea has a strong basis in the Prophet's teachings. That said, there is no reliable evidence for the Hadith that specifically equates the least serious form of *Riba* with fornication with one's mother. The fact that this statement was also attributed to Companions like 'Abdallāh bin Salām suggests that it might originally have been a saying in the early Muslim community. The problematic transmitters above may have confused Abū Hurayra's saying this with a prophetic Hadith.

CITATIONS FOR THE HADITH

Sunan Ibn Mājah: *kitāb al-tijārāt, bāb al-taghlīẓ fī al-ribā*; al-Ḥākim, *al-Mustadrak*, 2:37; Abū Bakr al-Bazzār, *Musnad al-Bazzār*, 5:318; al-Ṭabarānī, *Mu'jam al-kabīr*, 9:321; idem, *Mu'jam al-awsaṭ*, ed. Ṭāriq 'Awaḍ Allāh and

'Abd al-Muḥsin al-Ḥusaynī, 10 vols (Cairo: Dār al-Ḥaramayn, 1995), 7:158; Ibn Abī al-Dunyā, *Kitāb al-Ṣamt*, 173; idem, *Kitāb al-Ghība*, 34; al-Bayhaqī, *Shu'ab al-īmān*, ed. Muḥammad Sa'īd Basyūnī Zaghlūl, 7 vols (Beirut: Dar al-Kutub al-'Ilmiyya, 1990), 4:394; Abū Bakr Ibn Abī Shayba, *al-Muṣannaf*, ed. Kamāl Yūsuf al-Ḥūt, 7 vols (Riyadh: Maktabat al-Rushd, [1989]), 4:448; 'Abd al-Razzāq al-Ṣan'ānī, *al-Muṣannaf*, ed. Ḥabīb al-Raḥmān al-A'ẓamī, 2nd edn, 11 vols (Beirut: al-Maktab al-Islāmī, [1983]), 8:314.

Appendix IV

The Hadith of the Seventy-Two Virgins

This Hadith has the Prophet promising that,

> The martyr receives six features with God: he is immediately forgiven, he sees his seat in Paradise, he is protected from the torment of the grave and the greatest terror of the Resurrection, he is given the crown of honor, whose ruby is greater than the world and all in it; he is given seventy-two heavenly beauties (*ḥūr al-ʿīn*) as wives and allowed to intercede on behalf of seventy of his relatives.

This Hadith appears in the *Sunan*s of al-Tirmidhī and Ibn Mājah as well as the *Musnad* of Ibn Ḥanbal and the *Muṣannaf* of his teacher ʿAbd al-Razzāq al-Ṣanʿānī. These sources generally record this Hadith through a number of *Isnād*s converging on the Syrian Ismāʿīl bin ʿAyyāsh and continuing to his teacher, the widely respected scholar Baḥīr bin Saʿd, then to Khālid bin Maʿdān, then continuing to the Prophet via a number of varied chains. Ismāʿīl, however, was well known as a problematic transmitter who, though he was honest, frequently erred in transmitting Hadiths. He often confused *Isnād*s or turned Companion opinions into prophetic Hadiths and vice versa. This is certainly the case for the Hadith of the Seventy-Two Virgins. Ismāʿīl is recorded as transmitting it via five contrasting paths:

1. Baḥīr ← Khālid ← Miqdām bin al-Maʿdīkarab ← Prophet
2. Baḥīr ← Khālid ← Kathīr bin Murra ← ʿUbāda bin Ṣāmit* ← Prophet

* The narration from ʿUbāda was probably a confusion with ʿUbāda's separate narration of a different version of this Hadith, one that lacked specification of seventy-two heavenly beauties and intercession for seventy relatives; see al-Bazzār, *Musnad al-Bazzār*, 7:143.

3. Baḥīr ← Khālid ← Kathīr bin Murra ← Nuʿaym bin Hammār (*sic*) ← Prophet
4. Baḥīr ← Khālid ← Kathīr bin Murra ← ʿUqba bin ʿĀmir (not a prophetic Hadith)
5. Saʿīd bin Yūsuf ← Yaḥyā bin Abī Kathīr ← Abū Sallām ← Abū Muʿāniq al-Ashʿarī ← Abū Mālik ← Prophet.

Amid this confusion of Ismāʿīl's varied narrations of the Hadith, there is only one source that confirms that his teacher Baḥīr transmitted the Hadith at all, namely the Hims Hadith scholar Baqiyya bin Walīd, who was generally favored as a source over Ismāʿīl by leading critics such as Abū Ḥātim al-Rāzī.

Baqiyya, though, was just as problematic as Ismāʿīl, meriting unusually lengthy entries in leading Hadith critical dictionaries like the *Mīzān al-iʿtidāl* and the *Tahdhīb al-Tahdhīb*. Although he was praised as upstanding and reliable (*thiqa*) by some leading Hadith critics of the ninth century, he was more often and more extensively criticized. He was lambasted in particular for narrating unselectively from many transmitters and, much more seriously, dropping the names of his immediate sources and insinuating that he received the material from figures earlier in the *Isnād* (*tadlīs*). Both Ibn Ḥanbal and, later, Ibn Ḥibbān al-Bustī engaged in extensive research into Baqiyya's infractions in this area, expressing great concern and regret for previous confidence in him. Ibn Ḥibbān observed that 'for less than this a person loses their upstanding status (*ʿadāla*).' Both Abū Ḥātim al-Rāzī and the leading Shāfiʿī jurist and Hadith scholar Ibn Khuzayma declared Baqiyya unfit for use as proof (*ḥujja*), a conclusion that al-Bayhaqī later described as a consensus position. Al-Jūzajānī declared that Baqiyya could not be used as proof if he narrated a report from a source uncorroborated, and al-Nasāʾī concluded that he should not be heeded if he did not specify that he heard material directly from his source.

All of these warnings apply exactly to the Hadith of the Seventy-Two Virgins. Besides Ismāʿīl's confused tangle of narrations, only Baqiyya transmits the Hadith from Baḥīr, and he does so by the ambiguous phrase 'from' – not evidence of direct audition. Al-Fasawī observed that one of Baqiyya's faults was that he enjoyed 'entertaining and bawdy (*milaḥ wa ṭarāʾif*)' – and unreliable – Hadiths too much. Al-Dhahabī called him 'a man of anomalous, surprising and unacceptable Hadiths' (al-Dhahabī, *Mīzān*, 1:339; Ibn Ḥajar, *Tahdhīb*, 1:435–37). Taken together, these criticisms mean that any narrations coming through Baḥīr cannot be accepted as reliable.

There is another Hadith cluster with a very similar text narrated from the Companion Abū Hurayra. It quotes the Prophet as saying:

> The martyr is forgiven upon the first shedding of his blood. He is married to the heavenly beauties and is made an intercessor for seventy of his family. He who mans a fort on the frontier, if he dies there, the rewards of all his deeds till the Day of Judgment are written for him, a breeze comes to him every morning with his sustenance, he is given seventy Huris as companions, and it is said to him 'Stand and intercede' until the Hour of Accounting is done.

This Hadith is found in the works of al-Ṭabarānī (*al-Mu'jam al-kabīr*, 3:326) but inspires little confidence. Even the notoriously lax critics al-Suyūṭī and al-Munāwī only rate it as *ḥasan* and weak respectively. The weakest point in the *Isnād* is al-Ṭabarānī's own teacher, Bakr bin Sahl, who is criticized by some as unreliable and as having inexact narrations (*muqārib al-ḥadīth*) in the eyes of al-Dhahabī (al-Suyūṭī, *al-Jāmi' al-ṣaghīr*, 305, no. 4963; al-Munāwī, *Fayḍ al-qadīr*, 7:3691-92; al-Dhahabī, *Mīzān*, 1:345–46).

There are also other versions of this overall tradition that do not include the specification of seventy-two heavenly beauties and come via chains of transmission unrelated to those mentioned above; one in the *Musnad* of al-Bazzār (7:143) and one in Ibn Ḥanbal's *Musnad* (4:200).

OVERALL RATING

The presence of 'heavenly beauties' in Paradise is established by the Qur'an, as are the accolades and place in Heaven awarded to martyrs. Moreover, the collection of all the above transmissions, whether or not they can be accurately traced back to the Prophet or just to a Companion or other members of the early Muslim community, strongly indicate that reports were circulating among the first Muslim generations enumerating several heavenly compensations given to martyrs and including the companionship of huris. This lies behind al-Albānī's decision to rate these narrations collectively as *ṣaḥīḥ* (al-Albānī, *Silsilat al-aḥādīth al-ṣaḥīḥa*, 7, part 1:647–50, no. 3213).

As for the specific number of seventy or seventy-two huris for each martyr, however, this hinges on the reliability of 1) the narrations via Baḥīr, and 2) the solitary narration from Abū Hurayra in al-Ṭabarānī's works. Baḥīr's narrations fell victim to Ismā'īl bin 'Ayyāsh's confusion and are only otherwise known by the unreliable and inaccurate Baqiyya, who was known to take liberties with precisely such extravagant contents. The narration from Abū Hurayra collected by al-Ṭabarānī is unreliable due to the questions surrounding Bakr bin Sahl, its solitary narrator. This collection of evidence does not seem to merit any rating higher than 'weak' (*ḍa'īf*) for both of the Hadith clusters above.

CITATIONS FOR THE HADITH OF THE SEVENTY-TWO VIRGINS

See *Jāmi' al-Tirmidhī*: *kitāb faḍā'il al-jihād, bāb thawāb al-shahīd*; *Sunan Ibn Mājah*: *kitāb al-jihād, bāb faḍl al-shadāha fī sabīl Allāh*; *Musnad Aḥmad Ibn Ḥanbal*: 4:131; Ibn Abī 'Āṣim al-Nabīl, *Kitāb al-Jihād*, ed. Musā'id Sulaymān al-Ḥamīd, 2 vols (Damascus: Dār al-Qalam, 1989), 2:532–38; al-Bazzār, *Musnad al-Bazzār*, 7:143; al-Ṭabarānī, *al-Mu'jam al-kabīr*, 3:326.

Notes

CHAPTER 1: THE PROBLEM(S) WITH ISLAM

1. Ṣafwat Ḥijāzī speaking on the Risāla channel, http://www.youtube.com/watch?v=Uo1fH5Szv6k&feature=related (last accessed 6/17/2012).
2. http://www.youtube.com/watch?v=OVnYu3rSLik&feature=related.
3. *Ṣaḥīḥ Muslim*: *kitāb al-imāra, bāb ḥukm man farraqa amr al-muslimīn wa huwa jamā'a.*
4. Al-Zurqānī, *Mukhtaṣar al-Maqāṣid al-ḥasana*, 206.
5. William Graham, 'Scripture,' in *Encyclopedia of Religion*, ed. Mircea Eliade (New York: MacMillan, 1987), 13:133–36.
6. Lucian of Samosata, 'A True Story,' in *Selected Satires of Lucian*, 14; G. W. Bowerstock, *Fiction as History*, 12, 23.
7. Voltaire, *Essai sur les moeurs*, 1:271–72.
8. Thomas Carlyle, 'Hero as Prophet: Mahomet: Islam,' in *Carlyle's Lectures on Heroes*, 58.
9. Georges Tartar, trans., *Dialogue Islamo-Chrétien sous le calife al-Ma'mûn*, 162.
10. See http://www.nashvillescene.com/pitw/archives/2010/07/16/ramsey-argues-freedom-of-religion-doesnt-apply-to-muslims; Glen Owen, 'Tony Blair says murder of Lee Rigby PROVES "there is a problem within Islam,"' *Daily Mail/Mail Online*, June 1, 2013 (http://www.dailymail.co.uk/news/article-2334451/Tony-Blair-says-murder-Lee-Rigby-PROVES-problem-Islam.html).
11. Montesquieu, *De l'Esprit des lois*, 2:800–802.
12. George Huntston Williams, 'Erasmus and the Reformers on Non-Christian Religions and Salus Extra Ecclesiam,' in *Action and Conviction in Early Modern Europe*, ed. Theodore K. Rabb and Jerrold E. Seigel, 342; Jonathan Lyons, *Islam through Western Eyes*, 62.
13. Pierre Bayle, *Dictionnaire historique et critique*, 3:262; Mary Montagu, *Letters*, 116 (Letter dated April 1, 1717).
14. Scott Kugle, 'Framed, Blamed and Renamed: The Recasting of Islamic Jurisprudence in Colonial South Asia,' 289; E. P. Thompson, *Whigs and Hunters*, 270–77.
15. Voltaire, *Le Siècle de Louis XIV*, 1009.
16. Thomas Macaulay, 'Minute on Indian Education.'

17. Montesquieu, *Lettres Persanes*, 27–28.
18. Ahmad Gunny, *Perceptions of Islam in European Writings*, 287, 290, 307.
19. Jonathan Lyons, *Islam through Western Eyes*, 76, 95.
20. Lyons, 91.
21. Henri Saint-Simon, 'Introduction to the Scientific Studies of the 19th Century (1808),' in *Social Organization, The Science of Man and Other Writings*, 16.

CHAPTER 2: A MAP OF THE ISLAMIC INTERPRETIVE TRADITION

1. Although I draw the general outline of the Islamic legal tradition from the *Inṣāf*, I also rely heavily on Shah Wali Allah's masterpiece, the *Ḥujjat Allāh al-Bāligha*, with which the *Inṣāf* overlaps a great deal, as well as on his other writings on Sufism.
2. *Sunan Abī Dāwūd*: *kitāb al-ṭahāra, bāb karāhiyat istiqbāl al-qibla 'ind qaḍā' al-ḥāja*.
3. Robert Kirschner, 'The Vocation of Holiness in Late Antiquity,' 118.
4. Shāh Walī Allāh, *Ḥujjat Allāh al-bāligha* (henceforth *HAB*), 2:460.
5. Robert Hoyland, *Seeing Islam as Others Saw It*, 221; Adamnan of Iona, *De Locis Sanctis*, ed. Denis Meehan (Dublin: Dublin Institute for Advanced Studies, 1958), 43.
6. Al-Khaṭīb explains that this Hadith was an egregious forgery; al-Khaṭīb al-Baghdādī, *Tārīkh Baghdād*, 9:455–56.
7. Cited from al-Madā'inī's *Kitāb al-aḥdāth*; Aḥmad bin Sa'd al-Dīn al-Miswarī, *al-Risāla al-munqidha min al-ghiwāya fī ṭuruq al-riwāya*, 51–55.
8. Jalāl al-Dīn al-Suyūṭī, *al-La'ālī al-maṣnū'a fī al-aḥādīth al-mawḍū'a*, 1:429–35.
9. Al-Suyūṭī, *al-Bāhir*, 30–31.
10. This opinion is attributed to 'Abdallāh Ibn al-Mubārak (d. 797) and other Khurasani scholars; Abū Ṭālib al-Makkī, *Qūt al-qulūb*, 1:130. See also, 'Abdallāh b. Aḥmad, *Masā'il al-imām Aḥmad Ibn Ḥanbal riwāyat ibnihi*, ed. Zuhayr Shāwīsh (Beirut: al-Maktab al-Islāmī, 1981), 438.
11. *HAB*, 1:476.
12. *Musnad Aḥmad Ibn Ḥanbal*: 5:12.
13. Muḥammad al-Khwārazmī, *Jāmi' masānīd al-imām al-a'ẓam*, 1:126.
14. Al-Khwārazmī, *Jāmi' masānīd*, 2:280, 283.
15. Al-Sarakhsī, *al-Mabsūṭ*, 9:153; Badr al-Dīn al-'Aynī and Nāṣir al-Islām al-Rāmpūrī, *al-Bināya sharḥ al-Hidāya*, 6:392.
16. Al-Sha'rānī, *al-Mīzān al-kubrā*, 1:124.
17. Al-'Aynī, *Al-Bināya sharḥ al-Hidāya*, 7:219–20; 'Alā' al-Dīn al-Kāsānī, *Badā'i' al-ṣanā'i'*, 5:142.
18. *HAB*, 1:442–43; Shāh Walī Allāh, *al-Juz' al-laṭīf*, 2–5.
19. *Muwaṭṭa'*: *kitāb al-buyū', bāb al-khiyār*; Ṣāliḥ 'Abd al-Salām al-Ābī, *al-Thamar al-dānī*, 386.
20. *HAB*, 2:336.
21. See, for example, Soraya Altorki and Donald P. Cole, *Arabian Oasis City*, 65–66.
22. *Muwaṭṭa'*: *kitāb al-buyū', bāb mā jā'a fī al-ribā fī al-dayn*.
23. Abū al-Rayḥān al-Bīrūnī, *Taḥqīq mā li'l-Hind*, 1, 16. For a translation, see *Alberuni's India*, trans. Edward Sachau (New York: Norton & Co., 1971), 3–22; Shāh Walī Allāh, *al-Irshād ilā muhimmat al-isnād*, 3.
24. *HAB*, 1:71, 74, 143. Shāh Walī Allāh actually cites this first report on the world

as an old woman incorrectly. It is not a prophetic Hadith but rather a report from the Companion Ibn ʿAbbās. See al-Ghazālī, *Iḥyāʾ ʿulūm al-dīn*, 3:2026.

25. Arthur Jeffery, 'Ghevond's Text of the Correspondence between ʿUmar II and Leo III,' 328–29.

26. Abū Hilāl al-ʿAskarī, *Kitāb al-Awāʾil*, 2:119.

27. Maimonides, *The Guide for the Perplexed*, 69; John Mair, 'The Text of the Opuscula Sacra,' in *Boethius, His Life, Thought and Influence*, 209–11.

28. Majid Fakhry, *A History of Islamic Philosophy*, 57.

29. Al-Zamakhsharī, *al-Kashshāf*, 4:754.

30. *Ṣaḥīḥ Muslim*: *kitāb al-qadar, bāb ḥijāj Ādam wa Mūsā.*

31. *HAB*, 1:481.

32. This statement was attributed to Maymūn bin Mihrān (d. 735–36); Shāh Walī Allāh, *al-Inṣaf*, 51.

33. Zafar Ishaq Ansari, 'Islamic Juristic Terminology before Shāfiʿī: A Semantic Analysis with Special Reference to Kūfa,' 282–87.

34. Al-Shāfiʿī, *al-Risāla*, 534–35; idem, *al-Umm*, 7:257.

35. *HAB*, 2:487.

36. Al-Shāfiʿī, *al-Umm*, 7:250; idem, *al-Risāla*, 177.

37. Al-Dārimī, *Sunan*, 1:153.

38. Al-Ṣanʿānī, *Subul al-salām*, 3:170.

39. Al-Khaṭṭābī, *Maʿālim al-sunan*, 1:174. See chapter 5 for more on this question.

40. Aḥmad al-Ghumārī, *Masālik al-dilāla ʿalā masāʾil matn al-Risāla*, 217–18; Ibn Rushd, *Distinguished Jurist's Primer*, 2:259–60.

41. *HAB*, 1:400.

42. Al-Shāfiʿī, *Risāla*, 89, 226, 403.

43. Abū Ṭālib al-Makkī, *Qūt al-qulūb*, 1:137; Shāh Walī Allāh, *al-Irshād ilā muhimmāt al-isnād*, 3.

44. '*Idhā ḥaddatha al-thiqa ʿan al-thiqa ḥattā yantahiya ilā rasūl Allāh (ṣ) fa-huwa thābit ʿan rasūl Allāh (ṣ)*'; al-Shāfiʿī, *al-Umm*, 7:177.

45. Al-Shāfiʿī, *al-Risāla*, 370–83; Ibn ʿAdī, *al-Kāmil*, 1:125.

46. This statement comes from the famous Basran Hadith critic ʿAbd al-Raḥmān bin Mahdī, at whose request al-Shāfiʿī supposedly wrote his *Risāla*; *Jāmiʿ al-Tirmidhī*: *kitāb faḍāʾil al-jihād, bāb mā jāʾa fī-man yuqātilu riyāʾan wa liʾl-dunyā.*

47. Al-Khwārazmī, *Jāmiʿ masānīd*, 2:236, 242.

48. Literally, '*az jihat-i ittibāʿ*;' Shāh Walī Allāh, *Musaffā*, 1:294.

49. *Musnad Aḥmad Ibn Ḥanbal*: 1:21, 46.

50. Ibn Qutayba, *Taʾwīl mukhtalif al-ḥadīth*, 208.

51. *HAB*, 1:51.

52. Jonathan Brown, 'How We Know Early Ḥadīth Critics Did *Matn* Criticism,' 154–55.

53. Jonathan Brown, 'The Rules of *Matn* Criticism: There Are No Rules.'

54. Christopher Melchert, 'The *Musnad* of Aḥmad Ibn Ḥanbal,' 32–51.

55. Abū Ṭālib al-Makkī, *Qūt al-qulūb*, 1:177.

56. Ibn Qudāma, *Mughnī*, 2:162–66; al-Buhūtī, *al-Rawḍ al-murbiʿ*, 115; al-Albānī, *Irwāʾ al-ghalīl*, 3:61–63.

57. Al-Buhūtī, *al-Rawḍ al-murbiʿ*, 104.

58. *Jāmiʿ al-Tirmidhī*: *kitāb al-zakāt, bāb mā jāʾa fī faḍl al-ṣadaqa*; cf. *kitāb ṣifat al-janna, bāb mā jāʾa fī khulūd ahl al-janna wa ahl al-nār.*

59. Ibn Abī Ḥātim, *Tafsīr*, apud al-Suyūṭī, *al-Durr al-manthūr*, 6:190; *Jāmiʿ al-Tirmidhī: kitāb al-daʿwāt, bāb fī ḥusn al-ẓann billāh.*

60. Some Mutazila considered the Antichrist to be an allegory for evil forces at the end of time. On the issue of the Punishment of the Grave, some early Mutazila denied it altogether while others argued it was only for unbelievers, not sinful Muslims; Ibn Qayyim, *Kitāb al-Rūḥ*, 112.

61. Al-Khaṭīb al-Baghdādī, *Tārīkh Baghdād*, 7:157.

62. Al-Dhahabī, *Siyar aʿlām al-nubalāʾ*, 11:125.

63. Abū Jaʿfar al-Ṭaḥāwī, *Sharḥ Mushkil al-Āthār*, 3:272–77.

64. ʿAlawī al-Saqqāf, *Majmūʿat sabʿat kutub mufīda*, 52.

65. Selma Zecevic, 'Missing Husbands, Waiting Wives, Bosnian *Muftis*,' 348; al-Shaʿrānī, *al-Mīzān al-kubrā*, 2:153–54.

66. Al-Dhahabī, *Bayān raghal al-ʿilm waʾl-ṭalab*, 12; Yossef Rapoport, 'Legal Diversity in the Age of Taqlīd,' 219–25.

67. Ibn al-Jawzī, *al-Muntaẓam*, 18:32; Tāj al-Dīn al-Subkī, *Ṭabaqāt al-shāfiʿiyya al-kubrā*, 8:231–33.

68. After the 1400s the Shafiʿi school allowed something similar, namely that, if the ruler ordered judges to apply the ruling from any of the four schools of law on some issue, the judge was required to obey; Ibn Ḥajar Haytamī, *al-Fatāwā al-kubrā al-fiqhiyya*, 4 vols. (Cairo: ʾAbd al-Ḥamīd Aḥmad al-Ḥanafī, n.d.), 4:331.

69. This was the famous debate between Sharīf al-Jurjānī and Saʿd al-Dīn al-Taftazānī; ʿAbd al-Ḥayy al-Laknawī, *Ṭarab al-amāthil bi-tarājim al-afāḍil*, 267–68; ʿAlāʾ al-Dīn al-Rūmī, *Risālat al-Nikāt waʾl-asʾila*, Istanbul Suleymaniye Library, Şehid Ali Paşa Ms. 277, 2a–2b.

70. This comes from the travel account of Ibn Faḍlān's embassy to the newly Muslim king of the Bulghars in the Volga region in 921 CE, perhaps better known as Antonio Banderas in *The 13th Warrior*, an adaptation of Michael Crichton's fictionalized *The Eaters of the Dead*; James Montgomery, 'Ibn Faḍlān and the Rūsiyyah,' 19–20.

71. Ḥujjat al-Islām Abū Ḥāmid al-Ghazālī, *Miʿyār al-ʿilm*, 127–28.

72. Jonathan Brown, 'Did the Prophet Say it or Not?,' 261–62.

73. Augustine, *Enchiridion*, 4; Saadia Gaon, *The Book of Beliefs and Opinions*, 16–19.

74. Brown, 'Did the Prophet Say it or Not?,' 262–63.

75. Ibn Nujaym, *al-Ashbāh waʾl-naẓāʾir*, 83.

76. For another fascinating case of an Egyptian Ḥanafī scholar allowing a man to follow the Hanafi school on one issue of ritual purity and the Maliki school on another, see Abū al-Ikhlāṣ Ḥasan al-Shurunbulālī (d. 1658), 'al-ʿIqd al-farīd fī bayān al-rājiḥ min al-khilāf fī jawāz al-taqlīd,' in *Majallat Jāmiʿat Umm al-Qurā*, ed. Khālid b. Muḥammad al-ʿArūsī, 17, no. 32 (1425/[2005]): 704–706.

77. Shāh Walī Allāh, *al-Tafhīmāt al-ilāhiyya*, 2:154; Mīr Ibrāhīm Siyālkotī, *Tārīkh-i Ahl-i Ḥadīs*, 658.

78. J. M. S. Baljon, 'Shah Waliullah and the *Dargah*,' in *Sufism and Society in Medieval India*, 111.

79. Al-Khaṭīb al-Baghdādī, *Tārīkh Baghdād*, 7:251.

80. *Ṣaḥīḥ al-Bukhārī: kitāb al-raqāʾiq, bāb al-tawāḍuʿ.*

81. Al-Albānī, *Silsilat al-aḥādīth al-ṣaḥīḥa*, 2:187–90 (no. 621); *Ṣaḥīḥ Muslim: kitāb al-faḍāʾil, bāb min faḍāʾil Mūsā.*

82. Simon Digby, 'The Sufi Shaikh as a Source of Authority in Medieval India,' in *India's Islamic Traditions, 711–1750*, 256.

83. Itzchak Weismann, *The Naqshbandiyya*, 66.

84. H. A. R. Gibb, trans., *The Travels of Ibn Battuta*, 2:273–74.
85. Al-Nabhānī, *Jāmiʿ karāmāt al-awliyā'*, 2:392.
86. Al-Shaʿrānī, *Ṭabaqāt al-kubrā*, 11. For an expanded version of this quotation, see Abū Ṭālib al-Makkī, *Qūt al-qulūb*, 1:121.
87. Some scholars agreed that the man did not have to pay the *Zakat*, but ʿIzz al-Dīn Ibn ʿAbd al-Salām overruled them; Muḥammad al-Zurqānī, *Sharḥ al-Muwaṭṭa'*, 2:139.
88. Shāh Walī Allāh, *Manāqib al-Bukhārī wa faḍīlat Ibn Taymiyya*, 26.
89. Muwaffaq al-Dīn Ibn Qudāma, 'Dhamm al-ta'wīl,' 87; idem, *Taḥrīm al-naẓar*, 32, 42, 65. See also Ibn Taymiyya, *Majmūʿat al-fatāwā*, 4:171.
90. The first book mentioned here is Ibn al-Jawzī's (d. 1201) famous 'The Misleading of Satan' (*Talbīs Iblīs*), the second is Abū Shāma al-Maqdisī's (d. 1268) 'Spurring the Rejection of Heresy' (*al-Bāʿith ʿalā inkār al-bida'*). Along with Ibn Taymiyya, a staunch critic of theosophical Sufism was his friend and colleague Shams al-Dīn al-Dhahabī (d. 1348); see al-Dhahabī, *Mīzān al-iʿtidāl*, 1:431.
91. This comes from the late fifteenth-century Moroccan scholar al-Maghīlī's answers to the sultan of Songhay, Askia Muhammad; John O. Hunwick, ed., *Sharīʿa in Songhay*, 76–78.
92. Shāh Walī Allāh, *al-Inṣāf*, 68; al-Makkī, *Qūt al-qulūb*, 1:159–60.
93. *HAB*, 1:224–25; Baljon, 'Shah Waliullah and the *Dargah*,' 110–17.
94. *HAB*, 2:25.
95. Shmuel Moreh, trans., *Napoleon in Egypt*, 36.
96. This scholar was William Muir (d. 1905); Avril Powell, *Scottish Orientalists and India*, 160–65.
97. Moreh, 153.

CHAPTER 3: THE FRAGILE TRUTH OF SCRIPTURE

1. *Ṣaḥīḥ al-Bukhārī: kitāb al-ṭibb, bāb idhā waqaʿa al-dhubāb fī al-inā'.*
2. *Ṣaḥīḥ al-Bukhārī: kitāb al-adhān, bāb faḍl al-ta'dhīn*; Umar Ryad, *Islamic Reformism and Christianity*, 55; G. H. A. Juynboll, *The Authenticity of Tradition Literature*, 41; Maḥmūd Abū Rayya, *Aḍwā' ʿalā al-sunna al-muḥammadiyya*, 199, 279, 301.
3. See, for example, Augustine, *City of God*, 16:9.
4. Ibn Ḥajar al-ʿAsqalānī, *Fatḥ al-Bārī*, 2:108–109; Muḥammad Zakariyyā al-Kāndhlawī, *Awjaz al-masālik*, 2:31–32.
5. Ibn Ḥajar, *Fatḥ al-Bārī*, 6:452–53; *Ṣaḥīḥ al-Bukhārī: kitāb aḥādīth al-anbiyā', bāb khalq Ādam wa dhurriyyatihi.*
6. Delchaye, *The Work of the Bollandists*, 48, 147.
7. Owen Chadwick, *Secularization of the European Mind*, 164.
8. The prediction of the 'return of the Virgin' and the 'birth of a child' is in Virgil's fourth Eclogue; Virgil, *Eclogues*, 29; Edward Gibbon, *Decline and Fall of the Roman Empire*, 1:651–52; David Cressy, 'Books as Totems in Seventeenth-Century England and New England,' 99.
9. Frank Kermode, *Sense of an Ending*, 58–63.
10. Moshe Halbertal, *The People of the Book*, 27–29.
11. Robert Grant, 'Historical Criticism in the Ancient Church,' 184.
12. Donald Russell and David Constant, trans., *Heraclitus: Homeric Problems*, xii, 111.
13. Kermode, *Genesis of Secrecy*, 57 ff.
14. Eusebius, *History of the Church*, 4–5 (1.2.4–12) (Genesis 18:1–2).
15. Beryl Smalley, *Study of the Bible in the Middle Ages*, xiv, 303, 306.

16. Spinoza, *Theological-Political Treatise*, 100–101, 114–15, 153, 164.
17. Such stories include the drunk Lot sleeping with his daughters: Origen, 'On First Principles,' in *Origen*, 180, 187–88.
18. Hermann Reimarus, *Fragments*, 231–32.
19. Cicero, *The Nature of the Gods*, I:60–62, 71–73 (pp. 94, 98); Gibbon, *Decline and Fall*, 1:27.
20. Voltaire, *Oeuvres Completes*, 26:511 (Letter VII 'Sur les Français').
21. Ogier de Busbecq, *Turkish Letters*, 82.
22. Ovamir Anjum, *Politics, Law and Community in Islamic Thought*, xiv.
23. Thomas Carlyle, *The French Revolution*, 28; Chadwick, *The Secularization of the European Mind*, 14; Timothy Larson, 'Bishop Colenso and His Critics,' in *The Eye of the Storm*, 45.
24. 'Abd al-Raḥmān al-Kawākibī, 'Umm al-Qurā,' 329; Muḥammad Bakhīt al-Muṭī'ī, 'Kitāb Aḥsan al-kalām fī-mā yata'allaqu bi'l-sunna wa'l-bid'a min al-aḥkām,' 3, 30.
25. Murtaḍā al-Riḍawī, *Ma'a rijāl al-fikr fī al-Qāhira*, 315–20.
26. Al-Juwaynī, *al-Kāfiya fī al-jadal*, 51; Ibn Amīr al-Ḥajj, *al-Taqrīr wa'l-taḥbīr*, 1:145.
27. Al-Nawawī, *Sharḥ Ṣaḥīḥ Muslim*, 1/2:331–32; Leo Lefebure, 'Violence in the New Testament and the History of Interpretation,' 76.
28. Jalāl al-Dīn al-Suyūṭī, *Badhl al-majhūd li-khizānat Maḥmūd*, 15a–15b.
29. The Hadith reads '*Āyat al-munāfiq thalāth, idhā ḥaddatha kadhaba, wa idhā wa'ada akhlafa wa idhā u'tumina khān*'; *Ṣaḥīḥ al-Bukhārī*: *kitāb al-īmān, bāb 'alāmat al-munāfiq*; *Jāmi' al-Tirmidhī*: *kitāb al-īmān, bāb mā jā'a fī 'alāmat al-munāfiq*.
30. Ibn Qudāma, *Mughnī*, 1:43; al-Nawawī, *Sharḥ Ṣaḥīḥ Muslim*, 3/4:306; al-Qurṭubī, *Jāmi'*, 4:448.
31. Al-Ḥākim al-Naysābūrī, *al-Mustadrak*, 2:313; Sulaymān Ibn 'Abd al-Wahhāb, *al-Ṣawā'iq al-ilāhiyya*, 20. An earlier attestation of Ibn 'Abbas' statement can be found in the context of another Hadith; see *Jāmi' al-Tirmidhī*: *kitāb al-īmān, bāb ma jā'a fi sibāb al-muslim fusūq*. See also Majid Khadduri, trans., *The Islamic Law of Nations: Shaybānī's Siyar*, 92–93.
32. Augustine, *Enarratio in Psalmum*, 45:7.
33. The Hadith reads, '*Shahrā 'īd lā yanquṣāni ramaḍān wa dhū al-ḥijja*'. See *Ṣaḥīḥ al-Bukhārī*: *kitāb al-ṣawm, bāb shahrā 'īd lā yanquṣān*; *Jāmi' al-Tirmidhī*: *kitāb al-ṣawm, bāb mā jā'a fī shahrā 'īd lā yanquṣān*; al-Khaṭṭābī, *Ma'ālim al-sunan*, 2:95.
34. Al-Nawawī, *Sharḥ Ṣaḥīḥ Muslim*, 1/2:374; al-Munāwī, *Fayḍ al-qadīr*, 12:6506–507; Ibn Ḥajar, *Fatḥ al-Bārī*, 1:83.
35. Babylonian Talmud Bava Mezia 59a–59b. The first quote, attributed to the Talmud (What is the Torah...) I found in D. S. Russell's *From Early Judaism to Early Church*, 34. I have not been able to find the original citation. I thank my colleague Jonathan Ray for his help.
36. Desiderius Erasmus, 'Concerning the Eating of the Fish,' in *The Essential Erasmus*, 292; '*Wa hādhā al-Qur'ān innamā huwa khaṭṭ masṭūr bayn daffatayn la yanṭiqu innamā yatakallamu bihi al-rijāl*'; al-Ṭabarī, *Tārīkh al-rusul wa'l-mulūk*, 3:110 (Year 36 AH, section on *i'tizāl al-khawārij 'Aliyyan*).
37. James Madison, *Federalist Papers*, 354–55 (Federalist 37).
38. Al-Juwaynī, *Waraqāt*, 26.
39. Al-Juwaynī, *Waraqāt*, 28–30.
40. Al-Juwaynī, *Waraqāt*, 36–38.
41. Al-Juwaynī, *Waraqāt*, 46.

42. Abū Shāma al-Maqdisī, *al-Bā'ith 'alā inkār al-bida'*, 16; al-Albānī, *Fatāwā*, 10, 49, 188; Shams al-Dīn al-Sakhāwī, *Takhrīj al-Arba'īn al-Sulamiyya*, 149–50.
43. *Jāmi' al-Tirmidhī: kitāb al-birr wa'l-ṣila, bāb mā jā'a fī raḥmat al-ṣibyān*; Ibn Ḥajar, *Fatḥ al-Bārī*, 13:30. See also Qur'an 2:249.
44. Al-Khaṭṭābī, *Ma'ālim al-sunan*, 4:198; *Ṣaḥīḥ al-Bukhārī: kitāb al-libās, bāb man jarra thawbahu ghayr khuyalā'*.
45. Ibn Taymiyya, *Majmū'at al-fatāwā*, 27:15–17; al-Khaṭṭābī, 2:222.
46. Khaṭīb al-Baghdādī, *Tārīkh Baghdād*, 6:115.
47. *'Al-'ibra bi-'umūm al-lafẓ lā bi-khuṣūṣ al-sabab'*; Ali Gomaa, *al-Ṭarīq ilā al-turāth*, 207; al-Shawkānī, *Nayl al-awṭār*, 8:112.
48. Al-Qurṭubī, *Jāmi'*, 10:442–45.
49. Al-Zarkashī, *al-Baḥr al-muḥīṭ*, 2:365.
50. Al-Bayhaqī, *al-Sunan*, 7:323; Muḥammad bin 'Alī al-'Umarī al-Dimashqī, *al-Naẓm al-mufīd al-aḥmad fī mufradāt madhhab al-imām Aḥmad*, 83; al-Shawkānī, 'Bulūgh al-munā fī ḥukm al-istimnā,' 163–64.
51. Al-Khaṭṭābī, *Ma'ālim al-sunan*, 3:181; *Jāmi' al-Tirmidhī: kitāb tafsīr al-Qur'ān, bāb min sūrat al-nūr*; al-Qurṭubī, *al-Jāmi'*, 6:470; Shihāb al-Dīn al-Zanjānī, *Takhrīj al-furū' 'alā al-uṣūl*, 237–38.
52. *Ṣaḥīḥ al-Bukhārī: kitāb al-janā'iz, bāb laysa minnā man ḍaraba al-khudūd.*
53. *Ṣaḥīḥ Muslim: kitāb al-janā'iz, bāb al-mayyit yu'adhdhabu bi-bukā' ahlihi 'alayhi; Jāmi' al-Tirmidhī: kitāb al-janā'iz, bāb mā jā'a fī karāhiyat al-bukā' 'alā al-mayyit.*
54. Al-Nawawī, *Sharḥ Ṣaḥīḥ Muslim*, 5/6:483–85; Ibn Qudāma, *Mughnī*, 2:412.
55. Ibn Qudāma, *Mughnī*, 2:411.
56. *Sunan Abī Dāwūd: kitāb al-manāsik, bāb al-raml.*
57. Ibn Qudāma, *Mughnī*, 2:696–98; al-Jāwī, *Qūt al-ḥabīb al-gharīb*, 109; al-Sha'rānī, *al-Mīzān al-kubrā*, 2:15.
58. Al-Suyūṭī, *al-Itqān*, 4:162.
59. *Jāmi' al-Tirmidhī: kitāb al-īmān, bāb mā jā'a fī-man yamūtu wa huwa yashhadu an lā ilāh illā Allāh.*
60. *Sunan Abī Dāwūd: kitāb al-janā'iz, bāb fī ziyārat al-qubūr.*
61. *Jāmi' al-Tirmidhī: kitāb al-ṭahāra, bāb mā jā'a fī tark al-wuḍū' mimmā ghayyarat al-nār.*
62. Abū al-Qāsim Ibn Salāma, *al-Nāsikh wa'l-mansūkh*, 16.
63. Al-Qurṭubī, *al-Jāmi'*, 8:512–13.
64. Ibn Salāma, *al-Nāsikh wa'l-mansūkh*, 46.
65. Ibn Qudāma, *Mughnī*, 10:367.
66. Ibn Ḥajar, *Fatḥ al-Bārī*, 1:113–15. Ibn Rushd claims that jurists agree that those to be fought in Jihad are only polytheists (*mushrikūn*). The Hanbali Ibn Qudāma disagrees, stating that the People of the Book are preferred targets on the basis of a prophetic Hadith in the *Sunan* of Abū Dāwūd to this effect. Other scholars merely note 'unbelievers' as a whole; Ibn Rushd, *Distinguished Jurist's Primer*, 1:455; Ibn Qudāma, *Mughnī*, 10:370; al-Buhūtī, *al-Rawḍ al-murbi'*, 221.
67. Al-Sha'rānī, *Kashf al-ghumma 'an jamī' al-umma*, 6–7; idem, *al-Mīzān al-kubrā*, 2:67; J. Baljon, *Religion and Thought of Shāh Walī Allāh Dihlawī*, 149.
68. Oliver Wendell Holmes, *The Common Law*, 3.
69. Mullā 'Alī al-Qāri', *Sharḥ Sharḥ Nukhbat al-fikar*, 59.
70. Al-Khaṭṭābī, *Ma'ālim al-sunan*, 1:115; al-Shāfi'ī, *Risāla*, 341.
71. Al-Shāfi'ī, *al-Umm*, 7:177; idem, *al-Risāla*, 280–81; al-Juwaynī, *Waraqāt*, 59–65.

72. Al-Bayhaqī, *al-Sunan*, 2:101.
73. Al-Bayhaqī, *al-Sunan*, 2:111.
74. Al-Bayhaqī, *al-Sunan*, 2:114.
75. Al-Bayhaqī, *al-Sunan*, 2:113, 116.
76. Abū Ja'far al-Ṭaḥāwī, *Sharḥ Mushkil al-Āthār*, 15:42–49.
77. Al-Ṭaḥāwī, 15:30–34, 46–50, 55–59.
78. Al-Ṭaḥāwī, 15:38.
79. Al-Ṭaḥāwī, 15:39.
80. Al-Haytamī, *al-Fatāwā al-ḥadīthiyya*, 266–70.
81. Burhān al-Dīn al-Bayjūrī, *Ḥāshiya 'alā Jawharat al-tawḥīd*, 229; Mullā 'Alī al-Qāri', *Sharḥ Nukhbat al-fikar*, 47.
82. Qāḍī 'Iyāḍ, *Kitāb al-Shifā*, 106–11; al-Bayjūrī, *Ḥāshiya*, 233.
83. Ryad, 'The Dismissal of A. J. Wensinck from the Royal Academy of the Arabic Language in Cairo,' 97.
84. Erasmus, *The Praise of Folly*, 89–102; Nikki R. Keddie, *An Islamic Response to Imperialism*, 64.
85. St. Anselm of Bec, *Monologion and Proslogion*, 99. Based on Augustine's saying 'Believe that you may understand (*crede ut intelligas*)'; *Sermon* 43.7, 9.

CHAPTER 4: CLINGING TO THE CANON IN A RUPTURED WORLD

1. Mehemmet Zahit Kevseri, *Maqālāt al-Kawtharī*, 192–94, 208, 265–67, 280–81.
2. Origen, 'On First Principles,' in *Origen*, 189–90; Voltaire, 'Miracles,' *Dictionnaire Philosophique*, 57:110–14.
3. Pseudo-Augustine, 'Mirabilis Sacrae Scripturae,' in *Operum S. Augustini: Appendix*, 2165.
4. I borrow this distinction from the late Mohammed 'Abed al-Jabri, *Arab-Islamic Philosophy*, 36.
5. Spinoza, *Theological-Political Treatise*, 119–51; Abraham Ibn Ezra, *The Commentary of Abraham ibn Ezra on the Pentateuch,* 5:181; Thomas Woolston, *A third discourse on the miracles of our Saviour,* 53. Woolston justifies applying the allegorical approach to the New Testament by referring to Origen's allegorical reading of certain miraculous occurrences in the life of Jesus, particularly the Parable of the Fig Tree.
6. Keith Thomas, *Religion and the Decline of Magic*, 57.
7. Lee I. Levine, *Judaism and Hellenism in Antiquity*, 96 ff.
8. J. S. Spink, *French Free-Thought*, 23, 31.
9. Ryad, 'The Dismissal of A. J. Wensinck,' 114.
10. Indira Falk Gesinke, *Islamic Reform and Conservatism*, 177–82.
11. Al-Suyūṭī, *al-Khaṣā'iṣ al-kubrā*, 1:53; Ibn Kathīr, *The Life of the Prophet Muhammad*, 1:149–50; Ibn al-Qayyim, *Zād al-mi'ād*, 1:81–82. Mullā 'Alī al-Qāri' and others agree; Aḥmad Shihāb al-Dīn al-Khafājī and Mullā 'Alī al-Qāri', *Nasīm al-riyāḍ sharḥ Shifā' al-Qāḍī 'Iyaḍ*, 1:364.
12. Rashīd Riḍā and Muḥammad 'Abduh, *Tafsīr al-Manār*, 5:201–209; Ibn Taymiyya, *Majmū'at al-fatāwā*, 11:196.
13. Sir Sayyid Ahmad Khan, 'Review on Hunter's Indian Musalmans,' 81; *Ṣaḥīḥ al-Bukhārī: kitāb al-jihād wa'l-siyar, bāb du'ā' al-nabī (ṣ) al-nās ilā al-islām wa'l-nubuwwa.*
14. Rashīd Riḍā, *The Muhammadan Revelation*, 121, 137–38. Riḍā relies especially on the Qur'anic verses 2:190 and 22:39–40.

15. Bruce Lawrence, ed., *Messages to the World*; 28, 119, 124–25.
16. D. M. Last and M. A. Al-Hajj, 'Attempts at Defining a Muslim in 19th-Century Hausaland and Bornu,' 239; Lawrence, *Messages to the World*; 93, 122 (based on Qur'an 5:51). I am grateful to my mother, Dr. Ellen Brown, and her incredible collection of material for some of these obscure references.
17. Sayyid Quṭb, *Milestones*, 58, 77, 83, 93.
18. See, for example, Bernard Haykel, trans., 'Al-Qaeda's Creed and Path,' in *Global Salafism*, 52–54.
19. Lawrence, *Messages to the World*, 28, 61, 115, 124–25.
20. Lawrence, *Messages to the World*, 24; *Ṣaḥīḥ al-Bukhārī*: *kitāb al-jihād wa'l-siyar, bāb hal yustashfa'u ilā ahl al-dhimma*.
21. *Sunan Abī Dāwūd*: *kitāb al-kharāj wa'l-imāra wa'l-fay', bāb fī ikhrāj al-yahūd min jazīrat al-'arab*; Ibn Ḥajar, *Fatḥ al-Barī*, 6:210; H. A. R. Gibb, trans., *The Travels of Ibn Battuta*, 1:163.
22. Al-Nawawī, *Minhāj*, 526; al-Sha'rānī, *al-Mīzān al-kubrā*, 2:211; Ibn 'Ābidīn, *Ḥāshiyat Radd al-muḥtār*, 4:208–209; Ibn al-Mundhir, *al-Ishrāf*, 4:56.
23. Karam Zuhdī, et al, *Ḥurmat al-ghuluww fī al-dīn*, 8–9.
24. Zuhdī, *Ḥurmat al-ghuluww*, 56–57, 112–13, 116–18, 160.
25. Al-Albānī, *Fatāwā al-Shaykh al-Albānī*, 252 ff., 296; idem, 'Hadith al-Bukhari,' recorded lecture 5/1990 from www.islamway.com/?iw_s=Scholar&iw_a=lessons&scholar_id=47, last accessed 5/28/2004.
26. This interpretation of the Hadith comes from the Yemeni Salafi teacher Muqbil bin Hādī al-Wādi'ī (d. 2001); al-Wādi'ī, *Majmū' fatāwā al-Wādi'ī*, 74. See also al-Qāri', *Mirqāt al-mafātīḥ*, 9:324.
27. Rāghib al-Sirjānī, *Kayfa takhtāru ra'īs al-jumhūriyya*, 11, 25.
28. Dalia Mogahed, 'What Egyptian Women and Men Want,' *Foreign Policy*, March 10, 2011 http://www.foreignpolicy.com/articles/2011/03/10/what_egyptian_women_and_men_want#3 (last accessed 9/10/2012); 'Egyptians Remain Optimistic, Embrace Democracy and Religion in Political Life,' *Pew Research Global Attitudes Project: Chapter 4*, http://www.pewglobal.org/2012/05/08/chapter-4-role-of-islam-in-politics/ (last accessed 9/2013).
29. Nathan Brown, *The Rule of Law in the Arab World*, 32–33.
30. Farhat Ziadeh, *Lawyers, the Rule of Law and Liberalism in Modern Egypt*, 34–35; Peter Mansfield, *The British in Egypt*, 128.
31. Clark Lombardi, *State Law as Islamic Law in Modern Egypt*, 92–98; Ziadeh, 144.
32. Aḥmad Shākir, *Maqālāt*, 2:592–622.
33. Muḥammad al-Ghazālī, *Turāthunā al-fikrī*, 169.
34. Yūsuf al-Qaraḍāwī, *al-Shaykh al-Ghazālī kamā 'araftuhu*, 54.
35. Al-Ghazālī, *al-Sunna al-nabawiyya*, 53, 58.
36. *Ṣaḥīḥ al-Bukhārī*: *kitāb al-maghāzī, bāb* 83; *kitāb al-fitan, bāb* 17; Ibn Ḥajar, *Fatḥ al-Bārī*, 13:69–71; al-Munāwī, *Fayḍ al-qadīr*, 10:5062; al-Ghazālī, *al-Sunna al-nabawiyya*, 53–58; idem, *Turāthunā al-fikrī*, 175; Abd al-Hosein Zarrinkub, 'The Arab Conquest of Iran and its Aftermath,' *Cambridge History of Iran*, 4:17.
37. Haifaa Khalafallah, 'Rethinking Islamic Law,' 162–68. On the issue of considering women's testimony in court equal to men's, al-Ghazālī was repeating an argument advanced by his reformist mentor, the Shaykh al-Azhar Maḥmūd Shaltūt, who also noted Ibn Taymiyya's and Ibn Qayyim's arguments mentioned below; Maḥmūd Shaltūt, *al-Islām 'aqīda wa sharī'a*, 239–41.
38. Al-Albānī, *Mukhtaṣar Ṣaḥīḥ al-Bukhārī*, 2:8–9.

39. Al-Qaraḍāwī, *al-Shaykh al-Ghazālī kamā 'araftuhu*, 173; Ibn Qayyim, *I'lām al-muwaqqi'īn*, 1:94–96.
40. Al-Qaraḍāwī, *al-Fatāwā al-shādhdha*, 33–35.
41. 'Alawī bin Aḥmad al-Saqqāf, 'Mukhtaṣar al-Fawā'id al-Makkiyya,' 104.
42. Al-Sirjānī, 25. See *Ṣaḥīḥ al-Bukhārī*: *kitāb al-maghāzī, bāb* 83.
43. Ryan Kisiel, 'British child brides: Muslim mosque leaders agree to marry girls as young as 12... as long as parents don't tell anyone' *MailOnline*, http://www.dailymail.co.uk/news/article-2200555/The-British-child-brides-Muslim-mosque-leaders-agree-marry-girl-12--long-parents-dont-tell-anyone.html?openGraphAuthor=%2Fhome%2Fsearch.html%3Fs%3D%26authornamef%3DSuzannah%2BHills (last accessed 9/10/12).
44. Wency Leung, 'She's 23. He's 69. What gives?', *The Globe and Mail*, August 28, 2012, http://www.theglobeandmail.com/life/the-hot-button/shes-23-hes-69-what-gives/article4504707/; 'al-Shaykh al-Qaraḍāwī yatazawwaju min maghribiyya taṣghuruhu bi-37 'ām' www.mbc.net, June 13, 2012 (last accessed July 2012); 'Nigerian Senator "Married" 13-year old girl,' *Independent*, April 30, 2010.
45. CNN World Jan. 17, 2009, http://articles.cnn.com/2009-01-17/world/saudi.child.marriage_1_saudi-arabia-deeply-conservative-kingdom-top-saudi-cleric?_s=PM:WORLD (last accessed July 2012).
46. For contemporary attempts to refute Aisha's marriage age, see David Liepert, 'Rejecting the Myth of Sanctioned Child Marriage in Islam,' *Huffington Post*, January 29, 2011, http://www.huffingtonpost.com/dr-david-liepert/islamic-pedophelia_b_814332.html (last accessed 10/2/2012); Myriam Francois-Cerrah, 'The Truth about Muhammad and Aisha,' *The Guardian*, September 17, 2012, http://www.guardian.co.uk/commentisfree/belief/2012/sep/17/muhammad-aisha-truth (last accessed 10/1/2012); Islām Buḥayrī, 'Zawāj al-Nabī min 'Ā'isha wa hiya bint 9 sinīn kadhiba kabīra fī kutub al-ḥadīth,' *al-Yawm al-sābi'*, October 16, 2008, http://www1.youm7.com/News.asp?NewsID=44788&SecID=137&IssueID=0 (last accessed July 2013).
47. See Mohammed Fadel, 'Reinterpreting the Guardian's Role in the Islamic Contract of Marriage,' 1–26.
48. A rare Hadith in which the Prophet annuls the marriage contract of a young virgin whose father had married her without consent is rejected as proof due to a break in the chain of transmission; *Sunan Abī Dāwūd*: *kitāb al-nikāḥ, bāb fī al-bikr yuzawwijuhā abūhā wa lā yasta'miruhā*; al-Bayhaqī, *Sunan*, 7:188–90.
49. Shaykh Niẓām, *al-Fatāwā al-Hindiyya*, 1:316.
50. Al-Nawawī, *Sharḥ Ṣaḥīḥ Muslim*, 9/10:218; al-Buhūtī, *al-Rawḍ al-murbi'*, 383; Ibrāhīm Bin Ḍuwayyān, *Manār al-sabīl*, 2:216; Alexander Russell, *A Natural History of Aleppo*, 1:281; Mahmoud Yazbak, 'Minor Marriages and *khiyar al-bulugh* in Ottoman Palestine,' 395. Evidence that the Prophet waited for Aisha to reach physical maturity before consummation comes from al-Ṭabarī, who says she was too young for intercourse at the time of the marriage contract; al-Ṭabarī, *Tārīkh al-Ṭabarī*, 2:211; Allan Christelow, *Muslim Law Courts and the French Colonial State in Algeria*, 62–63, 124–28.
51. See Liat Kozma, *Policing Egyptian Women*, 31–38.
52. Tatar, *Dialogue Islamo-Chrétien*, 150–51; Ludovico Marracci, 'Prodromus,' in *Alcorani textus universus*, 23. The original report about the Prophet seeing Aisha in a dream contains nothing prurient or suggestive: 'I was shown you in a dream on two occasions. I saw a man carrying you [veiled] in white silk, and he said, "This is your wife." Then he unveiled you and I saw you and said, "If this is from God, he will make it so"'; Ibn Isḥāq, *Sīrat Ibn Isḥāq*, ed. Muḥammad Ḥamīd Allāh (Rabat: Ma'had al-Dirāsāt wa'l-Abḥāth, 1976), 239.

53. Edward Lane, *Manners and Customs of the Modern Egyptians*, 160; D. S. Margoliouth, *Mohammad and the Rise of Islam*, 29–30, 234. See also Simon Ockley, *History of the Saracens*, 19; Washington Irving, *Life of Mohammed*, ed. Charles Getchell (Ipswich, MA: Ipswich Press, 1989), 55.

54. Alan Macfarlane, *The Origins of English Individualism*, 27–28; *Encyclopaedia Britannica*, 11th ed., s.v. 'Rape'. The England of Margoliouth's youth saw a further increase in the average age of women marrying; J. A. and Olive Banks, *Feminism and Family Planning in Victorian England*, 45; Najm al-Dīn al-Ghazzī, *al-Kawākib al-sā'ira*, 1:160.

55. Macfarlane, 155–58.

56. Daniel Klerman, 'Rape: English Common Law,' *Oxford International Encyclopedia of Legal History*, 5:68–69.

57. Leila Ahmed, *Women, Gender and Islam*, 152–53; Kozma, *Policing Egyptian Women*, 31–38.

58. 1923 Update to Article 101 of Law 31, 1910; Muḥammad Abū al-Faḍl al-Gīzāwī, 'Qānūn Taḥdīd sinn al-zawāj,' *al-Muḥāmāt* 4, no. 4 (1924): 398. Ziadeh has it as Law 56, December 11, 1923; Ziadeh, 123; Leila Ahmad, 176–77; Beth Baron, 'Making and Breaking Marital Bonds in Modern Egypt,' 282.

59. 'Abduh, *al-A'māl al-kāmila*, 2:76–92.

60. 'Āmir al-'Aqqād, *Lamaḥāt min ḥayāt al-'Aqqād*, 369.

61. 'Abbās Maḥmūd al-'Aqqād, *al-Ṣiddīqa bint al-Ṣiddīq*, 66–67.

62. Aḥmad Shākir, *Maqālāt*, 1:196; 353–69.

63. 'Abduh, *al-A'māl al-kāmila*, 2:80.

64. Kevseri, *Maqālāt*, 82, 167–68, 192, 208.

65. 'Abd al-Ḥalīm Maḥmūd, *Fatāwā*, 2:132, 434.

66. David Ayalon, 'The Great Yasa of Chingiz Khan,' 124–25.

67. Gibb, *The Travels of Ibn Battuta*, 3:545; 2:378. See Guy Burak, 'The Second Formation of Islamic Law,' 594 ff.

68. Ayalon, 108–109, 115.

69. Rudolph Peters, *Crime and Punishment in Islamic Law*, 11.

70. 'Abd al-Ghanī Nābulusī, *al-Ḥadīqa al-nadiyya*, 2:234. Here al-Nābulusī is either modifying or clarifying an opinion he expressed earlier in a treatise arguing for the permissibility of smoking. One of the arguments he notes against him was that the 'sultan had prohibited it.' Al-Nābulusī objects that the ruler can only forbid what is prohibited by God's law; idem, *Risāla fī ibāḥat al-dukhān*, 8.

71. Alan Guenther, 'Hanafi *Fiqh* in Mughal India: The *Fatāwá-i 'Ālamgīrī*,' 212–16, 223–24. There is a major discrepancy in a much-relied-upon translation of Aurangzeb's aims. The Elliot translation of the *Mir'āt al-'ālam*, a history attributed to Bakhtawar Khan, one of the emperor's courtiers, states that the *Fatawa* would 'render everyone independent of Moslem doctors [i.e., ulama].' The original Persian text, edited by Sajida Alvi, reads that the *Fatawa* 'will make the other books of jurisprudence unnecessary (*az sāyir-i kutub-i fiqhī moghnī khwāhad*)...' See Bakhtawar Khan, 'Mirat-i Alam,' in *The History of India as Told by its Own Historians*, ed. H. M. Elliot and John Dawson, 7:160. Cf. Bakhtāvar Khān, *Mir'āt al-'ālam*, ed. Sajida Sultana Alvi, 2 vols (Lahore: Research Society of Pakistan, 1969), 1:388.

72. Gīzāwī, 397–98; Ziadeh, 124.

73. J. N. D. Anderson, 'The Syrian Law of Personal Status,' 36–37.

74. In his discussion of Aisha's marriage age, al-Ghazālī insists that, whatever her age, Aisha was suitable and fit when the marriage was consummated: Ghazālī, *Qaḍāyā al-mar'a*, 77.

75. 'Alī al-Ṭanṭāwī, *Dhikrayāt*, 4:290–92, 296; idem, *Fatāwā*, 122–23.

76. Muḥammad Abū Zahra, *Fatāwā*, 447–50; *Sunan al-Nasā'ī: kitāb nikāḥ, bāb tazawwuj al-mar'a mithlihā fī al-sinn*; Abū al-Ḥasan al-Sindī, *Ḥāshiya 'alā Sunan al-Nasā'ī*, 2:29. Abu Zahra's argument about the harm of legally ignoring Shariah-valid marriages, which would effectively result in undocumented marriages, had been used in 1924 by the former Mufti of Egypt, Muḥammad Bakhīt al-Muṭī'ī, in his objections to the 1923 law restricting marriage age; al-Muṭī'ī, "Taḥdīd sinn al-zawāj," *al-Muḥāmāt* 4, no. 4 (1924): 410–11.

77. Justin McCarthy, *The Ottoman Turks*, 387.

78. Hugh Poulton, *Top Hat, Grey Wolf and Crescent*, 190–91, 206.

79. Mahmoud El-Gamal, *Islamic Finance*, 141–42.

80. *Planned Parenthood of Southeastern Pennsylvania v. Casey* 833 U.S., 864–5 (1991) (Justice O'Connor writing).

CHAPTER 5: MUSLIM MARTIN LUTHERS AND THE PARADOX OF TRADITION

1. Robin Wright, 'Scholar Emerges As The Martin Luther Of Islam – His Interpretation: Freedom Of Thought, Democracy Essential,' *Seattle Times* February 12, 1995, http://community.seattletimes.nwsource.com/archive/?date=19950212&slug=2104526; http://rosemarieberger.com/2009/06/13/the-mosque-in-morgantown-finding-our-religion-within-american-pluralism/; http://www.salon.com/2002/02/15/ramadan_2/. It should be noted that early Islamic modernists like Sir Sayyid Ahmad Khan and Jamāl al-Dīn al-Afghānī also called for a Muslim Martin Luther; Michaelle Browers and Charles Kurzman, *An Islamic Reformation?*, 4–6.

2. 'The Online Ummah,' *The Economist* August 18, 2012.

3. Hermann von Kerssenbrock, *Narrative of the Anabaptist Madness*, 2:576–80, also 534, 546–47. On the other hand, a law interpreted from the New Testament made even sexual desire for a non-spouse punishable by death in Munster; Lyndal Roper, 'Sexual Utopianism in the German Reformation,' 407.

4. Earl Morse Wilbur, *A History of Unitarianism*, 345–47.

5. Samuel Fisher, 'Rusticus ad Academicos (The Rustic's Alarm to the Rabbis),' 33. See also Travis L. Frampton, *Spinoza and the Rise of Historical Criticism of the Bible*, 216–19.

6. Thomas More, *Responsio ad Lutherum*, 153.

7. This quote comes from Sylvester Prierias' rebuttal of Luther; David Bagchi, *Luther's Earliest Opponents*, 34; Richard Popkin, *History of Skepticism*, 68.

8. Bagchi, *Luther's Earliest Opponents*, 34–45.

9. Judah Halevi, *The Kuzari*, 161–62, 168.

10. Plato, *Phaedrus*, 96–98 (lines 275–76).

11. 'The First Apology of Justin, the Martyr,' trans. Edward Rochie Hardy, *Early Christian Fathers*, 263, 266.

12. Eusebius, *History of the Church*, 102 (3.39.2)

13. Saadia Gaon explained that the rabbis set down the Mishna because they feared the consequences of the cessation of prophecy and diaspora; Samuel Poznanski, *The Literary Opponents of Saadiah Gaon*, 41.

14. Robert M. Grant, 'Historical Criticism in the Ancient Church,' 188–89.

15. Irenaeus, 'Refutation and Overthrow of the Knowledge Falsely So Called,' *Early Christian Fathers*; 360, 370–71, 382.

16. John R. McKae, *Seeing Through Zen*, 2–4.
17. Martin S. Jaffee, *Torah in the Mouth*, 126, 142.
18. The term for one who relied on written pages was *ṣaḥafī*. This is attributed to Sulaymān bin Mūsā; Abū Zur'a al-Dimashqī, *Tārīkh Abī Zur'a al-Dimashqī*, 133.
19. Al-Ahdal, *al-Nafas al-Yamānī*, 63.
20. Ibn 'Uthaymīn, *Kitāb al-'Ilm*, 150, 240–41; al-'Awda, *Ḍawābiṭ li'l-dirāsāt al-fiqhiyya*, 42.
21. Al-Suhrawardī, *'Awārif al-ma'ārif*, 105.
22. Al-Ash'arī, *al-Ibāna*, 138.
23. Al-Mūsawī, *al-Murāja'āt*, 82, 88.
24. Al-Qummī, *Tafsīr al-Qummī*, 2:13, 429.
25. Ayatollah Khomeini, *Hadīth-i velāyat*, 1:130.
26. Heinz Halm, *Empire of the Mahdi: The Rise of the Fatimids*, 17–18.
27. Halm, *Empire of the Mahdi*, 127, 242–43, 373.
28. Halm, *Empire of the Mahdi*, 195, 248–61, 383.
29. The scholar recounting this story is Muḥammad bin 'Alī Rizām al-Kūfī; Muḥammad Ṭāhir Ibn 'Āshūr, *Maqālāt*, 42.
30. Halm, *Empire of the Mahdi*, 204.
31. Lapidus, *History of Islamic Societies*, 164, 173–74.
32. Al-Kāshānī, *Tafsīr al-ṣāfī*, 1:34.
33. St. Augustine, 'Letters of St. Augustine,' in *Nicene and Post Nicene Fathers*, trans. J. G. Cunningham, 1:612 (Letter 36 to Causulanus); idem, *The Essential Augustine*, 162 (Letter 54 to Januarius).
34. Eusebius, *History of the Church*, 66, 89, 94, 97, 101.
35. Eusebius, *History of the Church*, 61, 65–66.
36. Jonathan Brown, *Hadith*, 221–39; see specifically, Harald Motzki, 'The *Muṣannaf* of 'Abd al-Razzāq al-Ṣan'ānī as a Source of Authentic *Aḥādīth* of the First Century A.H.,' 8–12; Andreas Görke, Harald Motzki and Gregor Schoeler, 'First Century Sources for the Life of Muḥammad? A Debate,' 2–59.
37. By the sixteenth century, Sunni scholars had all agreed that this Hadith was totally sound, even 'transmitted profusely via parallel chains' (*mutawātir*). Yet all evidence from al-Dāraquṭnī's numerous surviving works suggests that the narration of Suwayd was the only one he accepted as admissible at all. The others come via Ḥārith al-A'war (a Shiite very problematic for Sunni Hadith scholars) from Ali and another via one Sayf bin Muḥammad, whom al-Dāraquṭnī discounts as weak; al-Dāraquṭnī, *al-'Ilal al-wārida fī al-aḥādīth al-nabawiyya*, 3:166, 11:193; al-Khaṭīb, *Tārīkh Baghdād*, 9:230–31; Ibn al-Ṣalāḥ, *Muqaddima*, 471; al-Albānī, *Silsilat al-aḥādīth al-ṣaḥīḥa*, 2:431–32 (#796); al-Munāwī, *Fayḍ al-qadīr*, 6:3008.
38. For Hanafis and Hanbalis, anything above forty days would be considered a case of chronic menstrual bleeding, during which a woman can perform her prayers. For Shafi'is and Malikis, the *nifās* period can last sixty days; al-Buhūtī, *Rawḍ al-murbi'*, 49–50; al-Qudūrī, *The Mukhtaṣar*, 22; al-Khaṭṭābī, *Ma'ālim al-sunan*, 1:95; al-Marwazī, *Ikhtilāf al-fuqahā'*, 194; al-Nawawī, *Minhāj*, 89.
39. The main Hadith is transmitted from the Prophet by the sole chain of his wife Umma Salama → Mussa → Abu Sahl Kathir. Mussa, however, is totally unknown other than by this Hadith, thus rendering her '*majhūl*' (unidentified) and automatically invalidating her chain; *Jāmi' al-Tirmidhī*: *kitāb al-ṭahāra, bāb mā jā'a fī kam tamkuthu al-nufasā'*; *Sunan Abī Dāwūd*: *kitāb al-ṭahāra, bāb mā jā'a fī waqt al-nufasā'*; *Musnad Aḥmad Ibn*

Ḥanbal: 6:300, 310; al-Dhahabī, *al-Mughnī fī al-ḍu'afā'*, 2:406. Ibn Mājah has a version of this Hadith via a separate *Isnād* from Anas bin Mālik (*Sunan Ibn Mājah*: *kitāb al-ṭahāra, bāb al-nufasā' kam tajlis*) that is very weak due to the presence of a totally unreliable narrator, Salām bin Salīm. Another narration via Ibn 'Abbās in al-Bayhaqī's *Sunan* suffers from a glaring break in the *Isnād*, which invalidates it; al-Bayhaqī, *Sunan*, 1:504. See overall, al-Bayhaqī, *Sunan*, 1:503–6; al-Shawkānī, *Nayl al-awṭār*, 1:390–91.

40. *Jāmi' al-Tirmidhī*: *kitāb al-zakāt, bāb mā jā'a fī zakāt al-khuḍrawāt*. Abū Ḥanīfa seems to have originally required some tax, but his position was eclipsed by that of his senior students; Ibn al-Mundhir, *al-Ishrāf*, 3:31–32; al-Qudūrī, 96.

41. Peters, *Crime and Punishment in Islamic Law*, 124.

42. Nihan Altınbaş, 'Honor-related Violence in the Context of Patriarchy,' 1–19.

43. *Ṣaḥīḥ Muslim*: *kitāb al-li'ān*; al-Nawawī, *Sharḥ Ṣaḥīḥ Muslim*, 9/10:375; http://www.qaradawi.net/fatawaahkam/30/1439.html; http://english.bayynat.org.lb/Archive_news/01082007.htm.

44. Al-Nabhānī, *Jāmi' karāmāt al-awliyā'*, 1:332–33. The couple may have been tortured into their confession; Najm al-Dīn al-Ghazzī, *al-Kawākib al-sā'ira*, 1:295.

45. Ibn Qudāma, *Mughnī*, 9:359; al-Bayhaqī, *Sunan*, 8:69.

46. Ibn al-Mundhir, *Ishrāf*, 7:351; Ibn Rushd, *Distinguished Jurist's Primer*, 2:485–86; al-Qurṭubī, *Jāmi'*, 1:639.

47. Yan Thomas, 'Vitae Necisque Potestas: Le Père, La Cité, La Mort,' 507.

48. Richard Saller, *Patriarchy, Property and Death in the Roman Family*, 115–17; Yan Thomas, 'Vitae Necisque Potestas,' 499–548, especially 500, 506. If a mother kills her child then she is liable; *Digest* 48, 9, 1.

49. Al-Nawawī, *al-Minhāj*, 337.

50. In the Hanafi school a relied-upon opinion was that, if one brother killed his father and another brother killed the mother, only one of the killers could be executed as punishment but both would have to pay compensation, presumably to the one brother who survived; Shaykh Niẓām, *al-Fatāwā al-Hindiyya*, 6:5.

51. The scholar in question was Fakhr al-Islām al-Shāshī (d. 1114); Abū Bakr Ibn al-'Arabī, *Aḥkam al-Qur'ān*, 1:94–95.

52. *Ṣaḥīḥ al-Bukhārī*: *kitāb al-jihād wa'l-siyar, bāb lā yu'adhdhabu bi-'adhāb Allāh*; *Ṣaḥīḥ al-Bukhārī, kitāb al-diyāt, bāb qawl Allāh ta'ālā al-nafs bi'l-nafs*; *Ṣaḥīḥ Muslim*: *kitāb al-qasāma... bāb mā yubāḥu bihi dam muslim.*

53. Spinoza, *Theological-Political Treatise*, 214.

54. Gomaa, *Bayān*, 78–82; al-Qaraḍāwī, *al-Ḥurriyya al-dīniyya wa'l-ta'addudiyya fī naẓar al-islām*, 20–51.

55. See *Ṣaḥīḥ Muslim*: *kitāb al-īmān, bāb bayān anna man māta 'alā al-kufr fa-huwa fī al-nār...*; al-Bayjūrī, *Ḥāshiyat 'alā Jawharat al-tawḥīd*, 68.

56. Juliane Hammer, *American Muslim Women, Religious Authority, and Activism*, 16–17, 42.

57. Gomaa, *al-Bayān*, 61; http://qaradawi.net/fatawaahkam/30/1316.html.

58. Muḥyī al-Dīn Ibn 'Arabī, *al-Futūḥāt al-makkiyya*, 6:428–29 (paragraphs nos 592–95); Sa'diyya Shaikh, *Sufi Narratives of Intimacy*, 91. I am grateful to Sa'diyya for pointing out this citation.

59. '*Wa lā ta'ummanna imra'a rajulan wa lā a'rābī muhājiran wa lā fājir mu'minan*'; Ibn Ḥajar al-'Asqalānī calls its *Isnād* 'feeble' (*wāh*) and al-Bayhaqī and al-Albānī note that all its narrations are weak; Ibn Ḥajar, *Bulūgh al-marām*, 173; al-Bayhaqī, *Sunan*, 3:128; al-Albānī, *Ḍa'īf Sunan Ibn Mājah*, 84. See al-Bayhaqī, *Sunan*, 3:127–28; Ibn Qudāma, *Mughnī*, 2:33; al-Buhūtī, *Rawḍ al-murbi'*, 100.

60. Ibn 'Arabī, *al-Futūḥāt al-makkiyya*, 6:428–29 (paragraphs 592–95).
61. Behnam Sadeghi, *The Logic of Law Making in Islam*, 58, 75. Ibn Ḥajar concluded that no evidence of note existed for this being a prophetic Hadith. It was only a Companion opinion; Ibn Ḥajar, *al-Dirāya takhrīj aḥādīth al-Hidāya*, 1:171; Ibn Rushd, *Distinguished Jurist's Primer*, 1:161; al-Khaṭṭābī, 1:174.
62. Ibn Qudāma, *Mughnī*, 2:22–29, 46. In theory, men in the congregation who did not believe their prayers would be accepted if they followed a female imam could simply make the intention of praying alone. Then there would only remain the question of whether their prayer was valid with a woman between them and the *qibla*, which even the late Mufti of Saudi Arabia, 'Abd al-'Azīz Bin Bāz, said posed no problem; 'Abd al-'Azīz Bin Bāz and Ibn 'Uthaymīn, *Fatāwā al-'ulamā' li'l-nisā'*, 29. The Lucknow jurist 'Abd al-Ḥayy al-Farangī Maḥallī noted that it had become common in his time for boys who had memorized the Qur'an to lead their older relatives in prayer, but he opposed this based on the standard Hanafi position; 'Abd al-Ḥayy al-Laknawī, *Majmū'at rasā'il 'Abd al-Ḥayy al-Laknawī*, 4:121–22.
63. Aḥmad al-Ghumārī, 'al-Iqnā' bi-ṣiḥḥat ṣalāt al-jum'a fī al-manzil khalf al-midhyā',' in *Silsilat al-sāda al-Ghumāriyya*, 23–28; al-Nawawī, *Minhāj*, 122.
64. Muḥammad Khiḍr Ḥusayn, *al-Sa'āda al-'uẓmā*, 163–64. This is the preferred Hanafi opinion and would only apply to a woman's voice during prayer; Ibn 'Ābidīn, *Ḥāshiya*, 1:406; 6:369.
65. Gomaa, *Fatāwā al-nisā'*, 486.
66. Al-Ba'lī, *Kashf al-mukhaddarāt*, 1:172. Ibn al-Jawzī was one of the Hanbalis who held this position; Ibn al-Jawzī, *Aḥkām al-nisā'*, 23.
67. A small number of scholars allowed up to three dissenting opinions; Ibn al-Nadīm, *The Fihrist*, 520; Shihāb al-Dīn al-Ramlī, *Ghāyat al-ma'mūl fī sharḥ Waraqāt al-uṣūl*, 281–82; Gomaa, *al-Ijmā' 'ind al-uṣūliyyīn*, 19.
68. Al-Zarkashī, *al-Baḥr al-muḥīṭ*, 3:574–77, al-Juwaynī, *al-Burhān*, 1:456.
69. http://qaradawi.net/fatawaahkam/30/1316.html; Hammer, 83.
70. Ibn Qudāma, *Mughnī*, 2:33. For the Hadith, see *Sunan Abī Dāwūd: kitāb al-ṣalāt, bāb imāmat al-nisā'*.
71. Ibn Ḥajar, *Bulūgh al-marām*, 176; al-Ḥākim, *al-Mustadrak*, 1:203; al-Bayhaqī, *Sunan*, 3:186–87; al-Albānī, *Silsilat al-aḥādīth al-ṣaḥīḥa*, 6, 1:548; idem, *Ṣaḥīḥ Sunan Abī Dāwūd*, 3:141–43. Al-Ḥākim remarks that this is a 'strange sunna' but does not dispute the reliability of the Hadith. Two fifteenth-century Hanafi scholars, al-Zayla'ī and Badr al-Dīn al-'Aynī refute criticism of the Hadith's transmitters leveled by Ibn al-Jawzī and Ibn al-Qaṭṭān; al-'Aynī, *Sharḥ Sunan Abī Dāwūd*, 3:93–95; al-Zayla'ī, *Naṣb al-rāya takhrīj ahādīth al-Hidāya*, 2:31. Ibn al-Mulaqqin and Ibn Ḥajar remark elsewhere that one of the transmitters in the *Isnād*, 'Abd al-Raḥmān bin Khallād, is not well identified, though other versions of the non-gender-specific version do not rely on him. Ibn Ḥajar also notes that the report about Umm Waraqa, with no gender specification for the congregation, also appears without the Prophet's involvement in the *Musnad* of al-Ḥārith bin Abī Usāma; Ibn al-Mulaqqin, *al-Badr al-munīr*, 4:389–93; Ibn Ḥajar, *Talkhīṣ al-ḥabīr*, 2:57.
72. *Sunan Abī Dāwūd: kitāb al-ṣalāt, bāb imāmat al-nisā'*; *Musnad Aḥmad Ibn Ḥanbal*: 6:405; al-Dāraquṭnī, *Sunan*, 1:279, 403. The question of why al-Dāraquṭnī included this minority version of the Hadith of Umm Waraqa in his *Sunan* is answered by the book's purpose. At best, it was a storehouse of legally interesting and useful Hadiths for followers of the Shāfi'ī school, not a collection following any standard of soundness. At worst, as the Syrian Hadith scholar 'Abd al-Fattāḥ Abū Ghudda argued, the book was actually a collection of flawed and weak Hadiths misnamed as a *Sunan*; see Abū Ghudda,

al-Ta'rīf bi-ḥāl Sunan al-Dāraquṭnī (Damascus: Maktab al-Maṭbū'āt al-Islāmiyya, 1992).

73. Jonathan Brown, 'Critical Rigor Vs. Juridical Pragmatism,' 22–32; Ibn Qudāma, *Mughnī*, 2:33; see al-Qaraḍāwī's fatwa above. Other ulama have tried to defuse the Hadith of Umm Waraqa by claiming that she was only permitted to lead her household in *optional* prayers, such as the nightly prayers held in Ramadan. But the versions of the Hadith in al-Ḥākim's *Mustadrak* and al-Bayhaqī's *Sunan* specify that she led them in *required* prayers. In addition, Ibn Qudāma, though an opponent of woman-led prayer, objects that nothing in any version of this Hadith suggests the Prophet intended only optional prayers. Moreover, a muezzin only performs the call to prayer for the obligatory five daily prayers; Ibn Qudāma, *Mughnī*, 2:33.

74. Al-Khaṭīb, *Tārīkh Baghdād*, 5:360; 11:210.

75. Al-Subkī, *Ṭabaqāt al-fuqahā' al-shāfi'iyya*, 3:311.

76. Gayatri Spivak, 'Can the Subaltern Speak?', in *Colonial Discourse and Post-Colonial Theory*, 93.

77. Leila Ahmed, *Women and Gender in Islam*, 128–30; Katherine Bullock, 'The Gaze and Colonial Plans for the Unveiling of Muslim Women,' 9.

78. Rudolph Peters, 'What Does it Mean to be an Official Madhhab?: Hanafism and the Ottoman Empire,' in *The Islamic School of Law*, ed. Peri Bearman, et al., 153.

79. Ibn al-Ḥājj, *al-Madkhal*, 2:12.

80. Al-Ṭaḥāwī, *Sharḥ mushkil al-āthār*, 13:57. Ibn Kathīr approves of the report; Ibn Kathīr, *Tafsīr*, ed. Muṣṭafā al-Sayyid Muḥammad, et al. (Giza: Mu'assasat Qurṭuba, 2000), 3:403.

81. Ibn Hishām, *al-Sīra al-nabawiyya*, 2:73; 3:44; al-Dhahabī, *Siyar*, 2:297.

82. Ibn Abī al-Wafā', *al-Jawāhir al-muḍiyya*, 4:120.

83. Al-Nabhānī, *Jāmi' karāmāt al-awliyā'*, 2:359, citing al-Munāwī, *al-Kawākib al-durriyya*, 3:48. There is an interesting disparity between al-Nabhānī's version of al-Munāwī's text and the published edition. The editor of al-Munāwī has the text saying 'she preached to women (*nisā'*)' and al-Nabhānī has it 'she preached to the people (*nās*).' I think the former reading may reflect a corruption, since the text following that clause in al-Munāwī's work reads '*fa-yathbutu li-wa'ẓihā wa y[u]qṭa'u man asā'a*', which I understand as 'so one [male or general] became firm due to her preaching, and whoever [male, general] acted badly was cut off.' This is odd, difficult language, but it makes even less sense if it follows the mention of a female-only audience. Also, it is unlikely that the area around the pulpit (*minbar*) of the mosque would be set aside for women only; cf. Ibn Kathīr, *al-Bidāya wa'l-Nihāya*, 14:72; Ibn Ḥajar, *al-Durar al-kāmina*, 3:226.

84. Ghulam Ahmad Parwez, *Islam: A Challenge to Religion*, 31, 139–40, 341 ff.

85. Shoaib A. Ghias, 'Defining Shari'a: The Politics of Islamic Judicial Review in Pakistan,' chapter four. I thank the author for sharing his forthcoming work with me. See also Ali Qasmi, *Questioning the Authority of the Past*, 253–58.

86. Fazlur Rahman, *Islamic Methodology in History*, 40.

87. Rahman, *Islam and Modernity*, 18–19.

88. Nasr Hamid Abu Zayd, *Naqd al-khiṭāb al-dīnī*, 193, 202; idem, *Critique du discours religieux*, 186–89; idem, *Reformation of Islamic Thought*, 94, 99.

89. Edip Yuksel, Layth Saleh al-Shaiban and Martha Schulte-Nafeh, *The Quran: A Reformist Translation*, 7, 10–11.

90. Spinoza, *Theological-Political Treatise*, 105–108, 111.

91. Parwez, *Islam*, 137, 342–45.

92. Rahman, *Islamic Methodology in History*, 44, 70.

93. Al-Suyūṭī, *al-Durr al-manthūr fī al-tafsīr bi'l-ma'thūr*, 5:196.

94. This is a paraphrase of the Hadith: *al-jīrān thalātha: jār lahu ḥaqq wa huwa al-mushrik lahu ḥaqq al-jiwār, wa jār lahu ḥaqqāni wa huwa al-muslim lahu ḥaqq al-jiwār wa ḥaqq al-islām, wa jār lahu thalāthat ḥuqūq jār muslim lahu raḥim lahu al-islām wa al-raḥim wa al-jiwār*. There is agreement on the weakness (*ḍaʿīf*) of this Hadith. Al-ʿAjlūnī cites it from the *Musnad* of al-Bazzār and the *Thawāb al-aʿmāl* of Abū al-Shaykh; al-ʿAjlūnī, *Kashf al-khafā*, 1:393; al-Albānī, *Silsilat al-aḥādīth al-ḍaʿīfa*, 7:488–90 (no. 3493).

95. *Miṣr Tantakhib* 12/16/11 on CBC, http://www.youtube.com/watch?v=oxoUrlDe8aY (last accessed 1/20/2013).

96. See also Qur'an 3:28, 118. See, for example, the show *Kifāyat al-dhunūb* with Shaykh Ayman Ṣīdaḥ on the Raḥma Channel (October 2011) and Muḥammad Zughbī on *Min al-Jānī* show on Egypt's Khalījiyya Channel (May 2011); http://www.youtube.com/watch?v=5RejZbRaymw; http://www.youtube.com/watch?v=FhCy-jYGSEU. For more examples, see http://www.youtube.com/watch?v=HsswsOiiA3o; http://www.youtube.com/watch?v=xeW_AVhrt34;
http://www.youtube.com/watch?v=Zp6G7kV3Gko;
See also a lesson by Shaykh Khālid ʿAbdallāh on the Death of Abū Ṭālib; www.way2allah.com/khotab/item-6174.htm (taped 5/31/2008).

97. Najm al-Dīn Ibn Qudāma, *Mukhtaṣar Minhāj al-qāṣidīn*, 108.

98. *ḥaqq al-jār in maraḍ ʿudtahu wa in māt shayyaʿtahu wa in istaqraḍaka aqraḍtahu wa in aʿwaza satartahu wa in aṣābahu khayr hanna'tahu wa in aṣābathu muṣība ʿazzaytahu wa lā tarfaʿ binā'aka fawqa binā'ihi fa-tasuddu ʿalayhi al-rīḥ wa lā tu'dhihi bi-rīḥ qidrika illā an taghrifa lahu minhā*; this Hadith is considered weak by many scholars, but Ibn Ḥajar al-ʿAsqalānī states that it has a basis (*aṣl*) from the Prophet; al-Zabīdī, *Itḥāf al-sāda al-muttaqīn*, 6:308–309.

99. Ibn Ḥajar, *Fatḥ al-Bārī*, 10:541–42; al-Ṣanʿānī, *Subul al-salām*, 4:217–18.

100. Auguste Comte, *A General View of Positivism*, 229, 429; Gesinke, *Islamic Reform and Conservatism*, 167.

101. Yāsir Burhāmī, *Faḍl al-ghanī al-ḥamīd*, 136; Rāghib al-Sirjānī, *Fann al-Taʿāmul al-nabawī maʿa ghayr al-muslimīn*, 157. This latter report about the Christian prayer is cited from Ibn Ishaq, *The Life of Muhammad*, 271. Although the Christian delegation from Najran did not embrace Islam, they asked Muhammad to send one of his trusted Companions back with them to act as an arbitrator in their internal disputes.

102. Ayaan Hirsi Ali, *Infidel*, 271.

103. Abu Zayd, *Critique du discours religieux*, 182–84.

104. Abu Zayd, *Naqd al-khiṭāb al-dīnī*, 204–205.

105. 'Al-Haqiqa,' September 2011, Dream TV http://www.youtube.com/watch?v=tiRzmUYoR44

106. Hannah Arendt, *Between Past and Future*, 13–14.

107. Stanley Fish, *There's No Such Thing as Free Speech, and It's a Good Thing, Too*, 135; apud Andrew March, *Islam and Liberal Citizenship*, 44.

108. Emily Yoffe, 'Brotherly Love: My twin and I share an earth-shattering secret that could devastate our family—should we reveal it?,' *Slate.com*, February 16, 2012, http://www.slate.com/articles/life/dear_prudence/2012/02/incestuous_twin_brothers_wonder_if_they_should_reveal_their_secret_relationship_.html (last accessed July 2013), also http://gawker.com/5885722/.

109. Sophia Rosenfeld, *Common Sense: A Political History*.

110. 'France and Islam: Fighting Fire with Fire,' *The Economist* 11/2/2011 http://www.economist.com/blogs/newsbook/2011/11/france-and-islam; Pregnant nun ice cream advert banned for 'mockery' 9/14/2010, http://www.bbc.co.uk/news/uk-11300552.

111. Muḥammad al-Bāz, *Du'āt fī'l-manfā*, 151–67, 181.

112. For a reference to this, see Ibn 'Uthaymīn, *al-Sharḥ al-mumti' 'alā Zād al-mustaqni'*, 1:140. Al-Laknawī (d. 1887) notes that it is prohibited to pray while holding a vial full of urine; al-Laknawī, *Majmū'at rasā'il*, 4:83.

113. Martin Luther, *The Large Catechism*, 4, 7.

114. http://www.coptreal.com/WShowSubject.aspx?SID=31695.

115. Gomaa, *Bayān*, 57–58.

CHAPTER 6: LYING ABOUT THE PROPHET OF GOD

1. 'Islamic Finance: Banking on the Ummah,' *The Economist*, January 5, 2013, http://www.economist.com/news/finance-and-economics/21569050-malaysia-leads-charge-islamic-finance-banking-ummah; 'Islamic finance: Calling the faithful,' *Economist*, December 7, 2006, http://www.economist.com/node/8382406 (last accessed August 2013).

2. Ibn al-Jawzī, *al-Muntaẓam*, 17:4. Rates in the Ottoman Empire ran from 10 to 20 percent; Suraiya Farooqhi, et al., *An Economic and Social History of the Ottoman Empire II: 1600–1914*, 492.

3. M. Afifi al-Akiti, 'Riba & Investing in Shares,' http://www.livingislam.org/maa/riba_e.html

4. Aḥmad al-Ghumārī considers this supposed link in the *Isnād* highly improbable. Al-Shiblī died in Baghdad in 946, at which time al-Makkī was still in Basra (he was still in Mecca as of 940, in fact). Al-Khaṭīb al-Baghdādī's description of al-Makkī's very limited scholarly activity and subsequent ostracism in Baghdad suggests that he did not visit the city until shortly before his death there in 996 CE. Al-Makkī mentions the next link in the *Isnād*, al-Junayd, as well as his main link to al-Junayd, Abū Sa'īd Ibn al-A'rābī, many times in his *Qūt al-qulūb* but never once mentions al-Shiblī; al-Ghumārī, *al-Burhān al-Jalī*, 44–45; al-Makkī, *Qūt*, 1:165.

5. The saying cited by Al-Attas is *al-nās niyām fa-idhā mātū intabahū*. See Abū Ḥāmid al-Ghazālī, *Iḥyā' 'ulūm al-dīn*, 4:2469–71. Tāj al-Dīn al-Subkī, Zayn al-Dīn al-'Irāqī and al-Albānī all say this saying has no basis whatsoever as a prophetic Hadith; al-Albānī, *Silsilat al-aḥādīth al-ḍa'īfa*, 1:219. For a discussion of the Hadith on *Riba* as Incest, see Appendix III.

6. Aristotle, *Metaphysics*, 1011b (Book Four).

7. Nietzsche, *Philosophy and Truth*, 81, 96.

8. Donald Davidson, 'A Coherence Theory of Truth and Knowledge,' in *Reading Rorty*, ed. Alan Malachowski, 123.

9. William James, 'The Meaning of Truth,' in *Pragmatism and Other Essays*, 133 ff.

10. Petrarch, *The Secret*, 83.

11. John W. Schroeder, *Skillful Means: The Heart of Buddhist Compassion*, 15; Michael Pye, *Skilful Means: A Concept in Mahayana Buddhism*, 37–38; *The Lotus Sutra*, 65 ff.

12. Ibn Rushd, *Averroes' Commentary on Plato's Republic*, 129. Cf. Charles Butterworth, 'Philosophy, Ethics and Virtuous Rule: A Study of Averroes' Commentary on Plato's "Republic,"' *Cairo Papers in Social Science* 9, no. 1 (1986).

13. Ibn Rushd, *The Book of the Decisive Treatise*, 201.

14. Al-Sakhāwī, *al-Maqāṣid al-ḥasana*, 102–103.

15. *Ṣaḥīḥ al-Bukhārī*: *kitāb al-'ilm, bāb man khaṣṣa bi'l-'ilm qawman dūn qawm karāhiyyatan an lā yafhamū*; *Ṣaḥīḥ Muslim*: *kitāb al-īmān, bāb man laqiya Allāh bi'l-īmān*; Ibn Ḥajar, *Fatḥ al-Bārī*, 1:300.
16. Al-Sha'rānī, *Ṭabaqāt al-kubrā*, 235.
17. *Jāmi' al-Tirmidhī*: *kitāb al-birr wa'l-ṣila, bāb mā jā'a fī iṣlāḥ dhāt al-bayn.*
18. Ibn Abī al-Dunyā, *Kitāb al-ṣamt wa ādāb al-lisān*, 511–12.
19. Abū Ṭālib al-Makkī, *Qūt al-qulūb*, 1:177–78.
20. Muḥammad bin 'Alī bin Wad'ān, *al-Arba'ūn al-wad'āniyya al-mawḍū'a*, 47.
21. Al-Dhahabī, *Mīzān al-i'tidāl*, 1:141.
22. Al-Haytamī, *al-Fatāwā al-ḥadīthiyya*, 391.
23. Brown, 'Did the Prophet Say it or Not?', 280.
24. Aḥmad al-Ghumārī, *al-Baḥr al-'amīq*, 1:227–28, 290. The two scholars in question were Aḥmad Rāfi' al-Ṭaḥṭawī and Fatḥallāh al-Bannānī.
25. Nelly Hanna, *In Praise of Books*, 95.
26. Muḥammad bin Sulaymān al-Jazūlī, *Guide to Goodness*, 12. My evaluation of the Hadiths in this chapter of the *Guide* is taken from al-Sakhāwī stating that a Hadith is undisputedly forged or lacks any basis whatsoever; al-Sakhāwī, *al-Qawl al-badī'*, 109 ff.
27. Muḥammad Ziyād al-Tukla, ed., *Majmū' fī kashf ḥaqīqat al-juz' al-mafqūd al-maz'ūm min Muṣannaf 'Abd al-Razzāq*, 69 ff. One famous late medieval scholar who cited this Hadith was Ibn Ḥajar Haytamī, *Fatāwā*, 85, 380.
28. Montagu, *Letters*, 300 (Florence, 1740).
29. Vico, *On the Study Methods of Our Time*, 38, 43–45.
30. The Hadith via Jābir: *'Man balaghahu 'an Allāh shay' fīhi faḍl fa-'amila bihi [īmānan bihi wa] rajā'an dhālik al-faḍl a'ṭāhu Allāh dhālik wa in lam yakun dhālik kadhālik'*; al-Khaṭīb, *Tārīkh Baghdād*, 8:293; Ibn 'Abd al-Barr, *Jāmi' bayān al-'ilm*, 1:22; al-Daylamī, *Firdaws al-akhbār*, 3:559–60. The Hadith is considered weak, forged or baseless by scholars from Ibn al-Jawzī and Ibn Ḥajar to al-Albānī. See Ibn al-Jawzī, *Kitāb al-Mawḍū'āt*, 1:258, 3:153; al-Sakhāwī, *al-Maqāṣid al-ḥasana*, 348, 411; Mullā 'Alī al-Qāri', *al-Asrār al-marfū'a*, 282, 322–24; al-Albānī, *Silsilat al-aḥādīth al-ḍa'īfa*, 1:647 ff. Ibn Taymiyya cited the Hadith, however, in his fatwas without noting any flaw, and his student Ibn Mufliḥ rated it *ḥasan*. Ibn Nāṣir al-Dīn also defends its authenticity; Ibn Nāṣir al-Dīn al-Dimashqī, *al-Tarjīḥ li-ḥadīth ṣalāt al-tasbīḥ*, 31 ff.; Ibn Taymiyya, *Majmū'at al-fatāwā*, 18:46; Ibn Mufliḥ, *al-Ādāb al-shar'iyya*, 2:278–79. Aḥmad al-Ghumārī points out that this Hadith is often confused with another weak Hadith that seems similar on its face but whose meaning is actually profoundly different, that of Anas from the Prophet: 'If some virtue reaches someone from God and he does not believe it, he will not attain it'; al-Suyūṭī, *al-Jāmi' al-ṣaghīr*, 520; al-Ghumārī, *al-Mudāwī*, 6:233–35.
31. Al-Sakhāwī, *al-Maqāṣid al-ḥasana*, 411.
32. Erasmus, *Opera Omnia*, 6:2:96; idem, *Erasmus' Annotations on the New Testament*, 735; Eusebius, *History*, 202; Bentley, *Humanists and Holy Writ*, 147.
33. Livy, *The Early History of Rome*, 34; Sallust, *Jugurthine War*, 36–37.
34. Aristotle, *Poetics*, 60–61; Cicero, *De Oratore*, 62–65; Polybius, *Histories*, I:14, VII: 25a; Jean Bodin, 'Method for the Easy Comprehension of History,' 70.
35. Leopold Von Ranke, *The Secret of World History*, 58 (from von Ranke's introduction to his *History of the Latin and Teutonic Nations*).
36. Thucydides, *The Peloponnesian War*, 14; Costas M. Proussi, 'The Orator: Isocrates,' 68; Cicero, *Brutus*, 47.
37. Tacitus, *Annales*, 6:28.

38. Plutarch, *Lives I*, 'Solon,' xxvii.1.

39. C. B. R. Pelling, 'Truth and Fiction in Plutarch's *Lives*,' 32, 36. For the opposing view, see Arnaldo Momigliano, 'Greek Historiography,' *History and Theory* 17, no. 1 (1978): 1–28, and Christopher Gill, 'Plato on Falsehood – not Fiction,' in *Lies and Fiction in the Ancient World*, ed. Christopher Gill and T. P. Wiseman (Austin: University of Texas Press, 1993), 38–87. For an excellent discussion that concurs with Pelling, see J. L. Moles, 'Truth and Untruth in Herodotus and Thucydides,' in *Lies and Fiction in the Ancient World*, 88–120.

40. Alan Spitzer, *Historical Truth and Lies about the Past*, 4.

41. David Lowenthal, *The Past is a Foreign Country*, 215.

42. Paul Veyne, *Comment on écrit l'histoire*, 23.

43. Episode VII: Peacefield.

44. Kevin Baker, 'You Have to Give a Sense of What People Wanted,' 56; Jane Mayer, 'Zero Conscience in "Zero Dark Thirty,"' *New Yorker* December 14, 2002, http://www.newyorker.com/online/blogs/newsdesk/2012/12/torture-in-kathryn-bigelows-zero-dark-thirty.html.

45. Aziz Al-Azmeh, 'Rhetoric for the Senses,' 215–31.

46. Gibbon, *Decline and Fall*, 3:92; Montesquieu, *Persian Letters*, 247 ff.; Jeffery, 'Ghevond's Text of the Correspondence between 'Umar II and Leo III,' 329; Voltaire, *Essai sur les moeurs*, 1:270; Maulana Abdullah Nana, *The Maidens of Jannat*, 16.

47. Pindar, *Pindar's Victory Songs*, 159; *Odyssey*, 24:90–110 (Fagles trans., p. 471).

48. Plato, *Symposium*, 208c–208e. The eleventh-century philosopher Ibn Miskawayh objects to the hedonism and desire for pleasure behind the masses' longing to enter Heaven; Ibn Miskawayh, *Tahdhīb al-akhlāq*, 42–43.

49. Al-Suyūṭī, *Abwāb al-sa'āda fī asbāb al-shahāda*; Abū Bakr al-Ājurrī, *Ṣifat al-ghurabā' min al-mu'minīn*, 20, 66–68.

50. 'Abdallāh bin 'Abd al-Raḥmān al-Dārimī, *Sunan*, 2:431; Al-Azmeh, 'Rhetoric for the Senses,' 227.

51. *Jāmi' al-Tirmidhī*: *kitāb ṣifat al-janna, bāb mā li-adnā ahl al-janna*; *Ṣaḥīḥ Muslim*: *kitāb al-janna wa ṣifāt na'īmihā, bāb awwal zumra tadkhulu al-janna 'alā ṣūrat al-qamar*; *Ṣaḥīḥ al-Bukhārī*: *kitāb bad' al-khalq, bāb mā jā'a fī ṣifat al-janna wa annahā makhlūqa*.

52. Al-Ṭabarānī, *al-Mu'jam al-kabīr*, 23:367–68. This Hadith is considered very weak; al-Mundhirī, *al-Targhīb wa'l-tarhīb*, 3:1377 (no. 2230).

53. A. J. Arberry, *Reason and Revelation in Islam*, 53.

54. Al-Ghazālī, *The Incoherence of the Philosophers*, 216–17. Ibn Sīnā had no compunction about drinking wine himself, as evidenced in his autobiography, but advocated upholding the Shariah punishments for such crimes in his *Kitāb al-Shifā'*; William Gohlman, *The Life of Ibn Sina*, 29; Ibn Sīnā, *Kitāb al-Shifā'*, 447–56. See also Peter Heath, *Allegory and Philosophy in Avicenna*, 121–22.

55. Lady Montagu, *Letters*, 108–109.

56. Al-Ghazālī, *The Incoherence of the Philosophers*, 1, 212, 218–19.

57. Ibn Taymiyya, *Majmū'at al-Fatāwā*, 13:132 ff.

58. Al-Ghazālī, *Iḥyā' 'ulūm al-dīn*, 4:2469–71.

59. *Ṣaḥīḥ Muslim*: *kitāb al-janna wa ṣifāt na'īmihā, bāb awwal zumra tadkhulu al-janna 'alā ṣūrat al-qamar*.

60. Al-Nawawī, *Sharḥ Ṣaḥīḥ Muslim*, 17/18:178; al-Qāḍī 'Iyāḍ, *Ikmāl al-mu'lim bi-fawā'id Muslim*, 8:366. The Hadith of the Poor in Heaven comes from the Prophet via 'Imrān bin Ḥuṣayn; *Ṣaḥīḥ al-Bukhārī*: *kitāb bad' al-khalq, bāb* 8; *Ṣaḥīḥ Muslim*: *kitāb al-riqāq, bāb* 1.

61. Ibn Ḥajar, *Fatḥ al-Bārī*, 6:400–401. Some scholars offered different explanations. Ibn Taymiyya's most influential disciple, Ibn Qayyim, suggested that the multiple partners enjoyed by men in Heaven are mostly huris as opposed to earthly women now in Paradise; Ibn al-Qayyim, *Ḥādī al-arwāḥ*, quoted in Muḥammad Bakhīt al-Ḥujaylī, *Ajwibat Ibn al-Qayyim 'an al-aḥādīth allatī ẓāhiruhā al-ta'āruḍ*, 1:488; al-Munāwī, *Fayḍ al-qadīr*, 5:2375.

62. The Hadith is found in *Ṣaḥīḥ al-Bukhārī: kitāb bad' al-khalq, bāb mā jā'a fī ṣifat al-janna wa annahā makhlūqa*. For Ibn 'Abbās' statement, see al-Ṭabarī, *Jāmi' al-bayān*, 1:172; al-Bayhaqī, *Kitāb al-Ba'th wa'l-nushūr*, 210; Ibn Taymiyya, *al-Fatwā al-Ḥamawiyya*, 107.

63. Abū al-Qāsim al-Suhaylī, *al-Rawḍ al-unuf*, 4:127–28. See also, Ibn Taymiyya, *al-Fatwā al-Ḥamawiyya*, 51–52.

64. David Nyberg, *The Varnished Truth*, 1–2.

65. Augustine, 'Lying,' 67–70.

66. Immanuel Kant, *On a Supposed Right to Lie because of Philanthropic Concerns*, published with *Grounding for the Metaphysics of Morals*, 64–65 (paragraphs 426–27).

67. Kant, 'What is Enlightenment,' in *On History*, 3, 9.

68. John Stuart Mill, *Utilitarianism*, 274–75.

69. Plutarch, *Lives I*, 'Solon,' xxix.5.

70. Lucian of Samosata, 'How to Write History,' in *Lucian: a Selection*, 211; Francis Bacon, 'Of Truth,' in *Francis Bacon*, 103; Augustine, 'Lying,' 78; Kant, *On a Supposed Right to Lie*, 64–65.

71. Ibn Jubayr, *The Travels of Ibn Jubayr*, 230–31; Ibn al-Jawzī, *Kitāb al-quṣṣāṣ wa'l-mudhakkirīn*, 147.

72. Jonathan Brown, 'Even If It's Not True It's True: Using Unreliable Ḥadīths in Sunni Islam,' 18.

73. Brown, 'Even If It's Not True It's True,' 23.

74. Ibn al-Jawzī, *Kitāb al-Mawḍū'āt*, 2:244–47.

75. Brown, 'Even If It's Not True It's True,' 20–22.

76. Brown, 'Even If It's Not True It's True,' 35–46.

77. Anthony Collins, 'A Discourse on Free Thinking,' 99; Kant, 'What is Enlightenment,' in *On History*, 3–4.

78. Dr. Ismā'īl al-Daftār, in personal discussion with author, July 2010. For this Hadith, see Ibn Qayyim, *al-Manār al-munīf*, 50–51; al-Suyūṭī, *al-La'ālī al-maṣnū'a*, 2:291.

79. Muḥammad al-Ghazālī, *al-Sunna Nabawiyya*, 35–36.

80. *Ṣaḥīḥ Muslim*: *kitāb al-riqāq, bāb akthar ahl al-janna al-fuqarā' wa akthar ahl al-nār al-nisā'*; *Jāmi' al-Tirmidhī*: *kitāb al-adab, bāb taḥdhīr fitnat al-nisā'*; *Sunan Ibn Mājah*: *kitāb al-fitan, bāb fitnat al-nisā'*; *Ṣaḥīḥ al-Bukhārī*: *kitāb al-manāqib, bāb 'alāmāt al-nubuwwa fī'l-islām*; *Ṣaḥīḥ Muslim*: *kitāb al-fitan, bāb* 18.

81. Zaid Shakir, in discussion with author at Critical Islamic Reflections conference, Yale University, April, 2003.

82. These originally appeared in the newspaper *Aḥdāth al-Maghrib*. Al-Baṭṭār echoed criticisms of earlier Islamic modernists like Abū Rayya such as the scientific problems of the Hadith of the Fly, religious objections over Hadiths describing the Prophet being bewitched (al-Baṭṭār and other reformists object that he was infallible) as well as a Hadith affirming the biblical story of David and Bathsheba, which similarly casts a prophet in an imperfect light. See al-Baṭṭār, *Fī naqd al-Bukhārī kāna baynahu wa bayn al-ḥaqq ḥijāb*.

83. For example, of the transmitters that Bukhari uses in his *Ṣaḥīḥ* but who are criticized by notable Hadith scholars (382 are listed by Ibn Ḥajar in his introduction to the *Fatḥ al-Bārī*), 19 percent of them only appear in the chapters dealing with the non-core issues, such as the chapters on *Maghāzī, Tafsīr, Daʿwāt, Adab, Ṣifat al-Nabī, Riqāq, al-Anbiyāʾ, Fitan* or the various *faḍāʾil* chapters (a small number also appeared in supporting narrations in other chapters, but I ignored this because supporting narrations typically include less impressive transmitters than the primary ones). But these twelve chapters only make up 12 percent of *Ṣaḥīḥ al-Bukhārī*'s ninety-seven chapters, and the *Tafsīr* chapter is one of the book's largest. The remaining 81 percent of the impugned transmitters are distributed across the other 88 percent of the book's chapters – not surprising or statistically significant.
84. Muḥammad Saʿīd Ramaḍān al-Būṭī, personal communication, Abu Dhabi, 4/15/2006.
85. Derek D. Rucker and David Dubois, 'The Failure to Transmit Certainty: Causes, Consequences, and Remedies,' *Advances in Consumer Research*, 36 (2009): 69–70.
86. *'muʿjiza tammat bi-tashīl rabbānī'*; http://www.shorouknews.com/columns/view.aspx?cdate=16042012&id=f1183b12-b343-48ed-b949-58a825afbed6 (last accessed 4/17/2012).
87. http://www.pewforum.org/Politics-and-Elections/Little-Voter-Discomfort-with-Romney%E2%80%99s-Mormon-Religion.aspx.
88. Erich Auerbach, *Mimesis*, 11–12.
89. Kevseri, *Maqālāt*, 46.
90. The critic cited here is al-Sakhāwī; Yāsīn al-Fādānī, *al-ʿUjāla fī al-aḥādīth al-musalsala*, 15.
91. Al-Nabhānī, *Jāmiʿ karāmāt al-awliyāʾ*, 1:188.
92. Al-Subkī, *Ṭabaqāt al-shāfiʿiyya*, 8:35–37.

CHAPTER 7: WHEN SCRIPTURE CAN'T BE TRUE

1. This can be verified in a speech given years later. See http://www.youtube.com/watch?v=pKMPVpjYrN4.
2. 'Abd al-Ḥamīd Abū Sulaymān, *Ḍarb al-mar'a wasīla li-ḥall al-khilāfāt al-zawjiyya*, 19, 25, 36, 65. Laleh Bakhtiar also translates *ḍaraba* as 'to leave'; Laleh Bakhtiar, trans., *The Sublime Quran* (Chicago: Islamicworld.com, 2007), 94.
3. Abū Sulaymān, *Ḍarb al-mar'a*, 82. See the Hadiths describing this, as referenced in Qur'an 66:3–5, in *Ṣaḥīḥ al-Bukhārī*: *kitāb al-nikāḥ, bāb mawʿiẓat al-ab ibnatahu li-ḥāl zawjihā*; *Ṣaḥīḥ Muslim*: *kitāb al-ṭalāq, bāb fī al-īlāʾ wa iʿtizāl al-nisāʾ*.
4. Abū Sulaymān, *Ḍarb al-mar'a*, 43–44, 62, 70–75.
5. Amina Wadud, *Qur'an and Woman*, 76; idem, *Inside the Gender Jihad*, 191–200. See also Nadeem Mohamed, 'Between "Yes" and "No": Amina Wadud and Scriptural Imperatives,' 73–87.
6. Kolawole Azeez Oyediran and Uche Isiugo-Abanihe, 'Perceptions of Nigerian Women on Domestic Violence,' 43–47; Kathryn Yount, 'Resources, Family Organization, and Domestic Violence against Married Women in Minya, Egypt.'
7. See Shakespeare's *The Two Gentlemen of Verona*, Act IV, Scene 1; Richard Trench, *Dictionary of Obsolete English* (New York: Philosophical Library, 1958), 228; see Warner Bros' *Confidential Agent* (1945).
8. Here I am drawing on Robert Gleave's excellent book *Islam and Literalism*, 1–21. See Stanley Fish, *Is There a Text in This Class?*, 14.

9. For the main body of this report, see *Sunan Abī Dāwūd*: *kitāb al-nikāḥ, bāb ḍarb al-nisā'*; *Sunan Ibn Mājah*: *kitāb al-nikāḥ, bāb ḍarb al-nisā'*. For the final statement about the best men not beating their wives, see the recensions in al-Ḥākim, *Mustadrak*, 2:188, 191.

10. *Ṣaḥīḥ Muslim*: *kitāb al-ḥajj, bāb ḥajjat al-Nabī*; *Sunan Abī Dāwūd*: *kitāb al-manāsik, bāb ṣifat ḥajjat al-Nabī*. The *Jāmi' al-Tirmidhī* identifies the crime deserving of beating as the wife committing 'a gross [sexual] transgression (*fāḥisha mubayyina*)'; *Jāmi' al-Tirmidhī*: *kitāb al-riḍā', bāb mā jā'a fī ḥaqq al-mar'a 'alā zawjihā*; idem, *kitāb al-tafsīr, bāb tafsīr sūrat al-tawba*.

11. *Ṣaḥīḥ al-Bukhārī*: *kitāb al-nikāḥ, bāb mā yukrahu min ḍarb al-nisā'*.

12. *Ṣaḥīḥ al-Bukhārī*: *kitāb al-nikāḥ, bāb* 94; *kitāb al-adab, bāb* 43; *Ṣaḥīḥ Muslim*: *kitāb al-faḍā'il, bāb mubā'adatihi (s) li'l-āthām*; *Sunan Abī Dāwūd*: *kitāb al-adab, bāb fī al-'afw wa'l-tajāwuz*. One Hadith that Aisha herself transmitted raises questions about her claim. In it, the Prophet gets up from Aisha's bed at night and leaves. Curious and 'jealous,' she follows him to the graveyard then sneaks back home before he arrives. The Prophet confronts her about following him and then tells her that he was praying for the dead and teaches her the prayer to say for them. When he confronts her, Aisha says that 'he pushed me with his palm on my chest in a way that caused me pain.' This appears via two wordings, '*lahadanī fī ṣadrī lahdatan awja'atnī*' (*Ṣaḥīḥ Muslim, Sunan al-Nasā'ī,* via Aisha → Muḥammad bin Qays → 'Abdallāh bin Kathīr) and '*lahazanī fī ṣadrī lahzatan awja'atnī*' (*Musnad Aḥmad, Sunan al-Nasā'ī*, via Aisha → Muḥammad bin Qays → 'Abdallāh bin Abī Mulayka). This may well be an orthographic error, but both words have been understood the same way: *Ṣaḥīḥ Muslim*: *kitāb al-janā'iz, bāb mā yuqālu 'ind dukhūl al-qubūr wa'l-du'ā' li-ahlihi*; *Musnad Aḥmad*: 6:221; *Sunan al-Nasā'ī*: *kitāb al-janā'iz, bāb al-amr bi'l-istighfār li'l-mu'minīn*.

13. This report can be found in the ninth- and tenth-century *Tafsīrs* of 'Abd bin Ḥumayd, al-Ṭabarī, Ibn Abī Ḥātim and others. See *Tafsīr Muqātil bin Sulaymān* (Beirut: Dār al-Kutub al-'Ilmiyya, 2003), 1:227 and al-Suyūṭī, *al-Durr al-manthūr*, 2:167.

14. Ibn Ḥajar, *Fatḥ al-Bārī*, 9:378–79.

15. Abū Bakr Ibn al-'Arabī, *Aḥkām al-Qur'ān*, 1:499–500.

16. Al-Jāwī, *Qūt al-ḥabīb al-gharīb*, 211; al-Nawawī, *Sharḥ Ṣaḥīḥ Muslim*, 7/8:434.

17. '*Lā yus'alu al-rajul fīmā ḍaraba imra'atahu*'; see *Musnad Aḥmad Ibn Ḥanbal*: 1:20; *Sunan Abī Dāwūd*: *kitāb al-nikāḥ, bāb fī ḍarb al-nisā'*; *Sunan Ibn Mājah*: *kitāb al-nikāḥ, bāb ḍarb al-nisā'*; al-Ḥākim, *Mustadrak*, 4:175; al-Bayhaqī, *Sunan*, 7:497; Ibn Ḥajar al-Haytamī, *Fatāwā*, 182; al-Munāwī, *Fayḍ*, 12:6409; 'Abd al-Karīm al-Rāfi'ī, al-*Tadwīn fī akhbār Qazwīn*, 1:152. Al-Suyūṭī considered it *ḥasan*, but it is judged weak by al-Albānī since it is known only through one transmitter, 'Abd al-Raḥmān al-Muslī, who is, in turn, known only from this Hadith. This was noted by al-Bazzār and al-Dhahabī, who also alerts us that only one transmitter narrates it from 'Abd al-Raḥmān; al-Albānī; *Silsilat al-aḥādīth al-ḍa'īfa*, 10:1:316 (no. 4776); al-Dhahabī, *Mīzān*, 2:602; al-Bazzār, *Musnad*, 1:356.

18. Khaled Abou El Fadl, *Conference of the Books*, 171–72, 180–86. Muḥammad al-Ghazālī shares this position; Ghazālī, *A Thematic Commentary on the Quran*, 61.

19. Abū Bakr Ibn al-'Arabī, *Aḥkām al-Qur'ān*, 1:499.

20. Gomaa, *Fatāwā al-nisā'*, 297–99; Gomaa, personal interview (6/16/2013).

21. Gomaa, personal communication 6/2012.

22. Muḥammad Ṭāhir Ibn 'Āshūr, *al-Taḥrīr wa'l-Tanwīr*, 5:43–44.

23. Ibn al-Faras, *Aḥkām al-Qur'ān*, 2:179–81.

24. Ibn al-Jawzī, *Aḥkām al-nisā'*, 80–81; al-Qurṭubī, *al-Jāmi' li-aḥkām al-Qur'ān*, 3:157.
25. This application of Qur'an 4:34–35 goes back to the Successor Sa'īd bin al-Jubayr; Ibn al-'Arabī, *Aḥkām al-Qu'rān*, 1:498–99.
26. Maribel Fierro, 'Ill-Treated Women Seeking Divorce,' 326. See also Manuela Marín, 'Disciplining Wives: A Historical Reading of Qur'ân 4:34,' 29–35. Ibn Taymiyya addresses this issue in a fatwa as well, citing Qur'an 4:19 as a basis for preventing such abuse; Ibn Taymiyya, *Majmū'at al-fatāwā*, 32:189.
27. Fierro, 324–33.
28. Elyse Semerdjian, *Of the Straight Path*, 138–44. Evidence from Ottoman court records supports this overall thesis. In one case in Istanbul in 1691 a man threatened to beat his wife to make her file for divorce. He succeeded, managing to make her not only decline any maintenance payments but also return her sizable dowry and a set of pillows and comforters. The wife, however, took the case to court, arguing that her decision was under duress and bringing neighborhood witnesses to her husband's threats. The judge ruled in her favor, returning her possessions and money to her. See BAB54 Vol. 20 page. 415, Hüküm no: 509, Orijinal metin no: [90a–1]; available at http://www.kadisicilleri.org/. Other evidence from legal practice comes from seventeenth-century Surat, India, where marriage contracts commonly included 'the four conditions,' one of which was that divorce would ensue automatically if the husband beat his wife such that there was bruising; Farhat Hasan, State and Locality in Mughal India (Cambridge: Cambridge University Press, 2004), 80–1.
29. Mathieu Tillier, 'Women before the Qāḍī under the Abbasids,' 284; Ibn Battuta, *Travels*, 2:354–55; Judith Tucker, *In the House of the Law*, 66; Yvonne Seng, 'Invisible Women: Residents of early Sixteenth-Century Istanbul,' 250.
30. Elke E. Stockreiter, 'Child Marriage and Domestic Violence: Islamic and Colonial Discourses on Gender Relations and Female Status in Zanzibar, 1900–1950s,' in *Domestic Violence and the Law in Colonial and Postcolonial Africa*, ed. Emily S. Burrill, et al., 138, 143–44. A British judge applying Anglo-Muhammadan law in 1886 notes that British law and Islamic law were very similar on this point in that they both prohibited real violence or apprehension of it; A.A.A. Fyzee, *Cases in the Muhammadan Law of India, Pakistan and Bangladesh*, ed. Tahir Mahmood (Delhi: Oxford University Press, 2005), 92–3 and also 32–3.
31. Emily Burrill and Richard Roberts, 'Domestic Violence, Colonial Courts, and the End of Slavery in French Soudan, 1905–12,' in Burrill, et al., 45–46.
32. Fierro, 336.
33. The Saudi Ministry of Justice, *Mudawwanat al-Aḥkām al-qaḍā'iyya*, 113–17. A similar ruling in the region of Qatif recently made headlines, with a man receiving thirty lashes and ten days in prison after he admitted hitting his wife; 'Saudi Arabia: Judge Ignores Wife, Sentences Husband to 30 Lashes for Domestic Violence,' *International Business Times*, June 6, 2013, http://www.ibtimes.co.uk/articles/475491/20130606/saudi-arabia-man-slaps-wife-domestic-violence.htm.
34. Shaham, *Family and the Courts in Modern Egypt*, 132–33.
35. Anna Würth, 'Stalled Reform: Family Law in Post-Unification Yemen,' 22–24.
36. Wadud, *Inside the Gender Jihad*, 191.
37. Eusebius describes his teacher as having taken the verse in 'an absurdly literal sense'; Eusebius, *History of the Church*, 186 (6.8.1).
38. This statement came from the Egyptian Maliki and diehard opponent of Salafism Aḥmad bin Muḥammad al-Ṣāwī (d. 1825); Aḥmad al-Ṣāwī, *Ḥāshiyat al-Ṣāwī 'alā Tafsīr al-Jalālayn*, 3:9.

39. Fariba Zarinebaf-Shahr, 'Women in the Public Eye in Eighteenth-Century Istanbul,' 302–304.

40. Galileo, 'Letter to Christina of Lorraine,' 85–88; Augustine, *De Genesi ad Litteram Libri Duodecim*, I:19:38.

41. Muhammad Qasim Zaman, trans., 'Studying Hadith in a Madrasa in the Early Twentieth Century,' 232–33. This is a translated excerpt from Manazir Ahsan Gilani's Urdu *Ihati-ya Dar al-'Ulum main bite huwa dine*.

Select Bibliography

SOURCES IN EUROPEAN LANGUAGES

Abou El Fadl, Khaled M. *Conference of the Books*. Lanham: University Press of America, 2001

Abu Zayd, Nasr Hamid. *Critique du Discours religieux*. Trans. Mohamed Chairet. Arles, France: Sindbad, 1999

——. *Mafhūm al-naṣṣ*. Cairo: al-Hay'a al-Miṣriyya al-'Āmma li'l-Kutub, 1990

——. *Reformation of Islamic Thought*. Amsterdam: Amsterdam University Press, 2006

Ahmed, Asad Q. 'Logic in the Khayrābādī School of India: A Preliminary Exploration.' In *Law and Tradition in Classical Islamic Thought*, ed. Michael Cook, et al., 227–46. New York: Palgrave, 2013

Ahmed, Leila. *Women and Gender in Islam*. New Haven: Yale University Press, 1992

Ali, Ayaan Hirsi. *Infidel*. New York: Free Press, 2007

Altınbaş, Nihan. 'Honor-related Violence in the Context of Patriarchy, Multicultural Politics and Islamophobia after 9/11.' *American Journal of Islamic Social Sciences* 30, no. 3 (2013): 1–19

Altorki, Soraya and Donald P. Cole. *Arabian Oasis City: The Transformation of 'Unayzah*. Austin, TX: University of Texas Press, 1989

Alvi, Sajida Sultana. *Perspectives on Mughal India*. Karachi: Oxford University Press, 2012

Anderson, J. N. D. 'The Syrian Law of Personal Status.' *Bulletin of the School of Oriental and African Studies* 17, no. 1 (1955): 34–49

Anjum, Ovamir. *Politics, Law and Community in Islamic Thought*. Cambridge: Cambridge University Press, 2012

Ansari, Zafar Ishaq. 'Islamic Juristic Terminology before Shāfi'ī: A Semantic Analysis with Special Reference to Kūfa.' *Arabica* 19, no. 3 (1972): 255–300

St. Anselm of Bec. *Monologion and Proslogion*. Trans. Thomas Williams. Indianapolis: Hackett, 1995

Arberry, A. J. *Reason and Revelation in Islam*. London: Allen & Unwin, 1957

Arendt, Hannah. *Between Past and Future*. Cleveland: Meridian Books, 1963

Aristotle. *Poetics*. Trans. Stephen Halliwell. Cambridge, MA: Harvard University Press, 1999

Aquil, Raziuddin, ed. *Sufism and Society in Medieval India*. Delhi: Oxford University Press, 2010

Augustine of Hippo. *Enchiridion on Faith, Hope and Love*. Trans. Henry Paolucci. Chicago: Gateway Edition, 1961

——. *The Essential Augustine*. Ed. Vernon J. Bourke. Indianapolis: Hackett, 1985

——. 'Lying (*De Mendacio*).' In *The Fathers of the Church* 16. Trans. Sister Mary Sarah Muldowney. New York: Fathers of the Church, 1952

Pseudo-Augustine. 'Mirabilis Sacrae Scripturae.' In *Operum S. Augustini: Appendix*. From Documenta Catholica Omnia, vol. MPL035 (available at http://www.documentacatholicaomnia.eu/04z/z_0354-0430__Augustinus__De_Mirabilis_Sacrae_Scripturae_Libri_Tres__MLT.pdf.html)

Auerbach, Erich. *Mimesis*. Trans. Willard Trask. New York: Doubleday, 1946

Ayalon, David. 'The Great Yasa of Chingiz Khan: A Reexamination (Part C2).' *Studia Islamica* 38 (1973): 107–56

Al-Azmeh, Aziz. 'Rhetoric for the Senses: A Consideration of Muslim Paradise Narratives.' *Journal of Arabic Literature* 26, no. 3 (1995): 215–31

Bacon, Francis. *Francis Bacon*. Ed. Arthur Johnston. New York: Schocken Books, 1963

Bagchi, David. *Luther's Earliest Opponents*. Minneapolis: Fortress Press, 1991

Baker, Kevin. 'You Have to Give a Sense of What People Wanted.' *American Heritage*. Nov/Dec (2001): 50–56

Baljon, J. M. S. *Religion and Thought of Shāh Walī Allāh Dihlawī 1703–1762*. Leiden: Brill, 1986

Banks, J. A. and Olive. *Feminism and Family Planning in Victorian England*. New York: Schocken Books, 1977

Barnes, Timothy D. *Constantine and Eusebius*. Cambridge, MA: Harvard University Press, 1981

Baron, Beth. 'Making and Breaking Marital Bonds in Modern Egypt.' In *Women in Middle Eastern History*, ed. Nikkie Keddie and Beth Baron, 275–91. New Haven: Yale University Press, 1991

Bayle, Pierre. *Dictionnaire Historique et Critique*. 5th edn, 4 vols. Amsterdam, Leiden, Utrecht: [no publisher], 1740

Bearman, Peri; Peters, Rudolph and Frank Vogel, ed. *The Islamic School of Law*. Cambridge, MA: Harvard University Press, 2005

Bentley, Jeremy H. *Humanists and Holy Writ: New Testament Scholarship in the Renaissance*. Princeton: Princeton University Press, 1983

Bodin, Jean. 'Method for the Easy Comprehension of History.' In *Historians at Work II*, ed. Peter Gay and Victor G. Wexler, 62–82. New York: Harper & Row, 1972

Bok, Sissela. *Lying*. 2nd edn. New York: Vintage Books, 1999

Bowerstock, G. W. *Fiction as History: Nero to Julian*. Berkeley: University of California Press, 1994

Browers, Michaelle and Charles Kurzman. *An Islamic Reformation?* Lanham: Lexington, 2004

Brown, Jonathan A. C. 'Critical Rigor Vs. Juridical Pragmatism: How Legal Theorists and Ḥadīth Scholars Approached the Backgrowth of *Isnāds* in the Genre of *'Ilal al-Ḥadīth*.' *Islamic Law and Society* 14, no. 1 (2007): 1–41

——. 'Did the Prophet Say it or Not?: The Literal, Historical and Effective Truth of Hadiths in Sunni Islam.' *Journal of the American Oriental Society* 129, no. 2 (2009): 259–85

——. 'Even If It's Not True It's True: Using Unreliable Ḥadīths in Sunni Islam.' *Islamic Law and Society* 18, no. 1 (2011): 1–52

——. *Hadith: Muhammad's Legacy in the Medieval and Modern World*. Oxford: Oneworld Publications, 2009
——. 'The Rules of *Matn* Criticism: There Are No Rules.' *Islamic Law and Society* 19, no. 4 (2012): 356–96
Brown, Nathan. *The Rule of Law in the Arab World*. Cambridge: Cambridge University Press, 1997
Bullock, Katherine H. 'The Gaze and Colonial Plans for the Unveiling of Muslim Women.' *Studies in Contemporary Islam* 2, no. 2 (2000): 1–20
Burak, Guy. 'The Second Formation of Islamic Law: The Post-Mongol Context of the Ottoman Adoption of a School of Law.' *Comparative Studies in Society and History* 55, no. 3 (2013): 579–602
Burrill, Emily S.; Roberts, Richard L. and Elizabeth Thornberry, ed. *Domestic Violence and the Law in Colonial and Postcolonial Africa*. Athens, OH: Ohio University Press, 2010
De Busbecq, Ogier. *Turkish Letters*. Trans. E. S. Forster. London: Eland, 2001
Carlyle, Thomas. *Carlyle's Lectures on Heroes*. Oxford: Oxford University Press, 1920
——. *The French Revolution*. New York: Heritage Press, 1956
Chadwick, Owen. *The Secularization of the European Mind*. Cambridge: Cambridge University Press, 1975
Chaudhry, Ayesha S. *Domestic Violence and the Islamic Tradition: Ethics, Law and the Muslim Discourse on Gender*. Oxford: Oxford University Press, 2014
Christelow, Allan. *Muslim Law Courts and the French Colonial State in Algeria*. Princeton: Princeton University Press, 1985
Cicero, Marcus Tullius. *Brutus*. Trans. G. L. Hendrickson. Cambridge, MA: Harvard University Press, 1952
——. *De Oratore I and II*. Trans. E. W. Sutton. Cambridge, MA: Harvard University Press, 1942
——. *The Nature of the Gods (De Natura Deorum)*. Trans. Horace C. P. McGregor. New York: Penguin, 1967
Cressy, David. 'Books as Totems in Seventeenth-Century England and New England.' *Journal of Library History* 21, no. 1 (1986): 92–106
Comte, Auguste. *A General View of Positivism*. New York: Robert Speller and Sons, 1957
Delchaye, Hippolyte. *The Work of the Bollandists*. Princeton: Princeton University Press, 1922
Draper, Jonathan A., ed. *The Eye of the Storm: Bishop John William Colenso and the Crisis of Biblical Criticism in Victorian Britain*. London: T&T Clark, 2003
Eaton, Richard M., ed. *India's Islamic Traditions, 711–1750*. Delhi: Oxford University Press, 2003
El-Gamal, Mahmoud. *Islamic Finance*. Cambridge: Cambridge University Press, 2006
Elliot, H. M. and John Dawson, ed. *The History of India as Told by its Own Historians: The Muhammadan Period*, vol. 7. New York: AMS Press, 1966
Erasmus, Desiderius. *Erasmus' Annotations on the New Testament: Galatians to the Apocalypse*. Ed. Anne Reeve. Leiden: Brill, 1993
——. *The Essential Erasmus*. Trans. John Dolan. New York: Mentor, 1964
——. *Opera Omnia*. Ed. Andrew J. Brown. Amsterdam: Elsevier, 2001
——. *The Praise of Folly*. Trans. John Wilson. Ann Arbor: University of Michigan Press, 1972
Eusebius. *The History of the Church*. Trans. G. A. Williamson. Ed. Andrew Louth. New York: Penguin, 1989
Fadel, Mohammed. 'Reinterpreting the Guardian's Role in the Islamic Contract of Marriage.' *Journal of Islamic Law* 3, no. 1 (1998): 1–26

Fakhry, Majid. *A History of Islamic Philosophy*. 2nd edn. New York: Columbia University Press, 1983

Farooqhi, Suraiya, et al. *An Economic and Social History of the Ottoman Empire Volume Two: 1600–1914*. Cambridge: Cambridge University Press, 1994

Fierro, Maribel. 'Ill-Treated Women Seeking Divorce: The Qur'ānic Two Arbiters and Judicial Practice amongst Malikis in Al-Andalus and North Africa.' In *Dispensing Justice in Islam: Qadis and their Judgments*. Ed. Muhammad Khalid Masud, Rudolph Peters and David Powers, 323–47. Leiden: Brill, 2006

Fish, Stanley. *Is There a Text in This Class?: The Authority of Interpretive Communities*. Cambridge, MA: Harvard University Press, 1980

——. *There's No Such Thing as Free Speech, and It's a Good Thing, Too*. New York: Oxford University Press, 1994

Fisher, Samuel. 'Rusticus ad Academicos (The Rustic's Alarm to the Rabbis).' In *The Testimony of the Truth Exalted*. [No place]: [no publisher], 1679

Frampton, Travis L. *Spinoza and the Rise of Historical Criticism of the Bible*. New York: T&T Clark, 2006

Francaviglia, Richard and Jerry Rodnitzky, ed. *Lights, Camera, History: Portraying the Past in Film*. College Station: Texas A&M University Press, 2007

Francisco, Adam S. *Martin Luther and Islam: A Study in Sixteenth-Century Polemics and Apologetics*. Leiden: Brill, 2007

Galileo. 'Letter to Christina of Lorraine, Grand Duchess of Tuscany.' In *The Seventeenth Century*. Ed. Andrew Lossky, 81–94. New York: Free Press, 1967

Geertz, Clifford. 'Common Sense as a Cultural System.' *Antioch Review* 67, no. 4 (2009): 770–90

Ghias, Shoaib A. 'Defining Shari'a: The Politics of Islamic Judicial Review in Pakistan.' PhD dissertation, University of California Berkeley, 2013

Gibb, H. A. R., trans. *The Travels of Ibn Battuta*, 3 vols. New Delhi: Munshiram Manoharlal, 2004

Gibbon, Edward. *Decline and Fall of the Roman Empire*, 3 vols. New York: Modern Library [no date]

Gesinke, Indira Falk. *Islamic Reform and Conservatism*. London: I. B. Tauris, 2010

Al-Ghazali, Abu Hamid. *The Incoherence of the Philosophers*. Trans. Michael F. Marmura. Provo: Brigham Young University Press, 1997

Gibson, Margaret, ed. *Boethius, His Life, Thought and Influence*. Oxford: Basil Blackwell, 1981

Gleave, Robert. *Islam and Literalism: Literal Meaning and Interpretation in Islamic Legal Theory*. Edinburgh: Edinburgh University Press, 2012

Gohlman, William E., trans. *The Life of Ibn Sina*. Albany: State University of New York Press, 1974

Görke, Andreas; Motzki, Harald; and Gregor Schoeler, 'First Century Sources for the Life of Muḥammad? A Debate.' *Der Islam* 89, no. 1 (2012): 2–59

Grant, Robert M. 'Historical Criticism in the Ancient Church.' *Journal of Religion* 25, no. 3 (1945): 183–96

Green, Arnold H. *The Tunisian Ulama 1873–1915*. Leiden: Brill, 1978

Guenther, Alan M. 'Hanafi *Fiqh* in Mughal India: The *Fatāwá-i 'Ālamgīrī*.' In *India's Islamic Traditions, 711–1750*. Ed. Richard M. Eaton, 209–30. Delhi: Oxford University Press, 2003

Gunny, Ahmad. *Perceptions of Islam in European Writings*. Chippenham, UK: The Islamic Foundation, 2004

Halbertal, Moshe. *People of the Book: Canon, Meaning, and Authority*. Cambridge, MA: Harvard University Press, 1997

Halevi, Judah. *The Kuzari*. Trans. H. Slonimsky. New York: Schocken Books, 1964
Halm, Heinz. *Empire of the Mahdi: The Rise of the Fatimids*. Trans. Michael Bonner. Leiden: Brill, 1996
Hammer, Juliane. *American Muslim Women, Religious Authority, and Activism: More than a Prayer*. Austin, TX: University of Texas Press, 2012
Hanna, Nelly. *In Praise of Books: A Cultural History of Cairo's Middle Class, Sixteenth to the Eighteenth Century*. Syracuse: Syracuse University Press, 2003
Heath, Peter. *Allegory and Philosophy in Avicenna (Ibn Sina): With a Translation of the Book of the Prophet Muhammad's Ascent to Heaven*. Philadelphia: University of Pennsylvania Press, 1992
Ho, Engseng. *The Graves of Tarim*. Berkeley: University of California Press, 2006
Holmes, Oliver Wendell. *The Common Law*. Chicago: American Bar Association, 2009
Homer. *Odyssey*. Trans. Robert Fagles. New York: Penguin, 1997
Hoyland, Robert. *Seeing Islam as Others Saw It*. Princeton: Darwin Press, 1997
Hunwick, John O., ed. *Sharīʿa in Songhay: The Replies of al-Maghīlī to the Questions of Askia al-Ḥājj Muḥammad*. London: Oxford University Press, 1985
Ibn Ezra, Abraham. *The Commentary of Abraham ibn Ezra on the Pentateuch, Volume 5: Deuteronomy*. Trans. Jay F. Schachter. Hoboken, NJ: Ktav Publishing, 2003
Ibn Jubayr, Abu'l-Husayn Muhammad. *The Travels of Ibn Jubayr*. Trans. Roland Broadhurst. London: Goodword Books, 2004
Ibn Rushd. *Averroes' Commentary on Plato's Republic*. Trans E. I. J. Rosenthal. Cambridge: Cambridge University Press, 1956
——. *The Book of the Decisive Treatise*. Trans. Charles Butterworth. Provo: Brigham Young University Press, 2001
——. *Distinguished Jurist's Primer*. Trans. Imran Khan Nyazee, 2 vols. Reading, UK: Garnet, 1996
Ivanhoe, Philip J, trans. *On Ethics and History: Essays and Letters of Zhang Xuecheng*. Stanford, CA: Stanford University Press, 2010
Al-Jabri, Mohammed 'Abed. *Arab-Islamic Philosophy: A Contemporary Critique*. Trans. Aziz Abbassi. Austin, TX: Center for Middle Eastern Studies, 1999
Jaffee, Martin S. *Torah in the Mouth*. Oxford: Oxford University Press, 2001
James, William. *Pragmatism and Other Essays*. Ed. Joseph Blau. New York: Washington Square Press, 1963
Al-Jazuli, Muhammad bin Sulayman. *Guide to Goodness*. Trans. Andrey (Hassan) Rosowsky. 2nd edn. Chicago: Kazi, 2006
Jeffery, Arthur. 'Ghevond's Text of the Correspondence between 'Umar II and Leo III.' *Harvard Theological Review* 37, no. 4 (1944): 269–332
Juynboll, G. H. A. *The Authenticity of Tradition Literature*. Leiden: Brill, 1969
Kant, Immanuel. *On History*. Ed. Lewis White Beck. Indianapolis: Bobbs-Merrill, 1963
——. *On a Supposed Right to Lie because of Philanthropic Concerns*. Published with *Grounding for the Metaphysics of Morals*. Trans. James W. Ellington. 3rd edn. Indianapolis: Hackett, 1993
Keddie, Nikki R. *An Islamic Response to Imperialism*. Berkeley: University of California Press, 1968
Kermode, Frank. *The Classic*. Cambridge, MA: Harvard University Press, 1983
——. *The Genesis of Secrecy*. Cambridge, MA: Harvard University Press, 1979
——. *Sense of an Ending*. 3rd edn. Oxford: Oxford University Press, 2000
von Kerssenbrock, Hermann. *Narrative of the Anabaptist Madness*. Trans. Christopher S. Mackey, 2 vols. Leiden: Brill, 2007

Khalafallah, Haifaa. 'Rethinking Islamic Law: Genesis and Evolution in the Islamic Legal Method and Structures.' PhD dissertation, Georgetown University, 1999

Khan, Sir Sayyid Ahmad. *Writings and Speeches of Sir Syed Ahmad Khan*. Ed. Shan Mohammad. Bombay: Nachiketa Publications, 1972

Kirschner, Robert. 'The Vocation of Holiness in Late Antiquity.' *Vigiliae Christianae* 38 (1984): 105–24

Klein, Michael L. *Anthropomorphisms and Anthropopathisms in the Targumim of the Pentateuch*. Jerusalem: Makor, 1982

Kozma, Liat. *Policing Egyptian Women*. Syracuse: Syracuse University Press, 2011

Kugle, Scott. 'Framed, Blamed and Renamed: The Recasting of Islamic Jurisprudence in Colonial South Asia.' *Modern Asian Studies* 35, no. 2 (2001): 257–313

Lane, Edward. *Manners and Customs of the Modern Egyptians*. New York: Cosimo, 2005

Lapidus, Ira. *A History of Islamic Societies*. New York: Cambridge University Press, 1988

Last, D. M. and M. A. Al-Hajj. 'Attempts at Defining a Muslim in 19th-Century Hausaland and Bornu.' *Journal of the Historical Society of Nigeria* 3, no. 2 (1965): 231–40

Lawrence, Bruce, ed. *Messages to the World: The Statements of Osama Bin Laden*. Trans. James Howarth. London: Verso, 2005

Lefebure, Leo. 'Violence in the New Testament and the History of Interpretation.' In *Fighting Words: Religion, Violence, and the Interpretation of Sacred Texts*, ed. John Renard, 75–100. Berkeley: University of California Press, 2012

Levine, Lee I. *Judaism and Hellenism in Antiquity: Conflict or Confluence*. Seattle: University of Washington Press, 1998

Lewis, Bernard. *Islam and the West*. Oxford: Oxford University Press, 1993

Livy, Titus. *The Early History of Rome*. Trans. Aubrey de Sélincourt. London: Penguin Books, 1960

Lombardi, Clark B. *State Law as Islamic Law in Modern Egypt*. Leiden: Brill, 2006

The Lotus Sutra. Trans. Burton Watson. New York: Colombia University Press, 1993

Lowenthal, David. *The Past is a Foreign Country*. Cambridge: Cambridge University Press, 1985

Lucian of Samosata. *Lucian: A Selection*. Ed. M. D. Macleod. Warminster, UK: Aris & Phillips, 1991

——. *Selected Satires of Lucian*. Trans. Lionel Lesson. New York: Norton, 1962

Luther, Martin. *The Large Catechism*. Trans. F. Bente and W. H. T. Dau. Penn State Electronic Classics, 2000 (available at *www2.hn.psu.edu/faculty/jmanis/m~luther/mllc.pdf*)

Lyons, Jonathan. *Islam through Western Eyes*. New York: Columbia University Press, 2012

Macfarlane, Alan. *The Origins of English Individualism*. Oxford: Basil Blackwell, 1978

Madison, James, et al. *Federalist Papers*. Ed. Lawrence Goldman. New York: Oxford University Press, 2008

Maimonides. *The Guide for the Perplexed*. Trans. M. Friedlander. 2nd edn. New York: Dover Publications, 1956

Malachowski, Alan R., ed. *Reading Rorty*. Oxford: Basil Blackwell, 1990

Mansfield, Peter. *The British in Egypt*. New York: Holt, Rinehart & Winston, 1971

Marracci, Ludovico. 'Prodromus.' In *Alcorani: Textus Universus*. [Padua]: (no publisher), 1698

Margoliouth, D. S. *Mohammad and the Rise of Islam*. New York: Cosimo, 2006, originally published 1905

Marín, Manuela. 'Disciplining Wives: A Historical Reading of Qur'ân 4:34.' *Studia Islamica* 97 (2003): 5–40

McCarthy, Justin. *The Ottoman Turks*. London: Longman, 1996

McKae, John R. *Seeing Through Zen*. Berkeley: University of California Press, 2003

Meijer, Roel, ed. *Global Salafism*. New York: Columbia University Press, 2009

Melchert, Christopher. 'The *Musnad* of Aḥmad Ibn Ḥanbal: How It Was Composed and What Distinguishes It from the Six Books.' *Der Islam* 82 (2005): 32–51

Metcalf, Barbara and Thomas. *A Concise History of India*. Cambridge: Cambridge University Press, 2002

Mill, John Stuart. *Utilitarianism, On Liberty, Essay on Bentham*. Ed. Mary Warnock. New York: Meridian Books, 1974

Montagu, Mary Wortley. *Letters*. New York: Everyman's Library, 1906.

Montesquieu, Charles Louis. *De l'Esprit des lois*. Ed. Laurent Versini, 2 vols. [Paris]: Gallimard, 1995

——. *Lettres Persanes*. Ed. Paul Vernière. Paris: Garnier Frères, 1960

——. *Persian Letters*. Trans. C. S. Betts. New York: Penguin, 1993

Montgomery, James. 'Ibn Faḍlān and the Rūsiyyah.' *Journal of Arabic and Islamic Studies* 3, no. 1 (2000): 1–25

More, Sir Thomas. *Responsio Ad Lutherum*. Trans. Gertrude Joseph Donnelly. Washington, D.C.: Catholic University of America Press, 1962

Moreh, Shmuel, trans. *Napoleon in Egypt*. Princeton: Markus Wiener, 1997

Motzki, Harald. 'The *Muṣannaf* of 'Abd al-Razzāq al-Ṣan'ānī as a Source of Authentic *Aḥādīth* of the First Century A.H.' *Journal of Near Eastern Studies* 50 (1991): 1–21

Mubarak, Hadia. 'Breaking the Interpretive Monopoly: A Re-Examination of Verse 4:34.' *Hawwa* 2, no. 3 (2005): 261–89

Nana, Maulana Abdullah. *The Maidens of Jannat*. 3rd edn. Karachi: Zam Zam, 2012

Nietzsche, Friedrich. *Philosophy and Truth*. Trans. Daniel Breazede. New Jersey: Humanitarian Press, 1979

Nyberg, David. *The Varnished Truth: Truth Telling and Deceiving in Ordinary Life*. Chicago: University of Chicago Press, 1993

Ockley, Simon. *History of the Saracens: Lives of Mohammed and His Successors*. London: Henry G. Bohn, 1847

Origen. *Origen*. Ed. and trans. Rowan Greer. New York: Paulist Press, 1979

Oyediran, Kolawole Azeez and Uche Isiugo-Abanihe. 'Perceptions of Nigerian Women on Domestic Violence: Evidence from 2003 Nigeria Demographic and Health Survey.' *African Journal of Reproductive Health* 9, no. 2 (2005): 38–53

Papaconstantinou, Arietta, ed. *Writing 'True Stories': Historians and Hagiographers in the Late Antique and Medieval Near East*. Turnhout: Brepols, 2010

Parwez, Ghulam Ahmad. *Islam: A Challenge to Religion*. Lahore: Tolu-e Islam Trust, 1968

Pelling, C. B. R. 'Truth and Fiction in Plutarch's *Lives*.' In *Antonine Literature*, ed. D. A. Russell, 19–52. Oxford: Clarendon Press, 1990

Peters, Rudolph. *Crime and Punishment in Islamic Law*. Cambridge: Cambridge University Press, 2005

Petrarch, Francesco. *The Secret*. Trans. William H. Draper. London: Chatto & Windus, 1911

Pindar. *Pindar's Victory Songs*. Trans. Frank Nisetich. Baltimore: Johns Hopkins University Press, 1990

Plato. *Phaedrus*. Trans. Walter Hamilton. London: Penguin, 1973

——. *Symposium*. Trans. Alexander Nehamas. Indianapolis: Hackett, 1989

Plutarch. *Lives I*. Trans. Bernadotte Perrin. Cambridge, MA: Harvard University Press, 1914

Polybius. *The Histories*. Trans. Mortimer Chambers. New York: Washington Square Press, 1966
Popkin, Richard. *History of Skepticism*. Oxford: Oxford University Press, 2003
Poulton, Hugh. *Top Hat, Grey Wolf and Crescent*. New York: New York University Press, 1997
Powell, Avril A. *Scottish Orientalists and India: The Muir Brothers, Religion, Education and Empire*. Woodbridge, UK: Boydell Press, 2010
Poznanski, Samuel. *The Literary Opponents of Saadiah Gaon*. London: Luzac, 1968
Proussi, Costas M. 'The Orator: Isocrates.' In *The Educated Man*, ed. Paul Nash, et al., 55–76. New York: John Wiley & Sons, 1965
Pye, Michael. *Skilful Means: A Concept in Mahayana Buddhism*. London: Duckworth, 1978
Qasmi, Ali Usman. *Questioning the Authority of the Past: The Ahl al-Qur'an Movement in the Punjab*. Karachi: Oxford University Press, 2011
Rahman, Fazlur. *Islam and Modernity*. Chicago: University of Chicago Press, 1982
——. *Islamic Methodology in History*. Karachi: Central Institute for Islamic Research, 1965
Rabb, Theodore K. and Jerrold E. Seigel, ed. *Action and Conviction in Early Modern Europe*. Princeton: Princeton University Press, 1969
Von Ranke, Leopold. *The Secret of World History: Selected Writings on the Art and Science of History*. Ed. Roger Wines. New York: Fordham University Press, 1981
Rapoport, Yossef. 'Legal Diversity in the Age of Taqlīd: The Four Chief Qāḍīs under the Mamluks.' *Islamic Law and Society* 10, no. 2 (2003): 210–28
Reimarus, Hermann. *Reimarus: Fragments*. Ed. Charles H. Talbert. Philadelphia: Fortress Press, 1970
Richardson, Cyril, ed. *Early Christian Fathers*. New York: Macmillan, 1979
Rida, Rashid. *The Muhammadan Revelation*. Trans. Yusuf T. DeLorenzo. Alexandria, VA: Al-Saadawi Publications, 1996
Roper, Lyndal. 'Sexual Utopianism in the German Reformation,' *Journal of Ecclesiastical History* 42, no. 3 (1991): 391–418
Rosenfeld, Sophia. *Common Sense: A Political History*. Cambridge, MA: Harvard University Press, 2011
Russell, Alexander. *A Natural History of Aleppo*, 2 vols. London: (no publisher), 1794
Russell, Donald A. and David Constant, trans. *Heraclitus: Homeric Problems*. Atlanta: Society of Biblical Literature, 2005
Russel, D. S. *From Early Judaism to Early Church*. Philadelphia: Fortress Press, 1986
Ryad, Umar. 'The Dismissal of A. J. Wensinck from the Royal Academy of the Arabic Language in Cairo.' In *The Study of Religion and the Training of Muslim Clergy in Europe*, ed. Willem B. Drees and Pieter Sjoerd van Koningsveld, 91–134. Leiden: Leiden University Press, 2008
——. *Islamic Reformism and Christianity*. Leiden: Brill, 2009
Saadia Gaon. *The Book of Beliefs and Opinions*. Trans. Samuel Rosenblatt. New Haven: Yale University Press, 1948
Sadeghi, Behnam. *The Logic of Law Making in Islam: Women in Prayer in the Legal Tradition*. Cambridge: Cambridge University Press, 2013
——. and Mohsen Goudarzi. 'Ṣan'ā' 1 and the Origins of the Qur'ān.' *Der Islam* 87, no. 1 (2012): 1–40
Saller, Richard P. *Patriarchy, Property and Death in the Roman Family*. Cambridge: Cambridge University Press, 1994
Sallust, Gaius Crispus. *Jugurthine War*. Trans. S. A. Handford. New York: Penguin Classics, 1967

Schaff, Philip, ed. *Nicene and Post Nicene Fathers*. Grand Rapids: Wm. B. Eerdmans Publishing, [1886]
Schroeder, John W. *Skillful Means: The Heart of Buddhist Compassion*. Honolulu: University of Hawaii Press, 2001
Semerdjian, Elyse. *Of the Straight Path: Illicit Sex, Law, and Community in Ottoman Aleppo*. Syracuse: Syracuse University Press, 2008
Seng, Yvonne. 'Invisible Women: Residents of early Sixteenth-Century Istanbul.' In *Women in the Medieval Islamic World*, ed. Gavin R. G. Hambly, 241–68. New York: St. Martin's Press, 1998
Shaikh, Sa'diyya. *Sufi Narratives of Intimacy: Ibn 'Arabi, Gender and Sexuality*. Chapel Hill, NC: University of North Carolina Press, 2012
Smalley, Beryl. *Study of the Bible in the Middle Ages*. 3rd edn. Oxford: Basil Blackwell, 1983
Spink, J. S. *French Free-Thought*. London: Athlone Press, 1960
Spinoza, Baruch. *Theological-Political Treatise*. Trans. Michael Silverthorne and Jonathan Israel. Cambridge: Cambridge University Press, 2007
Spitzer, Alan. *Historical Truth and Lies about the Past*. Chapel Hill: University of North Carolina Press, 1996
Saint-Simon, Henri. *Social Organization, The Science of Man and Other Writings*. Ed. Felix Markham. New York: Harper Torchbooks, 1952
Stevens, Laura M. 'Civility and Skepticism in the Woolston-Sherlock Debates over Miracles.' *Eighteenth-Century Life* 21, no. 3 (1997): 57–70.
Sunstein, Cass R. *Legal Reasoning and Political Conflict*. New York: Oxford University Press, 1996
Tartar, Georges, trans. *Dialogue Islamo-Chrétien sous le calife al-Ma'mûn* (813–34). Paris: Nouvelles Éditions Latines, 1985
Thomas, Keith. *Religion and the Decline of Magic*. New York: Oxford University Press, 1971
Thomas, Yan. 'Vitae Necisque Potestas: Le Père, La Cité, La Mort.' *Publications de l'École Française de Rome* (1984): 499–548
Thompson, E. P. *Whigs and Hunters: The Origin of the Black Act*. New York: Pantheon Books, 1975
Thucydides. *The Peloponnesian War*. Trans. John F. Finley. New York: Random House, 1951
Tillier, Mathieu. 'Women before the Qāḍī under the Abbasids.' *Islamic Law and Society* 16 (2009): 280–301
Tucker, Judith. *In the House of the Law: Gender and Islamic Law in Ottoman Syria and Palestine*. Berkeley: University of California Press, 1998
Veyne, Paul. *Comment on écrit l'histoire*. Paris: Éditions du Seuil, 1971
Vico, Giambattista. *On the Study Methods of Our Time*. Trans. Elio Gianturco. New York: Bobbs-Merrill, 1965
Virgil. *Eclogues, Georgics, Aeneid 1–6*. Trans. H. R. Fairclough. Cambridge, MA: Harvard University Press, 1994
Voltaire. *Dictionnaire Philosophique*. Paris: Boudouin Frères, 1829
——. *Essai sur les moeurs*. Paris: Éditions Garnier Frères, 1963
——. *Le Siècle de Louis XIV*. Ed. Jacqueline Hellegouarch and Sylvain Menant. Paris: Le Livre de Poche, 2005
——. *Oeuvres Complètes*. Paris: Garnier Frères, 1879
Wadud, Amina. *Inside the Gender Jihad*. Oxford: Oneworld Publications, 2006
——. *Qur'an and Woman*. Oxford: Oxford University Press, 1999

Weismann, Itzchak. *The Naqshbandiyya*. London: Routledge, 2007

Wilbur, Earl Morse. *A History of Unitarianism*. Cambridge, MA: Harvard University Press, 1947

Williams, Patrick and Laura Chrisman, ed. *Colonial Discourse and Post-Colonial Theory*. New York: Columbia University Press, 1994

Woolston, Thomas. *Third Discourse on Miracles of our Savior (A third discourse on the miracles of our Saviour, in view of the present controversy between infidels and apostates)*. 4th edn. London: [no publisher], 1729

Würth, Anna. 'Stalled Reform: Family Law in Post-Unification Yemen.' *Islamic Law and Society* 10, no. 1 (2003): 12–33

Yazbak, Mahmoud. 'Minor Marriages and *khiyar al-bulugh* in Ottoman Palestine: a Note on Women's Strategies in a Patriarchal Society.' *Islamic Law and Society* 9, no. 3 (2002): 386–409

Yount, Kathryn M. 'Resources, Family Organization, and Domestic Violence against Married Women in Minya, Egypt.' *Journal of Marriage and Family* 67, no. 3 (2005): 579–96

Yuksel, Edip; al-Shaiban, Layth Saleh and Martha Schulte-Nafeh. *Quran: A Reformist Translation*. [No place]: Brainbow Press, 2011

Zaman, Muhammad Qasim. 'Studying Hadith in a Madrasa in the Early Twentieth Century.' In *Islam in South Asia in Practice*, ed. Barbara Metcalf, 225–39. Princeton: Princeton University Press, 2009

Zarinebaf-Shahr, Fariba. 'Women in the Public Eye in Eighteenth-Century Istanbul.' In *Women in the Medieval Islamic World*, ed. Gavin R. G. Hambly, 301–24. New York: St. Martin's Press, 1998

Zecevic, Selma. 'Missing Husbands, Waiting Wives, Bosnian *Muftis*: *Fatwa* Texts and the Interpretation of Gendered Presences and Absences in Late Ottoman Bosnia.' In *Women in the Ottoman Balkans*, ed. Amila Buturovic and Irvin Cemil Schick. New York: I. B. Tauris, 2007

Ziadeh, Farhat. *Lawyers, the Rule of Law and Liberalism in Modern Egypt*. Stanford, CA: Hoover Institution, 1968

ARABIC AND PERSIAN-LANGUAGE SOURCES

'Abduh, Muḥammad. *Al-A'māl al-kāmila li'l-imām al-shaykh Muḥammad 'Abduh*. Ed. Muḥammad 'Amāra, 6 vols. Cairo: Dār al-Shurūq, 1993

Al-Ābī, Ṣāliḥ 'Abd al-Salām. *Al-Thamar al-dānī fī taqrīb al-ma'ānī Ḥāshiyat Risālat Ibn Abī Zayd al-Qayrawānī*. 2nd edn. Cairo: Muṣṭafā al-Bābī al-Ḥalabī, 1944

Abū Rayya, Maḥmūd. *Aḍwā' 'alā al-sunna al-muḥammadiyya*. Cairo: Dār al-Ta'līf, 1958

Abū Sulaymān, 'Abd al-Ḥamīd. *Ḍarb al-mar'a wasīla li-ḥall al-khilāfāt al-zawjiyya*. Cairo: Dār al-Salām, 2003 (original printing, 2001)

Abū Zahra, Muḥammad. *Fatāwā*. Ed. Muḥammad 'Uthmān Shabīr. Damascus: Dār al-Qalam, 2006

Abū Zayd, Nāṣir Ḥāmid. *Naqd al-khiṭāb al-dīnī*. Cairo: Sīnā, 1996

Abū Zur'a al-Dimashqī. *Tārīkh Abī Zur'a al-Dimashqī*. Ed. Khalīl al-Manṣūr. Beirut: Dār al-Kutub al-'Ilmiyya, 1996

Al-Ahdal, 'Abd al-Raḥmān b. Sulaymān. *Al-Nafas al-Yamānī*. Sana: Markaz al-Dirāsāt wa'l-Abḥāth al-Islāmiyya, 1979

Al-'Ajlūnī, Ismā'īl b. Muḥammad. *Kashf al-khafā 'ammā ishtahara min al-aḥādīth 'alā alsinat al-nās*. Ed. Aḥmad al-Qalāsh, 2 vols. Cairo: Maktabat Dār al-Turāth, 1997

Al-Ājurrī, Abū Bakr. *Ṣifat al-ghurabā' min al-mu'minīn*. Ed. Badr 'Abdallāh al-Badr. Kuwait: Dār al-Khulafā', 1983

Al-Albānī, Muḥammad Nāṣir al-Dīn. *Ḍa'īf Sunan Ibn Mājah*. Riyadh: Maktabat al-Ma'ārif, 1997

——. *Fatāwā al-Shaykh al-Albānī*. Ed. 'Ukāsha 'Abd al-Mannān al-Ṭayyibī. Cairo: Maktabat al-Turāth al-Islāmī, 1994

——. *Irwā' al-ghalīl takhrīj aḥādīth Manār al-sabīl*. Ed. Muḥammad Zahīr al-Shāwīsh. Beirut: Al-Maktab al-Islāmī, 1979

——. *Mukhtaṣar Ṣaḥīḥ al-Bukhārī*, 4 vols. Riyadh: Maktabat al-Ma'ārif, 2002

——. *Ṣaḥīḥ Sunan Abī Dāwūd*, 7 vols. Kuwait: Mu'assasat Gharās, 2002

——. *Silsilat al-aḥādīth al-ḍa'īfa wa'l-mawḍū'a*. 2nd edn, 14 vols. Riyadh: Maktabat al-Ma'ārif, 2000–2005

——. *Silsilat al-aḥādīth al-ṣaḥīḥa*, 7 vols. Riyadh: Maktabat al-Ma'ārif, 1995–2002

Al-'Aqqād, 'Abbās Maḥmūd. *Al-Ṣiddīqa bint al-Ṣiddīq*. 3rd edn. Cairo: Dār al-Ma'ārif, [1966]

Al-'Aqqād, 'Āmir. *Lamaḥāt min ḥayāt al-'Aqqād*. 2nd edn. Cairo: Dār al-Sha'b, 1970

Al-Ash'arī, Abū al-Ḥasan. *Al-Ibāna 'an uṣūl al-diyāna*. Ed. Fawqiyya Ḥusayn Maḥmūd. Cairo: Dār al-Anṣār, 1977

Al-'Askarī, Abū Hilāl. *Kitāb al-Awā'il*. Ed. Walīd Qaṣṣāb and Muḥammad al-Miṣrī, 2 vols. [Cairo]: Dār al 'Ulūm, 1981

Al-'Awda, Salmān. *Ḍawābiṭ li'l-dirāsāt al-fiqhiyya*. Riyadh: Maktabat al-Rushd, 2004. This book was originally written in 1983

Al-'Aynī, Badr al-Dīn, and Muḥammad 'Umar Nāṣir al-Islām al-Rāmpūrī. *Al-Bināya sharḥ al-Hidāya*. 2nd edn, 12 vols. Beirut: Dār al-Fikr, 1990

——. *Sharḥ Sunan Abī Dāwūd*. Ed. Khālid Ibrāhīm al-Miṣrī, 7 vols. Riyadh: Maktabat al-Rushd, 1999

Al-Baghdādī, al-Khaṭīb Abū Bakr. *Tārīkh Baghdād*. Ed. Muṣṭafā 'Abd al-Qādir 'Aṭā, 14 vols. Beirut: Dār al-Kutub al-'Ilmiyya, 1997

Al-Ba'lī, 'Abd al-Raḥmān. *Kashf al-mukhaddarāt*. Ed. Muḥammad Nāṣir al-'Ajmī. Beirut: Dār al-Bashā'ir al-Islāmiyya, 2002

Al-Baṭṭār, Khadīja. *Fī naqd al-Bukhārī kāna baynahu wa bayn al-ḥaqq ḥijāb*. [Casablanca]: Manshūrāt al-Aḥdāth al-Maghribiyya, 2003

Al-Bayhaqī, Abū Bakr Aḥmad. *Kitāb al-Ba'th wa'l-nushūr*. Ed. 'Āmir Aḥmad Ḥaydar. Beirut: Markaz al-Khadamāt wa'l-Abḥāth al-Thaqāfiyya, 1987

——. *Al-Sunan al-kubrā*. Ed. Muḥammad 'Abd al-Qādir 'Aṭā, 11 vols. Beirut: Dār al-Kutub al-'Ilmiyya, 1999

Al-Bayjūrī, Burhān al-Dīn Ibrāhīm. *Ḥāshiyat al-imām al-Bayjūrī 'alā Jawharat al-tawḥīd*. Ed. 'Alī Jum'a. Cairo: Dār al-Salām, 2006

Al-Bāz, Muḥammad. *Du'āt fi'l- manfā*. Cairo: Fāris, 2004

Al-Bazzār, Abū Bakr. *Musnad al-Bazzār*. Ed. Maḥfūẓ al-Raḥmān al-Salafī, 10 vols. Beirut, Medina: Mu'assasat 'Ulūm al-Qur'ān, 1989

Bin Bāz, 'Abd al-'Azīz and Muḥammad Ibn 'Uthaymīn. *Fatāwā al-'ulamā' li'l-nisā'*. Cairo: Maktabat al-Sunna, 1995

Al-Bīrūnī, Abū al-Rayḥān. *Taḥqīq mā li'l-Hind min maqūla maqbūla fi'l-'aql aw mardhūla*. Hyderabad: Dā'irat al-Ma'ārif al-'Uthmāniyya, 1958

Al-Buhūtī, Manṣūr b. Yūnus. *Al-Rawḍ al-murbi'*. Ed. Bashīr Muḥammad 'Uyūn. Damascus: Maktabat Dār al-Bayān, 1999

Burhāmī, Yāsir. *Faḍl al-ghanī al-ḥamīd ta'līqāt hāmma 'alā Kitāb al-Tawḥīd*. Alexandria: Dār al-Khulafā' al-Rāshidīn, 2009

Al-Dāraquṭnī, 'Alī b. 'Umar. *Al-'Ilal al-wārida fī al-aḥādīth al-nabawiyya*. Ed. Maḥfūẓ al-Raḥmān al-Salafī, 11 vols. Riyadh: Dār Ṭība, 1985

——. *Sunan*. Ed. 'Abdallāh Hāshim Yamānī, 4 vols in 2. Beirut: Dār al-Ma'rifa, 1966

Al-Dārimī, 'Abdallāh b. 'Abd al-Raḥmān. *Sunan*. Ed. Fawāz Aḥmad Zamarlī and Khālid al-'Alamī, 2 vols. Beirut: Dār al-Kitāb al-'Arabī, 1987

Al-Daylamī, Shīruwayh b. Shahrudār. *Firdaws al-akhbār*. Ed. Sa'īd Basyūnī Zaghlūl, 6 vols. Beirut: Dār al-Kutub al-'Ilmiyya, 1986

Al-Dhahabī, Shams al-Dīn. *Bayān raghal al-'ilm wa'l-ṭalab*. Ed. Muḥammad Zāhid al-Kawtharī. Cairo: al-Maktaba al-Azhariyya [no date]

——. *Mīzān al-i'tidāl fī naqd al-rijāl*. Ed. 'Alī Muḥammad al-Bijāwī, 4 vols. Beirut: Dār al-Ma'rifa [no date], reprint of 1963–64 Cairo 'Īsā al-Bābī al-Ḥalabī edn

——. *Al-Mughnī fī al-ḍu'afā'*. Ed. Ḥāzim al-Qāḍī, 2 vols. Beirut: Dār al-Kutub al-'Ilmiyya, 1997

——. *Siyar a'lām al-nubalā'*. Ed. Shu'ayb al-Arnā'ūṭ, et al., 25 vols. Beirut: Mu'assasat al-Risāla, 1992–98

Al-Dimashqī, Muḥammad b. 'Alī al-'Umarī. *Al Naẓm al-mufīd al-aḥmad fī mufradāt madhhab al-imam Aḥmad*. Ed. Fayṣal Yūsuf al-'Alī. Beirut: Dār al-Bashā'ir al-Islāmiyya, 2006

Al-Fādānī, Yāsīn. *Al-'Ujāla fī al-aḥādīth al-musalsala*. 2nd edn. Damascus: Dār al-Baṣā'ir, 1985

Al-Ghazālī, Ḥujjat al-Islām Abū Ḥāmid. *Iḥyā' 'ulūm al-dīn*. Ed. Muḥammad Wahbī Sulaymān and Usāma 'Ammūra, 5 vols. Damascus: Dār al-Fikr, 2006

——. *Mi'yār al-'ilm*. Cairo: al-Maṭba'a al-Munīriyya [no date]

Al-Ghazālī, Muḥammad. *Al-Sunna al-nabawiyya bayn ahl al-fiqh wa ahl al-ḥadīth*. 11th edn. Cairo: Dār al-Shurūq, 1998

——. *Turāthunā al-fikrī*. 8th edn. Cairo: Dār al-Shurūq, 2003

——. *Qaḍāyā al-mar'a*. 5th edn. Cairo: Dār al-Shurūq, 1994

Al-Ghazzī, Najm al-Dīn. *Al-Kawākib al-sā'ira bi-a'yān al-mi'a al-'āshira*. Ed. Jibrā'īl Jabbūr, 3 vols. Beirut: Dār al-Āfāq al-Jadīda, 1979

Al-Ghumārī, Aḥmad bin al-Ṣiddīq. *Al-Baḥr al-'amīq fī marwiyāt Ibn al-Ṣiddīq*, 2 vols. Cairo: Dār al-Kutubī, 2007

——. *Burhān al-jalī fī taḥqīq intisāb al-ṣūfiyya ilā 'Alī*. Ed. Aḥmad Mursī. Cairo: Maktabat al-Qāhira [no date]

——. *Masālik al-dilāla 'alā masā'il matn al-Risāla*. 3rd edn. Cairo: Maktabat al-Qāhira, 1995

——. *Al-Mudāwī li-'ilal al-Jāmi' al-ṣaghīr wa sharḥay al-Munāwī*, 6 vols. Cairo: Dār al-Kutub, 1996

——. *Silsilat al-sāda al-Ghumāriyya*. Ed. Muḥammad 'Alī Yūsuf. Cairo: Maktabat al-Qāhira [no date]

Gomaa, Ali. *Al-Bayān li-mā yashghalu al-adhhān*. Cairo: al-Muqaṭṭam, 2005

——. *Fatāwā al-nisā'*. Cairo: Al-Muqaṭṭam, 2010

——. *Al-Ijmā' 'ind al-uṣūliyyīn*. Cairo: Dār al-Risāla, 2002

——. *Al-Ṭarīq ilā al-turāth al-islāmī*. 4th edn. Cairo: Nahḍat Miṣr, 2009

Al-Ḥākim Muḥammad b. 'Abdallāh al-Naysābūrī. *Al-Mustadrak 'alā al-Ṣaḥīḥayn*. Hyderabad: Dā'irat al-Ma'ārif al-'Uthmāniyya

Al-Hamadhānī, Abū Naṣr Muḥammad b. 'Abd al-Raḥmān. *Al-Sab'iyyāt fī mawā'iẓ al-barriyyāt*. MS 1378, King Saud University, Riyadh

Ḥusayn, Muḥammad Khiḍr. *Al-Sa'āda al-'uẓmā*. Ed. 'Alī al-Riḍā al-Tūnsī, 1973

Al-Haytamī, Aḥmad Ibn Ḥajar. *Al-Fatāwā al-ḥadīthiyya*. Ed. Muḥammad 'Abd al-Raḥmān al-Mar'ashlī. Beirut: Dār Iḥyā' al-Turāth al-'Arabī, 1998

Al-Ḥujaylī, Muḥammad Bakhīt. *Ajwibat Ibn al-Qayyim 'an al-aḥādīth allatī ẓāhiruhā al-ta'āruḍ*, 2 vols. Riyadh: Sunan, 2011

Ibn 'Abd al-Barr, Abū 'Umar Yūsuf. *Jāmi' bayān al-'ilm wa faḍlihi*, 2 vols. Cairo: Dār al-Ṭibā'a al-Munīriyya [no date]

——. *Kitāb al-Tamhīd li-mā fī al-Muwaṭṭa' min al-ma'ānī wa'l-asānīd*. Ed. Muṣṭafā Aḥmad al-'Alawī and Muḥammad 'Abd al-Kabīr al-Bakrī, 2nd edn, 26 vols. Rabat: Wizārat 'Umūm al-Awqāf wa al-Shu'ūn al-Islāmiyya, 1982-.

Ibn 'Abd al-Wahhāb, Sulaymān. *Al-Ṣawā'iq al-ilāhiyya fī al-radd 'alā al-Wahhābiyya* [no place, publisher or date]

Ibn Abī al-Dunyā. *Kitāb al-Ghība*. Ed. 'Amr 'Alī 'Umar. Bombay: al-Dār al-Salafiyya, 1989

——. *Kitāb al-ṣamt wa ādāb al-lisān*. Ed. Najm 'Abd al-Raḥmān Khalaf. Beirut: Dār al-Gharb al-Islāmī, 1986

Ibn Abī al-Wafā' al-Qurashī. *Al-Jawāhir al-muḍiyya fī ṭabaqāt al-ḥanafiyya*. Ed. 'Abd al-Fattāḥ Muḥammad al-Ḥalw, 5 vols. Giza: Mu'assasat al-Risāla, 1978–88

Ibn 'Ābidīn, Muḥammad Amīn. *Ḥāshiyat Radd al-muḥtār*, 8 vols. Beirut: Dār al-Fikr, 1992. A reprint of the 1966 Cairo Muṣṭafā al-Bābī al-Ḥalabī edn

Ibn 'Adī, Abū Aḥmad 'Abdallāh. *Al-Kāmil fī ḍu'afā' al-rijāl*, 7 vols. Beirut: Dār al-Fikr, 1985

Ibn Amīr al-Ḥajj, Muḥammad. *Al-Taqrīr wa'l-taḥbīr*, 3 vols. Beirut: Dār al-Fikr, 1996

Ibn al-'Arabī, Abū Bakr. *Aḥkam al-Qur'ān*. Ed. Muḥammad 'Abd al-Qādir 'Aṭā, 4 vols. Beirut: Dar al-Fikr, 2008

Ibn 'Arabī, Muḥyī al-Dīn. *Al-Futūḥāt al-makkiyya*. Ed. 'Uthmān Yaḥyā and Ibrāhīm Madkūr, 14 vols. Cairo: al-Hay'a al-Miṣriyya al-'Āmma, 1972–92

Ibn 'Āshūr, Muḥammad Ṭāhir. *Maqālāt*. Ed. 'Alī Riḍā Ḥusaynī. Tunis: [no publisher], 2001

——. *Al-Taḥrīr wa'l-Tanwīr*, 17 vols. Tunis: al-Dār al-Tūnisiyya, 1984

Ibn Ḍuwayyān, Ibrāhīm b. Muḥammad. *Manār al-sabīl fī sharḥ al-Dalīl*. Ed. Zuhayr Shāwīsh. 7th edn, 2 vols. Damascus: al-Maktab al-Islāmī, 1989

Ibn al-Faras, 'Abd al-Mun'im b. 'Abd al-Raḥīm. *Aḥkām al-Qur'ān*. Ed. Ṭāhā 'Alī Būsarīḥ, 3 vols. Beirut: Dār Ibn Ḥazm, 2006

Ibn Ḥajar al-'Asqalānī, Aḥmad. *Bulūgh al-marām*. Ed. Ṭāriq 'Awaḍ Allāh. Beirut: Dār Ibn Ḥazm, 2008

——. *Fatḥ al-Bārī sharḥ Ṣaḥīḥ al-Bukhārī*. Ed. 'Abd al-'Azīz b. 'Abdallāh b. Bāz and Muḥammad Fu'ād 'Abd al-Bāqī, 16 vols. Beirut: Dār al-Kutub al-'Ilmiyya, 1997

——. *Al-Dirāya takhrīj aḥādīth al-Hidāya*. Ed. 'Abdallāh Hāshim al-Yamānī. Beirut: Dār al-Ma'rifa [no date]

——. *Al-Durar al-kāmina fī a'yān al-mi'a al-thāmina*, 4 vols. Beirut: Dār al-Jīl, 1993

——. *Lisān al-mīzān*, 7 vols. Beirut: Dār al-Fikr [no date]

——. *Tahdhīb al-tahdhīb*. Ed. Muṣṭafā 'Abd al-Qādir 'Aṭā, 12 vols. Beirut: Dār al-Kutub al-'Ilmiyya, 1994

——. *Talkhīṣ al-ḥabīr fī takhrīj aḥādīth al-Rāfi'ī al-kabīr*, 4 vols. Ed. Abū 'Āṣim Ḥasan 'Abbās. Cairo: Mu'assasat Qurṭuba, 1995

Ibn al-Ḥājj, Muḥammad al-Mālikī. *Al-Madkhal*, 4 vols. Beirut: Dār al-Fikr, [1990]

Ibn Hishām, 'Abd al-Malik. *Al-Sīra al-nabawiyya*. Ed. Jamāl Thābit and Muḥammad Maḥmūd, 5 vols. Cairo: Dār al-Ḥadīth, 1998

Ibn al-Jawzī, 'Abd al-Raḥmān. *Aḥkām al-nisā'*. Cairo: Dār al-Hady al-Muḥammadī, 1985

——. *Kitāb al-Mawḍū'āt*. Ed. 'Abd al-Raḥmān Muḥammad 'Uthmān, 3 vols. Medina: al-Maktaba al-Salafiyya, 1966–68

——. *Kitāb al-Quṣṣāṣ wa'l-mudhakkirīn*. Ed. Merlin Swartz. Beirut: Dar El-Machreq, 1986

——. *Al-Muntaẓam fī tārīkh al-mulūk wa'l-umam*. Ed. Muḥammad 'Abd al-Qādir 'Aṭā and Muṣṭafā 'Abd al-Qādir 'Aṭā, 18 vols in 16. Beirut: Dār al-Kutub al-'Ilmiyya, 1992

Ibn Kathīr, Ismāʻīl. *Al-Bidāya wa'l-Nihāya*, 14 vols. Beirut: Maktabat al-Maʻārif, 1966
——. *The Life of the Prophet Muhammad*. Trans. Trevor Le Gassick. Reading, UK: Garnett, 1998
Ibn Miskawayh, Aḥmad b. Muḥammad. *Tahdhīb al-akhlāq*. Ed. Qusṭanṭīn Zurayq. Beirut: American University in Beirut, 1966
Ibn Mufliḥ al-Maqdisī. *Al-Ādāb al-sharʻiyya*. Ed. Shuʻayb al-Arnā'ūṭ, et al., 3 vols. Beirut: Mu'assasat al-Risāla, 1996
Ibn al-Mulaqqin, ʻUmar b. ʻAlī. *Al-Badr al-munīr fī takhrīj al-aḥādīth wa'l-āthār al-wāqiʻa fī al-Sharḥ al-kabīr*. Ed. Muṣṭafā Abū al-Ghayṭ, et al., 10 vols. Riyadh: Dār al-Hijra, 2004
Ibn al-Mundhir, Muḥammad b. Ibrāhīm. *Al-Ishrāf ʻalā madhāhib al-fuqahā'*. Ed. Abū Ḥammād Saghīr Aḥmad al-Anṣārī, 10 vols. Mecca: Maktabat Makka al-Thaqāfiyya, 2004
Ibn Nadīm, Abū al-Faraj Muḥammad. *The Fihrist*. Ed. and trans. Bayard Dodge. Chicago: Kazi Publications, 1998. Reprint of the 1970 Columbia University Press edn
Ibn Nāṣir al-Dīn al-Dimashqī. *Al-Tarjīḥ li-ḥadīth ṣalāt al-tasbīḥ*. Ed. Maḥmūd Mamdūḥ. Beirut: Dār al-Bashā'ir, 1985
Ibn Nujaym al-Ḥanafī. *Al-Ashbāh wa'l-naẓā'ir*. Ed. Muḥammad Muṭīʻ al-Ḥāfiẓ. Damascus: Dār al-Fikr, 1986
Ibn Qayyim al-Jawziyya. *Iʻlām al-muwaqqiʻīn ʻan rabb al-ʻālamīn*. Ed. Muḥammad ʻIzz al-Dīn Khaṭṭāb, 5 vols. Beirut: Dār Iḥyā' al-Turāth al-ʻArabī, 2001
——. *Kitāb al-Rūḥ*. Ed. ʻĀrif al-Ḥājj. Beirut: Dār Iḥyā' al-ʻUlūm, 1988
——. *Al-Manār al-munīf fī al-ṣaḥīḥ wa'l-ḍaʻīf*. Ed. ʻAbd al-Fattāḥ Abū Ghudda, 12th edn. Beirut: Maktab al-Maṭbūʻāt al-Islāmiyya, 2004
——. *Zād al-miʻād*. Ed. Shuʻayb and ʻAbd al-Qādir al-Arnā'ūṭ. Beirut: Mu'assasat al-Risāla, 1986
Ibn Qudāma, Muwaffaq al-Dīn. ʻDhamm al-ta'wīl.' In *Rasā'il dīniyya salafiyya*, ed. Zakariyyā ʻAlī Yūsuf, 64–91. Cairo: Maṭbaʻat al-Imām [no date]
——. *Al-Mughnī*. Ed. ʻAbdallāh al-Turkī and ʻAbd al-Fattāḥ al-Ḥalw, 12 vols. Cairo: Hujr, 1986
——. *Taḥrīm al-naẓar fī kutub ahl al-kalām*. Ed. George Makdisi. London: Luzac, 1962
Ibn Qudāma, Najm al-Dīn Abū al-ʻAbbās Aḥmad. *Mukhtaṣar Minhāj al-qāṣidīn*. Ed. Muḥammad Aḥmad Dahmān, Shuʻayb al-Arnā'ūṭ and ʻAbd al-Qādir al-Arnā'ūṭ. Damascus: Maktabat Dār al-Bayān, 1978
Ibn Qutayba, ʻAbdallāh al-Dīnawarī. *Ta'wīl mukhtalif al-ḥadīth*. Ed. Muḥammad Zuhrī al-Najjār. Beirut: Dār al-Jīl, 1973
Ibn al-Ṣalāḥ, Abū ʻAmr. *Muqaddima*. Ed. ʻĀ'isha ʻAbd al-Raḥmān. Cairo: Dār al-Maʻārif, 1989
Ibn Salāma, Abū al-Qāsim Hibat Allāh. *Al-Nāsikh wa'l-mansūkh*. 2nd edn. Cairo: Muṣṭafā al-Bābī al-Ḥalabī, 1967
Ibn Sayyid al-Nās, Muḥammad. *ʻUyūn al-athar fī funūn al-maghāzī wa'l-shamā'il wa'l-siyar*, 2 vols. Dār al-Āfāq al-Jadīda, 1977
Ibn Sīnā. *Kitāb al-Shifā': Ilāhiyyāt*. Ed. Ibrāhīm Madkūr. Cairo, 1960
Ibn Taymiyya, Taqī al-Dīn Aḥmad. *Al-Fatwā al-Ḥamawiyya*. Ed. Muḥammad Riyāḍ al-Atharī. Beirut: ʻĀlam al-Kutub, 2005
——. *Majmūʻat al-fatāwā*. Ed. Sayyid Ḥusayn al-ʻAffānī and Khayrī Saʻīd, 35 vols. Cairo: al-Maktaba al-Tawfīqiyya [no date]
Ibn ʻUthaymīn, Muḥammad Ṣāliḥ. *Kitāb al-ʻIlm*. Ed. Fahd bin Nāṣir al-Sulaymān. Riyadh: Dār al-Thurayyā, 2002
——. *Al-Sharḥ al-mumtiʻ ʻalā Zād al-mustaqniʻ*. Riyadh: Dār Ibn al-Jawzī, 2002

Ibn Wad'ān, Muḥammad b. 'Alī al-Mawṣilī. *Al-Arba'ūn al-wad'āniyya al-mawḍū'a*. Ed. 'Alī Ḥasan 'Abd al-Ḥamīd. Beirut: al-Maktab al-Islāmī, 1986

Al-Jāwī, Muḥammad Nawawī b. 'Umar. *Qūt al-ḥabīb al-gharīb*. Cairo: Maṭba'at Muṣṭafā al-Bābī al-Ḥalabī, 1938

Al-Juwaynī, Imām al-Ḥaramayn 'Abd al-Malik. *Al-Burhān fī uṣūl al-fiqh*. Ed. 'Abd al-'Aẓīm Maḥmūd al-Dīb, 3 vols. Mansoura: Dār al-Wafā', 1998

——. *Al-Kāfiya fi al-jadal*. Ed. Fawziya Ḥusayn Maḥmūd. Cairo: Dar Iḥyā' al-Kutub al-'Arabiyya, 1979

——. *Al-Waraqāt bi-sharḥ al-imām Jalāl al-Dīn al-Maḥallī*. Ed. 'Abd al-Salām 'Abd al-Hādī Shannār and Riyāḍ Khaṭṭāb. Damascus: Dār al-Farfūr, 2002

Kāndhlawī, Muḥammad Zakariyyā. *Awjaz al-masālik ilā Muwaṭṭa' Mālik*. Ed. Taqī al-Dīn al-Nadwī, 29 vols. Damascus: Dār al-Qalam, 2003

Al-Kāsānī, 'Alā' al-Dīn. *Badā'i' al-ṣanā'i'*. 2nd edn, 7 vols. Beirut: Dār al-Kutub al-'Ilmiyya, 1982

Al-Kāshānī, Mawlā Muḥsin Fayḍ. *Tafsīr al-ṣāfī*. Ed. Ḥusayn al-A'lamī, 3 vols. Beirut: Mu'assasat al-A'lamī, 1979

Al-Kawākibī, 'Abd al-Raḥmān. *Al-A'māl al-kāmila*. Ed. Muḥammad 'Amāra. 2nd edn. Cairo: Dār al-Shurūq, 2009

Al-Khafājī Aḥmad Shihāb al-Dīn and Mullā 'Alī al-Qāri'. *Nasīm al-riyāḍ sharḥ Shifā' al-Qāḍī 'Iyaḍ*, 4 vols. Beirut: Dār al-Kitāb al-'Arabī [no date]

Kevseri, Mehemmet Zahit. *Maqālāt al-Kawtharī*. Cairo: Dār al-Salām, 2007

Al-Khaṭṭābī, Abū Sulaymān Ḥamd. *Ma'ālim al-sunan*. 3rd edn, 4 vols. Beirut: al-Maktaba al-'Ilmiyya, 1981

Khomeini, Ayatollah Ruhollah. *Hadīth-i velāyat*. Tehran: Markaz-i Chāp va Nashr-i Sāzamān-i Tablīghāt-i Islāmī, 1999

Al-Khwārazmī, Muḥammad b. Maḥmūd. *Jāmi' masānīd al-imām al-a'ẓam*. Ed. Abū Bakr Muḥammad al-Hāshimī. 2nd edn, 3 vols. Hyderabad: Dā'irat al-Ma'ārif al-'Uthmāniyya, 2008

Al-Laknawī, 'Abd al-Ḥayy. *Majmū'at rasā'il 'Abd al-Ḥayy al-Laknawī*, ed. Nu'aym Ashraf Aḥmad, Karachi: Idārat al-Qur'ān wa'l-'ulūm al-Islāmiyya, [1998]

——. *Ṭarab al-amāthil bi-tarājim al-afāḍil*. Karachi: Qadīmī Kutubkhāne [no date]

Maḥmūd, 'Abd al-Ḥalīm. *Fatāwā*, 2 vols. Cairo: Dār al-Shurūq, 2002

Al-Makkī, Abū Ṭālib. *Qūt al-qulūb*. Cairo: Maṭba'at al-Anwār al-Muḥammadiyya, [1985]

Al-Maqdisī, Abū Shāma. *Al-Bā'ith 'alā inkār al-bida'*. Ed. 'Uthmān Aḥmad 'Anbar. Cairo: Dār al-Hudā, 1978

Al-Marwazī, Muḥammad b. Naṣr. *Ikhtilāf al-fuqahā'*. Ed. Muḥammad Ṭāhir al-Ḥakīm. Riyadh: Aḍwā' al-Salaf, 2000

Al-Miswarī, Aḥmad b. Sa'd al-Dīn. *Al-Risāla al-munqidha min al-ghiwāya fī ṭuruq al-riwāya*. Ed. Ḥamūd al-Ahnūmī. Sanaa: Maktabat Badr, 1997

Al-Munāwī, Shams al-Dīn 'Abd al-Ra'ūf. *Fayḍ al-qadīr sharḥ al-Jāmi' al-ṣaghīr*. Ed. Ḥamdī al-Damardāsh Muḥammad, 13 vols. Mecca: Maktabat Nizār Muṣṭafā al-Bāz, 1998

Al-Mundhirī, 'Abd al-'Aẓīm. *Al-Targhīb wa'l-tarhīb*. Ed. Mashhūr Ḥasan Āl Salmān, 4 vols. Riyadh: Maktabat al-Ma'ārif, 2004

Al-Mūsawī, 'Abd al-Ḥusayn Sharaf al-Dīn. *Al-Murāja'āt*. 5th edn. Tehran: Dār al-Usra, 2008

Al-Muṭī'ī, Muḥammad Bakhīt. *Majmū'at rasā'il al-'allāma Muḥammad Bakhīt al-Muṭī'ī*. 2nd edn. Cairo: Maktabat al-Qāhira, 1932

Al-Nabhānī, Yūsuf. *Jāmi' karāmāt al-awliyā'*. Ed. 'Abd al-Wārith Muḥammad 'Alī. 2nd edn, 2 vols. Beirut: Dār al-Kutub al-'Ilmiyya, 2002

Al-Nābulsī, ʻAbd al-Ghanī. *Al-Ḥadīqa al-nadiyya sharḥ al-Ṭarīqa al-muḥammadiyya*, 2 vols. [India]: Dār al-Ḥadīqa, [1860]
——. *Risāla fī ibāḥat al-dukhān*. Damascus: Maṭbaʻat al-Iṣlāḥ, 1924
Al-Nawawī, Muḥyī al-Dīn Zakariyyā. *Minhāj al-ṭālibīn*. Ed. Muḥammad Ṭāhir Shaʻbān. Jeddah: Dār al-Minhāj, 2000
——. *Sharḥ Ṣaḥīḥ Muslim*, 15 vols. Beirut: Dār al-Qalam, 1987
Al-Qāḍī ʻIyāḍ b. Mūsā. *Ikmāl al-muʻlim bi-fawāʼid Muslim*. Ed. Yaḥyā Ismāʻīl, 9 vols. Mansoura: Dār al-Wafāʼ, 1998
——. *Kitāb al-Shifā bi-taʻrīf ḥuqūq al-muṣṭafā*. Beirut: Dār Ibn Ḥazm, 2000
Al-Qāriʼ, Mullā ʻAlī. *Mirqāt al-mafātīḥ*. Ed. Jamāl Ayṭānī. Beirut: Dār al-Kutub al-ʻIlmiyya, 2001
——. *Sharḥ Sharḥ Nukhbat al-fikar*. [No place]: al-Maktaba al-Islāmiyya, 1972
Al-Qaraḍāwī, Yūsuf. *Al-Fatāwā al-shādhdha*. Cairo: Dār al-Shurūq, 2010
——. *Al-Ḥurriyya al-dīniyya wa'l-taʻaddudiyya fī naẓar al-islām*. Beirut: al-Maktab al-Islāmī, 2007
——. *Al-Shaykh al-Ghazālī kamā ʻaraftuhu*. Cairo: Dār al-Shurūq, 2000
Al-Qudūrī, Aḥmad b. Muḥammad. *The Mukhtaṣar*. Trans. Ṭāhir Maḥmood Kiānī. London: Ta-Ha Publishers, 2010
Al-Qummī, ʻAlī b. Ibrāhīm. *Tafsīr al-Qummī*. Ed. Sayyid Ṭayyib al-Mūsawī al-Jazāʼirī, 2 vols. [Beirut]: Maṭbaʻat Najaf, 2009
Al-Qurṭubī, Muḥammad b. Aḥmad. *Al-Jāmiʻ li-aḥkām al-Qurʼān*. Ed. Muḥammad Ibrāhīm al-Ḥifnāwī and Maḥmūd Ḥāmid ʻUthmān, 20 vols in 10. Cairo: Dār al-Ḥadīth, 1994
Al-Rāfiʻī, ʻAbd al-Karīm b. Muḥammad. *Al-Tadwīn fī akhbār Qazwīn*. Ed. ʻAzīz Allāh al-ʻUṭāridī, 4 vols. Beirut: Dār al-Kutub al-ʻIlmiyya, 1987
Al-Ramlī, Shihāb al-Dīn Aḥmad b. Ḥamza. *Ghāyat al-maʼmūl fī sharḥ Waraqāt al-uṣūl*. Cairo: Muʼassasat Qurṭuba, 2005
Riḍā, Rashīd and Muḥammad ʻAbduh. *Tafsīr al-Manār*. 2nd edn, 10 vols. Beirut: Dar al-Maʻrifa, [1970]
Al-Riḍawī, Murtaḍā. *Maʻa rijāl al-fikr fī al-Qāhira*. Cairo: Maṭbaʻat Ḥassān, 1974
Al-Sakhāwī, Shams al-Dīn ʻAbd al-Raḥmān. *Al-Maqāṣid al-ḥasana*. Ed. Muḥammad ʻUthmān al-Khisht. Beirut: Dār al-Kitāb al-ʻArabī, 2004
——. *Al-Qawl al-badīʻ fī al-ṣalāt ʻalā al-ḥabīb al-shafīʻ*. Giza: Dār al-Rayyān [no date]
——. *Takhrīj al-Arbaʻīn al-Sulamiyya*. Ed. ʻAlī Ḥasan ʻAbd al-Ḥamīd. Beirut: al-Maktab al-Islāmī, 1988
Al-Ṣanʻānī, Muḥammad Ibn al-Amīr. *Subul al-salām sharḥ Bulūgh al-marām*. Ed. Muḥammad ʻAbd al-Raḥmān al-Marʻashlī. 3rd edn, 4 vols. Beirut: Dār Iḥyāʼ a-Turāth al-ʻArabī, 2005
Al-Saqqāf, ʻAlawī bin Aḥmad. *Majmūʻat Sabʻa kutub mufīda*. Cairo: Muṣṭafā al-Bābī al-Ḥalabī, 1940
Al-Sarakhsī, Muḥammad b. Aḥmad. *Al-Mabsūṭ*, 30 vols in 15. Beirut: Dār al-Maʻrifa, [1978]
The Saudi Ministry of Justice. *Mudawwanat al-Aḥkām al-qaḍāʼiyya*. 2nd edn. Riyadh: Wizārat al-ʻAdl, 2007 (available at http://www.moj.gov.sa/ar-sa/ministry/versions/Pages/Modona.aspx).
Al-Ṣāwī, Aḥmad b. Muḥammad. *Ḥāshiyat al-Ṣāwī ʻalā Tafsīr al-Jalālayn*. Ed. ʻAlī Muḥammad al-Ḍabbāʻ, 4 vols in 3. Bombay: Surtis Sons, [1981]
Al-Shāfiʻī, Muḥammad b. Idrīs. *Al-Risāla*. Ed. Aḥmad Shākir. Beirut: al-Maktaba al-ʻIlmiyya [no date]
——. *Al-Umm*, 7 vols. Cairo: Dār al-Shaʻb, 1968

Shāh Walī Allāh al-Dihlawī. *Ḥujjat Allāh al-Bāligha*. Ed. Sayyid Aḥmad Balanpūrī, 2 vols. Deoband: Maktabat Ḥijāz, 2010

——. *Al-Inṣāf fī bayān asbāb al-ikhtilāf*. Ed. 'Abd al-Fattāḥ Abū Ghudda. Beirut: Dār al-Nafā'is, 1983

——. *Al-Irshād ilā muhimmat al-isnād*. Ed. Aḥmad Ḥasankhān. [Lahore]: Maṭba'at Aḥmadī [no date]

——. *Al-Juz' al-laṭīf fī tarjamat al-'abd al-ḍa'īf*. Ed. Abū al-Ṭayyib 'Aṭā' Allāh al-Fujyanī. Lahore: [no publisher], 1951

——. *Manāqib Muḥammad b. Ismā'īl al-Bukhārī wa faḍīlat Ibn Taymiyya*. Delhi: Maṭba' Aḥmad Rāfi' [no date]

——. *Al-Tafhīmāt al-ilāhiyya*, 2 vols. Bijnor, India: Madīna Barqī Press, 1932

——. *Muṣaffā sharḥ al-Muwaṭṭa'*. Delhi: Maṭba'at-i Fārūq, 1876

Shākir, Aḥmad. *Maqālāt al-'allāma al-shaykh Aḥmad Muḥammad Shākir*. Ed. 'Abd al-Raḥmān al-'Aql, 2 vols. Giza: Dār al-Riyāḍ, 2005

Shaltūt, Maḥmūd. *Al-Islām 'aqīda wa sharī'a*. 18th edn. Cairo: Dār al-Shurūq, 2001

Al-Sha'rānī, 'Abd al-Wahhāb. *Kashf al-ghumma 'an jamī' al-umma*. Cairo: Maṭba'at al-Kastiliyya, 1864

——. *Al-Mīzān al-kubrā*, 2 vols in 1. Cairo: Maktabat Zahrān [no date]. Reprint of 1862 Cairo edn from Maktabat al-Kastiliyya

——. *Al-Ṭabaqāt al-kubrā; or, Lawaqiḥ al-anwār fī ṭabaqāt al- akhyār*. Ed. Sulaymān al-Ṣāliḥ. Beirut: Dār al-Ma'rifa, 2005

Al-Shawkānī, Muḥammad b. 'Alī. 'Bulūgh al-munā fī ḥukm al-istimnā.' In *al-Rasā'il al-fiqhiyya li'l-imām al-Shawkānī*, ed. Aḥmad Farīd al-Mazīdī, 161–69. Beirut: Dār al-Kutub al-'Ilmiyya, 2005

——. *Nayl al-awṭār*. Ed. 'Izz al-Dīn Khaṭṭāb, 8 vols. Beirut: Dār Iḥyā' al-Turāth al-'Arabī, 2001

Shaykh Niẓām, et al. *Al-Fatāwā al-Hindiyya; or, Fatāwā 'Ālamgīrī*. Ed. 'Abd al-Laṭīf Ḥasan 'Abd al-Raḥmān, 6 vols. Beirut: Dār al-Kutub al-'Ilmiyya, 2001

Al-Sirjānī, Rāghib. *Fann al-Ta'āmul al-nabawī ma'a ghayr al-muslimīn*. Cairo: Aqlām, 2010

——. *Kayfa takhtāru ra'īs al-jumhūriyya*. 5th edn. Cairo: Aqlām, 2011

Al-Subkī, Tāj al-Dīn 'Abd al-Wahhāb. *Ṭabaqāt al-shāfi'iyya al-kubrā*. Ed. 'Abd al-Fattāḥ Muḥammad al-Ḥalw and Maḥmūd Muḥammad al-Ṭanāḥī. 2nd edn, 10 vols in 6. Cairo: Hujr, 1992

Al-Suhaylī, Abū al-Qāsim 'Abd al-Raḥmān. *Al-Rawḍ al-unuf*. Ed. Majdī Fayṣal al-Shūrā, 4 vols. Beirut: Dār al-Kutub al-'Ilmiyya, 1997

Al-Suhrawardī, Abū Ḥafṣ 'Umar. *'Awārif al-ma'ārif*. Ed. 'Abd al-Ḥalīm Maḥmūd and Maḥmūd al-Sharaf. Cairo: al-Īmān, 2005

Al-Suyūṭī, Jalāl al-Dīn. *Abwāb al-sa'āda fī asbāb al-shahāda*. Ed. Muṣṭafā 'Abd al-Qādir 'Aṭā. Beirut: Dār al-Kutub al-'Ilmiyya, 1987

——. *Badhl al-majhūd li-khizānat Maḥmūd*. MS 334547, Al-Azhar Library (available at www.alazharonline.org)

——. *Al-Bāhir fī ḥukmihi ṣallā Allāh 'alayhi wa sallam bi'l-bāṭin wa'l-ẓāhir*. Cairo: Maktabat al-Qāhira, [1999]

——. *Al-Durr al-manthūr fī al-tafsīr bi'l-ma'thūr*, 6 vols. Cairo: Maṭba'at al-Anwār al-Muḥammadiyya, 1990

——. *Al-Itqān fī 'ulūm al-Qur'ān*. Ed. Ṭāhā 'Abd al-Ra'ūf Sa'd, 4 vols in 2. Cairo: al-Maktaba al-Tawfīqiyya [no date]

——. *Al-Jāmi' al-ṣaghīr fī aḥādīth al-bashīr al-nadhīr*. 2nd edn. Beirut: Dār al-Kutub al-'Ilmiyya, 2004

——. *Al-Khaṣā'iṣ al-kubrā*, 2 vols. Beirut: Dār al-Kitāb al-'Arabī [no date]. Reprint of 1902 Hyderabad edn from Dā'irat al-Ma'ārif al-'Uthmaniyya

——. *Al-La'ālī al-maṣnū'a fī al-aḥādīth al-mawḍū'a*. Ed. Ṣalāḥ Muḥammad al-'Uwayḍa, 3 vols. Beirut: Dār al-Kutub al-'Ilmiyya, 1996

Al-Ṭabarānī, Abū al-Qāsim Sulaymān. *Al-Mu'jam al-kabīr*. Ed. Ḥamdī 'Abd al-Majīd al-Salafī, 25 vols. Beirut: Dār Iḥyā' al-Turāth al-'Arabī [no date]

Al-Ṭabarī, Muḥammad b. Jarīr. *Jāmi' al-bayān 'an ta'wīl āy al-Qur'ān*, 30 vols. Beirut: Dār al-Fikr, 1985

——. *Tārīkh al-Ṭabarī*, 6 vols. Beirut: Dār al-Kutub al-'Ilmiyya, 2003

Al-Ṭaḥāwī, Abū Ja'far Aḥmad. *Sharḥ Mushkil al-Āthār*. Ed. Shu'ayb al-Arnā'ūṭ, 15 vols. Beirut: Mu'assasat al-Risāla, 1987

Al-Ṭanṭāwī, 'Alī. *Dhikrayāt*, 6 vols. Jeddah: Dār al-Manāra, 1985–86

——. *Fatāwā*. Ed. Mujāhid Dayrāniyya. Jeddah: Dār al-Manāra, 1985

Al-Tukla, Muḥammad Ziyād, ed. *Majmū' fī kashf ḥaqīqat al-juz' al-mafqūd al maz'ūm min Muṣannaf 'Abd al-Razzāq*. Riyadh: Dār al-Muḥaddith, 2007

Al-Wādi'ī, Muqbil bin Hādī. *Majmū' fatāwā al-Wādi'ī*. Ed. Ṣādiq Muḥammad al-Bayḍānī. [No place, no publisher] 2005

Al-Zabīdī, Murtaḍā Muḥammad. *Itḥāf al-sāda al-muttaqīn bi-sharḥ Iḥyā' 'ulūm al-dīn*, 10 vols. Beirut: Mu'assasat al-Tārīkh al-'Arabī, 1994

Al-Zamakhsharī, Maḥmūd b. 'Umar. *Al-Kashshāf*. Ed. 'Abd al-Razzāq Mahdī. Beirut: Dār Iḥyā' al-Turāth al-'Arabī, 2001

Al-Zanjānī, Shihāb al-Dīn. *Takhrīj al-furū' 'alā al-uṣūl*. Ed. Muḥammad Adīb Ṣāliḥ. Riyadh: Maktabat 'Ubaykān, 1999

Zarkashī, Badr al-Dīn Muḥammad. *Al-Baḥr al-muḥīṭ fī uṣūl al-fiqh*. Ed. Muḥammad Muḥammad Tāmir, 4 vols. Beirut: Dār al-Kutub al-'Ilmiyya, 2007

Al-Zayla'ī, Jamāl al-Dīn. *Naṣb al-rāya takhrīj ahādīth al-Hidāya*. Ed. Muḥammad Yūsuf al-Banūrī, 4 vols. Cairo: Dār al-Ḥadīth, 1939

Zuhdī, Karam; Nājiḥ Ibrāhīm, et al. *Ḥurmat al-ghulūw fī al-dīn wa takfīr al-muslimīn*. Riyadh: Maktabat al-'Ubaykān, 2004

Al-Zurqānī, Muḥammad b. 'Abd al-Bāqī. *Mukhtaṣar al-Maqāṣid al-ḥasana*. Ed. Muḥammad Luṭfī al-Ṣabbāgh. Beirut: al-Maktab al-Islāmī, 1989

——. *Sharḥ al-Muwaṭṭa'*. Beirut: Dār al-Kutub al-'Ilmiyya, 1991

Index